Happy Birthday Mum,
from Simon + Lizzie
1997.

NORTHUMBRIAN PANORAMA

NORTHUMBRIAN PANORAMA

Studies in the History and Culture of North East England

Edited by

T.E. Faulkner

Department of Historical and Critical Studies, University of Northumbria at Newcastle

OCTAVIAN PRESS
LIMITED

Published by Octavian Press Limited, 1996
13 Charlotte Mews, London W1P 1LN

Typeset by Keyline, Newcastle upon Tyne

Printed and bound by Statex Print & Design, Boldon, Tyne & Wear

British Library Cataloguing-in-Publication Data
A catalogue record for this book is
available from the British Library.

ISBN 0 9527237 0 0

CONTENTS

LIST OF COLOUR PLATES

LIST OF ILLUSTRATIONS IN THE TEXT

PHOTOGRAPHIC ACKNOWLEDGEMENTS

Amber Films: figs. 88, 91

Authors' photographs: figs. 1, 2, 6, 8, 13, 14, 24, 31, 32, 33, 35, 36, 37, 38, 39, 47, 54, 79.

The Baltimore Museum of Art: figs. 19, 21, 23, 25.

R. Baston: figs. 3, 4, 5, 7.

Beamish. The North of England Open Air Museum, Stanley, Co. Durham: figs. 27, 29, 84.

The Bowes Museum, Barnard Castle, Co. Durham, U.K.: figs. 55, 56, 57, 58, 59, 60, 62.

The Brooklyn Museum, New York: fig. 68.

City Library and Arts Centre, Sunderland: fig. 34.

"City Repro" (Newcastle upon Tyne): figs. 46, 49.

The Cooper-Hewitt Museum, New York: fig. 70.

L. J. Couves & Partners: fig. 80.

The Dean and Chapter of Durham (photographs by M. W. Smith): figs 9, 10.

Department of the Environment: colour plate v.

The Dorman Museum, Middlesborough Borough Council: fig. 83.

Editor's photographs: cover illustration; figs. 19, 21, 23, 25.

The Evening Chronicle: fig. 44.

Fenwick Ltd: fig. 85.

Peter Fryer: figs. 86, 87, 89, 90.

David Hill: colour plate i.

The Independent: fig. 53.

The Journal: fig. 77.

The Laing Art Gallery, Newcastle upon Tyne: colour plates ii, iii; figs. 22, 65, 66, 67.

Layton Art Collection, Milwaukee Art Museum: colour plate vii.

John Lewis Partnership Archives: fig. 81.

Marks & Spencer's Archive: fig. 82.

Metropolitan Museum of Art, New York: fig. 76.

The National Gallery of Art, Washington, D.C.: fig. 74.

The National Trust: colour plate iv.

Newcastle City Libraries: figs. 26, 28, 30, 40, 43, 48, 63, 64, 78.

Sterling and Francine Clark Art Institute, Williamstown, Mass.: colour plate vi.

Tynemouth Volunteer Life Brigade: fig. 72.

Worcester Art Museum, Worcester, Mass.: fig. 73.

NOTES ON THE CONTRIBUTORS

T.E. Faulkner is a Senior Lecturer in the History of Design at the University of Northumbria. He was Chairman of the Victorian Society (North East Group), 1986-89, and represents the Georgian Group on the Conservation Areas Advisory Committee of Newcastle upon Tyne. He is co-author of *John Dobson: Newcastle Architect, 1787-1865* (1987) and is a Fellow of the Society of Antiquaries of London.

E.M. Atkins graduated with first class honours in the History of the Visual Arts in the Modern Period from the University of Northumbria in July 1993. Since then she has been lecturing in Communication and Study Skills at Wearside College, and in Art History at Hartlepool College of Further Education and for the WEA.

Cheryl Buckley is Reader in Design History at the University of Northumbria, where she has worked since 1980. She is currently working on Women and Fashion between the Wars in Britain and on theories of Design and Gender. Her previous publications include *Potters and Paintresses: Women Designers in the Pottery Industry, 1870-1955* (1990), and articles and book chapters on women designers and the theoretical relationship between women and design history, theory and practice.

P.R. Coss is Professor of Medieval History at the University of Wales, Cardiff, and formerly Professor and Head of History at the University of Northumbria. He is a Fellow of the Society of Antiquaries of London and of the Royal Historical Society, and is a member of the editorial board of the leading historical journal *Past and Present.* His books include *Lordship, Knighthood and Locality: a Study in English Society* c.*1180* – c.*1280* (1991) and *The Knight in Medieval England 1000-1400* (1993).

Constance M. Fraser is a graduate of King's College, Durham University, her doctoral thesis being published by the Clarendon Press, Oxford, in 1957 as *A History of Antony Bek, Bishop of Durham, 1283-1311.* Until her retirement in 1989 she taught local history in the Centre for Continuing Education, University of Newcastle upon Tyne. She has edited four volumes of documents for the Surtees Society and two for the Newcastle Society of Antiquaries (of which she has served as President), and is General Editor of the Wakefield Court Roll Section of the Yorkshire Archaeological Society. She is a consultant supervisor for postgraduate students at the University of Northumbria.

Peter Hutchings lectures in Film Studies at the University of Northumbria. He is the author of *Hammer and Beyond: The British Horror Film* (1993), and has also published articles on Hitchcock, the films of Ridley and Tony Scott, genre theory and the aesthetics of horror.

Sarah Kane was educated at Oxford University and the Courtauld Institute of Art, London. She has been a Research Assistant at the University of Northumbria, investigating the history of the Bowes Museum, Barnard Castle, on which she has published several articles and conference papers. She has organised the annual conference of the Association of Art Historians, held in Newcastle in 1996.

Angela Long grew up in Sunderland. She has lectured in Design History at both Newcastle and Sunderland Polytechnics and worked as a tutor-counsellor for the Open University. For many years she taught Contextual Studies at Hong Kong Polytechnic, and was a consultant to the Open Learning Institute of Hong Kong. She is currently teaching Design History at the University of Northumbria and researching into the environmental meaning of the domestic landscape.

Phoebe Lowery is a graduate of East Anglia University and worked for the National Trust in Norfolk before coming to the University of Northumbria to undertake research on 'The Northumbrian Country House'. Since 1992 she has worked for the Northumbria Region of the National Trust, as Property Manager of Washington Old Hall and, now, of Wallington Hall.

Kenneth McConkey is Professor of Art History and Dean of the Faculty of Arts and Design at the University of Northumbria. His initial research into naturalistic painting in Britain in the 1880s has led to many books and exhibition catalogues. Most recently these have included volumes on Irish Art, Edwardian Portraiture and British Impressionism, and the standard monograph on Sir John Lavery. In 1995 he selected and catalogued the major exhibition *Impressionism in Britain* at the Barbican Art Gallery, London.

Paul Usherwood is leader of the B.A. degree course in the History of the Visual Arts in the Modern Period at the University of Northumbria. His previous publications include *Art for Newcastle: Thomas Miles Richardson and the Newcastle Exhibitions, 1822-1843* (1984) and *Lady Butler: Battle Artist, 1846-1933* (1987), as well as book chapters and articles on aspects of nineteenth-century British military painting, and art in the North East. He is Chair of the Public Monuments and Sculpture Association North East Recording Project and also writes on contemporary art for *Art Monthly*.

Ian Willis is a Senior Lecturer in History at the University of Northumbria. He has taught history at all levels from secondary school to university. His research interests include visual imagery and history, and various aspects of local and regional history. He is currently working on market towns in Northumberland in the modern period.

INTRODUCTION

This book is about the history and culture of North East England – 'Northumbria', defined as the historic counties of Durham and Northumberland. Its origin lies in the work of an inter-disciplinary research group in the Department of Historical and Critical Studies at the University of Northumbria, Newcastle upon Tyne. The Department was formed from the merger of the subject areas of English, History, and the History of Art, Design and Film. It soon became obvious that a good proportion of its staff had research interests in the history of the North East and that there existed considerable potential for collaborative work. In 1990, therefore, a research group was set up on the initiative of Professor P.R. Coss to work in the general area of "North Eastern Cultural Identity". Its aims were three-fold: to initiate new work in the field; to develop existing research; and to synthesise and co-ordinate the two, via a series of staff seminars and conferences. This book is the result.

It consists of twelve chapters, by members of staff and associates of the Department, on various aspects of the North East. The topics covered, described in more detail later in this Introduction, comprise medieval heraldry and effigies, the diocese of Durham, the country house, studies of Morpeth, Sunderland and Newcastle upon Tyne, interpretations of Hadrian's Wall, the evolution of two of the region's major museums, the work of a nineteenth-century American artist in Northumberland, women and fashion in the North East, and ways in which the region has been represented in film and television. These, while emphasizing a number of common themes – identity, image, class, status, gender, and the insularity or otherwise of the region – bring to bear a multiplicity of points of view not attempted in this form before. Some break new ground; others re-examine and reinterpret subject matter in the light of modern perceptions and ideas.

The book is divided into four sections: *Medieval to Eighteenth Century*; *Urban Identity*; *Heritage and Regional Culture*; and *Representations*. These in turn reflect some of the approaches and areas of interest implicit in much that is taught and studied at the University of Northumbria, including empirical investigation, visual analysis, feminist history, and what might be termed a 'post modern' approach. In the latter, the changing perceptions of historical facts and events are regarded as being of almost as much importance as the facts and events themselves. The range of subject matter covered by the book is also considerable, including social, demographic and political history, and the visual arts, represented by painting and sculpture, architecture, fashion and film (hence the 'panoramic' element of the title of the book). So too is the time-scale covered: from the Middle Ages to the present day.

Northumbrian Panorama, of course, makes no attempt to present a comprehensive history of the region; nor is it written from the point of view of any single ideology or theoretical position. No single view, we believe, can do justice to a region which, however distinctive, is arguably more varied and diverse than is sometimes supposed. Instead, the aim is to explore aspects of this diverse yet distinctive identity in a variety of ways, emphasizing – although not exclusively – its cultural manifestations, particularly as expressed in visual and material terms. Indeed, some of the chapters examine ways in which received notions of the region's identity began to influence and be utilised in forms of cultural production, most recently in film and television, from about the late eighteenth century onwards; they suggest ways in which the Northumbrian past has been rewritten and represented, and thus, it is hoped, may clarify the understanding of regional stereotypes and myths.

The North East has been remarkably well served by historians. The upsurge of antiquarian and historical endeavour in the eighteenth and early nineteenth centuries gave us the work of, among others, Henry Bourne, John Brand and Eneas Mackenzie on Newcastle, George Allan, Robert Surtees and William Fordyce on County Durham, and John Wallis and John Hodgson on Northumberland. Mackenzie also tackled the counties of both Durham and Northumberland, as did an earlier historian, William Hutchinson. The great fifteen-volume *History of Northumberland* came a century or so later (although not under the auspices of the *Victoria County History*). This has been described as "the best modern multi-volume survey in the whole of England".[1] In modern times, for the period we are concerned with here, we have, for example, the work of Norman McCord, D.J. Rowe and Constance Fraser (the last-named represented in this book). If these historians have emphasised social, economic and political themes, other areas have been less fully explored although there have been a number of specialist, if not comprehensive, studies on aspects of the region's art and architecture. Very recently, too, the Literary and Philosophical Society of Newcastle upon Tyne's *Bicentenary Lectures* have illuminated cultural and institutional aspects of the North East's history; it is hoped that the present volume may make an additional contribution in this field, even though we are aware that there is still much to do, particularly in the areas of women's history, regional literature, and the modern art and architecture of the North East.

There now seems to be a renewed awareness of regionality, both politically and academically; certainly interest in the culture and history of the North East is now stronger than ever. At the time of writing, a new journal of regional and cultural affairs, *Northern Review*, has just been launched, and proposals to create a Durham and North East England History Centre and to revive the *Victoria County History* of Durham (begun in 1905 but in abeyance since the late 1920s) are further evidence of this. All this does not mean, however, that there is unanimity as to the approaches which should be adopted in studying the North East or, indeed, the elements of which the region consists. For example, one of the most recent studies of the North East is *Geordies: Roots of Regionalism* (1992), edited by Robert Colls and Bill Lancaster. This is a significant and thought-provoking book which makes substantial claims as to the region's distinctiveness. It suggests that the North East, defined as the old counties of Durham and Northumberland, has as much claim to "regional, political and cultural identity within the new Europe as, for example, Catalonia, Brittany or Bavaria".[2] Less credibly, however, it contends that the notion of the 'Geordie' applies to the region as a whole, rather than merely to industrial Tyneside. As Fraser and Emsley say, "the Geordie is really a Tynesider",[3] and it is hard to imagine residents of, say, Alnwick, Hexham, Morpeth or Durham seeing themselves as Geordies. Even those of an industrial town like Sunderland would probably reject the term, given their intense rivalry with Newcastle, not only on the football field, but also, as suggested in Chapter Five of the present work, commercially. All might, however, accept the label 'Northumbrian'. The problem is, surely, that not all North Easterners can possibly share the urban, industrial working-class identity usually associated with the Geordie and to which *Geordies* seems to be committed. As Norman McCord has said: "All of the writers here seek to be committed in varying degrees to a belief in a romanticized and idealized 'working class' which has never existed in reality in anything like the form in which it is worshipped by its most fervent disciples".[4] Significantly, most of the contributions in *Geordies* deal with subjects connected with Tyneside and tend to perpetuate an urban, industrial, working class image and identity for the North East, despite their claims to banish stereotypes.

That the North East is (particularly from c.1850 to c.1950), or has been, a region of mass industrialisation, famous for technological innovation, is indisputable. Nor can the importance of the coal trade, from the Middle Ages onwards, be underestimated. By the 1880s the Durham coalfield employed over 130,000 men, reaching a peak of 170,000 by the mid-1920s. (Throughout this period about half the going number were simultaneously employed in Northumberland). Even in the mid-1950s there were still over 100,000 miners in Durham alone. This industrial heritage has given rise to what tends to be the dominant modern image of the North East, described as early as the 1930s by writers like J.B. Priestley and Thomas Sharp. Sharp wrote in 1937:

> For the production of fine machines, a miserable mixture of drab buildings was spread thick over a wide terrain till every vestige of physical beauty and seemliness disappeared from the scene; and Newcastle, Gateshead, Felling, Hebburn, Jarrow, Wallsend, Walker and North and South Shields have all become names indicative of the worst depths of dreariness to which town-building can fall.[5]

However, the North East is also extensively agrarian and, in the late eighteenth century, was noted for its agricultural improvements. Moreover, unfashionable though it may be to make the point, the region has had an important middle class and even aristocracy, whose contributions to local government, to the creation of civic and cultural institutions and to the patronage of art and architecture are detailed in several chapters of the present work. The region is also important for its ecclesiastical heritage, for its antiquities and for traditions which substantially pre-date its major industrial phase; indeed, in the broader scheme of things, this phase may come to be seen as comparatively short lived, as we enter a 'post-industrial' society. Even *Geordies* admits to celebrating, if not defending, a culture that is disappearing – tacit admission, perhaps, of the concomitance of the 'Geordie' with the industrial working class. It also makes a virtue of the region's alleged provinciality, its geographical remoteness justifying a vision of the North East having separate status within an enlarged federal Europe. Yet, over the centuries, it is noticeable how the region has frequently been in touch with the most up-to-date, polite, metropolitan forms, particularly in architecture and the arts. The coal trade ensured more communication with the south than tends to be acknowledged and there seems to exist a duality between the remoteness of the North East, a region even today with few major inland towns, and the unexpected sophistication of its institutions and culture.

The present work shares the same geographical focus as *Geordies* but revives the concept of 'Northumbria', one which still has considerable resonance today. It is frequently adopted for commercial and institutional use, often to denote some measure of shared identity for the counties of both Durham and Northumberland. There is, for example, the Northumbria region of the National Trust, the Northumbria Police, the Northumbrian Constituency of the European Parliament, Northumbrian Water Ltd and many more. This usage can be said to have the weight of tradition and history on its side. *Northumbrian Panorama* also seeks to redress the balance by postulating for the North East a more complex and varied identity, both industrial and rural, and evolving over a much wider spread of time. Thus we examine both the city and the market town, the country house and the terraced street. At this point it may be useful to look at aspects of this identity in a historical context and in the light of some of the themes explored in the chapters of this book, before giving a more detailed summary of the specific topics under review.

A sense of regional identity for the North East (the historic counties of Durham and Northumberland) is underpinned by both geography and history. Indeed, the historian Patrick Wormald has argued that 'Northumbria', defined in this way, is one of only two regions (the other being Yorkshire) which have constituted definable entities throughout English history and might even have achieved more independence.[6] The Anglo-Saxon kingdom of Northumbria, obviously, always included the area of the two counties (even if extending from the Humber to the Forth at its greatest extent in the seventh and eighth centuries A.D.), and, indeed, by the late tenth century, had become reduced to little more than this area. Of the two previously independent kingdoms from which Northumbria was created, Bernicia and Deira, the former, for much of its existence, also approximated to the area we have defined as the modern North East. The boundary between these two kingdoms was almost certainly the Tees.[7] With the coming into being of an English state, and for centuries thereafter, Northumbrian customs and institutions survived, as Professor Jolliffe famously showed, together with what he called "a distinctive Northumbrian civilisation of unique interest".[8] As Frank Musgrove has pointed out:

> The kings of all England in fact ruled the North through viceroys who were members of the house of Bamburgh: previously kings, they were now earls of Northumbria, with scarcely diminished powers. It was the earls of Northumbria and not the kings of England who determined who would be bishops of Durham. They were not appointed earls of Northumbria by the king of England: they succeeded by hereditary right. And they appear to have paid no tribute to the English king.[9]

This sense of independence led to the need for repression after the Norman conquest but, in spite of this, it has been suggested that "the ancient kingdom of Northumbria retained its identity as a single administrative area throughout the Middle Ages".[10]

The region contained numerous palatinates and 'liberties' over which the king did not have jurisdiction, and later attempts to govern the north via a series of councils and lieutenancies culminated in the establishment of the King's Council of the North in 1484, revived by Henry VIII in 1525 and 1537. The fact that this had supreme authority north of the Trent, the Council itself ultimately being based in York, suggests a basis in a surviving concept of 'Northumbria' in its earlier, larger form. However, historians such as Richard Lomas and Edward Miller agree that "to treat the historic counties of Durham and Northumberland during the Middle Ages as a single region . . . is fully justified and thoroughly worthwhile".[11] On the other hand, A.J. Pollard, in his *North Eastern England During the Wars of the Roses,* includes parts of Yorkshire in his definition of the North East and contends that during the fifteenth century the Tees, far from being a barrier, actually brought people from north and south of the river closer together; many landowners of all classes owned property on both sides. (Incidentally, and I think significantly, he also argues that at this time the North East was less remote and culturally backward than is usually supposed.) What Professor Pollard does concede, however, is that from the point of view of jurisdiction and administration the diocese and palatinate of Durham, the latter containing much land in Northumberland as well as County Durham itself, did set these counties apart.[12] The consolidation of the palatinate by 1189 gave the 'Prince-Bishop' of Durham jurisdiction over eastern England between the Tees and the Tweed; he represented the king, with regalian powers of justice and prerogative, and had a primary responsibility for defence against the Scots. In practice, if not in theory, he even had authority to deal with foreign powers. Thus Cuthbert Tunstall (referred to in Chapter Two of the present work) was the first President of the newly created Council of the North in 1537. He was frequently used by Henry VIII to negotiate with the Scots and as an adviser to the Lieutenant Generals appointed by the king to defend the border or invade across it. In 1544, Tunstall was stationed in Newcastle to support Hertford's invasion of Scotland and in the following year was employed by Henry to negotiate peace with France. However, after Tunstall's death in 1559, the powers of the Prince-Bishop were somewhat reduced.

If the power and authority of the Prince-Bishops held the region together for a very considerable time, this further declined, and by the eighteenth century the identities of Durham and Northumberland were becoming more separate. Thus, as early as the 1720s, in his *A Tour Through the Whole Island of Great Britain,* Daniel Defoe seems to have found the two counties geographically distinct (which actually makes sense in that the hills of County Durham are typical rolling fells – part of the Northern Pennines – and very different from the Cheviots). He says little or nothing about County Durham (although much about the city and its bishopric) but finds in Northumberland "abundant business for an Antiquary; every place shows you ruined Castles, Roman altars, Inscriptions, Monuments of Battles, of Heroes killed and Armies routed, and the like".[13] (He even comments on the distinctive Northumberland dialect.) A century or so later, this general perception is echoed in the kind of publication typified by John Hodgson's *Topographical and Historical Description of the County of Northumberland* (1817), containing "an account of its towns, cathedral, castles, antiquities, churches, monuments, public edifices, picturesque scenery, the residences of the nobility, gentry, &c. Accompanied with biographical notices of eminent and learned men to whom this county has given birth". The death of Van Mildert, the last Prince-Bishop, in 1836, seemed to symbolise the two counties' further distinctiveness by this time, a factor reflected also in the separate county histories of Hodgson himself, Hutchinson, Fordyce and others. This was later accentuated by the creation of the separate diocese of Newcastle (1882). This divergence continued. In the mid-nineteenth century, the two counties had approximately equal populations, but throughout the period of nineteenth- and early twentieth-century industrialisation, the rate of population growth was always considerably greater in Durham than in the less completely industrialised county of Northumberland. Thus, by the 1881 census, the population of Durham was almost exactly twice that of its northern neighbour (875,000 to 434,000).

Paradoxically, the process of industrialisation may have encouraged a renewed (if different) sense of regional identity for the North East. Indeed, A.J. Pollard goes so far as to claim that the sense of identity created in this way is the only significant one the region is ever likely to have possessed.[14] According to Robert Colls in *Geordies*, the North East found "its modern identity" after about 1860. He goes on:

> the later nineteenth century saw the birth of a distinctive regional identity and this identity was accompanied by momentous developments in industry, communications, population growth and urban living. Prompted by national re-evaluations of what it was like to be 'English', the regional intelligentsia struggled to establish their 'northernness' . . . People started talking again about 'Northumbria'.[15]

The region did celebrate its burgeoning industrial might with the Newcastle Exhibition of 1887, ostensibly commemorating Queen Victoria's jubilee but concentrating on armaments, shipbuilding and the railways. At the same time came a revival of antiquarianism, both in a new, popular form typified by such publications as *The Monthly Chronicle of North County Lore and Legend* (which, incidentally, issued a compendium of essays in 1887) and in its traditional, scholarly guise. People had indeed started talking about 'Northumbria', but it is important to remember that by this they were increasingly likely to mean Northumberland alone. This is the case, for example, with *Northumbria,* a volume based on lectures delivered to the Literary and Philosophical Society of Newcastle upon Tyne in 1898. Robert Spence Watson, on "Northumbrian Folk and Speech", typifies the self-conscious, if deeply felt 'patriotism' of the lectures:

> I am a devoted Northumbrian, with an intense love for and belief in the Northumbria of old and the Northumberland of today. I have wandered through every nook and into every cranny of the grand old county since I was a little child, and still visit with ever renewed delight the hills and vales, the peles and castles, which are so abundant, so varied, and so full of interest for us all . . .

> Northumbria was, in many a great emergency, the saviour of England. Northumbria was the cradle of its religion, and decided the form of its religious faith. Northumbria strikes the keynote of the poetic song which is one of England's greatest glories. Northumbria led the van of Christendom in learning as in art. And what Northumbria did Northumberland has continued to do in some measure, and will continue to do in full measure when we all fully recognise and live up to the privilege and responsibility which are implied in the proud boast, "I am a Northumbrian".[16]

However, by this time unitary bodies such as the Architectural and Archaeological Society of Durham and Northumberland had been formed (in 1862; it still exists today) and as late as 1949 the planner Thomas Sharp, a native of County Durham, stressed the importance of inter-county institutions in his perception of the two counties as a social and economic unit which could be referred to as 'Northumbria'.[17]

These issues of regionality provide an appropriate context for a more detailed discussion of the contents of the present work. In its first section, *Medieval to Eighteenth Century,* the theme of the region's geographical remoteness or otherwise comes to the fore. Chapter One examines chivalric culture during the thirteenth, fourteenth and fifteenth centuries and shows how the region's elite expressed their status through the medium of heraldry. In "Heraldry and Monumental Effigies in the North East" P.R. Coss also shows how, during this period, there were workshops in the North East producing sepulchral monuments of regionally distinctive character, while others were substantially influenced by fashionable techniques and styles from the south. In Chapter Two, "The Diocese of Durham in 1563", Constance Fraser analyses a little-known diocesan survey ordered by the Privy Council which provides information about the population and ecclesiastical condition of the parishes. Many livings were empty at this crucial stage of the Church's history. The purging of dissenters was slow, even after the appointment of the Calvinistic James Pilkington as bishop of Durham in 1561 and there seems to have been little enthusiasm for Anglicanism in the North East, less than thirty years after the Pilgrimage of Grace. This sense of residual independence is perhaps not surprising, given that the Rising of the Earls (of Northumberland and Westmorland) was so soon to come (1569). Much later, there was considerable backing for James II in the region in 1688 and it was still possible for the Catholic James Radcliffe, third earl of Derwentwater, of Dilston Castle, Northumberland, to raise a certain amount of local support for his ill-fated participation in the Jacobite Rebellion of 1715. By 1745, however, the North East seems to have become reconciled to Hanoverian rule.

The third chapter, "Patronage and the Country House in Northumberland" by Phoebe Lowery, brings us to a major theme of the book, the architecture of the North East. This has often been assessed as idiosyncratic and parochial, with essentially utilitarian and defensible structures resulting from the region's comparative inaccessibility and its constant conflict with the Scots. Certainly we are familiar with the North East's castles, pele towers and bastle houses (the latter almost unique to Northumberland) and its small, rugged medieval churches, usually 'Early English' with Norman or even Saxon elements, containing few suggestions of splendour or display. Therefore, even after the union of the crowns in 1603 and the evolution of Northumberland, in S.J. Watts's phrase, "from border to middle shire",[18] the development of, for example, the country house in the North East was impeded by border conflict and other factors until the eighteenth century. At this time, as Ms Lowery suggests, it at last "began to evolve in tandem with national developments".

Yet, as we have seen, the region has been perceived as being far from culturally impoverished even in the fifteenth century, and, earlier still, its apparently utilitarian and defensible buildings repay further examination. Philip Dixon has recently argued that much of the conflict with the Scots came only after the aggressive campaigns of Edward I and that some of the greatest castles of the North East, such as the one at Newcastle itself, were built as much for display as for defence;[19] also, as Lesley Milner points out, pele towers were not only defensible but also "stylish, sophisticated and beautiful pieces of architecture".[20] Indeed, as if to belie its alleged insularity, the North East has been in the vanguard of later architectural movements like the Gothic Revival, since the eighteenth century. (Perhaps the patronage of architecture and design, particularly after 1660, by Bishop Cosin, a Laudian sympathiser, may have anticipated a taste for this.) Classicism, too, became important here from this time on and later developed in the hands of mainly local architects like John Dobson (1787-1865) to a point when it is now perceived as a major element of the region's identity, with regard to both country houses and urban architecture (particularly that of Newcastle upon Tyne). Hence it is no surprise to find that by the eighteenth (and nineteenth) centuries a series of country houses in the most up-to-date, polite and fashionable styles came to be built, underpinned by the wealth of an increasingly prosperous landed elite and that of new patrons enriched by trade. Both local and national architects played their part.

Three of the most significant and representative of the region's cities and towns, Morpeth, Sunderland and Newcastle, are examined in Section Two, *Urban Identity*. Ian Willis explains in Chapter Four ("Morpeth: A Northumbrian Market Town in the Nineteenth Century") how this "solid old town", in Cobbett's phrase,[21] was near but not really part of an area of heavy industry; it survived on the basis of a mixed economy, with agriculture remaining important. Its population grew much more slowly than that of a highly industrialised town like Sunderland which, as Angela Long describes in Chapter Five, epitomised Victorian prosperity and civic pride. Sunderland developed not only a distinctive form of working-class housing ("The Sunderland Cottage") but also important civic institutions such as a museum and art gallery, one of the earliest municipal ones in England, in contrast to the Laing Art Gallery, Newcastle, founded only in 1904.

Newcastle upon Tyne, the region's acknowledged capital, is different in so many ways. It too developed a distinctive housing type, the Tyneside flat; but the name of this reminds us that although the city's population rose from about 28,000 to 215,000 during the nineteenth century, its growth during the industrial revolution came comparatively late and tended to be peripheral, along the banks of the Tyne, particularly to the east. Newcastle's importance, of course, was also pre-industrial. It was always an important commercial centre, achieving separate county status in Elizabethan times. As early as 1334 its wealth, founded on the coal and to a lesser extent the wool trades, was ranked third amongst English towns.[22] By 1700 it had become the fourth largest English city (a century later, it was only ninth)[23] and at about this time the traveller Celia Fiennes commented that: "it most resembles London of any place in England, its buildings lofty and large of brick mostly or stone" with shops that "are good and are of distinct trades, not selling many things in one shop as is the custom in most country towns".[24] In the 1720s Defoe found it "a spacious, extended, infinitely populous place".[25] The eighteenth century was a boom period for Newcastle. Elegant structures were being built and its newspapers were filled with reports of the latest London gossip and events. The city's Literary and Philosophical Society was founded in 1793 and the Society's recent *Bicentenary Lectures* give a fascinating account of the remarkable upsurge of achievement during this period, not only in art, architecture and historical research, but also in science, engineering, mathematics, music, medicine and law. This general development continued into the first half of the next century and was symbolised, and indeed climaxed, by the metropolitan style city centre 'improvements' of Richard Grainger and his architects.

In Chapter Six ("Conservation and Renewal in Newcastle upon Tyne"), I examine changes in the 'urban landscape' of Newcastle over the last two centuries and the city's inconsistent record in the field of architectural conservation. It seems that by about 1960 Newcastle's prestige and prosperity had declined to such an extent that its leaders were prepared to sacrifice an unacceptable proportion of its classical heritage in their rather unsuccessful search for a new image. Although, ironically, inspired by a sense of the city's former greatness, these leaders appear to have lacked confidence in its status as a regional capital. In more general terms, this pattern of behaviour typifies a long-standing tendency to uncertainty and inconsistency, whether on the part of the nineteenth century oligarchy or the party political representatives of modern times. It is true that, as we have seen, the city expanded more slowly during the period most associated with the growth of civic and municipal aspirations and the fact that its culture and population would appear to have been less homogeneous than that of, for example, Sunderland, may also have been a factor in all this. In any event, councillors' timidity seems to have been responsible for, among other things, the non-appearance of a civic art gallery until Edwardian times and for the fact that even Grainger's improvements had been a largely commercial, rather than municipal, initiative. Even before this, the historian Eneas Mackenzie had lamented that the Corporation of Newcastle had not adopted "a comprehensive and rational plan of improvement".[26]

The third section of the book is entitled *Heritage and Regional Culture.* Allusion has already been made to the rediscovery or reinvention, in the later nineteenth century, of a sense of regionality for the North East, whether in terms of the region as a whole or Northumberland alone. One of the most potent symbols of that regionality has been the Roman Wall; its mystique seems stronger than ever today. Indeed, images of it are constantly used in tourist brochures, on the covers of books about the North East, or commercially (as on the label of a well-known brand of 'Northumbrian' mineral water!). In Chapter Seven ("Hadrian's Wall and the New Romans"), Paul Usherwood examines the changing perceptions of the wall and its symbolic value at three specific moments in modern times: the early nineteenth century, the early part of this century, and today. He argues that the Wall can be seen to have had a continuing role of defining social space, as much as geographic space, for many of the region's inhabitants.

Also important in defining and re-evaluating a sense of national and local heritage, since the nineteenth century, has been the role of museums. The Bowes Museum, Barnard Castle, and the Laing Art Gallery, Newcastle upon Tyne, present an interesting contrast in terms of their origin, history, purpose and location. Yet neither, until recent years, has emphasised the expression of locality or regionality. The Bowes Museum, as Sarah Kane points out in Chapter Eight ("When Paris Meets Teesdale"), has had an anomalous identity, being "an essentially urban institution in the depths of the countryside", projecting a continental image in its architecture and seeking a national, even European dimension in its exhibits. Thus, after its foundation in 1869 and belated opening to the public in 1892, writers and others interested in rediscovering and promoting a sense of regional tradition and identity, found it difficult to incorporate the Museum into this. Ms Kane also examines the ambiguous identities and intentions of the Museum's founders, John and Josephine Bowes, who appear to have conceived of the building partly as a country house.

Meanwhile, as we have seen, the region's largest city continued to lack a municipal art gallery or museum. The Laing Art Gallery, Newcastle upon Tyne, was established only in 1904 and then almost fortuitously, as a result of an unexpected donation of £20,000 from a Scottish-born wine merchant, Alexander Laing. In Chapter Nine, "The Genesis of the Laing Art Gallery", E.M. Atkins attributes Newcastle's comparative lateness in establishing such a gallery largely to the earlier existence of similar but private institutions, such as the Central Exchange Gallery (part of Grainger's central redevelopment) and the Northern Academy of Arts; also, to the rivalry between the supporters of local artists and those with a more international reputation. Another major factor was confused hegemonic decision making. It seems that the city's ruling elite lacked civic confidence and pride; certainly there was neither a wholehearted commitment to 'high art' nor any great desire, after the formation of the Laing, to promote or celebrate regional culture and art. Significantly, the Laing started with no established collection of paintings, either from the Corporation or from bequests.

If the region's capital was tardy in creating an official art gallery, the North East has long had considerable attraction for artists themselves. Closely linked to the growing interest in antiquarianism, historical research and regional affairs during the late eighteenth and early nineteenth centuries, mentioned earlier, was the Picturesque Movement. This sought, through art, literature and tourism, to celebrate the increasing appeal of wild and rugged scenery, or that imbued with historical associations. As explained in Chapter Eight, the North East, increasingly accessible because of the new and improved turnpike roads, became almost as popular as the Lake District for the 'Picturesque Tour'. Artists such as Cotman, Girtin, Turner and Varley (who taught John Dobson watercolour painting) depicted the region at this time. A century or so later artists seeking escape from what was now an increasingly industrialised society, found refuge in 'art colonies' in the more remote parts of Europe. Such a colony was at Cullercoats, Northumberland. Here the American Winslow Homer came and worked in 1881-82. He is the subject of Chapter Ten, the first in the final section of this book, entitled *Representations.* Thus in "Winslow Homer at Cullercoats", Kenneth McConkey shows how the artist became fascinated with depicting not only the sea and ships, but also the village's fisherwomen, in their traditional dress. Homer's heroic, idealised portrayals of these working women at their daily tasks, such as mending nets or carrying baskets of fish, are a remarkable outcome of his sojourn in Northumberland. They also serve to remind us that the North East, contrary to the impression conveyed by modern stereotypes, was never a region of exclusively male employment.

Working women are also discussed in the next chapter, "Modernity, Femininity and Regional Identity: Women and Fashion in the North East of England". Here Cheryl Buckley explains how, with many of the North East's traditional heavy industries starting to decline even before the Second World War, the employment of women became more and more significant: in department stores, in the growing retail and service sectors generally and in the region's new light industries, particularly clothing manufacture. Women's increased independence, and importance both as producers and consumers, meant that they "played a large part in stimulating the growth of new shopping facilities and the design and manufacture of a plethora of lower priced, available, fashionable goods". Through fashion, women were able to experience modernity at first hand and to re-evaluate, consciously or unconsciously, the meaning of femininity within modern life. Dr Buckley develops a theory of a 'feminine modernity' which calls into question both national and regional concepts of women's place within society and the accuracy of many conventional representations of the North East.

The analysis of such representations, at the present time, provides a fitting conclusion to this book. In the final chapter, "When the Going Gets Tough . . .", Peter Hutchings shows how films and television programmes of recent years have presented an image of the North East as grim, hard, urban, working-class and male, although with essentially female undercurrents of 'caringness', the family and community – the region of the 'Geordie', in other words. Even the products of Amber Films, an important independent Tyneside film-making co-operative, tend to perpetuate this image, however sensitively and affectionately. Despite their gritty, 'authentic' settings and dialogue, these films, such as *Seacoal* and *In Fading Light*, may have more in common than we would think with the stylised, albeit powerful representations by Winslow Homer a century before. One has the feeling that, like the book *Geordies*, such films are attempting to record and celebrate a culture that is vanishing fast. *Geordies* is written "by Geordies, about Geordies";[27] the film-makers of Amber Films have lived and worked in the region for many years but in most cases originated elsewhere. This study of films and television programmes about the North East establishes that all of these representations, whether produced within the region or in some way 'imposed' on it from outside, draw upon "quite a narrow range of stereotypical assumptions about, amongst other things, class and gender", rather than providing a genuinely 'authentic' picture of the North East. Perhaps this is inevitable, given, as this book attempts to show, the region's complexity and variety; however, this should not cause us to shy away from our responsibility to examine critically not only all the representations and perceptions of the region which we encounter, but also our own.

Finally, before giving the reader long overdue encouragement to explore what follows, it is my pleasant duty to acknowledge the invaluable contribution of many people to the production of this book. Our thanks go to Professors Kenneth McConkey and Christopher Bailey, respectively Dean of the Faculty of Arts and Design and Head of the Department of Historical and Critical Studies at the University of Northumbria, for their support; and, among others, to Martha Asher of the Sterling and Francine Clark Art Institute, Williamstown, Mass., Russell Baston, Ian Chilvers, Elizabeth Conran of the Bowes Museum, Gillian Dickinson, Lavinia Down, Toby Ek, Dr Malcolm Gee, Dr Jeremy Gregory, Dr Martin Harrop, Adrian Jenkins of the Laing Art Gallery, Newcastle upon Tyne, Valerie Levitt, Grace McCombie, Jennifer Mulherin of Octavian Press, Roger Norris of the Dean and Chapter Library of Durham, Dolly Potter, Margaret Reay, Ron Scott and Simon Davidson at 'Keyline', Barbara Sweet, and Alistair Yule, Warden of Auckland Castle.

T.E. Faulkner

References and Notes

1. L. Stone and J.C.F. Stone, *An Open Elite?: England, 1540-1880* (Oxford, 1986), p.36.
2. R. Colls and B. Lancaster (eds.), *Geordies: Roots of Regionalism* (Edinburgh, 1992), p.i.
3. C. Fraser and K. Emsley, *Northumbria* (London, 1978), p.11.
4. Norman McCord, review of *Geordies: Roots of Regionalism*, in *Northern History*, vol. xxx (1994), p.245.
5. Thomas Sharp, "The North-East – Hills and Hells" in Clough Williams-Ellis (ed.), *Britain and the Beast* (London, 1937), p.143.
6. Patrick Wormald, "The Making of England", *History Today* (February 1995), pp.26-32; he further developed his ideas during an appearance on "Start the Week" (BBC Radio Four, 6 February 1995).
7. See Peter Hunter Blair, "The Boundary between Bernicia and Deira", *Archaeologia Aeliana*, 4th ser., vol. xxvii (1949), pp.46-59.
8. J.E.A. Jolliffe, "Northumbrian Institutions", *The English Historical Review*, vol. xli no. clxi (January 1926), p.42.
9. Frank Musgrove, *The North of England: a History from Roman Times to the Present* (Oxford, 1990), pp.56-57.
10. R.R. Reid, *The King's Council in the North* (London, 1921), p.1.
11. Edward Miller, review of Richard Lomas, *North-East England in the Middle Ages* (Edinburgh, 1992), in *Northern History*, vol. xxix (1993), p.218.
12. See A.J. Pollard, *North Eastern England During the Wars of the Roses* (Oxford, 1990), esp. chapter 1.

13. Daniel Defoe, *A Tour Through the Whole Island of Great Britain* (1724-26, edition with an introduction by G.D.H. Cole, London, 1927), vol.II, pp.661-62.

14. Pollard, op. cit., p.10.

15. Colls and Lancaster, op. cit., p.10.

16. Robert Spence Watson, "Northumbrian Folk and Speech", in *Northumbria: Lectures delivered to the Literary and Philosophical Society of Newcastle upon Tyne, on Northumbrian History, Literature and Art* (Newcastle upon Tyne, 1898), pp.26-27.

17. Thomas Sharp, *Northumberland and Durham: 'Shell' Guide* (London, 1949), p.5.

18. S.J. Watts with Susan J. Watts, *From Border to Middle Shire: Northumberland 1586-1625* (Leicester, 1975).

19. As, for example, in "Northern Castles", lecture delivered to the Society of Antiquaries of Newcastle upon Tyne, at the University of Newcastle upon Tyne, 26 April 1995.

20. Lesley Milner, "Pele Towers", *Northern Architect*, 5th ser., no.1 (Winter 1994/95), p.7.

21. William Cobbett, *Rural Rides* ("Progress in the North", 1 October 1832).

22. Musgrove, op. cit., p.147.

23. Ibid., p.255.

24. C. Morris (ed.), *The Journeys of Celia Fiennes* (London, 1949), pp.209-11.

25. Defoe, op. cit., p.659.

26. E. Mackenzie, *A Descriptive and Historical Account of Newcastle upon Tyne* (Newcastle upon Tyne, 1827), p.197.

27. Colls and Lancaster, op. cit., p. ix.

Part I

MEDIEVAL TO EIGHTEENTH CENTURY

The Castelle of Barnard stondith stately apon Tese. The first area hath no very notable thing yn it, but the fair chapelle, wher be 2 cantuaries. In the midle of the body of this chapel is a fair marble tumbe with an image and an inscription about it yn French. Ther is another in the south waul of the body of the chapelle of fre stone, with an image of the same. Sum say that they were of the Bailliolles.

JOHN LELAND

Itinerary

(compiled c.1535-43)

I

HERALDRY AND MONUMENTAL EFFIGIES IN THE NORTH EAST

P.R. Coss

Medieval society was an intensely visual one. Among the most evocative expressions of that visuality which has been bequeathed to the modern world is heraldry. Heraldry has long fascinated antiquarians. Its study, however, is of far more than antiquarian interest, for its development and deployment take us to the very heart of medieval and early modern social history. As far as the North East is concerned, the groundwork for the modern study of heraldry and associated subjects was undertaken many years ago by C.H. Hunter Blair, President of the Literary and Philosophical Society of Newcastle upon Tyne for forty-two years and editor of *Archaeologia Aeliana* from 1924 until 1961.[1] Consequently, any reassessment of the subject inevitably becomes something of a commentary upon his work. Each generation, however, reinterprets the past – and present traces of the past – in the light of deepening knowledge and changing concerns.

Heraldry has been defined as "the systematic use of hereditary devices centred upon the shield".[2] The Bayeux Tapestry, of the late eleventh century, shows that shields were already painted with devices at that time, although their precise significance remains obscure.[3] Thereafter their purpose shifted from decoration to recognition and it is hardly to be doubted that the chief causes of this were the rise of the tournament and advances in armour which concealed the individual participant's features. An hereditary tendency soon developed and is clearly discernible from around 1140.

Not surprisingly, heraldry became increasingly systematized. Its function was primarily one of social display. It was also an expression of noble solidarity. Heraldry was to be found everywhere: on dress, for example, on manuscripts, on domestic plate, on caskets and chests, on tiles and wall paintings. And, of course, it was found in churches. Here a family displayed its singular importance. The higher nobility, in particular, sported their elevated status in cathedrals and other great churches, including monastic ones, especially those to which their families were benefactors. Lesser families had often to be content with demonstrating their status in their own parish churches, particularly through heraldic glass.

It is no accident that the very time when chivalric knighthood was becoming a dominant force within English landowning classes also saw the rise of the knightly effigy in churches. From the middle of the thirteenth century they became increasingly common throughout southern and middle England.[4]

Before the end of the century they had spread to northern England too. Styles were diffused from two centres, one being the west country and the other London, with overlap and cross-fertilization between the two. The cross-legged knight, for example, seems to have spread from the west country. The romantic idea that this style was reserved for crusaders has now generally been discarded. By the close of the thirteenth century, the sword-handling, cross-legged knight was becoming something of a national model, although it was never the only one. By this time, too, the effigy of the deceased lady was becoming commoner, to be followed increasingly during the fourteenth century by the joint effigy. The early fourteenth century, moreover, saw another new development, the monumental brass. The first figure brasses date from the end of the previous century but had been for ecclesiastical patrons. At the opening of the fourteenth century a workshop was in operation in London catering for customers wanting secular effigies in brass.[5] The market steadily expanded during the course of the century.

During the fourteenth and fifteenth centuries churches became literally festooned with heraldic arms, both in glass and in stone, and graced with images of the deceased. Many contained what were, in effect, family mausolea, with chapels and chantries often reserved for these. But this world was by no means a static one. During the course of the fourteenth century, the social reach of heraldry widened. By the middle decades esquires, socially below the knights, were becoming accepted as heraldic, and by the end of the century, if not before, they were being joined by those of merchant stock. One local witness to this is the fine early fifteenth-century Flemish brass to the Newcastle merchant Roger Thornton and his wife, now in the Cathedral. The adoption of heraldic arms and the proliferation of sepulchral monuments of various kinds are significant manifestations of social change. Inevitably, this caused reaction, in terms of a fear of upward mobility. This became stronger in the sixteenth century, as the size of the gentry expanded: as the most recent commentators have said, "The vigorous land market of the century after 1540, swelled by the vast estates released by the Crown, particularly after the Dissolution of the Monasteries, provided opportunities for those who sought to invest in land and to secure the status that pertained to its possession".[6] In a Commission of 1530, Henry VIII gave authority to the heralds to police the situation in order to prevent the assumption of arms by those "of vyle blood". The results were the heralds' 'visitations', which occurred on average in most counties every forty years. Those who claimed arms were to bring before the heralds their pedigrees and other proofs of ancient usage, and the resulting records are a goldmine to the genealogist and historian. They register, of course, not only the increase in the size of the gentry but society's deeply neurotic concern with such matters. In Northumberland, thirty-one families claimed gentle status at the visitation of 1563/4; no less than sixty did so in 1615.[7] The same story is found in County Durham. In 1575, fifty-six families produced pedigrees and claimed coats of arms, and the number had doubled by 1615. For one historian the phenomenon of prosperous yeomen acquiring arms is summed up by the Punshons of Herrington, with the arms: *a fess embattled between three sheeps' heads.*[8]

The related phenomena of heraldry and the sepulchral monument offer a series of important themes for the historian to pursue. The North East was seldom – although it was occasionally – in the van, but its records and surviving monuments do allow the historian an entrée into the elite mentality of the medieval and early modern past. Let us begin with heraldry and the important but rather mysterious phenomenon of dissemination of coats of arms during its formative period. There can be little doubt that the most primitive and, therefore, the primary means of dissemination of coats of arms within the nobility was among kin. Roger fitz Richard, twelfth-century lord of Warkworth, for example, bore a version of the arms of Geoffrey de Mandeville, earl of Essex (d. 1144), to whom he was related by marriage. The earl of Essex bore *quarterly or and gules* (that is, gold in the first and fourth quarters, red in the second and third). Roger fitz Richard and his descendants bore *quarterly or and gules, a baston sable.* (A *baston* or *baton* is a form of *bend* – the charge which runs diagonally across the shield – but which is cut short at the ends). Transmission of arms through kin can be shown very clearly in the North East through the arms of the Balliols (colour plate i). The Balliols, lords of Bywell and Barnard Castle, bore *gules, an orle argent.* The *orle* is a simple device but one which is not easy to describe in words. Known alternatively as a false escutcheon, it is a narrow border or *bordure* following the exact outline of the shield and in a different 'tincture' from the main body of the shield. Borne by John Balliol, the regent of Scotland who died in 1268, it can be traced back to at least the time of Hugh Balliol, who died in 1228. Undoubtedly, however, the arms go back to the twelfth century, and it was then that they were adopted by the Bertrams. Hawise, daughter of Guy de Balliol, had married William Bertram of Mitford. In the thirteenth century Roger de Bertram of Mitford bore *gules crusily, an orle or.* (A field *crusily* is one powdered with *cross crosslets.*)

The Bertrams of Bothal, descendants of William de Bertram's second son, Richard, bore *or, an orle azure.* By the thirteenth century, family arms 'differenced' were being borne by members of immediate kin. John de Balliol's brother, Eustace, for example, bore *azure crusily, an orle or,* while Hugh de Balliol, John's son, bore *gules, an orle argent,* with an escutcheon representing the arms of his mother, Devorguilla of Galloway, viz. *azure, a lion rampant argent crowned or.*[9] Younger sons sometimes took their arms from their wife's family rather than their own if the former was deemed to be more prestigious. The Umfravilles of Prudhoe and Redesdale, for example, bore *gules crusily, a cinquefoil or.* (A *cinquefoil* is a leaf with five petals.) Ingram de Umfraville, however, who was related by marriage to the king of Scotland, chose to bear not his brother's arms 'differenced' but a variant of the Balliol arms, viz. *gules, an orle ermine with a label of five points azure.*[10]

Another means of dissemination of heraldic design is by association with a higher lord, either through tenancy or through service. It is highly probable, in fact, that the primary dissemination of arms below the ranks of the great lords was their use by members of their retinues at tournaments. Traces of such dissemination remain, but less systematically than one might wish and it is difficult to be sure just how important these factors were. Means used to difference arms were clearly in use from an early date. These included changes in tincture and marks, or *brisures* as they were known. Among these were the *bend*, the *bordure* and the *label.* There were probably no rules governing these in the early days. Nonetheless, even though we may know only the charges on the field, we can sometimes see the social reasons for the adoption of arms. Two of the families which held by knight's service of the barony of Wark held the arms of its lord 'differenced'. The arms of Ros of Wark were *or, three bougets sable.* (Water-bougets or buckets were leather bags or bottles, two of which were carried on a stick over the shoulder.) The Lilburns and the Ildertons, who were their tenants, both bore *bougets*: in the case of the Lilburns *sable, three bougets argent,* and of the Ildertons *argent, three bougets sable,* arms very close to those of their overlord.[11] Several Northumberland families bear cinquefoils, indicating a likely relationship with the Umfravilles: the Burradons bore *argent, three cinquefoils sable* and the Farendons *gules, three cinquefoils or.*[12] It is certain, however, that such factors were not universal. Families had their own reasons for their choice of arms, many of which are certainly not recoverable. A minority were canting arms, that is to say the arms directly reflected the family name. An obvious example is that of the Herons, lords of Hadston, Northumberland, whose arms were *gules, three herons argent.*[13] Another difficulty is that some families undoubtedly changed their arms in these early years. We have clear evidence of this during the late thirteenth century and it may well have been relatively common in heraldry's formative years.

Given the vitality and significance of heraldry, it is sad indeed that so little remains of the glass which adorned medieval and early modern churches, especially in the North East; the most spectacular loss locally is from Durham Cathedral itself. However, this makes it all the more precious that armorial shields were depicted in stone on the outer walls of its castles and towers.[14] One of the leaders here was Sir Roger Bertram of Bothal, with a fine series of shields on the battlements above his gatehouse, completed by 1343.[15] A few years later, Henry lord Percy followed suit on his octagon towers which formed the gateway to his inner bailey at Alnwick.[16]

For obvious reasons the gatehouse was a favourite repository for arms. It is hardly surprising, therefore, that when Ralph de Lumley, after being created the first baron Lumley in 1385, turned his house into a castle a few years later, he had six shields of arms carved above the gatehouse. In addition to that of his royal lord, Richard II, which has centre place, and his own, there are the arms of his great northern contemporaries: Henry Percy, first earl of Northumberland; Sir John Neville, third lord Neville of Raby, to whose daughter, Eleanor, Ralph was married; Sir Thomas Grey of Heaton; and Sir William Hilton. When the latter built his own castle a few years later, he returned the compliment.[17] When emblazoned these six coats of arms are spectacular. On the Lumley gatehouse, moreover, they were depicted couched (that is, on the slant), to allow the inclusion of the helms, with mantles and crests, as in the full fashion of the day (fig. 1). Along with the castle, the associated arms advertised that Lumley had now wholly arrived as a power in the far north.

The linked subjects of heraldry and the effigy in the North East are best approached, in fact, via a detailed consideration of the Lumleys. John, lord Lumley, who died in 1609, was a man much concerned with ancestry. On the gateway of the inner court at Lumley Castle (see fig. 2) he placed a series of nineteen shields, which still survive today, though sadly in deteriorating condition. Sixteen of them represent his ancestors, while the final three give the family arms – *argent, a fess gules between three popinjays vert* – flanked by the arms of his two wives, Jane Fitzalan, daughter of the earl of Arundel, and Elizabeth, daughter of John, lord Darcy of Chick. In the nearby church of St Mary

Fig. 1 Gatehouse, Lumley Castle, Co. Durham (detail).

Fig. 2 Inner Court, Lumley Castle, Co. Durham (detail).

and St Cuthbert, Chester-le-Street, John arranged for fourteen effigies to be placed along the north aisle, representing most of the generations of the family-from Liulph, its supposed founder, to his grandfather. Above each of them was placed a tablet recording the knight's name and arms. A long inscription in Latin, apparently Lord John's own composition, records the history of the family. In the Great Hall of the castle itself he had a mantelpiece erected with the full arms of himself and his first wife impaled, that is placed side by side in true heraldic fashion. Portraits of his ancestors once adorned the walls. Near to the portrait of his second wife hung the family pedigree.[18] Besides being passionately interested in his family's past, Lord John was himself something of a general antiquarian. He seems to have been a collector of manuscripts. He certainly owned British Library Royal C. XII, a fourteenth-century manuscript which contains, among other things, the French romance *Fouke Fitz Warin* and the *Short English Metrical Chronicle.*[19] In 1585 he gave a considerable number of Greek and Latin books to the University of Oxford.[20] With such a keen sense of ancestry, it was no doubt a matter of great sadness to him that he was to die childless. His three children by his first wife died in infancy and he had no offspring by his second. With him passed what Surtees refers to as the first race of Lumley. His estates passed to a kinsman, Richard Lumley, ancestor of the earls of Scarborough.[21]

Lord John Lumley's interest, however, was more than antiquarian. At Chester-le-Street he provided the Lumleys with something they had hitherto, and rather surprisingly, lacked: a family mausoleum. The family was already commemorated in the church. An octagonal font bears the quartered arms of George, third lord Lumley, and his wife, Elizabeth, the daughter and heiress of Roger Thornton, the last of the great Newcastle mercantile dynasty. Their arms were also depicted separately, the Thornton arms being *sable, a chief and a chevron indented argent.* Also depicted were several impaled arms, the most significant being Neville impaling Lumley, denoting the first lord Lumley's important marriage to the sister of the earl of Westmorland. The font probably dates from shortly after the death of George, lord Lumley, in 1507. John, lord Lumley, now proceeded to gather together artificially what in many families would have accrued piecemeal and more naturally. Eleven of the effigies were, in fact, made to order. Only three were genuine medieval effigies, two of them imported from the graveyard of Durham Cathedral, by license of the bishop, granted in 1594.[22] The third is of unknown provenance. The whole setting not only indicated social prominence, but also suggested antiquity. The same was true of the castle's courtyard shields and Lord Lumley's pedigree which inspired them.

According to the latter, the Lumleys were descended from the Saxon nobleman Liulph, who had fled from southern England in the wake of the Norman invasion and had settled on the Wear, marrying the daughter of Earl Aeldred of Northumbria. Their son, Uchtred, was said to have been a baron and, therefore, a man of some standing within the palatinate of Durham, while his son, William, is supposed to have assumed the name Lumley. The Lumleys were claiming to be of ancient and, indeed, of Anglo-Saxon lineage. In reality, the story of Liulph and his family was probably grafted upon the Lumley pedigree, the early generations of which are almost certainly bogus. Hunter Blair, however, was over-pessimistic in extending this to the first five generations. A William de Lumley was certainly in evidence during the last decade of the twelfth century and he was, most probably, the head of the supposed fourth generation.[23] Either he or his son, another William, is recorded as a knight of the county of Durham during 1210-12.[24] It was a common occurrence for minor landowners to adopt toponymic names during this period. In truth, however, the Lumleys seem to have owed their rise to successful marriage rather than anything else. William de Lumley 'III' married the daughter and co-heiress of Walter de Audre, who probably held the major estate at Lumley, while his son, Sir Roger de Lumley, married Sybil, daughter and co-heiress of Hugh de Morwick of Northumberland. In 1279, in widowhood, she was said to be worth £50 land in Northumberland and her son, Robert, £50 in this county and £100 in the bishopric of Durham.[25] Another prestigious marriage was that of Robert de Lumley, no mean landowner in his own right, to Lucy, daughter and co-heiress of Marmaduke, lord Thweng, of Kilton, Yorkshire. Their grandson, Ralph, married Eleanor Neville and was raised to the parliamentary peerage as the first lord Lumley in 1385. He it was who built Lumley Castle. Licenses to crenellate were issued by the bishop in 1389 and by the Crown in 1392.

If John, lord Lumley, was an indifferent genealogist, he was nevertheless an accomplished herald. The shields which he added to the inner courtyard are impaled, correctly, with the husband's arms on the dexter side (i.e. the left facing the viewer) and the wife's on the sinister. From Roger de Lumley onwards the arms on the sinister side are certainly authentic. The Lumley arms themselves, however, are doubtful. Up to and including Sir Robert they are given as *gules, six popinjays argent.* There is no known contemporary justification for these arms. They may well have been derived from non-heraldic family seals. Robert's son, Marmaduke de Lumley, is shown bearing his mother's arms, *argent, a fess gules between three popinjays vert,* and these became the family arms from then on. The Parliamentary Roll of Arms of c.1308 indicates that these were the arms borne by Robert's father-in-law, Sir Marmaduke de Thweng. They were indeed ancient. They figure in the very earliest lists of arms – those of Matthew Paris – and in Glover's and Walford's Rolls. Marmaduke de Lumley sealed with the Thweng arms in 1365[26] and it was these which descended in the Lumley family. If Marmaduke de Lumley bore them undifferenced, this was no doubt because, with the extinction of the Thwengs, he became, in effect, the head of the line. John, lord Lumley, understood the significance of this well enough in the sixteenth century. In the church of St Mary and St Cuthbert, Chester-le-Street, he devoted an unusually long tablet to Marmaduke, which was effectively a mini genealogy. "This Marmaduke", it says, "after the death of his said mother, did beare and use the armes of Thwinge".[27] Whether Robert de Lumley himself bore the Thweng arms is unknown. What is clearly the case is that the Lumleys adopted the arms of the more illustrious family into which they had married.

The Lumleys were far from being the only family which adopted new arms at this time. A more illustrious example is that of the Percies. Henry de Percy, lord of Topcliffe, Yorkshire, fought at Falkirk in 1298 and at Carlaverock in 1300 where he bore the famous arms *or, a lion rampant azure* (see colour plate i). In 1309 he purchased the barony and castle of Alnwick from Antony Bek, bishop of Durham.[28] The Percy lion is to be found throughout Northumberland and Durham. However, these were not inherited arms. In fact, they were probably adopted from Henry's father-in-law, for the lord of Topcliffe had married Eleanor, daughter of the Richard Fitz Alan, earl of Arundel, who bore *gules, a lion rampant or.*[29] The traditional family arms were *azure, a fess of five fusils or.* (Fusils are tall lozenges.) Glover's roll informs us that Henry's father, another Henry (d.1272), had borne *azure, a fess engrailed or,* another way of expressing *azure, a fess of five fusils or,* and that the related Piers Percy had borne *or, a fess engrailed azure.* Matthew Paris tells us that a generation earlier Richard de Percy (d.1244) had borne *azure, a fess of five fusils argent,* while his nephew and successor, William, bore the fusils on his seal. William's own father, Henry (d.1198), may arguably have borne *azure, a fess of five fusils or,* the arms later in evidence; although this is speculative, the Percy arms clearly go back some way.[30]

That the Lumleys bore arms in the thirteenth century is not, therefore, to be doubted, but these appear to have been lost. The late arrival and comparative rarity of early rolls of arms, and the capacity of some families to switch arms, complicates the early history of heraldry. It may not be inconceivable, but it is most unlikely that the Lumleys had independently borne popinjays – and plain popinjays at that – prior to their association with the Thwengs.

The Parliamentary Roll of Arms, however, does reveal the existence of related arms. Sir John Fitz Marmaduke bore *gules, a fess between three popinjays argent,* arms very close to those of Thweng (see colour plate i). Sir John, who had borne these arms at the siege of Carlaverock in 1300, was head of the Fitz Marmadukes of Horden, a family undoubtedly related to the Thwengs. It seems probable that Sir John's grandfather, Geoffrey fitz Geoffrey, married a Thweng, which would account for both the arms and for his son's name, Marmaduke; Fitz Marmaduke now became the family name. Sir Richard Fitz Marmaduke bore yet another version of these arms: *gules, a fess between three popinjays argent and a baston azure.*[31] The tinctures are changed and a baston is added to the fess, but the derivation of the arms is clear. The Parliamentary Roll of Arms gives many instances of blood relatives bearing their family arms differenced.

Another set of related arms which figure in the Parliamentary Roll are those of Sir Robert de Lumley, who bore: *gules, a fess between three popinjays argent and in the fess three mullets sable*[32]. These are, in fact, the earliest recorded Lumley arms. What is immediately striking is that they are closer to the arms of Fitz Marmaduke than to Thweng. This suggests that the Sir Robert de Lumley who figures on the roll is not the man who married the Thweng heiress, Lucy, but another Robert. It is tempting to see him as a collateral of the Lumley family and to associate him with the man who married the sister of John Fitz Marmaduke of Horden from whom he acquired the manor of Ravensworth. A separate line, the Lumleys of Ravensworth, was established, whose pedigree was given by Robert Surtees. Its members continued to bear the Fitz Marmaduke arms differenced. The Fitz Marmaduke line, meanwhile, came to an end with the murder of John's son Richard, steward to the bishop of Durham, by his kinsman, Robert de Neville, on the old bridge in Durham in 1318.[33] The Parliamentary Roll of Arms contains, in fact, no list of knights for the county of Durham. Sir Robert de Lumley and Sir Richard Fitz Marmaduke figure under the list for Northumberland and Cumberland, while Sir John Fitz Marmaduke of Horden and Sir Marmaduke de Thweng appear under the national list of barons and bannerets. This could explain why Sir Robert de Lumley of the main line seems not to occur.

All of this, however, is to take John, lord Lumley's pedigree and the pedigree of the Lumleys of Ravensworth as reconstructed by Robert Surtees at face value. In fact, they are both in error. In 1919, W.H.B. Bird showed, convincingly, that there were two consecutive Robert de Lumleys, father and son, and that they died respectively in 1308 and 1325. Marmaduke de Lumley, son of the latter, was proved to be of age (i.e. 21) ten years later. In 1391, Ralph, lord Lumley, traced his own ancestry to Mary, sister of Richard Fitz Marmaduke, and her son Robert. It is clear, therefore, that the Robert de Lumley who married Mary Fitz Marmaduke was the son and heir of Roger de Lumley of the main line and that his own son, a second Robert, married Lucy de Thweng.[34] This second Robert was under age at the time of the Parliamentary Roll of Arms and the question of the Thweng arms simply does not arise at that date. His father, as we have seen, bore the Fitz Marmaduke arms, differenced. The Lumleys of Ravensworth were, indeed, a collateral line but they were descended, almost certainly, from a younger son of the elder Robert who was given Ravensworth, his mother's dower. A further implication is that the Lumleys effectively changed their arms not once but twice, in each case as a result of a prestigious marriage.

Genealogy: Fitz Marmaduke and Lumley

Geoffrey fitz Geoffrey of Horden = de Thweng
Marmaduke fitz Geoffrey = Isabella
Isabella Brus = John Fitz Marmaduke
Richard Fitz Marmaduke, steward of the bishop of Durham
Mary = Robert de Lumley son of Roger de Lumley
Robert de Lumley = Lucy de Thweng
Marmaduke de Lumley
John de Lumley of Ravensworth
Ralph, lord Lumley

In the end we are no closer to the problem of the original Lumley arms. What is clear is that Marmaduke de Lumley, son of Sir Robert de Lumley the younger and Lucy Thweng, ultimately bore the Thweng arms. He once sealed, in 1343, with six birds on a shield.[35] It may well have been this which John, lord Lumley, had sight of and which caused him to ascribe these arms to his ancestors. One has to be extremely wary, however, in the interpretation of seals. The borrowing of seals was a common phenomenon in this period. This particular seal has no clear inscription, so that one cannot be absolutely sure that it was Marmaduke's own, let alone that he bore such arms. The device is almost certainly derived from either the Fitz

Marmadukes or the Thwengs.[36] There is no need to assume that these are the Lumley arms of old. This was an understandable mistake on the part of John, lord Lumley, and later antiquaries have almost certainly followed him into this trap. Even more insecure is the evidence of a very fine, probably late thirteenth-century, seal of one Matthew de Lumley, shown on horseback in civilian dress looking back towards a bird in his hand. There is nothing to suggest that this bird reflects a coat of arms.[37]

The popinjays figure prominently again when one examines the effigies which Lord John had removed to Chester-le-Street church. One of these is of a fully mailed figure, cross-legged with a sleeveless surcoat. A single popinjay is carved upon his breast (fig. 3). It is certainly not William son of Uchtred, as the tablet pretends, and even the identification with Sir Roger de Lumley, or his father, as suggested by Hunter Blair, seems unlikely[38], as the Lumley popinjays very probably derived, as we have seen, from their association with the Fitz Marmadukes and the Thwengs. Moreover, had they actually borne six popinjays as charges, a single specimen on the surcoat would hardly seem to suffice. However, it could conceivably be Robert de Lumley the elder, or even his son.

Fig. 3 Effigy of knight, Chester-le-Street; perhaps Robert de Lumley.

The popinjays are found again in St Mary's church, Easington, where they are found on the heater-shield of a crossed-legged knight (fig. 4).[39] As with the Lumley effigy mentioned above, his feet rest on a lion fighting with a

Fig. 4 The Easington knight; probably Richard Fitz Marmaduke.

dragon; otherwise the effigies have little in common. It clearly represents one of the Fitz Marmaduke knights, quite probably Richard Fitz Marmaduke.[40] Two further effigies of Fitz Marmaduke knights survive. They are those which John, lord Lumley, brought from Durham to Chester-le-Street and which for him depicted Ralph, first lord Lumley, himself, who was killed in rebellion against Henry IV in 1400, and his son, Sir John, who was killed at Baugé in 1421. Once again, they carry the Fitz Marmaduke arms. They are in Frosterley marble, a dark limestone quarried in Weardale.

The image they convey is a crudely martial one. They bear pot helms, with a slit for the eyes. The sword is held upright behind the shield in a rather unusual fashion (fig. 5). As Hunter Blair pointed out,[41] they bear a strong resemblance to three other local effigies, at Whitworth, Pittington and Hurworth. They are not, however, identical. The figure at All Saints' church, Hurworth, has the shield at a much broader angle, for example, revealing a good deal more of the sword. His shield has three bougets on a fess, suggesting the arms of the Ros family, either of Wark or of Helmsley, or of course a variant of these. The effigy apparently came from Neasham Abbey, nearby. It is undoubtedly the finest and the most attractive of the effigies in this style. The figure at St Lawrence's church, Pittington, is said to have once carried the Fitz Marmaduke arms, although these are no longer visible.[42] At Whitworth the knight lies in the churchyard exposed to the weather (fig. 6) and close to the effigy of a lady. Behind her head is a shield with the same arms as on the knight's shield, viz. two bars with a bordure charged with roundels. The two Chester-le-Street effigies differ from the others in having straight rather than crossed legs. However, even these two are not identical

Fig. 5 Effigy of knight, Chester-le-Street; possibly Geoffrey fitz Geoffrey.

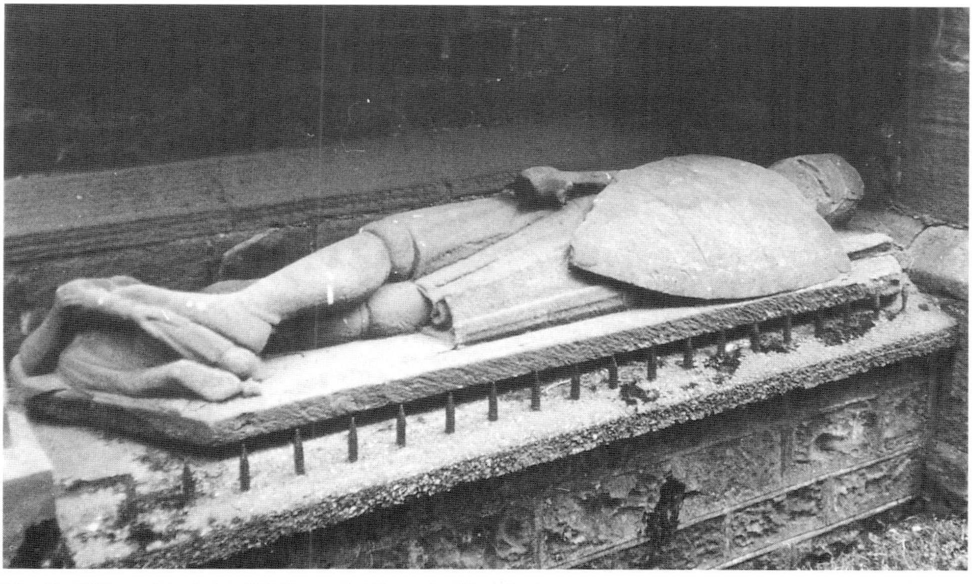

Fig. 6 Effigy of knight, Whitworth Church, Co. Durham.

with one another. One has a cushion beneath the head and is carved in higher relief. The shield is flat across the chest and the sword is alongside rather than in front of the helm (fig. 7). There cannot be any doubt, however, that these effigies are to be considered as a group and their style seems not to

Fig. 7 Effigy of knight, Chester-le-Street; possibly Marmaduke fitz Geoffrey.

be replicated anywhere else in England. Among the unusual features are the surcoats, which are strikingly short. Even allowing for the wide variety across the country and across time in this respect, it is difficult to find surcoats ending above the knee elsewhere. These effigies are quite clearly the products of a local workshop, with a style of its own.

This is not to suggest that the style is uninfluenced by effigies elsewhere. The various elements which combine to produce their effect – a stiff, frontal attitude – can be found earlier, either separately or in combinations, and seem to be among the various products of the London Purbeck marblers. The unsheathed sword, held in the right hand, is shown at Thruxton, Hampshire, for example, while there are a number of other examples of the closed helm and others with the shield covering the chest. At Blyth, Notts., it is these last two features which are combined.[43] Nevertheless, these North Eastern effigies are undoubtedly distinctive.

Hunter Blair dated these effigies as follows: Pittington, c.1280; Whitworth, c.1290; Chester-le-Street I, c.1300; Chester-le-Street II, c.1310; Hurworth, c.1310. It is surprising that this dating has been accepted uncritically, as it appears to be based upon little that is substantial.[44] The dating of effigies by reference to costume and armour is something of a minefield. The length of surcoats, for example, appears to be variable throughout the century. What is striking, however, is that almost all the other effigies with the great helm are considerably earlier in date.[45] Even the two effigies with the great helm from

Furness Abbey are considered to belong to the third quarter of the thirteenth century. In these cases, the body is turned to give a 'three-quarters view', which would seem to suggest a later style.[46] Furthermore, those products of the London Purbeck marblers which share the stiff, frontal attitude with the North Eastern effigies tend to date from mid century, or even earlier. All of this should put us on our guard. There may well be a time-lag before the secular stone effigy reached the North East, but it seems improbable that what was almost certainly its first workshop should have developed a style based on features that were entirely out of fashion. It would seem much more likely, therefore, that this workshop was in existence during the third quarter of the thirteenth century.

Blair's dating seems to have been based largely on genealogy. He assumed that the Pittington effigy and those from Chester-le-Street represented Fitz Marmadukes, an assumption that was surely correct. The Pittington effigy he ascribed to Geoffrey fitz Geoffrey, while the sometime Durham effigies he ascribed to Marmaduke fitz Geoffrey and John Fitz Marmaduke. Two of these knights, however, flourished considerably earlier than he allowed for. Geoffrey fitz Geoffrey occurs from the end of the twelfth century until 1242 and was a justice within the bishopric of Durham.[47] Marmaduke occurs in 1251 and as a knight in 1260. In that year he was given permission by the crown to fortify his house at Horden with ditches and a wall of stone and to crenellate it. In 1267 he occurs in a witness list with Sir Richard de Thweng and Sir Roger de Lumley.[48] His son, John Fitz Marmaduke, occurs as a knight as early as 1277 and 1282, by which time Marmaduke fitz Geoffrey seems no longer in evidence.[49] In short, the genealogical evidence tends to support the second half of the thirteenth century as the time of production of these effigies.

To ascribe particular effigies to individuals is extremely hazardous. There seems a very strong probability that one of the Chester-le-Street effigies represents Marmaduke fitz Geoffrey. It is tempting to believe that the other is John Fitz Marmaduke himself, given that his remains were brought from Scotland to Durham for burial.[50] Everything suggests, however, that this group of effigies dates from well before his death in 1311. It is perfectly possible, of course, that Sir John commissioned an effigy for himself at the same time as he purchased one for his father. It is extremely unlikely that it was constructed after his death. It is just conceivable that the workshop remained in existence and continued to produce its peculiar product over such a long space of time, but it is very improbable. A stronger possibility is that the two effigies represent Marmaduke and his father. The Pittington effigy may represent another male of the Fitz Marmaduke family.

The products of this workshop differ markedly from two other styles found widely in County Durham during the early decades of the fourteenth century. Both of these styles conform, broadly speaking, to national models. The one is the well-known cross-legged and sword-handling effigy. The head tends to rest upon a single cushion. In the majority of cases, the shields lack carved arms, and these were very probably indicated by colour upon gesso. Representative of this type is the supposed effigy of William son of Uchtred at Chester-le-Street. The alternative style has the hands clasped in prayer and the head resting on two cushions. The arms may or may not be carved on the shield. Among the examples are the Marmaduke effigy at St Mary's church, Easington, and Robert de Neville, 'the Peacock of the North' at St Brandon's, Brancepeth. This style is generally much more decorative. In addition to carved figures, there is decoration on the swords, sword belts and shield straps. The surcoats tend to be shorter. The style appeared later than the sword-handling effigy and, as far as County Durham is concerned, it seems to have been introduced a little before 1320.[51]

The number of military effigies expanded everywhere during the first decades of the fourteenth century and it was then that they penetrated into Northumberland. Here, however, it was the more serene, praying knight that was fashionable. Many of them have the knight's arms carved upon his shield. Among them is the Umfraville effigy at Hexham Abbey, with the arms *gules crusily, a cinquefoil or.* The fact that the chain mail of these effigies is shown by interlaced rings rather than by curved lines cut into the stone indicates that they did not come from the workshops that produced the County Durham effigies. It is quite likely that they were produced in Newcastle and that the major influence came from Yorkshire and Lincolnshire, where this manner of depicting mail is common.[52]

Less attention is sometimes paid to the effigies of ladies than to their male counterparts, except perhaps in the matter of costume. Yet, what they lack in vigour as compared to the military effigy in particular, they often make up for in serenity. When it came to style, drapery folds were clearly important, and these tend to be a major determinant of quality. The mantle was sometimes tucked up between arm and body, and perhaps this too was designed to give some sense of movement. Moving outwards from the body, the basic garments were the kirtle, gown and mantle, although some effigies lack the latter. Like the knightly effigies, they were generally painted.

Not surprisingly, Durham's earliest workshop also produced effigies of ladies. The Hurworth knight, in particular, bears some resemblance to the lady at Easington church, except that the latter is undoubtedly of greater quality. One can hardly fail to agree with Hunter Blair that "it is indeed difficult to think that it has come from the same workshop as the rudely carved contemporary figures at Pittington and Chester-le-Street." She is the only surviving female effigy of this workshop in Frosterley marble. There are

Fig. 8 The Easington Lady; probably Isabella Brus, wife of John Fitz Marmaduke (detail).

others, however, in sandstone that are of similar style, namely the well-preserved effigy at St Michael's church, Esh, and the earliest of the ladies at St Mary's, Staindrop.[53] The Easington lady displays the popinjays, once again, and there can be little doubt that Hunter Blair was correct in identifying her as a wife of one of the Fitz Marmaduke, lords of Horden.[54] By far the most likely candidate is Isabella Brus, first wife of John Fitz Marmaduke.[55] Elegant and engaging, the effigy appears at first sight to be simple and unadorned. She wears a long mantle, elegantly draped. Her left hand holds a fold, whilst her right lies across her waist with her mantle draped in multiple folds beneath her forearm. Her headdress is quite complex. She wears a fillet and a barbette (respectively a circlet and a band passing under the chin and pinned on the top of the head), with her hair in a crespine visible at the sides (fig. 8). But she is also wearing a veil with, seemingly, a wimple (a neck covering) beneath. These last may be there to denote her widowhood. Her head lies on a cushion. The overall effect is most charming and graceful. She appears to be personally at rest. Moreover, she seems socially comfortable, with her husband's arms displayed proudly on her body. It is noteworthy that she is bearing solely her husband's arms, that is to say her adoptive arms. She wears them, instructively perhaps, on the garment nearest to her body.

The same feature is to be seen sometimes on the seals of aristocratic ladies.[56] For example, the lady Agnes, second wife of William de Vesci, lord of Alnwick, is depicted on her seal (fig. 9) in a gown embroidered with the arms, the cross patonce, of her husband. Standing under a canopy, she is holding in her right hand a shield bearing the Vesci arms: *gules, a cross patonce argent.* On her left side is depicted her own family's arms: *vairy, or and gules.*[57] She was the daughter of William de Ferrers, earl of Derby. (The seal does not of course reveal the blazons, which are added from the rolls of arms.) Moreover, while the cross patonce is depicted on her gown, her mantle is lined with the Ferrers vair, signifying on her person the union of the two families. Her adopted family, however, clearly has precedence, both heraldically (dexter versus sinister) and personally.

Fig. 9 Seal (obverse) of Agnes de Vesci (by courtesy of the Dean and Chapter of Durham Cathedral).

More interesting still, arguably, is the reverse of the seal (fig. 10), which illustrates pride in her own ancestry. Here is shown a tree from which hang three shields – due to damage to the seal, a fourth has been destroyed. One of them is for her mother, Sibyl, daughter of the great William the Marshal, earl of Pembroke: *party or and vert, a lion rampant gules.*[58] Another represents her paternal grandmother, Agnes, sister and one of the co-heiresses of Ranulf III, earl of Chester: *azure, three garbs or.* She was related, the seal reminds us, to two of the greatest (arguably, the two greatest) aristocrats of the early thirteenth century. One can only speculate as to whether the fourth shield was the Ferrers shield or whether it represented her mother-in-law. She was Margaret, illegitimate daughter of William the Lion, king of Scotland.[59]

At Staindrop there are no less than three fourteenth-century effigies of ladies, together with one of a small boy. They are all, no doubt, of the Neville family. The earliest has a voluminous mantle gathered in folds under the arms and does seem to be stylistically similar to the Esh and Easington figures.[60] The Staindrop figures, however, tend to be more ornate, with carvings more in evidence. Thus the second figure, chronologically speaking, has, in addition to a canopy above the lady's head, an angel supporting a pillow on each side of her head and a dog with collar and bell on her left side near her feet. She has a lion at her feet. Her mantle lies in long graceful folds and her hands are clasped in prayer. The ornamental

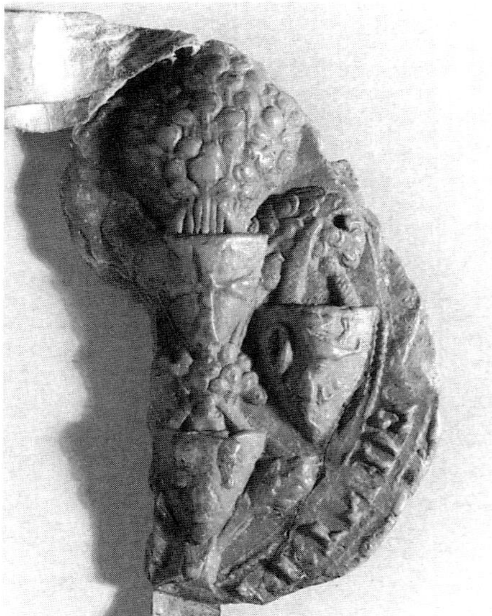

Fig. 10 Seal (reverse) of Agnes de Vesci (by courtesy of the Dean and Chapter of Durham Cathedral).

buttons of her tight-fitting kirtle are clearly visible. She wears a wimple, with a veil hanging over her shoulders and fastened by a jewelled fillet. She is thought to be Euphemia, the mother of Ralph, lord Neville, who built the south aisle c.1343.

Unlike the Easington lady, however, there is nothing about these effigies, other than their location, which connects them with their families or with their menfolk. Indeed, Staindrop appears to have been something of a female Neville mausoleum for much of the fourteenth century, with male members of the family preferring, it seems, to be buried elsewhere. The fine effigy of Robert de Neville, 'the Peacock of the North', son of Ralph, first lord Neville, for example, is at Brancepeth. He was killed fighting the Scots in 1319. Robert de Neville, his grandfather, was buried at Covenham Abbey.[61]

By the final quarter of the fourteenth century, the double effigy had arrived in the North East, rather later than elsewhere. Often these were in alabaster and very finely carved. The Nevilles here were in the van. Ralph, second lord Neville, and his wife Alice (who died in 1374) and John, lord Neville (d.1388), and his wife, Maud, are commemorated in two high-quality alabaster tombs in Durham Cathedral, infamously mutilated by Scottish prisoners in the seventeenth century. The tomb of Ralph Neville, first earl of Westmorland and his two wives at Staindrop appears to have been made about 1400, although he did not die until 1425 (fig. 11). Of fifteenth-century tombs, a magnificent example is that of Sir Ralph Grey (died 1443) and his wife in Chillingham church. The tomb table itself is

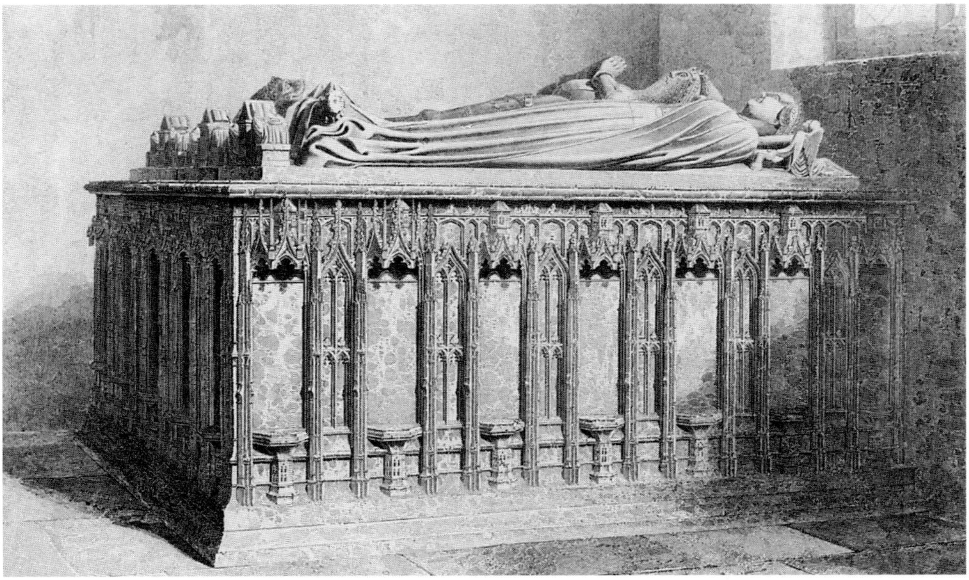

Fig. 11 Church of St. Mary, Staindrop, Co. Durham: Ralph Neville, first earl of Westmorland and wives (from Blore's *Monumental Remains,* 1826).

finely decorated with the statues of fourteen male and female saints. The arms of Grey of Heaton and Chillingham – *gules, a lion rampant in a border engrailed argent* – are carved on both sides of the tomb. On the end, below the couple's feet a shield impales Grey's arms with those of his wife, Elizabeth, daughter of Henry, lord Fitz Hugh of Ravensworth. The figures themselves are in alabaster, beautifully attired. He is in full plate armour, she in costume of the period. The figures are striking in their opulence. But, typically as far as the great families of the North East are concerned, they show nothing of the relationship between the couple, except the formal one, depicted armorially. They lie side by side, detached from one another, in an attitude of prayer. There is no suggestion of the intimacy that we sometimes find elsewhere, for example in the hand-holding effigy of Ralph Greene and Katherine his wife at Lowick, Northants.[62] Seen occasionally in double effigies, this relationship is depicted more often and more finely in brass, which medium, relatively lacking in the North East, lends itself more easily to it.

There is, however, one exception, which may well show a marital relationship. At St Mary's church, Norton, now in Cleveland, there is a very fine effigy of a knight "carved", as Blair says, "with great decorative detail".[63] He is cross-legged and mail-clad, with a flowing surcoat (fig. 12). There are many fine touches, including his jewelled sword-belt and a fine scabbard. Small shields are carved on his poleyns or knee-pieces. Pre-eminent among the carvings is the lion fighting with a dragon, on which the knight rests his

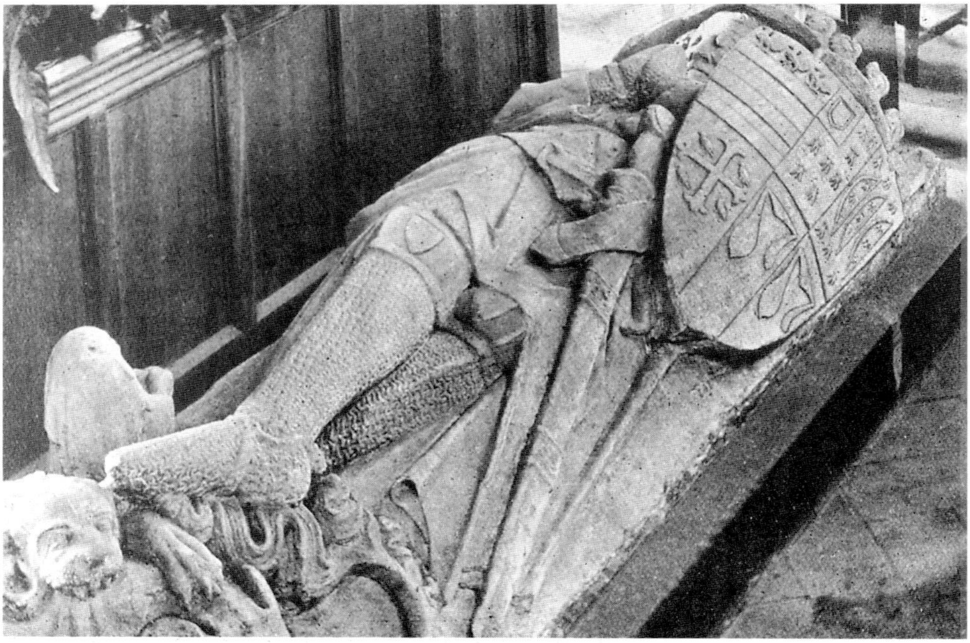

Fig. 12 The Norton Knight (from *Archaeologia Aeliana*, 4th ser. vol. vi, 1929).

Fig. 13 The Norton Knight (detail).

feet. A small grotesque figure looks over the shield. More importantly, a lady sits above his feet on his right side. She is evidently looking towards him, in dutiful if not reverential fashion; she is clearly intended to be devout (fig. 13) and could well represent his widow. The knight himself lies with his hands joined in an attitude of prayer.

The Norton monument has strong stylisitic similarities with the effigy of Sir Richard de Goldsborough IV in the chancel of St Mary's at Goldsborough in Yorkshire. Both belong, in fact, to a group which has been referred to as the work of the "Cheyne atelier" at York or, more recently, as Yorkshire "Series B".[64] This group includes the Goldsborough, Bedale and Escrick effigies, together with the effigy at Norton. All four of the knights depicted in these wear long-sleeved gowns which, it has been pointed out, are to be found depicted in various media "in the twenty years either side of 1300".[65] Once again, the Norton knight has his chain mail depicted by interlaced rings, unusual in County Durham and suggestive of a more southerly origin. Among the many other features which the Goldsborough and Norton effigies share are wide, wrist-length sleeves and the knee-piece which is reinforced in like manner with a small shield set on each side of the central strap. Both knights are mail-clad and cross-legged, in an attitude of prayer, with plain shields. Moreover, the Goldsborough effigy has three small attendant figures. One of them is seated in a similar position to the lady of the Norton effigy. Sadly, the upper part of the figure is lost, so that it is not now clear whether it is male or female. Clearly, though, it corresponds to the Norton figure. In fact, such figures were a characteristic feature of the effigies emanating from this atelier. The magnificent effigy to Brian Fitz Alan at Bedale has two such figures, located on either side of the knight at his feet. Both are damaged. The figure on his left is reading from a book, like the Norton lady. Although the head is missing, this figure appears to be male. His cowl is clearly visible and he may well be a member of a religious order. The figure is open to interpretation. It seems most likely that he is there to invoke prayers for the knight's soul. But, whatever one's interpretation in precise terms, these figures are surely symbolic as well as decorative. The Norton figure suggests a further refinement. Although she could represent a member of a religious order, her singularity strongly suggests the representation of a devout widow, who will now devote the remainder of her life to contemplation, living in chastity and probably eschewing remarriage.

The book on her lap is probably intended to denote this. She may be, in fact, one of those women who formalised their situation by making a vow and who came to be known, in consequence, as vowesses. The vow was made before a bishop prior to mass. The woman in question would place her written vow at the bishop's feet and read from it (or, if she were illiterate, her reading would be led by the bishop). She then marked the document with a cross and gave it to the bishop for safe-keeping.[66] The woman's clothes were blessed and asperged, followed by her ring with which she was then invested.[67] The open book may also be taken to indicate literacy, although this possibility should not be pushed too far.[68] Rather it expresses her piety.[69]

Many gentle women were the possessors of devotional books, however, and often they bequeathed them in their wills.[70] In Darlington parish church there is a badly preserved effigy of a lady; in her right hand she holds a book. She is veiled. Her probable widowhood does not preclude some nice touches. From her girdle there hangs her purse, while her gown is fastened at the neck by a magnificent diamond-shaped brooch.[71] Living in chastity did not necessarily mean being divorced from the world and from a normal social life.[72]

It is unfortunate that the knight and lady at Norton cannot be identified with any certainty. There is, however, an apparent clue to their identity. It lies not where one would expect it at first sight, in the arms on the knight's shield, for in one respect the Norton effigy is reminiscent of the local Lumley effigies. Like them, it was appropriated in the latter part of the sixteenth century. As no arms were carved on the knight's shield, the Blakistons were able to add their own, rather complex, arms to it. Quarterly of six, they are the Blakiston arms after the marriage between John Blakiston and Elizabeth, daughter and co-heiress of Sir George Bowes of Streatlam.[73] The perpetrator was probably Sir William Blakiston, son of John and Elizabeth. In all likelihood, the shield had only painted arms in the fourteenth century, although an original carving could conceivably have been removed, as Blair suggested. The appropriation of the Norton knight belongs, then, to the same cultural climate, of intense concern with antiquity and genealogy, as the knights of Chester-le-Street and the shields of Lumley Castle.

Behind the canopy at the knight's head, however, are two shields side by side. These are integral to the monument and contemporary with it. The fact that they are side by side suggests that the monument dates from before the system of impaling had got under way, and indicates, therefore, an early fourteenth-century date. There is good reason to suppose that these may be the arms of the knight and the lady who sits above his feet. They are: (i) an orle, overall a bend; (ii) a cross moline. Without the blazon, identification is difficult. As Blair points out, both of these arms are borne by more than one family. The former shield was clearly a Balliol shield 'differenced', while the cross moline was borne by, among others, the family of Bek, lords of nearby Redmarshall. This manor was held in the time of Antony Bek, bishop of Durham from 1284 to 1311, by his brother John Bek, baron of Eresby, Lincolnshire.[74] John Bek bore *gules, a cross moline argent,* and his clerical brother, not surprisingly, a variant upon this, viz. *gules, a cross moline ermine.*[75] The manor soon passed, however, through an intermediary, to Sir Henry de Lisle (of the Isle in Sedgefield). Similar arms were borne, meanwhile, by a local family, the Fulthorpes, with estates at Fulthorpe, Grindon and Norton; they bore *argent, a cross moline sable.*[76] Another local family which bore the Bek arms differenced, at least later in the fourteenth century, was that of Carrow, the lords of Seton Carew.[77] It seems most likely that their adoption stems from the time of Bishop Antony Bek.

Local tradition has it that the knight is Sir Roger de Fulthorpe who died in 1337, and that the arms represent the union of the Fulthorpes with the Langtons of Wynyard. A Ralph de Langton is later recorded as bearing *gules, an orle argent, overall a bend sable.* This identification would neatly connect two local families. Unfortunately, there are severe problems with it. It is far from certain that the orle was borne by the Langtons of Wynyard at this time. Ralph de Langton does not figure in their known pedigree, while Thomas de Langton of Wynyard, Henry's grandson, bore a lion rampant. Moreover, supposing the positioning of the arms to be the same as in the later rule of impalement, the knight's arms would be dexter and the wife's sinister. It is, in fact, the 'Langton' arms which are dexter and 'Fulthorpe' arms sinister. The families were, however, connected by marriage in the next generation. Margery, daughter of Roger de Fulthorpe, was married to Henry de Langton. It could be argued, therefore, that the knight does indeed represent Roger de Fulthorpe but that the arms are those of his daughter and son-in-law, who erected the monument. Alternatively, the knight could be Henry de Langton himself. The Langtons do not appear to have owned property in Norton, but they did hold estates in the locality and this church, with its attached college of secular canons, was the most prestigious in the area.[78] Henry's father was Alan de Langton, burgess of Newcastle and Berwick, to whom Sir Henry de Lisle had conveyed the manor of Redmarshall with his niece, Catherine, in 1306.[79] What better way could there have been for the Langton family to advertise their arrival and their acceptance within county society?

The strongest argument against the Fulthorpe/Langton identification, however, is chronological. The products of the "Cheyne atelier" have recently been dated quite closely. The Goldsborough effigy seems to represent Richard de Goldsborough IV, who died in or before 1303, and the Escrick and Bedale effigies men who died c.1300 and c.1306 respectively.[80] The Norton effigy is clearly contemporary with them. This dating has not been accepted unreservedly, however, and an alternative scheme would place the effigies around the 1320s.[81] Even so, it would hardly encompass Roger de Fulthorpe, let alone Henry de Langton who was living in 1344.

There is an alternative candidate. He is the justice, John Lithegraynes, a close associate of Anthony Bek, who bore *gules, an orle argent, overall a bend sable.*[82] Of obscure origins, Sir John was himself a powerful figure in the north of England. He died in 1303.[83] Furthermore, there are clear associations between the Goldsboroughs and the Beks, which may help to explain the migration northwards of the products of a Yorkshire workshop. Richard de Goldsborough's wife was herself a Bek, while several members of the family gained ecclesiastical preferment through their association with the powerful bishop of Durham, who was high in the counsel of the king.

The identification of the effigy with John de Lithegraynes, however, is far from certain. There is no known connection between John de Lithegraynes and the collegiate church at Norton. In fact, in 1290 John and his wife Alice had founded their own collegiate chapel at their manor of Lazenby in Yorkshire.[84] Alice's family is unknown. Perhaps she was a Fulthorpe, but there is no evidence to that effect. Alternatively, it could be argued that the juxtaposition of the arms does not represent a marriage at all, but rather the close relationship between Lithegraynes and Anthony Bek himself. In short, the mysteries of the Norton knight, the little lady and the associated arms are extremely difficult to resolve.

One final possibility has also to be floated, and then most probably dismissed. This is that the effigy represents one of the Lisles of Sedgefield. Neither the arms of Sir Henry nor Sir John de Lisle seem to be recorded. However, Sir Walter de Lisle who conveyed the manor of Edmundbyers to John de Cotum, chaplain, in 1325 may well have been a relative. Walter sealed heraldically with a *chevron between three ivy leaves slipped.*[85] These arms appear in brass in the church at Sedgefield. It was in this parish that their manor of the Isle lay, and from whence they appear to have sprung. If these were indeed their arms, it would of course rule out the Lisles as far as the Norton effigy is concerned.

It would, on the other hand, bring us closer to resolving a similar puzzle. In St Edmund's church, Sedgefield, there is a very fine brass of a lady, no doubt a widow, wearing wimple and veil over a gown and flowing mantle (fig. 14). She is a tiny figure, only a few inches high, but of fine workmanship. Two heraldic brasses were once either side of her in the south transept and were probably associated with her.[86] One would expect the arms on her left to be her own family's and those on her right to be her husband's. It is, indeed, the former which correspond to the Lisle arms; it looks, therefore, as

Fig. 14 Brass of a lady, St Edmund's, Sedgefield, Co. Durham.

though 'the little lady of Sedgefield' belongs to the Lisle family. The arms to her right bear an equally rare charge. They are a gyronny of twelve, the tinctures being *or* and a now faded colour. No local family has been identified with these arms. They were borne in the fourteenth century most prominently by the Bassingbournes (*or and azure, or and gules*), with interests in Hertfordshire and Cambridgeshire but also in Lincolnshire, and by the families of Bruton (*or and azure*), Cudemers (*or and sable*), Ertingdene (*or and sable*) and Spayne (*or and azure, with an escutcheon argent*). It has been argued recently that the lady bears a resemblance, both facially and in her drapery, to brasses made in a London workshop – and now referred to as the Setvans style – during the 1320s. Despite this, it is suggested that it was made in a northern workshop, under southern influence, on the grounds that the London trade did not reach so far.[87] But if the lady was connected with Hertfordshire and Cambridgeshire – as would be the case if she were a Lisle married to, say, a Bassingbourne – then she would have been associated with the heartland of the London trade. Her brass would hardly have been difficult to transport. Surviving secular brasses in the North-East, moreover, are not generally of the same quality.[88] On balance, a London provenance seems more probable.

The lady's precise identity, however, will probably remain unknown. She is unlikely to be Catherine de Langton, née Lisle. The arms on the lady's left side are probably her husband's, and there is nothing to connect them with the Langtons. It seems safe to conclude that she was a member of the Lisle family, and probably of the generation after Catherine.

The very best of the North East's sepulchral monuments were undoubtedly made further south. This is not to say, however, that the local products were necessarily of poor quality; indeed, the quality is variable. The products of the earliest stone workshop were certainly distinctive. In general, however, styles moved from south to north and the craftsmen of the North East were by no means isolated from fashions and from techniques developed elsewhere. With careful handling by the historian, sepulchral monuments, like heraldry, can be both an indicator of social values and a barometer of social change.

References and Notes

1. His most significant publications, in the present context, include: "Medieval Effigies in the County of Durham", *Archaeologia Aeliana*, 4th ser., vol. vi (1929), pp.1-51; "Medieval Effigies in Northumberland", *Archaeologia Aeliana*, 4th ser., vol. vii (1930), pp.1-32; "Northern Knights at Falkirk, 1298", *Archaeologia Aeliana*, 4th ser., vol. xxv (1947), pp.68-114; and "Baronys and Knights of Northumberland, A.D. 1166-1266", *Archaeologia Aeliana*, 4th ser., vol. xxx (1952), pp.1-54. He also contributed two volumes for the Newcastle upon Tyne Records Committee, namely *Northumbrian Monuments* and *Durham Monuments*, in 1924 and 1925 respectively, and with William Greenwell he catalogued the seals in the muniments of the Dean and Chapter of Durham Cathedral, in *Archaeologia Aeliana*, 3rd ser., vols vii-ix, xi, xiv-xv, xviii (1910-15). There is a brief *Memoir* to him, by I.A. Richmond, in *Archaeologia Aeliana*, 4th ser., vol. xli (1963).

2. A.R. Wagner, *Heralds and Heraldry*, 2nd. ed. (Oxford, 1956), p.12.

3. What follows is drawn largely from chapter four of my recent book, *The Knight in Medieval England* (Stroud, 1993). See also Maurice Keen, *Chivalry* (Yale, 1984).

4. On this subject see, in particular, H.A. Tummers, *Early Secular Effigies in England in the Thirteenth Century* (Leiden, 1980).

5. The most recent major work on this subject is John Coales (ed.), *The Earliest English Brasses: Patronage, Style and Workshops 1270-1350* (London, 1987). But see also Malcolm Norris, *Monumental Brasses: The Memorials*, 2 vols (London, 1977) and *Monumental Brasses: The Craft* (London, 1978).

6. Felicity Heal and Clive Holmes, *The Gentry in England and Wales 1500-1700* (London, 1994), p.27.

7. W. Percy Hedley, *Northumberland Families*, 2 vols (Gateshead, 1968-70) vol. ii, pp.91-92.

8. Mervyn James, *Family, Lineage and Civil Society: a Study of Society, Politics and Mentality in the Durham Region, 1500-1640* (Oxford, 1974), pp.71-72. A fess is a horizontal band across the centre of the shield.

9. Some versions have the Galloway arms in a canton (i.e. in one or other corner) of the escutcheon. See A. R. Wagner (ed.), *Aspilogia II: Rolls of Arms, Henry III* (London, 1967), p.122.

10. A label is narrow band across the shield from which three, or five, short bands descend at right angles.

11. Blair, "Baronys and Knights of Northumberland", pp.27, 45, has both bearing the latter arms, but see Joseph Foster, *Some Feudal Coats of Arms* (London, 1901, repr. 1984), p.153.

12.Walter de Burradon was one of those appointed to assign dower to Maud, the widow of Gilbert de Umfraville, in 1245. See Blair, "Baronys and Knights", pp.31, 35.

13. Another example is Bowes of Streatlam, viz. *ermine, three longbows gules.*

14. *Durham Monuments,* p.xx.

15. For a discussion of the Bertrams and their castle see Roland Bibby, *Bothal Observed* (Newcastle, 1973).

16. See Blair, *Northumbrian Monuments,* pp. 10-15, 18-23.

17. The Lumley, Grey and Percy arms are all to be seen above his gateway. They are not, however, in their original positions.

18. For details see Robert Surtees, *The History and Antiquities of the County Palatine of Durham,* 4 vols (London, 1816-40), vol. ii, pp.139-42, and W. Fordyce, *The History and Antiquities of the County Palatine of Durham,* 2 vols (London, 1857) vol. ii, pp.610-11.

19. G.F. Warner and J. Gilson, *Catalogue of Western Manuscripts in the Old Royal and King's Collections,* 4 vols (London 1921), ii, pp.26-29.

20. Surtees, *History and Antiquities,* vol. ii, p.159.

21. Surtees, *History and Antiquities,* vol. ii, pp.142, 159.

22. See also Blair, *Durham Monuments,* pp.99-101.

23. Joseph Walton (ed.), *Calendar of the Greenwell Deeds* (Newcastle, 1927), nos. 6,7.

24. *Curia Regis Rolls,* vol. vi, p.220.

25. W. Page (ed.), *Northumberland Assize Rolls,* Surtees Society, vol. lxxxviii (1891) pp.351, 354.

26. Greenwell and Blair, *Durham Seals,* no. 1662.

27. Surtees, *History and Antiquities,* vol. ii, p.140.

28. I.J. Sanders, *English Baronies: A Study of Their Origin and Descent, 1086-1327* (Oxford, 1963), p.103; Lord Howard de Waldon (ed.), *Some Feudal Lords and their Seals* (pub. by the De Waldon Library, 1903, and repub. Bristol, 1984), pp.41-42.

29. Some association with the Crown may also have been intended. Percy was not alone in adopting the lion at this time. The Segraves, Sir John and Sir Nicholas, similarly bore *sable, a lion rampant argent crowned or.* They had abandoned the three garbs (wheatsheafs) worn by their ancestors, which had been derived from their association with the now extinct Norman earls of Chester.

30. Wagner, *Aspilogia II,* pp.46, 123, 138.

31. For seals of the members of this family, from Geoffrey fitz Geoffrey to Richard Fitz Marmaduke, see *Durham Seals,* nos. 1064, 1708-9, 1711. They all show a fess between three popinjays. Interestingly, Marmaduke is called *de* Thweng.

32. A *mullet* or *molet* is a star shape, originally denoting a spur.

33. For his accounts of the Fitz Marmadukes and the Lumleys of Ravensworth see Surtees, *History and Antiquities,* vol. i, pp.24-26 and vol. ii, pp.208-11. The main Fitz Marmaduke estates passed to Thomas, earl of Lancaster, and from him to the Hollands. For the murder of Richard Fitz Marmaduke see H.S. Offler, "Murder on Framwellgate Bridge", *Archaeologia Aeliana,* 5th ser., vol. xvi (1988), pp.193-211.

34. W.H.B. Bird, "Lumley. Some Female Descents.", *The Genealogist,* new ser., vol. xxxv (1919), pp.3-7. Hunter Blair referred to this essay when discussing the female effigy at Easington (*Durham Monuments,* p.121), but rather strangely he took no account of it in his discussions of the Lumleys.

35. *Durham Seals,* no.1661.

36. However, the document is a quitclaim made jointly by Thomas de Thweng, clerk, and Marmaduke de Lumley. As its other seal is clearly the clerk's, there can be no doubt that the seal depicting popinjays was appended by (or for) Marmaduke.

37. *Durham Seals*, no.1664. Hunter Blair, however, seems to accept this evidence; see *Durham Monuments*, p.100.

38. *Durham Monuments*, p.100.

39. A heater-shield is one shaped like the base of a flat-iron.

40. Blair originally opted for Marmaduke fitz Geoffrey in 1925 but revised this in favour of Richard Fitz Marmaduke in 1929: *Durham Monuments*, p.121 and "Medieval Effigies in the County of Durham", p.21.

41. *Durham Monuments*, p.25.

42. Blair, "Medieval Effigies in the County of Durham", p.13. According to J.R. Boyle, *A Comprehensive Guide to the County of Durham* (London, 1892), p.477, one of the birds was distinctly visible on the shield in his day.

43. These features are discussed by Tummers, *Secular Effigies*, pp.90-91.

44. The dates are those given in "Medieval Effigies in the County of Durham", pp.13-16.

45. There are not, in fact, very many. Tummers notes a total of eleven from the thirteenth century (*Secular Effigies*, p. 64).

46. Tummers, *Secular Effigies*, p.91.

47. Bird, "Lumley. Some Female Descents", p.3.

48. *Calendar of Charter Rolls*, i, p.409 and ii, pp.140, 141; *Calendar of Patent Rolls 1258-66*, p.132.

49. *Calendar of Patent Rolls 1272-81*, p. 201; *Calendar of Close Rolls 1279-88*, p.188. In the latter year he acted as a surety for a debt, in the company of Robert and Marmaduke de Thweng. In the same year he was called upon for military service from the bishopric of Durham. See Francis Palgrave (ed.) *Parliamentary Writs*, vol. i (London, 1827), p.604.

50. Surtees, *History and Antiquities*, vol. i, p.25.

51. For more detail and for a list of the effigies see the discussion by Blair in "Medieval Effigies in the County of Durham", pp.4-6. Elsewhere, however, the later style was in existence before the end of the thirteenth century.

52. For a discussion of the Northumberland effigies see Blair, "Medieval Effigies in Northumberland", pp.1-18. At Egglescliffe, County Durham, there is also a knight with interlaced rings. He is unlikely to have come from a local workshop.

53. "Medieval Effigies in the County of Durham", p.10. The fact that these are in sandstone does not indicate a separate workshop. Among the military effigies of this school, the Whitworth effigy is also sandstone. The choice of material may, however, have been a factor in cost.

54. *Durham Monuments*, p. 121.

55. She was dead by 1285, when John married Ida, widow of Robert de Neville (*Calendar of Close Rolls 1279-88*, p.318). Ida, on the other hand, survived her husband and was living in 1315 (*Complete Peerage*, vol. ix, p.496.).

56. For an introduction to this subject see P.D.A. Harvey and A.F. McGuinness, *A Guide to British Medieval Seals* (London, 1995).

57. A field vairy is one composed of two tinctures arranged in the manner used to denote vair (squirrel-fur).

58. *Party* indicates a vertically divided field.

59. See *Durham Seals*, no.2537, *Archaeologia Aeliana*, 3rd ser. vol. xi (1914), depicted on plate 29. The charter confirms her husband's grant of grain to the monks of Farne Island. It is printed in J. Raine, *The History and Antiquities of North Durham* (London, 1852), Appendix p.123, no.700. For the genealogy see I.J. Sanders, *English Baronies*, p.103. The lady's husband died in 1253.

60. Blair, however, also notes a remarkable affinity with Countess Aveline, in Westminster Abbey (*Durham Monuments*, p.125). For Countess Aveline see Tummers, *Secular Effigies*, plates 134 and 136.

61. *Complete Peerage*, vol. ix, p.496. His father died in 1331; where he was buried seems not to be recorded.

62. See the photograph in Nigel Saul (ed.), *Age of Chivalry: Art and Society in Late Medieval England* (London, 1992), p.49.

63. *Durham Monuments*, p.171.

64. For what follows see Brian and Moira Gittos, "The Goldsborough Effigies", *Church Monuments: the Journal of the Church Monuments Society*, vol. ix for 1994, pp.3-32.

65. Ibid., p.26.

66. Sometimes these professions were copied into bishops' registers. For the details see Mary C. Erler, "Three Fifteenth-Century Vowesses", in Caroline M. Barron and Anne F. Sutton (eds.), *Medieval London Widows 1300-1500* (London, 1994), pp.165-67.

67. In some cases, the woman associated herself with a religious house, as for example did Elizabeth de Burgh, lady of Clare, who was associated with the Minoresses (the Franciscan nuns) of Aldgate outside London. In 1343 she received a papal indulgence allowing her to enter their enclosure with two ladies. She had earlier taken a vow of chastity. See Jennifer C. Ward, "Elizabeth de Burgh, lady of Clare (d. 1360)" in Barron and Sutton, *Medieval London Widows*, pp. 37-41.

68. For female literacy see Julia Boffey, "Women authors and women's literacy in fourteenth- and fifteenth-century England", in Carol M. Meale, *Women and Literature in Britain* (Cambridge, 1993), ch.8.

69. Compare the seal of Margaret, Lady Hungerford and Botreaux, discussed by Carol Meale (op. cit., pp.128-30). This shows her looking down at an open book on her lap, in a manner which "recalls contemporary Continental representations of the Virgin of Humility".

70. For women's book owning see Meale (ed.), *Women and Literature*, ch.7.

71. See Tummers, *Secular Effigies*, p.55 and plates 159, 161, who regards her as late thirteenth-century, and Blair, *Durham Monuments*, p.106, who says no identification is possible.

72. See the essays from *Medieval London Widows* cited above, and Jennifer C. Ward, *English Noblewomen in the Middle Ages* (London, 1992), ch.8.

73. Blair, *Durham Monuments*, p.172. Joseph Foster (ed.), *Pedigrees Recorded at the Visitations of the County Palatine of Durham* (London, 1887), p.19 gives the arms exactly as on the monument. For the early history of the Blakistons, who seem to have risen from the tenantry of the del Parks at Blakiston, see Robert Surtees, *History and Antiquities*, vol. iii, pp.159-60.

74. Surtees reports that John was given the manor by the bishop. However, a Henry Bek had held a manor here as early as 1208-10 (*Book of Fees*, p.28).

75. At the battle of Falkirk and at the siege of Carlaverock, however, his arms were said to have been *gules, a fer de moline ermine.* See Blair, "Northern Knights at Falkirk", pp.78-81. The same arms are found against his name in the Parliamentary Roll of Arms. *Fer de moline* denoted a mill-rind, the iron boss of a millstone.

76. For the details which follow see Robert Surtees, *History and Antiquities*, vol. iii, pp.26, 70, 75-79, 152-53. See also the pedigree "Langton and Conyers of Wynyard" in Joseph Foster, *Pedigrees Recorded at the Visitations of the County Palatine of Durham*, p. 203.

77. Blair, *Durham Monuments*, p.173; *Durham Seals*, no. 540.

78. For the college see W. Page (ed.) *The Victoria History of the County of Durham*, vol. ii (London, 1907), p.127. The college was in existence in 1227 and had eight prebends attached to it.

79. In addition to Redmarshall, Catherine acquired the greater part of Wynyard, an estate which had been divided on the death of Sir Hugh Capell, but which had been largely reconstructed by the Lisles.

80. See B. and M. Gittos, "The Goldsborough Effigies", pp.25-27.

81. See Claude Blair, "Yorkshire Effigies and Ring Scabbard-Attachments", *Church Monuments Society Newsletter*, vol. 11, no. 1, pp.4-5.

82. Hunter Blair himself came to prefer this identification, probably because of Lithegraynes's elevated station within the palatinate and the high quality of the effigy ("Medieval Effigies in the County of Durham", pp.25-26). B. and M. Gittos also favour John Lithegraynes.

83. For a brief account of his career, see W. Brown (ed.), *The Registers of John de Romeyn and Henry of Newark*, Surtees Society, vol. 128 (1917), pp.44-45. He had been sheriff of Northumberland and of Yorkshire. He became steward to John le Romeyn, bishop of Durham in 1286, and was a justice in the time of Anthony Bek. His surname occurs earlier in the century in the region of Barnard Castle and he may well have had some early association with the Balliols, which would explain his arms.

84. W. Page (ed.) *The Victoria History of the County of Yorkshire*, vol. iii (London, 1913), pp.363-64.

85. *Durham Seals*, no.1612. See Durham Dean and Chapter Muniments, 4-5 Spec. 2, 14 and 15.

86. They are now placed in a glass case above one another and alongside her on the wall of the nave.

87. By Paul Binski and John Blair, in John Coales (ed.), *The Earliest English Brasses* (London, 1987), pp.90, 134.

88. For North-Eastern brasses see, in addition to the above, pp.59-62, 159-60, S. Badham, *Brasses from the North East* (London, 1979), especially pp.24-25.

II

THE DIOCESE OF DURHAM IN 1563

Constance M. Fraser

In 1563, in response to an order of the Privy Council, a return was made of the number of households in every parish of every diocese in England and Wales, and unusually, the Durham returns are among the few to survive.[1] This source provides information not only about the number of households per parish but also about the names of the incumbents and the presence or absence of a curate. It also indicates which parishes were totally without a minister.

If one seeks to use the return as a guide to population it is necessary first to interpret the meaning of 'household'. It might mean more than 'family', including any servants attached thereto. It is useful, however, to refer to the numbers of communicants or 'houseling folk' returned by these parishes in an earlier survey of 1548, returned by Sir Thomas Hilton of Hylton, Sir Robert Brandlynge, Robert Mennell, serjeant-at-law, and Henry Whitreson, esq., as commissioners for the survey of all colleges, deaneries, chantries, stipendiary priests, free chapels, brotherhoods, guilds, obits, anniversaries and lights in the diocese of Durham, with the yearly value of all their land and other assets.[2] Dividing the number of adult communicants in 1548 by the estimated number of households in 1563 gives an average of three adults, which would suggest that servants were not a significant element in any household.

There were eighteen parishes in the archdeaconry of Durham with a population of over 540 adults or 180 households, namely, St Andrew Auckland with its 3,818 households, to which should be added its chapelry of St Helen Auckland with a further 182 households; the city of Durham, subdivided into its parishes of St Oswald (465), St Nicholas (205), and St Giles (107), totalling 959 households; and a further fourteen consisting in descending order of Stanhope with St John's Chapel (456), Darlington (366), Gateshead (307), Staindrop (294), Chester-le-Street (260) with its chapelry of Tanfield (32), Houghton-le-Spring (286), Ryton (250), Brancepeth (218), Gainford (208), Billingham (203), Sedgefield (195), Middleton-in-Teesdale with Eggleston chapel (192), Bishopwearmouth (190), and Hart and Hartlepool (186).

This contrasts with the only eleven populous parishes returned for the archdeaconry of Northumberland, although the nil returns need to be taken into account, the reasons for which will be considered presently. While Newcastle in its divisions of St Nicholas (269), All Saints (688), St

John's (383) and St Andrew's (305), and chapelries of Gosforth (91) and Cramlington (11) accounted for 1,747 households, the only other parishes to exceed 190 households were Holy Island (502), Bolam (428), Simonburn (which covered the whole of North Tynedale) with 401, Bamburgh (380), Ford (300), Warden with Haydon Bridge (250), Morpeth (224), Rothbury (204), Norham (194), and Embleton (190).

Before reacting to the unexpected results of this survey, for one does not expect Auckland to be more populous than Newcastle upon Tyne, one needs to remember that the parishes of the diocese of Durham, as in other upland dioceses, tended to cover a large acreage. Excluding Newcastle and its chapelries, the parishes highlighted by their large population tended to be manorial centres with mining activities. Many of them were valuable livings.[3] This applies to Auckland, Chester-le-Street, Darlington, Haughton-le-Skerne, Houghton-le-Spring, Bishopwearmouth, Norton with Stockton, Stanhope and Sedgefield, which were controlled by the bishop of Durham, and Middleton-in-Teesdale, Barnard Castle and Gainford, then in the Queen's hands as forfeiture, but originally a Balliol and later a Beauchamp/Neville barony. The size of these parishes is indicated by their sub-divisions into chapelries, Auckland with its chapels of St Helen, Escomb, Hamsterley and Witton-le-Wear, Chester-le-Street with its chapelries of Lamesley and Tanfield, Gainford with its chapelries of Barnard Castle, Whorlton and Denton, and the Durham parish of St Oswald with its chapelries of St Margaret, Croxdale, Witton Gilbert and Whitworth.

Much the same can be said about the Northumberland parishes, which also may be identified as lordships. The oddest perhaps is Bolam, now the county's most notable lost village, represented only by a church and manor-house. How could it have had 428 households in 1563? The answer might be the laconic explanation given in the survey of 1584 into depopulation in the county: "The towne was burnt".[4] The barony had long been subdivided among heiresses. Its area ran into three wards, and consisted of the townships of Trewick, Bolam, Gallow-hill, Belsay, Bradford, Harnham and Shortflatt. At the time of the Hearth Tax of 1664 the parochial tally was 36 householders, with a further 36 householders and a chapel at Belsay.[5] The Wansbeck valley is an area of lost villages, which were recorded in the Lay Subsidy Roll of 1296, but otherwise may be located only through the evidence of rig-and-furrow.

Simonburn, with its chapelries of Haughton, Wark, and Bellingham, represented the old liberty of North Tynedale, and had once been one of the wealthiest livings in England, which Edward III had purposed to appropriate to the chapel of Windsor Castle.[6] The Scottish wars had brought a steep decline in its fortunes, and in 1570 it was valued at £34 6s 8d. In 1563 it was served by a parson and a curate, with a Scottish curate based at Bellingham with its 303 households at the head of the North Tyne. Such numbers are feasible, as the overpopulation of the area was a source of worry to the inhabitants of Newcastle, who were sure that if they were allowed membership of the town's guilds they would murder their masters in their beds and open the town gates to their thieving kinsmen to loot the town.[7]

Bamburgh had been the ancient capital of Northumbria. There were three chapels under it, Belford, Lucker, and Tughall. Adjoining it were the ancient 'shires' of Norham and Holy Island, administered until 1540 by the bishops of Durham. Rothbury had been a royal estate based on mid-Coquetdale. Embleton had been the endowment of the hereditary sheriff of the county. Warden included the barony of Langley.

A glance at the map of the medieval diocese of Durham (fig. 15) indicates vividly that while the archdeaconry of Durham was adequately served with parsons able to supply returns, in the archdeaconry of Northumberland much of the uplands and nearly all the coastline provide no such information. In the archdeaconry of Durham out of a possible 58 parishes with 31 dependent chapels, only Lamesley in the parish of Chester-le-Street and Lanchester with its chapels of Medomsley and Esh failed to make returns. In the archdeaconry of Northumberland, Felton and Kirkharle were totally without parson or curate. Out of 57 parishes, with 50 dependent chapels, 41 made no returns, including Elsdon, Haltwhistle, Hartburn, Woodhorn and Newbiggin, Lesbury and Alnwick, Warkworth, Wooler, and Berwick-upon-Tweed. Hexham was omitted because it was included in the archdiocese of York. If the incumbent were not resident he might not know how many households lived within his parish; and it has been said that the livings in Northumberland were so poor that it was difficult to fill them, for which reason some were held in plurality. Lesbury with Alnwick was worth only £8 4s 10d, Wooler £5 8s, and the vicarage of Berwick £6 13s 4d; and it would seem that Robert Selby had doubled Berwick with Norham, finding a Scottish priest to serve the latter, and John Hall had doubled Wooler with Kirknewton. At Bamburgh, where there was "neither parson nor vicare", the curate had made the return of households, as did the men serving its three chapelries.

The Privy Council was interested in the distribution of population within the English counties, and turned to the Church for clerical assistance. The use of the pulpit to disseminate government information was another way to utilise its services. Defective returns highlighted weaknesses. Auckland had neither parson nor vicar, but *was* served by a curate. The same information was returned from Chester-le-Street, Lanchester, Monkwearmouth, Castle Eden, Durham St Nicholas and St Giles, and Jarrow. The name of Boldon's parson was unknown, although he submitted a return.

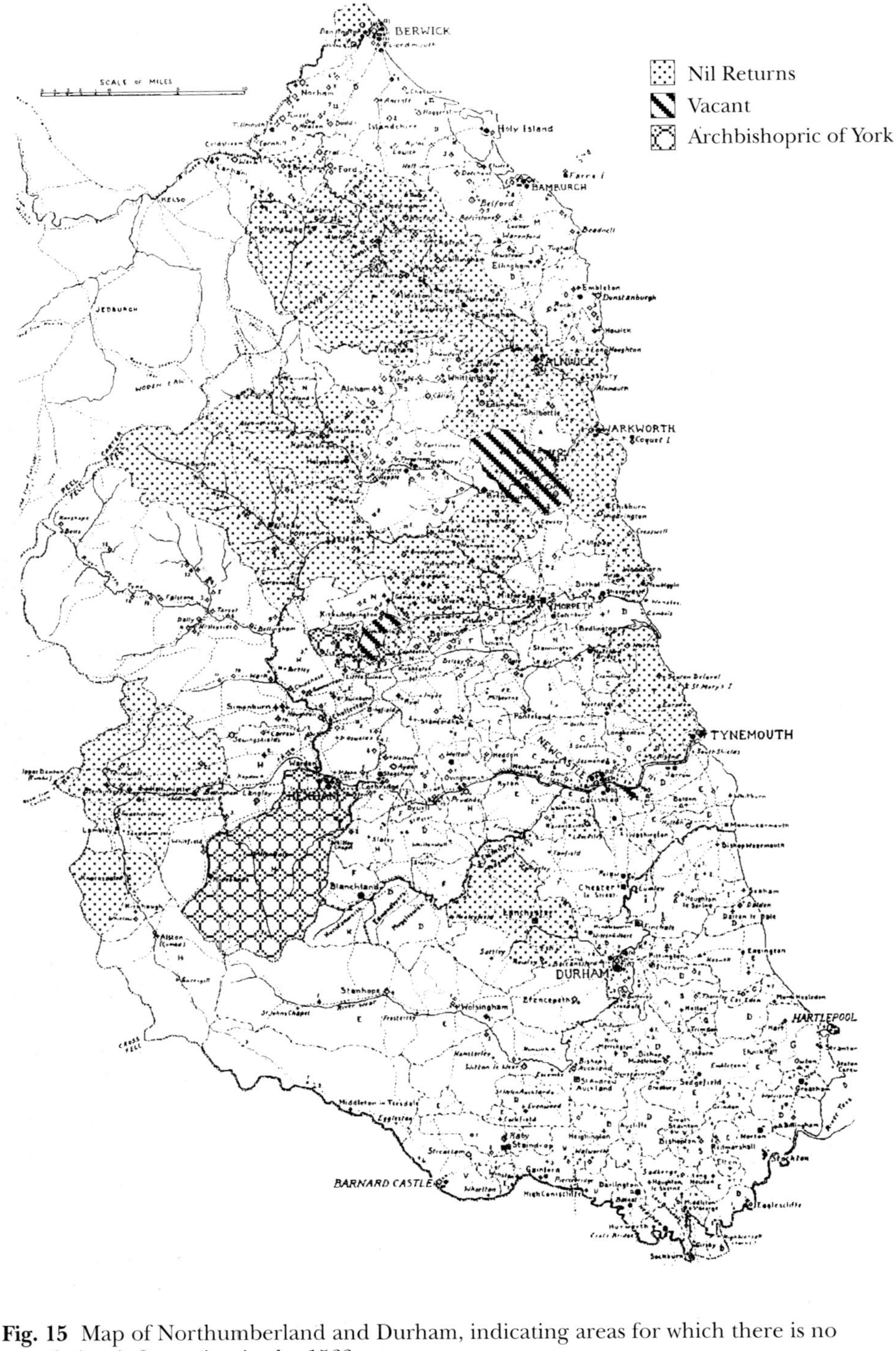

Fig. 15 Map of Northumberland and Durham, indicating areas for which there is no population information in the 1563 return.

In Northumberland there were vacancies at Felton, Bamburgh and Kirkharle, although at the last there was at least a curate: but in view of the possible non-residence of the incumbent there must have been disquiet at the number of parishes served by "a skotishe preste". Many of these may have been professed Catholics, seeking asylum after the Scottish Reformation of 1560. They were to be found in Durham at the chapels of Medomsley, Trimdon, Stockton, Satley and Jarrow. Many more were to be found in Northumberland, at Newburn, Morpeth, Hebron, Corbridge, Slaley, Bellingham, Kirkheaton, Haltwhistle, Hartburn, Hartington/Cambo, Shilbottle, Ingram, Chatton, Alwinton, Corsenside/Holystone, North Charlton, Kirknewton, Lucker, Tughall, Ancroft, Kyloe, and Lowick. The solution for absentee incumbents and Scottish curates was to be stipendiaries, who would be licenced by the bishop.[8]

The bishop's agent apparently knew the names of all the incumbents, except for Boldon, and the names of most of the curates; hence it is possible to identify many of these blind shepherds. Thomas Sparke, parson of Wolsingham, who figured on the list of those who failed to appear before the royal commissioners in 1559 to take the oaths of Supremacy and Uniformity, was also parson of Holy Island, and in 1563 was described as "now striken in the palsye".[9] Nicholas Foster of Brancepeth and Richard Marshall of Stainton-le-Street were similar defaulters. William Bennett of Aycliffe and George Cliffe of Elwick and Billingham positively denied the right of Queen Elizabeth to ecclesiastical jurisdiction. Cliffe, however, was installed at Billingham after the ejection of Robert Dalton for affirming "that he belevith that he who sittithe in the seate of Rome hath and oughte to have the jurisdiction ecclesiasticall over all Christian Realmes".[10] It is possible that the William Garnett, parson of Ryton and Egglescliffe, is identical with the rector of Crayke in Yorkshire who also defaulted at the 1559 visitation. Similarly, Robert Pearson, vicar of Sockburn, had defaulted in 1559, with John Foster of Edmundbyers and John Sayer of Elton. One wonders about any relationship between William Whithede, vicar of Heighington, who refused in 1559 to subscribe to the new Articles of Religion, and Hugh Whitehead, last prior and first dean of Durham.[11] John Tunstall, parson of the substantial living of Haughton-le-Skerne, was kin to Cuthbert Tunstall the bishop. He had come to the diocese on an exchange with Dr Thomas Barrett of the living of Laindon and a canonry of St Paul's, London (where Cuthbert Tunstall had been bishop).[12] Leonard Pilkington, brother of Bishop Pilkington, was a conspicuous pluralist, holding the livings of Whitburn and Middleton-in-Teesdale simultaneously, in addition to a prebend in the cathedral.

Pluralists in Northumberland included William Heryson, who held Bothal and Chatton, Robert Ogle, who held Sheepwash and Shilbottle, Robert Selby, who held Norham and Berwick (where his kinsmen held the office of Gatekeeper or Porter), Oliver Selby, who held Branxton and Tynemouth, and Ralph Tod, who held Woodhorn and Hartburn. Defaulters in that county in 1559 included Richard Marshall at Corbridge, Thomas Holyman at Ponteland, Giles Robinson at Newburn, Nicholas Maughan, stipendary curate at Warden, Robert Tesedaill, who was rector of Knaresdale, William Watson of Bedlington, John Dacre at Morpeth, and Thomas Thompson of Longhoughton.[13] The fact these men were still in office four years later supports the idea that there was little zeal for Anglicanism in the North East.

On the other hand, Bernard Gilpin of Houghton-le-Spring was a most active labourer in the vineyard. His reputation has lately come under criticism on the grounds that he must have been a time-server to start his career as a protégé of Bishop Tunstall and end it as a trusted instrument of Queen Elizabeth to win the North for the Church of England.[14] If, however, one regards him as a pragmatist wishing to educate a Godless population quite literally, as he founded Kepier Grammar School at Houghton, and endowed studentships at Queen's College, Oxford, he may surely be forgiven his dogmatic U-turn. He had been part of the diocesan administration briefly as archdeacon of Durham between 1556 and 1558, but in his preferred career as rector of Houghton-le-Spring (1557-83) was a licenced preacher and missioner throughout the diocese, striving to instil the fear of God into the hearts of the wayward inhabitants of the wild north-west of Northumberland as well as the more sober burgesses of Newcastle upon Tyne. He recognised the need to educate promising local young men to train as clergy by founding the Kepier Grammar School, largely helped through an endowment by the same John Heath who was blamed in the survey as the impropriator of Kepier Hospital who refused to nominate parsons at St Nicholas and St Giles at Durham and at the chapel of Satley. This concern with education was shared by William Birch, who in his will of 29 May 1575 included among his charitable bequests £2 for the poorest scholars in Latin at the grammar schools at Durham and Houghton-le-Spring, £2 for 20 poor scholars in Latin at Manchester School, £4 for eight poor scholars at St John's College or Clare Hall, Cambridge, and as much for poor scholars at Oxford, and £6 for the benefit of a specific scholar. His Latin grammar-books were to be given to three poor scholars at any grammar school, and his Latin divinity-books to those two of his nephews "that first be teachers in Ecclesiastical Ministry".[15]

What else may be learnt about the Durham diocesan clergy in 1563? It would appear from the ordination lists of Bishop Tunstall that at least twenty-one had started their careers as monks or canons, or as chaplains to a nunnery.[16] Of these the most successful had been Thomas Sparke, who at the dissolution of Lindisfarne priory in 1537, where he was prior, had been consecrated suffragan bishop of Berwick-upon-Tweed and given the lease of the priory estate, to be supplemented by the third prebend on the dissolution of Durham priory and its re-constitution as the cathedral chapter there in 1541. The same year he had been presented to the mastership of Greatham Hospital, and in 1547 was collated to Wolsingham. He remained in possession of all these until his death in 1572, leaving the administration of the northern cures to three "Scottish curates".[17] William Norton had been presented to Ovingham while still a canon of Hexham in 1532, where he remained until his death in 1567.[18] The same applied to Henry Spragayn, a canon of Blanchland, presented to St Andrew's, Bywell, in 1535 and remaining there until 1564.[19]

The Premonstratensian house at Alnwick provided a title for eight parish clergy, and not necessarily to livings in its own gift. Cuthbert Watson was presented to Ellingham, which was in the gift of Durham priory.[20] Oliver Selby had negotiated in 1534 the promise of the vicarage at Tynemouth, but had to wait until 1540 before he gained possession.[21] This had been in the gift of Tynemouth priory. William Hall went to Elsdon in 1543.[22] Thomas Thompson went to Longhoughton in 1551.[23] John Graye went to Chillingham in 1554, and John Hall to Kirknewton in 1554, having Wooler added in 1561.[24] Thomas Middleton was presented to Bishop Middleham in 1558.[25]

William Reseley, presented to Kirkwhelpington in 1551, was a former canon of Brinkburn.[26] Geoffrey Glenton, William Hardinge, and Robert Crawfurthe were canons of Eggleston, who were found livings at Heddon-on-the-Wall (1548), Hart (1554), and Kimblesworth (1560) respectively.[27] Roland Prat from Coverham was presented to Wooler in 1549, but was promised Washington, which he eventually secured in 1558.[28] William Bennett of Aycliffe, George Cliffe of Elwick and Billingham, John Foster of Edmundbyers and Henry Yates at Alston had all been Durham monks.[29]

The collation or institution of most of the incumbents recorded in 1563 can be traced in the registers of Bishop Tunstall (1530-59) and Bishop Pilkington (1561-75). Tunstall was essentially a political bishop, used by Henry VIII as President of the Council of the North (1536-8), mildly Catholic, but no hunter of heretics during the reign of Mary Tudor. One assumes a family interest with the acquisition by John Tunstall of the valuable rectory of Haughton-le-Skerne. Between 1527 and 1534 John Tunstall was the Principal of New Inn Hall, Oxford. He also held the livings of Basildon, and St Olave's, Southwark, and was an executor of Bishop Tunstall's will.[30]

One of the few clergy to be directly affected by the religious turmoil of the Henrican reformation was John Rudd, D.D. In 1540 he was collated to the collegiate church of Norton, and by 1550 he was a royal chaplain to Edward VI, who presented him to the tenth stall at Durham. The following year he was presented to a prebend at Winchester, but with the accession of Queen Mary

Fig. 16 Cuthbert Tunstall (1474 – 1559), the last Catholic bishop of Durham (from W. Hutchinson's *History of Durham*, i, 1785).

he was deprived of his livings. He was restored on the accession of Queen Elizabeth.[31] Nicholas Crawhall was collated to Haltwhistle in 1554, on the deprivation of his predecessor.[32] Robert Ogle similarly was collated to Sheepwash in 1555 on the deprivation of Alexander Brown, instituted in 1548.[33] When the pendulum swung back with the accession of Elizabeth, Hugh Hochonson, B.D., of St Oswald, Durham, was turned out in 1562 in favour of Thomas Pentland.[34]

One of the choicest Durham prebends was the seventh stall. Queen Elizabeth presented to it in September 1560 Thomas Sampson, dean of Christ Church, Oxford. He was succeeded in July 1562 by William Birch, A.M., earlier Warden of Manchester College. In 1561 Birch had been presented to Gateshead, which he resigned in 1564 preparatory to his presentation to Stanhope. He was deprived of his prebend in 1567 because of his scruples as to vestments, and replaced by Leonard Pilkington, D.D., the bishop's brother.[35]

Lowering one's sights to the level of curate, one finds in the return that several large parishes had been left without rector or vicar, with the comment that the Queen had not chosen to fill the living. These were the former collegiate churches of Auckland, Chester-le-Street, Lanchester and Darlington, with their dependent chapels. Auckland was making do with three chaplains, Chester with two, Lanchester with three, and Darlington with two. It was the same with Monkwearmouth, with one curate, and St Nicholas, Durham, where the impropriator was John Heath, "a cooper of London", who also held St Giles, Durham. Three curates were left to serve the 316 households. The chapelry of Heworth had the occasional Sunday service. These livings were in the archdeaconry of Durham. In the archdeaconry of Northumberland Felton was vacant, with the Queen as patron, as was Kirkharle.

The career prospects of curates were bleak. Few mentioned in the return can be found in Pilkington's register as being instituted to a living at a later date. One of these happy few was James Lakenby, curate of Stranton in 1559, who had been advanced by 1563 to vicar there. Other curates subsequently instituted were Thomas Benson of Stanhope, ordained in 1554 and collated to Edmundbyres in 1571; Thomas Marshall of Beltingham, collated to Haltwhistle in 1564; and Edmund Stapleton of Sedgefield, collated to Longbenton in 1570.[36] Some can be found in the lists of ordinands in Tunstall's register. John Blythe of Dissington had been ordained in 1532. Ralph Heghley of Whorton was ordained the same year (when he was a canon of Eggleston), as was Oswald Masleyone of Belsay (when he was a canon of Brinkburn). Richard Milner of Lancaster was ordained in 1533 (when he was a canon of Alnwick). John Clapham of Darlington had been ordained in 1543, and John Bron of Witton Gilbert in 1547. Anthony Barro, at Haydon Bridge in 1563, was ordained in 1556, the same year as Nicholas Maughen of Newbrough and Geoffrey Marley of Pittington, ordained on a title provided by Sherburn Hospital. George Rayn of Haughton-le-Skerne was ordained in 1558. John Welche, curate of South Shields in 1563, had been rector of St Mary le Bow, Durham, where he was instituted in 1544.[37]

In this survey of the clergy of the diocese in 1563 one is torn between despair at the empty livings, served by "Scottish priests" or underpaid English curates, with the underlying presumption that the Queen had not seen fit to appoint because the revenue was being pocketed by the Crown, and re-assurance that a highly trained cadre of senior clergy had firm control of church administration. (A number of "empty" churches and chapelries were still able to make a return of households, and in very few cases were the names of the incumbent or chaplain unknown.) Some twenty-four were graduates, with degrees attributed to them on their appearance in the registers of Bishop Tunstall or Bishop Pilkington, either on their institution or when they made way for their successor by resignation, deprivation, or death. Of these, three do not figure in the lists of alumni of Oxford or Cambridge, namely Claude Rent of Whickham, William Garnet of Ryton, and Edward Mitchell of Rothbury. Their degrees may have been awarded on the continent. Rent and Mitchell had legal qualifications.

It would be unsurprising if Oxford had been favoured by the elder clergy holding livings in the gift of the cathedral chapter, itself the re-incarnation of the Durham priory. The monks had had their own dependent cell at that university, and Dr Sparke held its degrees of B.D. (1528/9) and D.D. (1535). Other graduates were William Whithede of Heighington, Ralph Tod of Hartburn and Woodhorn, Thomas Palmer of Embleton, a fellow of Merton College, which was the patron, Dr William Bennet of Aycliffe, Bernard Gilpin of Houghton-le-Spring, William Salkeld of Newcastle upon Tyne, George Cliffe of Billingham, and Thomas Pentland of St Oswald, Durham.[38] Cambridge had educated Edmund Beane of Stanhope, Nicholas Foster of Brancepeth,

Nicholas Hertbern of Simonburn, Richard Marshall of Corbridge, Robert Tailour of Lesbury, George Wynter of Greatham, Dr John Rudd of Norton, William Birch of Gateshead, Edward Banck of Long Newton, William Stevynson of Gainford, William King, archdeacon of Northumberland, and Robert Swift of Sedgefield, Pilkington's spiritual chancellor.[39]

These were the high-fliers, many holding prebends in Durham Cathedral. Thomas Sparke held the second prebend from the beginning in 1541 to his death in 1564, and William Bennett, another former monk, similarly held the fourth prebend from 1541 to 1579. William Birch held the seventh prebend between 1562 and 1567. John Rudd held the tenth prebend from 1550 to 1553, when he was deprived as a married man under the Marian reaction. He was restored in 1559, and continued there until his death in 1578. Adam Holiday of Bishopwearmouth, not a graduate, held the eleventh prebend from 1561 to 1590. Robert Swift held the first prebend from his appointment to the diocese in 1562 until his death in 1599.[40] One may assume that all were involved in diocesan administration. Sparke was suffragan bishop of Berwick, and Swift, in addition to being spiritual chancellor, was a justice of the peace and on occasion a justice at the Durham assizes.[41]

It is more difficult to pierce the facade to discover the real opinions of the clergy in this difficult decade in the Church's history. If one turns to the Royal Visitation of 1559, one finds that the curates of Darlington, Billingham, Cockfield, Egglescliffe, Elton, Stranton, Muggleswick, Chollerton, Corbridge, Warden and Morpeth had scruples about subscription to the Queen's claims to supremacy over the Church in England: a stand similarly maintained by the rectors of Long Newton, Egglescliffe, Sockburn, Middleton-in-Teesdale, Wolsingham, Brancepeth, Edmundbyers, Knaresdale, Morpeth, Sheepwash, Bothal and Ford, and the vicars of Stranton, Tynemouth, Newburn, Ponteland, Corbridge, Bedlington, Longhoughton and Alnham.[42] Four years later there had been replacements at Egglescliffe, Middleton-in-Teesdale, Bothal, Ford and Alnham. Robert Crawfurthe had been downgraded, and George Rayn, John Chair and Robert Eltringham had been transferred. Elsewhere there had been no change. George Cliffe, who had positively asserted papal supremacy, was subsequently deprived in 1564/5, but nevertheless was presented to Brancepeth in 1571. Possibly it took time to purge the dissenters. Certainly an examination of dates of appointment indicates ten institutions between 1546 and 1551, when one would expect a sympathetic promotion of radical thinkers, a similar promotion of twenty-nine between 1554 and 1558, when one would expect Catholic sympathisers, and twenty-three appointed after the death of Bishop Tunstall and either during the vacancy or after the appointment of the Calvinistic James Pilkington as bishop.

Wills can provide a good insight into the convictions of the testator. At least twenty-six wills survive of clergy mentioned in the 1563 survey. Fifteen specifically bequeath their souls to God and express their hopes of salvation through Christ's redemptive power. Such may be regarded as of a "Protestant" persuasion. Edmund Beane of Stanhope, William Bennett of Aycliffe, Richard Farro of Winston, Leonard Pilkington of Whitburn, Adam Holiday of Bishopwearmouth and John Rudd of Norton were all married, and bequeathed legacies to their widows and children.[43] Many left money to the poor of their parish, William Birch of Stanhope, Bernard Gilpin of Houghton-le-Spring, Edward Mitchell of Rothbury and Leonard Pilkington of Whitburn being particularly generous. Birch remembered the poor tradesmen in Gateshead, poor prisoners in the gaols of Durham, Newcastle and Lancaster, poor householders in Stanhope and Durham, poor widows and tradesmen in Manchester and Salford, and left £3 to be distributed among twenty poor girls in Manchester as marriage-portions. He also remembered the poor in *Stopperd, Risshun* [?Rushton, Lancashire], Withington in Cheshire, and Didsbury in Lancashire, where he may have had a family connection.[44] Gilpin was born in Westmorland, and his benefactions went to the poor of Houghton-le-Spring, Easington, Newcastle, Sunderland, Auckland, Barnard Castle, Kentmire, Staveley, Kendal, and Lancaster. Mitchell remembered the poor of Carlisle, Aspatria and Rothbury.[45] Pilkington remembered the poor of Whitburn, Durham and Middleton-in-Teesdale, the dole to be distributed at the discretion of his widow.[46] Books were bequeathed by Birch, Gilpin, William Hardinge of Hart, and Robert Richardson of Redmarshall.[47] A funeral feast is specified by Thomas Middleton of Bishop Middleham and Henry Plomer of Conisliffe.[48] Edward Mitchell, who was also a prebendary of Carlisle Cathedral, left money for a funeral dinner for those attending "of reputation". The poor attending were to be given a penny each.[49] Pilkington left 20 nobles [£6.66] to mend the highways around Durham, while Birch left £3 to repair the bridges and highways within three miles of *Birch* [?Bruche, Lancashire].[50]

Fig. 17 Arms of James Pilkington (1520? – 75), the first Protestant bishop of Durham (from W. Hutchinson's *History of Durham*, i, 1785).

In a very few cases the inventories of the incumbents have also survived, taken at the date of probate. According to these, Dr Bennett of Aycliffe left assets worth £203 6s 6d: which diminishes the value of his donation of 10s to the poor of his parish.[51] Most of his goods went to his family. Richard Farro had assets of £66 4s 5d, most of which were bequeathed to his family.[52] The same might be said of Robert Lighton of Longhorsley.[53] Richard Marshall's effects were valued at £225 4s 8d, and his will referred to property in Yorkshire, Morpeth, Newcastle, Elswick and Corbridge. His namesake was registrar of the Dean and Chapter of Durham. His legacies were mainly to family.[54] Arthur Shaftoe of Stamfordham had assets worth £67 3s 4d, which similarly were passed to his family.[55] David Taillour of Bolam gave 3s 4d to his church, and passed on the residue, assessed at over £45 4s 6d, to his "servant" and cousin William Taillour of Prestwick.[56] Wealthiest among them, not unexpectedly, was Thomas Sparke, bishop of Berwick, master of Greatham Hospital, and rector of Wolsingham. His plate alone was assessed at £64 16s 1d, including a mitre set with stones and pearls, silver-gilt, worth £13 6s 8d. Among other items belonging to him at Greatham was "a wainscott chair to bear a man in that is sick or diseased, 6s 8d". His effects at Durham were appraised at £61 14s 11d: while sundry debts owed to him amounted to £400 2s 6d, including £40 owed by Henry, late earl of Westmorland, £20 owed by Bishop Cuthbert Tunstall, £46 owed by Dean William Whittingham, £26 13s 4d owed by the executors of Mr Anthony Salvin, and £4 owed by the mayor and brethren of Hartlepool.[57] In this case, any accompanying will has not survived.

The survey of 1563 provides an opportunity to investigate the Durham diocesan clergy at the moment that they were drawing breath, after the possibilities of the Marian reaction and before the renewed missionary zeal from the Continent. The moment of truth for some came with the Rising of the Earls (of Northumberland and Westmorland) in late autumn 1569 with the immediate object of releasing Mary, queen of Scots, from her captivity in Castle Bolton in Wensleydale. This was accompanied by an enthusiastic repudiation of the Anglican Settlement, with the celebrations of several High Masses in Durham Cathedral. Retribution on those who participated in the services and the burning of Bibles, Homilies, and Books of Common Prayer followed the collapse of the rebellion and the rounding up of the insurgents. Dr Swift, as diocesan chancellor, led the proceedings in the consistory court to examine those charged with defying the act of parliament prescribing the Book of Common Prayer as the sole recognised form for services within England, abolishing services in Latin, and requiring the defacement of all stone altars, books and ornaments required for the latter. Action was to be taken against all who from the end of November until 10 December 1569 set up a stone altar or holy-water stoup in any parish church, took part in the proscribed services, went to confession, or attended a sermon of William Holmes which concluded with a papal absolution for all who recognised that England had been in a state of schism.[58]

The apostate clergy were then cited before the consistory court and required to admit their fault. Mr George Cliffe, aged 57, admitted attending services in the cathedral, and was present at the Mass, "but dyd not singe at ytt nor loke at the elevation". As for Holmes's sermon, "he hard his voce, but understode not one sentence of that which was saide by the preacher". (The acoustics of Durham cathedral are notoriously poor.) "He receyved no hallibread nor halliwater, nor used no other rite or ceremonye; for he, this examinate, was aither redinge of his testament or holdinge talke with one or another".[59]

Oliver Eshe, now curate at St Giles, Durham, aged 41, had sought direction from Holmes about how to conduct future services in his church, and admitted administering the sacraments to his parishioners in their mouths, "bycause they wold not take yt into their hands".[60] Willliam Watson, chaplain to the hospital of St Mary Magdalen, aged 60, like Cliffe, had attended services, but did not sing, and could not hear the sermon. He was sorry for what he did "and never intendith to doo the lyk again by God's grace". John Baxter, rector of St Mary in the South Bailey, Durham, had also attended the services and been "reconciled" by the preacher, but was now "hartly sory for this his offence".[61] William Hardinge, here described as a minor canon, declared that he had been forced to attend by two soldiers, who said it would be the worse for him if he absented himself.[62] William Headlam, curate at St Nicholas, admitted saying matins and evensong in Latin, conducting a Mass, and being given the papal absolution in William Holmes's chamber on Palace Green.[63]

A second charge was levied against certain clergy that they had administered the Easter communion in 1570 according to illegal rites. This brought in Oliver Eshe, now at St Giles, Durham, and Thomas Pentland at St Oswald's.[64] Thomas Wright, vicar of Seaham, admitted that he had said daily the matins of the Blessed Virgin in his chamber, in the presence of George Wynter and others. John Nicholson, curate of Heighington, had read the psalms in Latin with the sanction of his vicar, Mr William Whithed. Robert Crawfurthe, as curate of Whitworth, had consecrated the elements by illegal rites. Richard Milner as curate of Lanchester had publicly declared the Anglican litany to be abolished. For these offences the latter two were sentenced to gaol.[65] The more usual punishment was a public expression of contrition in their parish church in a plain shirt, with bare head and feet.[66]

Fig. 18 Secular canon from W. Dugdale's *Monasticon Anglicanum*, iii (1673).

In proceedings against Roger Venis of Mitford for non-residence, one of his churchwardens testified that he had been absent since 30 November 1569, since when there had been no services, including funerals and baptisms. Another affirmed that Venis had been away since February 1569, "since which tyme he never served ther but by a Scotishe preiste"; and a third said "the vicar is absent emong the rebells".[67]

The local reaction at Sedgefield to the chance for change must have been particularly galling to its rector, Dr Swift. In 1567 he had prosecuted his churchwardens in the consistory court for removal of the communion table and desks in the church. From the testimony later heard in court, it appears that during the Rising a stone altar was built with the aid of many, although subsequently demolished by troops of Queen Elizabeth, when the holy-water stoup which had been resurrected was removed and hidden.[68]

Proceedings in the consistory court draw attention to other problems confronting the clergy of 1563. Christopher Thorobye, still vicar of Stannington in 1573, found himself in the middle of a brawl in church after Communion, concerning custody of goods taken from some gypsies. A dagger was drawn, or rather "it shott out of the sheithe by yt selff", and the vicar had to hustle the parties out of the church, aided by the parish clerk.[69] Thomas Marshall, now vicar of Haltwhistle, was put in a still more delicate situation at Beltingham, his old chapel. It was Easter communion, 1575, and the Ridleys of Willimontswick were first to receive communion. Beatrice Crawhall, gentlewoman, aged about 60, came forward and received her bread. She then asked for the wine immediately, because the "dry bread wolde not goo down with hir, and that she feired that hir decease wold arise of hir yf she had not drinke shortly after". The vicar took no notice, but continued administering the sacraments to a further sixty persons before returning to her. Meanwhile she "frothed at the mouth, and therby was enforsed to spit, which she saith upon hir oothe was of no evill intent, nor dyd not att all (praised be God) spitt out the communion bread". She also denied that she had chided the vicar for failure to pray for the harvest, when it was hit by much rain. She justified the telling her beads in church "for that she cannot se upon hir boke".[70] The reaction of the court to her explanations is not recorded.

Meanwhile Dr Leonard Pilkington was having problems collecting his tithes at Whitburn in respect of Robert Chambers's windmill at Cleadon. The rector wanted a tithe of the multure exacted from clients, and also from five bee-hives.[71] It is not clear whether he wanted a tithe from the swarms, or from the honey. A commutation for every item was offered. The matter of tithes also was raised at Newburn, where, however, the matter at issue was the non-residence of the vicar, Giles Robinson. The curate and one of the churchwardens were unable to swear that Robinson had actually taken an oath to reside, but his visits tended to coincide with tithe collection, including the tenths of calves, hens, pigs and fish, and when he came he stayed in Newcastle.[72]

A final case also touches on tithes and vicarages. Robinson had failed to provide hospitality in Newburn. Ralph Tod had died as vicar of Hartburn in

1569 and the living had been given to William Stevynson, who tried to sue Tod's executors for dilapidations. It was testified that Tod had enlarged the vicarage by a cross-chamber, newly built, and a stone chimney. He had also built a new water corn-mill, yielding more profit than any possible decays to the vicarage. (The valuation of these at £60 was ridiculous, for one could build a new house for as much.) What with extending the vicarage, paying forty shillings a year to the poor of the parish, paying various taxes, providing a wage for his curate, and the costs of a law suit in London about his mill-race, Tod had been out of pocket, as he still had £40-worth of tithes outstanding; "for that the parishioners ther ar very evill payers of ther duyties".[73]

There was much more than dogma to worry a clergyman.

References and Notes

1. British Library, Harleian MS 594.
2. J. Raine (ed.), *The Ecclesiastical Proceedings of Bishop Barnes* (Surtees Society 22, 1850), pp.lix-xxxvi.
3. Their estimated value was noted by Bishop Barnes (*Barnes*, 1-10).
4. Public Record Office, S.P.15/28, f. 105v.
5. Public Record Office, E.179/158/103 m. 10.
6. *Northumberland County History* XV, pp.167-73.
7. J.R. Boyle and F.W. Dendy, *Extracts from the Records of the Merchants of Newcastle upon Tyne* (Sur Soc 93, 1895), pp. 27-29.
8. BL, Harl. MS 594, ff. 188-195. *Barnes*, 3, 5, 7-10.
9. C.J. Kitching (ed), *The Royal Visitation of 1559* (Sur. Soc. 187, 1975), pp.102-3; BL, Harl. MS 594, f. 195.
10. *Roy. Vis.*, pp.22-23, 26; G. Hinde (ed.), *The Registers of Cuthbert Tunstall and James Pilkington* (Sur. Soc. 161, 1952), p.133.
11. *Roy. Vis.*, p.23.
12. D.S. Boutflower, *Fasti Dunelmenses* (Sur. Soc. 139, 1926), p.131.
13. Ibid., p.103.
14. D. Marcombe, "Bernard Gilpin: anatomy of an Elizabethan legend", *Northern History*, XVI (1980), pp.20-39.
15. *Barnes*, pp.cx-xiv.
16. *Reg.*, pp.27-29, 42, 44-45, 47-48, 52-55, 57-58, 62-66, 78-81, 87-89, 106-7, 111, 114, 121-23, 126-29. Cf. S.L. Greenslade, "The Last Monks of Durham Cathedral Priory", *Durham University Journal*, XLI (New Series, vol. X), 1948-49, pp. 107-13.
17. BL, Harl. MS 594, f. 195; *Reg.*, pp.77, 93, 171, 172.
18. *Reg.*, pp.40, 167.
19. Ibid., pp.59-60, 146.
20. Ibid., pp.71, 126.
21. Ibid., pp.63, 75, 126.
22. Ibid., pp.43, 57, 81, 85.
23. Ibid., pp.47, 57, 101.
24. Ibid., pp.66, 103, 104, 143, 146.
25. Ibid., pp.44, 54, 116.
26. Ibid., pp.111, 126, 148.
27. Ibid., pp.42, 44, 47, 58, 65, 66, 93, 105, 127, 133, 171, 178.
28. Ibid., pp.27, 42, 95, 102, 116, 128, 143, 164.

29. Ibid., pp.57, 58, 64, 66, 114, 119, 170; Greenslade, art. cit., pp. 107-13.
30. *Fasti*, p.131.
31. W. Hutchinson, *History of Durham*, ii (Newcastle upon Tyne, 1787), p.209.
32. *Reg.*, pp.104, 147.
33. Ibid., pp.93-94, 105.
34. Ibid., pp.145, 175.
35. Ibid., pp.144, 146, 147, 166, 176.
36. Ibid., pp.106, 145, 147, 168, 170; *Roy. Vis.*, p.103.
37. *Reg.*, pp.28, 52, 82, 84, 88, 105-6, 111, 114, 128.
38. J. Foster, *Alumni Oxonienses*, 4 vols (Oxford, 1891), pp.108, 290, 569, 1302, 1394, 1491, 1619.
39. A. & A.E. Venn, *Alumni Cantabrigienses*, Part I, 4 vols (Cambridge, 1922-27), i, pp.79, 116, 154: ii, pp.162, 320: iii, pp.21, 148: iv, pp.159, 192, 208, 439, 496.
40. W. Hutchinson, *History of Durham* ii, p.196.
41. C.M. Fraser (ed.), *Durham Quarter Sessions Rolls, 1471-1625* (Sur. Soc. 199, 1991), p.345.
42. *Roy. Vis.*, pp.21-28, 102-3. Cf. Greenslade, art. cit., pp.112-13.
43. J. Raine (ed.), *Wills and Inventories* (Sur. Soc. 2, 1834) I, pp.221-22; *Barnes*, pp.cviii-x, cxviii-xxii, cxxxiv-ix; Newcastle Central Library, Raine's Testamenta Dunelmensia A-F and I, ff.. 5, 11.
44. *Barnes*, pp.cx-xiv.
45. *Wills* (Sur. Soc. 38, 1860) II, pp.83-94.
46. *Barnes*, pp.cxxxiv-ix.
47. Ibid., pp.cx-xiv. cxxii-v, cxxix-xxx; *Wills*, II, pp.83-94.
48. *Barnes*, pp.cvii, cxxv-vii.
49. *Wills* I, pp.229-32.
50. *Barnes*, pp.cx-xiv, cxxxiv-ix.
51. Ibid., pp.cxix-xxii.
52. Ibid., pp.cviii-x.
53. Ibid., pp.cxxvii-ix.
54. *Wills* II, pp.318-22.
55. *Barnes*, pp.cx-vi-vii.
56. *Wills* I, pp.393-94.
57. Ibid., I, pp.379-82.
58. J. Raine, (ed.), *Depositions and Other Ecclesiastical Proceedings* (Sur. Soc., 21, 1845), pp.127-35.
59. Ibid., pp.136-37.
60. Ibid., pp.137-38.
61. Ibid., pp.147-48.
62. Ibid,, pp.158-59.
63. Ibid., pp.162-63.
64. Ibid., pp.169, 172.
65. Ibid., p.199.
66. Ibid., pp.143n, 168-69.
67. Ibid., pp.200-1.
68. Ibid., pp.118-20, 183-94.
69. Ibid., pp.258-61.
70. Ibid., pp.300-2.
71. Ibid., pp.304-5.
72. Ibid., pp.217-18.
73. Ibid., pp.211-12; *Reg.*, p.168.

III

PATRONAGE AND THE COUNTRY HOUSE IN NORTHUMBERLAND

Phoebe Lowery

This chapter concentrates on the country houses of Northumberland that were built or substantially altered between 1740 and 1840. In doing so, it seeks to evaluate what, if anything, distinguished these and earlier country houses from the English mainstream. Given the rigours of local terrain, climate and tradition and the distance of Northumberland from fashionable London, it is not unrealistic to suppose that this geographical divide should manifest itself in cultural terms. However, this chapter seeks to refute this notion to a certain extent – particularly after the middle of the eighteenth century, when, after slow beginnings, the Northumbrian country house began to evolve in tandem with national developments, rather than lagging behind them.

The country house provides the focus for this evaluation for several reasons. It has been observed that the study of the country house is a particularly effective way of examining the development of architectural style at least until the accession of Queen Victoria, when public buildings began to proliferate.[1] Prior to this date, country house design was unregulated, money was frequently available for both patron and architect to indulge their fantasies, and, perhaps most importantly, country house building provided a competitive arena for architects to demonstrate their skills. This last was especially true after the introduction of publications such as William Watts's *Seats of the Nobility and Gentry* (1779-86) and William Angus's book of the same title published in 1787, which were gazetteers of country houses often containing illustrations.

Thus we have the focus of this examination, which should answer questions on architectural style, pace and cost of building, choice of architect, sources of finance and architectural development generally within the county, placing the answers against a national backcloth. However, in a wider context, such a study of architectural patronage is also a revealing means of assessing a regional elite. Historians of the eighteenth century are presently reconsidering the nature of English society during the period. A relatively new development in the debate has been the assertion of social, political and, most importantly, cultural domination by the elite – domination which collapsed only towards the middle decades of the nineteenth century following the passage of the 1832 Reform Act. This contrasts with the traditional Marxist interpretation of the English Civil War as an event of decisive significance in social and political terms, a "Bourgeois Revolution" that resulted in a major shift of power in the 1640s, some two hundred years before the collapse of the elite hegemony identified by J.C.D. Clark.[2]

Both Clark and John Cannon[3] emphasise the forces of tradition which characterised the Hanoverian era, asserting that the domination of the landed elite survived and indeed increased in most areas during the eighteenth century. Elite hegemony, as far as they see it, existed with the aquiescence of the 'middling orders', who did not begin to challenge it until the later nineteenth century. Such a hegemony of course meant that the cultural values of the elite were pervasive in society, the middling ranks being only too keen to emulate their social superiors rather than challenge them. As Cannon observes:

> many brewers, bankers, coal owners and merchants having made their fortune were only too anxious to purchase a country estate and turn gentry.[4]

Research on the merchants of Leeds[5] has already demonstrated this to be true in West Yorkshire, and similar conclusions can be reached about Northumberland. A substantial number of the county's country house patrons had wealth founded on non-landed sources which they used to build suitable residences and establish themselves as gentry. Robert Lisle, the son of a cabinet-maker, inherited a fortune from his kinsman, a successful lawyer, and invested in Neo-classical Acton House, built in 1781, probably to the designs of William Newton. Isaac Cookson, a glass manufacturer with a wide range of other industrial interests, commissioned John Dobson to design Meldon Park in the Greek Revival style in 1832. These are but two examples amongst many more in Northumberland which would indicate that cultural domination by the elite was operating in this regional context.

Thus this chapter seeks not only to establish the distinguishing characteristics of the country house in Northumberland during the Hanoverian era, but also to identify and analyse the patrons who commissioned such houses, enabling a picture of elite society in the county to be constructed.

If there are several key points that must be grasped in any discussion of the development of the country house in Northumberland, the county's proximity to Scotland must be seen as the crucial distinguishing factor, since it stifled country house building until the latter part of the seventeenth century. As Thomas Fuller observed in his *Worthies of England,* published in 1662:

> One cannot rationally expect fair fabricks here where the vicinity of the Scots made not to build for state but strength.

The county's position as a frontier province, forming the major part of the border with Scotland, has been the dominant factor in the evolution of its architecture. Cross border conflict necessitated the construction of fortified buildings for defence and protection. During the three centuries prior to the Union of Crowns in 1603, the dominant architectural form was the tower house, often referred to as a pele. The function of such buildings was primarily fortification rather than comfort, their design guided by the best means of defence, although it is wrong to assume that aesthetic considerations had no bearing, as recent research has shown.[6]

For more southerly counties, the end of civil discord following the conclusion of the Wars of the Roses meant that fortification was no longer necessary, and by the sixteenth century the progression from castle to unfortified manor house (bearing many of the characteristics of country houses) was largely complete. The last quarter of the sixteenth century was particularly important in the development of the non-defensive house and has as a consequence become known as 'The Great Rebuilding', a period which really lasted until the Civil War. This was the age of the 'Prodigy Houses', of Longleat, Hatfield and Burghley, built to raise the esteem in which their owners were held, acting as clear demonstrations of political and social power or perhaps, more importantly, of the desire to obtain such power. The transformation of the southern parts of England during the later Tudor and early Stuart periods was not mirrored in Northumberland. No really substantial country seats were constructed at this time; it was only at Ford Castle that the typical E-plan of the period made an appearance and this was within the relative safety of the original castle's curtain walls, when a new south front was built some time before 1589.

Border conflict nominally ended with the accession of James VI of Scotland to the English throne; however, it took many years for it to end in actuality. While the Union did put an end to large-scale conflict, a degree of caution was essential to ensure the survival of a family and their property. This is demonstrated by the domestic building that took place in the county in the early seventeenth century, which showed some signs of development but made no great strides forward. Primarily it was confined to unfortified wings which were attached to the older tower houses, providing a element of refuge if the property came under attack. At Belsay in 1614 a two-storey house with large mullioned and transomed windows was built to adjoin the tower, and similar additions were made at Welton and West Bitchfield. At Chipchase, a three-storey symmetrical wing was added to the existing tower in 1621, with a three-tower frontispiece much like that found at Chillingham Castle, which was also constructed around the same date. The only examples of independent, new Jacobean manor houses built outside the protection of a town or city's walls (Anderson Place, Newcastle upon Tyne, constructed just before the Jacobean era, was of course sited within the walls) were built quite close to them. For example, Stote's Manor was built devoid of fortification in 1607 in what is now the suburb of Jesmond (the building was demolished c.1961) and Denton Hall to the west of Newcastle, was built beyond its boundaries in 1622.

However, just as Northumberland appeared to be making tentative steps forward, the Civil War arrested the development of such new polite architectural forms. The county historian John Hodgson was convinced of the deleterious effects of the Civil War, observing that the "beneficial change"[7] in the security of property that he perceived between the Union and the outbreak of the Great Rebellion was drastically undermined by the conflict and that life and property were almost as precarious as when the two realms had been ruled separately. Certainly the economic effects of the Civil War and the resulting Commonwealth were keenly felt in Northumberland. Sequestration affected many of Northumberland's leading families and those that did manage to retain their property often did so only by the payment of a heavy fine. The coal trade was particularly impaired, with disastrous consequences. Parliament blockaded the Tyne from 1643 and in the following year only 3,000 tons of coal were shipped as opposed to the usual annual export of 450,000 tons, and fewer than two hundred ships entered the Tyne compared with the three thousand of a normal year.[8] Other sources of finance were also detrimentally affected. The salt trade suffered from free Scottish competition; several of the Tyneside glass houses were damaged by the Scots and farming land laid waste by marauding armies. Revenue was therefore drastically constrained and this is indicated in the complete lack of building activity that took place during this troubled time. Not only would it have been foolhardy to commission a new country residence in a time of political uncertainty, the economic wherewithal to do this was sadly lacking.

After the Restoration, the real story of the Northumberland country house begins to unfold, albeit still slowly and tentatively. It commences with a Yorkshire mason, Robert Trollope (d.1686), the first truly identifiable figure on the Northumbrian architectural stage. His style can only be described as exuberantly vital, being an enthusiastic juxtaposition of the old established Gothic mode injected with classical devices which were not yet properly understood but were used with such confidence and vigour that the end product, however unconventional, is eminently appealing. He was responsible for Capheaton, which dates from 1668 (fig. 19), and probably also for Bockenfield Manor (c.1660), Callaly Castle, completed in 1676, and Netherwitton Hall (1672). He is thought to have descended from a long line

Fig. 19 Capheaton Hall, Northumberland (by Robert Trollope, 1668), from the south-west.

of stonemasons and was described as of the "cittie of York" in his contract with the city corporation of Newcastle to design and build the new Guildhall, to replace the existing medieval building, which was badly in need of repair. This rebuilding took place between 1655 and 1658.

Trollope's employment in the design of such a prominent building would naturally bring him to the attention of the wider populace. Certainly he caught the eye of Sir John Swinburne of Capheaton, who commissioned him to build a new mansion house. The Swinburnes were experiencing a resurgence in family fortunes at this time; their loyalty to the Stuarts had been rewarded by a baronetcy on the restoration of Charles II and the building of the new house symbolised their new importance within the county. Trollope's architecture has been called "idiosyncratic, rural, humorous and decorative".[9] This is certainly the case at Capheaton, which incorporates classical forms but in a totally original manner. Thus, while the house is symmetrical, with giant pilasters, the pilasters are bulgily rusticated, and the windows, which were originally mullioned and transomed, have cable mouldings surrounding them. Similiar anomalies occur at other properties attributed to Trollope. While he uses columns, they were worked in a spiral form, as at Bockenfield, or carved with vines as at Capheaton. Indeed, even Norman 'dog tooth' makes an appearance in his work.

This architect can really be fitted into the loose umbrella term 'Artisan Mannerism', first coined by Sir John Summerson[10] to describe the move away from the Gothic tradition towards classicism, as classical modes of expression began to be insinuated into English architecture. Summerson observed that the broken pediment was an architectural feature particularly beloved of such architects. At Callaly, Trollope employed trophies and even dolphins interposed between the two broken segments of his open pediments. At Capheaton he was content to make his pediment fantastically curly and ornamented. However, it appears that he was an isolated practitioner of the new architectural modes; Callaly, Capheaton and Netherwitton are fairly isolated examples of country house building in the late seventeenth century. An earlier house, now incorporated into the present mansion, was constructed at Wallington around 1688, but really it was the smaller, vernacular manor houses built for the yeoman class which predominate during this period.

The eighteenth century has been referred to as the 'Great Awakening' in terms of the construction of the country house in Northumberland, and is where our detailed analysis of houses and their patrons begins. Even so, it was not until the third or fourth decade of that century that country houses began to be built in any number, representing a stylistic gap from Trollope's work in the latter part of the preceding century. Country houses such as Roddam, Eslington, Hesleyside and Blagdon were constructed or substantially remodelled in the early years of the eighteenth century, but they are stylistically plain and remain anonymous in terms of authorship. All were extensively altered later in the century.

The one great exception, however, is a house of major architectural significance which was begun c.1720 and thus, in addition to several fine examples of Artisan Mannerism, Northumberland can also lay claim to an example of the work of perhaps the finest exponent of the English Baroque – Sir John Vanbrugh. Blenheim and Castle Howard are well known examples of this extraordinary man's sense of the dramatic. Seaton Delaval, near Blyth (fig. 20), is less well known, but, like the aforementioned, astounds with its uncompromisingly bold silhouette. Admiral George Delaval, its patron, expressed a desire in 1719

> to divert myself a little in my old age repairing the old house making a garden and planting forest trees for which we may expect prayers when we are no more.[11]

Perhaps the Duke of Marlborough's example encouraged the Admiral, seeking to erect a similar monument to his own illustrious career, to settle upon Vanbrugh. The result embodies the spirit of the English Baroque. A product of an intensely theatrical imagination, its classical mass is particularly suited to its exposed position a mile or two from the North Sea.

Fig. 20 Seaton Delaval Hall, Northumberland (by Sir John Vanbrugh, c.1720-29). The north front, from William Hutchinson's *A View of Northumberland* (1778). The south-east wing shown here was built c.1770 and destroyed by fire in 1822. Its counterpart (to the right in this view) was never actually built.

Quite surprisingly for such an imposing and original creation, Seaton Delaval did not inspire a wave of Baroque influenced architectural forms as Castle Howard did in North Yorkshire. Only Eglingham Hall, which was possibly designed by William Etty, Vanbrugh's Clerk of Works, bears any striking resemblance to it and really it must be regarded as an isolated incident, outside the mainstream of the county's architectural development – although, paradoxically, it is very much within the mainstream nationally. Consequently, if Seaton Delaval is discounted, there is little that distinguishes the architecture of the country house in Northumberland for almost half a century after Trollope's death. Country house building activity increased only slowly and it was not until the second half of the eighteenth century that steady progress began to be made. Thus the county again lagged behind national developments, not experiencing the general upsurge in building activity in the late seventeenth and early eighteenth century that has been identified.

One of the reasons for this was financial deprivation. Trollope's patrons could obviously afford to commission large mansions. Sir John Swinburne agreed to pay Trollope five hundred pounds for Capheaton, according to a contract which still survives at the house. Many of Sir John's peers, however, could not find sufficient funds even if they had wanted to. Naturally, landed income improved with political stability, but as late as 1770 the agricultural commentator Arthur Young bemoaned being obliged to

> ride through such extensive tracks of uncultivated good land, as are found in every part of this county.[12]

Young, however, noted approvingly the agricultural improvements undertaken by Abraham Dixon of Belford Hall.[13] And less than a decade later the county topographer William Hutchinson remarked:

> Improved husbandry makes a rapid progress, and enclosures take place of the wide extended tracts where many Herdsmen were heretofore necessarily employed to keep the cattle and flocks within their bounds.[14]

The effects of agricultural improvement began to be felt during the second half of the eighteenth century. Many of Northumberland's country house patrons were active improvers, like Charles Bigge of Linden and, of course, Abraham Dixon of Belford; indeed, Matthew Culley purchased his estate at Fowberry on the strength of his success in this area. New husbandry methods and newly invented machinery were widely adopted throughout the county with beneficial effects. In 1794 a Report prepared for the Board of Agriculture noted that "extensive" plantations were "rising in every part of the county" and that those parts of it which were capable of cultivation were "in general well inclosed by live hedges"; it observed in the lower parts of the county especially:

> a more pleasing prospect of inclosed country, extensive farms, scattered villages, populous towns, and busy scenes of trade.[15]

Furthermore, land rental values in the county were also improving, far outstripping the national average. Between 1795 and 1804, the value of coastal grazing pasture rose from forty shillings per acre to somewhere around sixty or seventy shillings and arable land from thirty-five to fifty-five shillings, an increase in one decade of more than forty per cent. Nationally, landed incomes rose by an equivalent percentage only over a fifty year period.

More importantly than landed income, however, was mineral income. Coal was the engine of country house building in Northumberland. As early as the mid-seventeenth century, the poet John Cleveland observed, referring to the coal mines that surrounded the city in his *News from Newcastle* (1651):

> England's a perfect world, has Indies too,
> Correct your maps. Newcastle is Peru.

In 1698, the traveller Celia Fiennes wrote: "Upon a high hill, 2 mile from Newcastle I could see all about the county which was full of coal pits".[16]

William Gray in his *Chorographia* of 1649 observed that the great trade in coal from Newcastle "began not past four score years since". Certainly by 1700 a substantial proportion of England's coal demands were being met by output from the Tyne and Wear coalfield, possibly as much as fifty per cent.[17] Demand for coal was increasing steadily during the period, firstly for use as domestic fuel and latterly due to increased demands made by the nascent industrial processes, which required coal rather than wood as fuel. Coal formed a proportion of many a patron's fortune, providing the wherewithal to build either by augmenting the income of established landed families or by enabling newcomers to establish themselves on estates as country gentlemen. A list of colliery owners around 1800[18] is scattered with familiar names: Bigge of Linden, Brandling of Gosforth, Bewicke of Close House, Ord of Fenham and Whitfield, Sir Francis Blake of Twizel and Tilmouth, Sir Matthew White Ridley of Blagdon and Heaton, Sir John Hussey (now Lord) Delaval of Ford and Seaton Delaval, and the Duke of Northumberland all appear as mine proprietors, amply demonstrating that those at the peak of landed society were as eager to exploit the mineral resources on their estates as those who had sprung from lesser origins.

In addition to its predominance in the coal trade, the North East was the leading area of glass production during the half century after 1780. This is not surprising since the industry utilised the poor quality small coal which could not be shipped out. The Cooksons of Meldon, the Cuthberts of Beaufront, the Williams of Killingworth, the Hargreaves of Shawdon and the White Ridleys of Blagdon all had glass interests. The value of such interests is demonstrated by the fact that the Newcastle Broad and Crown Glass Co. paid a dividend of one hundred pounds per share in 1815. In 1825 William Hargreave Pawson, who inherited Shawdon Hall from his cousin and rebuilt Titlington Hall, sold his twelve shares for seven hundred and ten pounds each.[19]

Edward Hughes observed:

> In the North, the rent roll is not a true index of economic power. Thanks to coal there was always a greater fusion of landed and merchant interests in these parts than elsewhere . . . the great age of the gentry was made possible only by the profits derived from trade.[20]

Hughes saw the Northumberland elite of the eighteenth century as predominantly 'nouveau riche' with trade based fortunes, largely replacing the old, heavily mortgaged, Northern recusant families on the occasion of their final collapse after the Jacobite rebellion of 1715. Northumberland was also one of three counties analysed by Lawrence Stone in his study of the English elite. Taking issue with Hughes's conclusions, Stone denied the existence of a substantial entry of new men into his elite class of building families between 1610 and 1870:

> What influx there was . . . was mainly of professionals and office holders, rather than merchants and bankers . . . as for industrialists they are simply not present except for some brewers in Hertfordshire.[21]

This is quite categorically not the case in Northumberland, although Hughes's version of an old elite being ousted by a new one with trade based fortunes is also very much open to question. It must be understood that Stone used a very narrow definition of the elite class, since he analysed only the largest country seats in each of the three counties as the basis for his research and steadfastly ignored those families who made their way to a substantial country estate by way of a smaller one, like the White Ridley family of Blagdon. Their wealth was founded on a fusion between the two merchant families of White and Ridley (the latter admittedly important since medieval times), who shared a common interest in coal and allied themselves by means of two marriages in the first half of the eighteenth century. They made their way to the Blagdon estate via Heaton Hall and, although a family who could be classed as a new entrant to the Northumbrian elite, they were discounted by Stone, who counted only those new entrants who jumped straight from a meagre town house to a substantial mansion in one fell swoop.

Typically, Northumberland's architectural patrons, particularly if they were new entrants to the elite, maintained links with both commerce and land over several generations, often marrying into both established landed families and families who were themselves primarily involved in trade and industry. This justifies the statement by Martin Postelthwayt in his *Dictionary of Trade and Industry* of 1765:

> Trade is so far here from being inconsistent with the character of a gentleman that trade in England makes gentlemen . . . after a generation or two, the children of traders or at least their grandchildren come to be as good gentlemen, statesmen, parliament men, privy councillors, judges, bishops and noblemen as those of the highest birth and most ancient families.

By grouping the country house patrons who built or substantially altered a country house between 1740 and 1840 by the method through which they acquired their estate, it is possible to gain a idea of the composition of Northumberland's elite society. As expected, the county had a high proportion of very well established families who passed their estates from father to son in the accepted manner. This linear descent of estates through a single family accounted for more than forty per cent of patrons. Such patrons had held their estate for more than three generations, this being what we may consider to be the length of time required for a family to consider itself established, although it could take less time in practice. Many families had held their estates for considerably longer, such as the Charltons of Hesleyside, who had lived in Tynedale since the thirteenth century, and the Claverings of Callaly, who are mentioned in a 1415 list of fortifications as being in the possession of a castle there. Thus such direct inheritors make up the largest category of patrons.

Indirect inheritors of estates make up the next largest section, accounting for around a quarter of the total. By indirect inheritors are meant those patrons who inherited their estate through brothers, wives, uncles, mothers and more distant kinfolk, due to the failure of the direct line from father to son. Again, this group is largely composed of well-established landed families who had held the property for many generations, such as those of Charles Brandling, who inherited the Gosforth estate due to the death of his childless brother, and William Ord, who inherited Fenham on his brother's early death.

In combination, these two groups of patrons represent about two thirds of the whole. Of the remaining third, about twenty per cent of these were what could be referred to as 'established purchasers' – usually building a second home and already possessing substantial landholdings elsewhere in the county. Thus, for example, Charles Bigge of Benton House also acquired Linden Hall, Longhorsley. A small number of patrons cannot be identified; this is particularly true of patrons building country houses in Benton, at that time not incorporated into Newcastle and highly desirable. Several substantial houses were built there in the early nineteenth century, quite probably for professional men who needed to be near Newcastle. These are now mainly demolished. Their owners are shadowy figures who defy accurate classification.

The remainder accounts for about a quarter of total patrons analysed. This is the most interesting group in terms of the wider context of this chapter, which seeks to shed some light on elite cultural hegemony and the relative openness of the upper strata to penetration from below; these patrons were what could be termed new entrants to the elite. Just under half of the patrons in this group bought large landed estates and immediately built country houses upon them. Examples are William Cuthbert, who commissioned John Dobson to remodel Beaufront, originally the family seat of the Erringtons, for him in 1837, and Isaac Cookson, Cuthbert's partner who, as we have seen, also employed Dobson in 1832. Both men were the third generation of families with widespread industrial and mercantile interests encompassing iron, coal, glass and chemicals. Medicine, trade, law and brewing enriched the other patrons in this category.

The patrons discussed above were in the very fortunate position of being able to purchase an estate and build a substantial country house in one generation. Our remaining new entrants inherited their estate within two generations of a purchaser who had bought the estate using funds from non-landed sources and who had been unwilling or unable to commence building operations immediately. Again, such patrons were enriched through trade and the law profession. Often a common denominator within both segments of the purchaser-patron group was coal.

To summarise then, the composition of Northumberland's elite society between 1740 and 1840 may be described as follows. Land ownership was fairly stable and the majority of patrons undertaking building activity were from well-established county families. However, over a quarter of the county's country house patrons engaged in building activity between 1740 and 1840 were what could be described as 'new men', entering the elite from below through a variety of non-landed sources of wealth underpinned by coal. Such new entrants did displace some of the older Northumberland families from their country seats. Thus the Reed family, who began as small time yeomen, replaced the ancient Heron family at Chipchase Castle, and the Hodgsons, successful traders and dealers, replaced the Jennisons at Elswick in 1742. However, by no means all of Northumberland's Catholic elite were uprooted in this fashion. Several Roman Catholic families survived the turmoil of the rebellions against the House of Hanover in 1715 and 1745 and can be found amongst those patrons engaged in building activity. For example, the Claverings of Callaly were modernising their ancient seat from 1727 onwards, William Charlton of Hesleyside added a new front to his mansion at the end of the eighteenth century, and in 1805 Carnaby Haggerston added new wings to a house (Haggerston Castle) which had been built by his father some time prior to 1777. The Riddell family of Swinburne Castle are a particularly good example of the survival of a Roman Catholic family. Through marriage with other Catholic families they acquired Cheeseburn Grange and Felton Park, commissioning the re-building of two of these houses and making substantial additions to the third. Thus while new families were rising in Northumbrian society, it was by no means at the expense of all the older Roman Catholic families.

Of all the sources of non-landed wealth utilised in the county for the purchase of estates by new entrants to the elite, coal and lucrative careers in the law appear to have been the most important. Due to the substantial proportion of patrons who were fairly newly enriched, linkages between the landed elite and commerce were strongly maintained. This is confirmed by the admission book of the Company of Merchant Adventurers, which reveals the names of several eventual patrons. Patrons may also be found acting as Mayor or Sheriff of Newcastle. Sir Walter Calverley Blackett, Wallington's great improver, was elected Mayor on no less than five occasions, only slightly in advance of Sir Matthew White Ridley of Blagdon who served three times. Intermarriage amongst the elite assured that landed and commercial wealth were also securely intertwined.

Another very common source of wealth enabling the building of the Northumbrian country house was advantageous marriage. At least a fifth of all patrons married heiresses or women blessed with very substantial dowries. A good example is George Craster who managed to obtain an heiress with a fortune of £30,000 as his bride in 1757; some of the money, no doubt, he utilised in the large improvements made to Craster Tower from 1763.

It was just as well there was such a variety of sources of finance available, as the costs of engaging in building activity were not small, with at least two patrons finding themselves overstretched. Estimates and accounts for building or altering houses in Northumberland during the Georgian era are sparse; however, some figures survive to give an indication of the amount of money that might be required during the century under examination. Fenham Hall, for example, was built from 1744 for William Ord, who inherited the estate from his brother; it is almost unique in that detailed accounts survive for the years that it was under construction.[22] William Ord practised as a lawyer and married an heiress, enabling him to spend some £4,000 on his new house (designed by Daniel Garrett). Some thirty years later the Newcastle architect William Newton estimated that it would cost £2,705 to build a new house at Backworth for Ralph William Grey. This sum excluded the building of the offices, the carriage of building materials and the quarrying of stone as well as the digging of the cellars, but did include the provision of all other materials. For this sum Grey obtained a mansion in the Palladian mode, with a central pediment crowning a five bay main block with lower arcaded wings (fig. 21). However, it is recorded by Horace St. Paul of Ewart Park that:

> Mr Grey told me that his house cost him a great deal more than the above sum and that besides the expense of the house his offices cost him a separate sum of above £700.[23]

A decade later, Newton charged just over £1,600 for alterations made at Capheaton (1789-90), which by this time must have looked distinctly unwieldy and outmoded to its proprietor, Sir John Swinburne, who commissioned a new Palladian front to update his Stuart mansion.[24] Moving into the nineteenth century, John Dobson estimated that it would cost £7,188 to build Meldon Park for Isaac Cookson in 1832.[25] Meldon was a large Neo-classical villa and was built on a 2,000-acre estate that Cookson had purchased from the Greenwich Hospital Trust the same year for 57,000 guineas, amply demonstrating the funds that the industrialist had at his disposal.

Fig. 21 Backworth Hall, Northumberland (by William Newton, 1778).

Very few patrons were fortunate to emulate Cookson's example of purchasing an estate and commissioning a new house in the same year. As has been noted earlier, quite often purchase would be made by one generation and building activity undertaken by another, once family coffers had been replenished. Such was the case with Matthew Bell, a clothier and eventual partner in the Old Newcastle Bank, who purchased the Woolsington estate in 1748. The house was originally constructed in the latter part of the seventeenth century and the first Matthew Bell was either content to live in it as it was or unable to find further funds for its alteration. He was succeeded by his grandson, who added classical wings to the old house at the end of the eighteenth century and also commissioned an elegant and fashionable orangery. Similarly, as we have seen, John Hodgson, a draper with coal interests, purchased the Elswick estate in 1742; it was embellished by a fine Neo-classical mansion designed by William Stokoe in 1803, commissioned by his grandson.

Insecurity and lack of capital prevented country house building from becoming firmly established in Northumberland until well into the eighteenth century. Thus, as has been observed, the county did not experience the general upsurge in country house building identified in the late seventeenth and early eighteenth centuries[26] and was therefore outside the mainstream. However, country house building activity also rose from the late 1790s, reaching a peak around the 1830s. By this time Northumberland had caught up with these national trends. Within the county, building activity reached a peak between the years 1810 and 1820, when at least twenty patrons were building new houses or beautifying old. The preceding decade was also distinguished by a high level of building activity. Attention has already been drawn to the improvements made in agriculture in the latter part of the eighteenth century, which no doubt contributed to the upswing in building activity. The Culleys, who completed alterations at Fowberry Tower in 1819, are an apt illustration of a family that profited from agricultural improvements. George and Matthew Culley began in a very humble way, but gradually built up substantial landholdings in the county. The Fowberry estate was purchased in 1807 for £45,000. George's son, the second Matthew Culley, used it as his country residence, continuing the alterations and additions begun by the Blake family in 1776. This was much to the amazed gratification of his father, who observed:

> whenever I am at Fowberry I am struck with astonishment, when I reflect on our beginning in Northumberland 43 years ago. To think of my son inhabiting a palace! altho' his father in less than fifty years since worked harder than any servant we have now and even drove a coal cart.[27]

Rising agricultural fortunes and the continuing presence of coal do not entirely account for the spurt in building activity in the early nineteenth century. Several of the patrons who built during the peak decade built completely new houses and, significantly, these houses were located on estates within easy reach of Newcastle. Such patrons tended to be professional men such as Sir Thomas Burdon, a partner in a brewery on the Quayside and heavily involved in civic affairs, who commissioned John Dobson to design West Jesmond House in 1817, and Thomas Headlam, Newcastle's senior physician, who also commissioned Dobson to design Black Dene House, Jesmond, in 1818.

Thus far we have drawn several conclusions about the building of the country house in Northumberland and the composition of the county's elite between 1740 and 1840. However, little has been said on the subject of motivation. Given the high cost of engaging in building activity, what prompted patrons to throw caution to the winds in their anxiety to build? In particular, what prompted new entrants into investing their hard-earned capital into a new or extensively altered country house? Writing about Belsay Hall, recently constructed by Sir Charles Monck, the county historian John Hodgson observed:

> the kitchens, stables and other offices are to the North; and they and the whole of this beautiful and unique structure are not more remarkable for the simplicity and elegance of their parts than for the fineness and solidarity of their masonry, which is calculated to continue them to remote generations as a splendid monument of the architectural skill of their designer and proprietor.[28]

This eloquently demonstrates that a new, altered, or rebuilt country house stood as a permanent memorial to the patron who commissioned it, distinguishing him from his ancestors and descendants.

John Wallis was the first historian to publish a large scale topographical study of Northumberland. *The Natural History and Antiquities of Northumberland*, published in 1769, is laced with admiring adjectives such as "handsome", "genteel" and "modern", and he refers to "ornamentation", "improvements" and "embellishments", mentioning properties that do not bear such signs of activity only briefly and then dismissively, as in the case of John Hodgson of Elswick, "whose seat is an old structure".[29] Half a century later, another county historian, Eneas Mackenzie, was even more effusive in his comments, referring to the "elegance", "stateliness", "noble appearances" and "commodious" nature of the various mansion houses that he describes. For example, Addison Baker Cresswell's Neo-classical mansion, Cresswell Hall, would, when finished, "rival in taste and magnificence the best in the county".[30]

Clearly, then, the country house did provoke comment. Contemporaries were obviously very aware of building activity, particularly on a large scale and would comment approvingly. Modernity and improvement were quite definitely in vogue. The country house and its owning family would be clearly linked in the eyes of the public; owners would be distinguished by their seats, for example, the Allgoods of Nunwick, the Brandlings of Gosforth and the White Ridleys of Heaton and Blagdon. A splendid seat would cast reflected rays in which its proud owner could bask, reinforcing a landowner's position at the forefront of society. Hutchinson observed of Alnwick in 1776:

> we found the Inn crowded with people of fortune, come from all parts of the county, to pay their compliments to the Duke and Duchess, it being their first public day, after their arrival at this palace for the summer recess.[31]

Not only would people pay their respects, they would also see a reconstructed castle of 'Gothick' splendour (fig. 22) which attempted to reinforce the ancient Percy lineage (this, incidently, had been weakened by passing twice through the female line in three generations) by all manner of heraldic device, both in the castle and the park.

More and more, as time progressed, the country house became a showpiece for its owner, designed to create an awe-inspiring and unassailable impression, not only among the owner's peers, but also among members of the public, of sufficient social status, who would be admitted to view the house by housekeepers when the family was away. People from lower down the social scale would also be brought into the immediate orbit of the big

Fig. 22 *View of the First Court in Alnwick Castle from the Porter's Lodge,* by J. Villet, c.1775. (The Laing Art Gallery, Newcastle upon Tyne).

house in their vicinity due to its role as a centre of consumption and employment in the area. Building provided employment for substantial numbers of labourers and craftsmen, who would mainly be drawn from the immediate locality. In 1770 it was observed that the Duke of Northumberland still had between one and two hundred men at work on both the park and the castle. Ties of deference and respect would be reinforced by the grandeur of the mansion house and also by the possibilities that it offered in terms of employment. Thus it can be seen that the country house acted as a vehicle for display, a very visible bulwark to a patron's social position, a statement of rank and superiority.

The holding of public office, particularly by new entrants to the elite, appears to be directly linked to the building of the country house. If the occupancy of the office of High Sheriff for the county is analysed it can be seen that newcomers often had the honour conferred upon them shortly after, or at the same time as, they were engaged in building activity.

Abraham Dixon's Palladian mansion at Belford (fig. 23) was completed by 1756 in a highly visible position near the main road. Three years after the completion of the house, Dixon was chosen for the office of High Sheriff, a sure sign that his merchant roots were forgotten and that he was now assimilated into the elite. Robert Lisle of Acton House acted as High Sheriff in 1789 only eight years after purchasing his estate. The son of a craftsman,

Fig. 23 Belford Hall, Northumberland (by James Paine, 1754-56; wings added by John Dobson, 1817, reflecting Paine's original design).

he inherited a fortune from a childless kinsmen who had practised as a lawyer in Morpeth, and invested it in the Acton estate. He commissioned a substantial Palladian mansion, perhaps designed by the fashionable Newcastle architect William Newton, which was probably just completed prior to his selection. Isaac Cookson was chosen six years after he commissioned Dobson to design Meldon Park, despite his continuing industrial interests. There are numerous other examples of this association between building activity and the office of High Sheriff, particularly amongst the less well established families. Members of Parliament also tended to have been engaged in substantial building activity. If the prestige of a landowning family depended on the extent of their acreage, the size and grandeur of their seat was also of considerable significance.

Between 1740 and 1840, five architects were successively prominent in the field of country house design in Northumberland. Their periods of prominence do not overlap; each architect dominated his own time. Through their individual contributions, it may be seen that, far from lagging behind in terms of architectural development, Northumberland could be considered to be in the vanguard of architectural fashion throughout the period, not suffering from its remote geographical position.

With the exception of Vanbrugh's solitary essay at Seaton Delaval, Daniel Garrett is the first identifiable country house architect to undertake several commissions here since Robert Trollope. In the main field of Palladian design, Garrett is seen as a relatively minor figure. Essentially he was a competent architect, well versed in Palladian motifs, which he applied to produce houses pleasing to the eye, but never remarkable or innovatory. Nevertheless, Garrett had an impeccable Palladian pedigree, acting as a man of business for no less a figure than the third earl of Burlington, the leading protagonist in the establishment of English Palladianism. Indeed it is recorded by Sir Thomas Robinson of Rokeby that:

> My Ld Burlington has a much better opinion of Mr Garrett's knowledge than of Mr Flitcroft's or any person whatever except Mr Kent.[32]

Garrett came to the North East as a direct result of Robinson's patronage. He worked extensively for Sir Walter Calverly Blackett at Wallington from the late 1730s onwards, drew up plans for Fenham Hall for William Ord and designed Nunwick in 1745 for Lancelot Allgood. He was probably also responsible for the south front of Blagdon for Sir Matthew White (this is dated 1752 on some of the rainwater heads) and possibly for the early stages of the restoration of Alnwick Castle. Nunwick is arguably the most accomplished of Garrett's designs and displays the obvious influence of Palladian prototypes.

However, it is as a pioneer of Rococo interior decoration that Garrett achieves most renown. So-called second generation Palladians began to move away from the heavy, Baroque-influenced decorative plasterwork used by their immediate predecessors, preferring livelier, lighter forms, with great emphasis on naturalistic forms such as flowers, shells and fruit. Garrett was in the forefront of this development. The best examples of his interiors survive at Wallington, adorning the state rooms that he created on the south front. The plasterer was Pietro Francini, who also worked at Fenham and quite possibly at Blagdon. The similarities between the Wallington plasterwork and that found in the magnificent saloon at Callaly also indicate that Garrett may have found employment there for the Clavering family.

Garrett died in 1753 and was succeeded by James Paine (1717-89) in too many of his commissions for it to have been coincidental. Paine is arguably the best known architect of his generation to have worked in the county. His commissions were additions to his already extensive northern practice and it may be that he came into contact with Garrett through mutual acquaintances in the Burlington circle; thus Paine is found working at Wallington, Blagdon and Alnwick, which were probably all Garrett commissions originally. He is important in terms of the Northumberland country house as one of the first architects to introduce the villa format for moderately wealthy country gentlemen. The idea of the villa had been introduced by Burlington and Colen Campbell in the first half of the eighteenth century, but the 1750s were perhaps its most significant period. By this time the idea of a villa, with wings housing the essential services, was prevalent. Paine designed three villas in the county during the 1750s. Gosforth House, designed for Charles Brandling around 1755, was the largest house of its period to be built in the villa form. Like Belford Hall for Abraham Dixon and Bywell Hall for William Fenwick, Gosforth had a *piano nobile*, given extra prominence by the addition of decorative detail, such as half columns, pilasters and pediments, which articulated the facade, giving it life and movement. Paine's influence within the county was acknowledged by the architect John Dobson, albeit in a scathing assessment:

> Mr Payne was unfortunately considered so great an authority, that all the country houses in the North were mere copies of his general plan . . .[33]

Paine was particularly influential upon William Newton (1730-98), who reproduces many of his characteristic motifs as well as using the villa format, both with and without wings, something that may be viewed as Paine's major contribution to Northumberland's country house architecture.

Both Paine and his predecessor Garrett worked extensively outside the region and were not local men. William Newton, the most successful and prolific country house architect in Northumberland in the latter decades of the eighteenth century,[34] was born in Newcastle and his practice was concentrated in Northumberland, with only the occasional foray into County Durham. Quite how many commissions he undertook is unknown; several houses, like Acton House (fig. 24), Togston Hall and the now demolished Broome Park and Bank House, can be attributed to him on stylistic grounds, although corroborating evidence is lacking. However, he was responsible for houses such as Howick Hall, Whitfield Hall, North Dissington Hall and Backworth Hall and for substantial alterations to Fenham Hall, Lemington Hall and Capheaton. His talents were also extensively utilised within Newcastle itself (see Chapter Six), as he designed (or made alterations to) several public buildings, the most notable being the Assembly Rooms.

Newton learnt his trade from his father, originally a shipwright who turned to architecture and first appears as the Clerk of Works at the Infirmary (built to designs by Garrett). Throughout the 1760s, father and son appear to have practised as a partnership. William Newton's selection as the architect of the Assembly Rooms in 1774 began a new phase in his career. A "very numerous and brilliant company"[35] attended the grand opening in 1776 and no doubt among their ranks were several of Newton's future patrons who would thus acquire first-hand knowledge of his skills. The front

Fig. 24 Acton House, Felton, Northumberland (by William Newton, 1781).

of the Assembly Rooms bears a striking resemblance to Paine's design for Gosforth. As well as drawing inspiration from Paine, however, Newton was also influenced by the work of Robert Adam, and his designs show a gradual movement away from strict Palladianism towards the kind of Neo-classicism popularised by Adam. Newton houses bear a recognisable stamp, with double string courses spanning an entrance front, which often has a slightly projecting centre capped with a pediment. Windows and doorways were often surrounded by relieving arches, and doorways were in the 'Venetian' style mirrored internally with a 'Venetian' screen. In general, his houses were characterised by a starkness of architectural detail which again mirrored national developments. Newton was also typical of a particular generation of architects in that he provided Northumberland's rising gentry with the type of country house that they wanted: conformist, compact and easy to build and maintain. Like Carr of Yorkshire, Smith of Warwickshire and Keck of Gloucestershire, he fits into the scheme of the provincial builder-architect who offered a comprehensive package of design, supervision and execution.

If William Newton owed some of his ideas to Robert Adam, John Paterson (d.1832) owed his career to the Adam brothers. Paterson was responsible for the design of two houses in Northumberland and for alterations to a third in the first decade of the nineteenth century. Originally he was employed by the Adams as their man in Edinburgh, overseeing the Scottish practice while Robert and James were in London. Sir Howard Colvin has commented on Paterson's prediliction for oval room shapes.[36] This was undoubtedly something he acquired during his supervision of Adam designs in Scotland. Paterson was intimately involved with the building of Seton Castle in East Lothian from 1790 and the design of Airthrey Castle, Stirlingshire, in 1791, both of which contained several oval or ovaloid rooms. His penchant for borrowing ideas appears to have been well known and was remarked upon by Adam's sister.[37] Unusual room shapes were a feature of the late eighteenth and early nineteenth centuries. Paterson's most complicated spatial manipulation was at Milbourne Hall, Northumberland, which, although a relatively small house, gives an impression of grandeur due to the skilful incorporation of the offices into the scheme. It is at Barmoor, also in Northumberland, however, that his Adam inheritance is most clearly demonstrated and thus the county can boast a romantic castle in the same spirit as Seton and Culzean (Ayrshire) to the north and the creations of John Nash, such as West Grinstead Park, Sussex, in the south.

The final architect achieving prominence before 1840 was another native Northumbrian. John Dobson (1787-1865) has been described as "the most eminent architect to have been born and to have worked in North East England".[38] His career was extensive and prolific and in line with many architects of his generation he mastered both classical and Gothic Revival forms. He began primarily as a classicist, working in the newly fashionable Greek Revival style, which had been much publicised in the county through Belsay Hall, a pure Greek Doric building begun in 1807 to the designs of its owner Sir Charles Monck. After training in Newcastle and London, Dobson established himself in practice in Newcastle and was much in demand, providing villa style residences in particular for the newly enriched industrialists and professional men. However, his clientele also numbered established families among its ranks. He designed manageably sized accommodation with excellent masonry unmarred by drains and pipes, which were concealed internally. His Neo-classical villas, such as Mitford, Meldon (fig. 25), Longhirst and Nunnykirk, all provided spacious reception areas for the gracious entertainment beloved by Regency England. With his expertise in siting houses in flattering positions, Dobson gave his properties pleasing aspects, important in an era predominated by Picturesque theories. Initially uneasy with the Gothic style, as demonstrated by Cheeseburn Grange of 1813, Dobson soon became a competent exponent, as Beaufront Castle, and Lilburn Tower (colour plate ii) testify, and there are some grounds for supporting his daughter's statement that:

> while Pugin and others were doing all they could to call the attention of architects from their beloved Greek temples to the beauties of Gothic, and Pugin himself supplied them with "Examples", it must be remembered that here was one practising what others taught almost in vain.[39]

Fig. 25 Meldon Park, Northumberland (by John Dobson, 1832).

Dobson's designs kept Northumberland firmly in the mainstream of national architectural development. He was an early practitioner of archaeologically correct Gothic architecture in national terms and it must also be noted that a Gothic Revival tradition was firmly rooted in Northumberland prior even to Dobson's birth. It began in the middle of the eighteenth century, about the same time that the aesthete Horace Walpole was beginning to toy with Strawberry Hill. The earl of Northumberland (as he was then) commenced work on Alnwick Castle in 1752, creating a confection of 'Gothick' splendour, in the end mainly by Robert Adam, apparently to please his wife (who may well have had a substantial say in the choice of designs). Now almost entirely swept away by later alterations, this work at Alnwick blazed a pathway for other Northumbrian patrons. At Craster Tower a new classical south front was added by George Craster from about 1767, but with alterations in the 'Gothick' taste made internally. Sir John Hussey Delaval gothicised Ford Castle during the 1770s. The Blake family of Fowberry and Twizel appear to have had a special predilection for 'Gothick'; in 1769 John Wallis recorded that Sir Francis was making "handsome additions" at Twizel in the "ancient Saxon-Gothic". Very pretty 'Gothick' additions were also made to Fowberry in 1776. About the same time Sir Matthew White Ridley commissioned William Newton to add a crenellated parapet and embattled towers to his house at Heaton, Newcastle. Barmoor Castle of 1801, an example derived from Robert Adam's castle style, has already been mentioned. Numerous smaller examples, such as the 'Gothick' kennels at Nunwick, are also evident in the county. Hence there was an unbroken stream of Gothic Revival architecture in Northumberland from at least the middle of the eighteenth century.

Northumberland's architectural distinctiveness was primarily due to its geographical position and the financial constraints which generally prevailed until the beginning of the eighteenth century. In combination these two elements stifled the development of the country house as an entity. However, once these constraints were removed and various sources of wealth became available, Northumberland quickly entered the mainstream of architectural fashion, following national trends. The county's elite of this period was neither exclusively composed of established landed families nor dominated by new entrants enriched by trade. Instead, it was a combination of the two with new entrants eager to follow the lead given by their peers, who were actively engaged in making improvements to their mansion houses in order to underline their superiority and assure their position at the peak of society.

References and Notes

1. See D. Cruickshank, *A Guide to the Georgian Buildings of England and Ireland* (London, 1985).

2. For elaboration of this point see J.C.D. Clark, *English Society 1688-1832: Ideology, Social Structure and Political Practice During the Ancien Regime* (Cambridge, 1985).

3. J.A. Cannon, *Aristocratic Century: the Peerage of Eighteenth Century England* (Cambridge, 1984).

4. Ibid., p.178.

5. R.G. Wilson, *Gentlemen Merchants, the Merchant Community in Leeds 1700-1830* (Manchester, 1971).

6. See for example L. Milner, "Pele Towers", *Northern Architect* (Winter 1994/95, 5th Series, Issue 1).

7. J. Hodgson, *A History of Northumberland* (Newcastle upon Tyne, 1858) vol. I, pp.392-93.

8. S. Middlebrook, *Newcastle upon Tyne: its Growth and Achievement* (Newcastle upon Tyne, 1950), p.77.

9. A.A. Tait, "Classicism in Eccentric Form", *Country Life*, vol.138 (1965).

10. J. Summerson, *Architecture in Britain 1530-1830* (Harmondsworth, 1991 edition), p.144.

11. Northumberland County History Committee, *History of Northumberland*, vol. IX (Newcastle upon Tyne, 1909), p.179.

12. Arthur Young, *A Six Months Tour through the North of England* (London, 1770), vol. III, pp.115-16.

13. Ibid., pp.50-62.

14. William Hutchinson, *A View of the County of Northumberland with an Excursion to the Abbey of Mailross in Scotland* (Newcastle upon Tyne, 1778), vol. II, p.450.

15. John Bailey and George Culley, *General View of the Agriculture of the County of Northumberland with Observations on the Means of its Improvement* (London, 1794), p.8; (see also pp.15 and 50).

16. C. Morris (ed.), *The Illustrated Journeys of Celia Fiennes*, 1685-c.1712 (London, 1982), p.176.

17. D. Levine and K. Wrightson, *The Making of an Industrial Society: Whickham 1560-1765* (Oxford, 1991).

18. T.V. Simpson, in *Journal of the Institution of Mining Engineers* (1832).

19. For a discussion of the Tyneside glass industry see C.M. Ross, "The Development of the Glass Industry on the Rivers Tyne and Wear 1700-1900" (Ph.D. thesis, University of Newcastle upon Tyne, 1982).

20. E. Hughes, *North Country Life in the Eighteenth Century: the North-East, 1700-1750* (Oxford, 1952), p.xix.

21. L. Stone and J.C.F. Stone, *An Open Elite: England 1540-1880* (Oxford, 1986), p.184.

22. Northumberland County Record Office, Ord Mss 324 E12, Fenham Journal 1745-55.

23. NCRO, Butler Mss ZBU B15, Horace St. Paul's Architectural Album.

24. NCRO, Swinburne Mss ZSW 451 & 452, Estimates and Accounts for Capheaton Hall.

25. M. Girouard, "Dobson's Northumbrian Houses", *Country Life* (17 February 1966).

26. See H.A. Clemenson, *English Country Houses and Landed Estates* (New York, 1982).

27. D.J. Rowe, "The Culleys, Northumberland Farmers 1767-1813", *Agricultural History Review* (vol. 19, 1971).

28. Hodgson, op. cit., pt.2 vol. I, p.366.

29. John Wallis, *The Natural History and Antiquities of Northumberland* (London, 1769), vol. II, p.177.

30. E. MacKenzie, *An Historical, Topographical and Descriptive View of the County of Northumberland and Those Parts of the County of Durham situated North of the River Tyne, with Berwick upon Tweed* (Newcastle upon Tyne, 1825), vol. II, p.127.

31. Hutchinson, op. cit., vol. II, p.194.

32. P. Leach, "Designs of a Practical Man: the Architecture of Daniel Garrett", *Country Life*, vol. 156 (1974).

33. Quoted by L. Wilkes, *John Dobson, Architect and Landscape Gardener* (Stocksfield, 1980), p.106.

34. For more on Newton see Phoebe Lowery, "William Newton – An Eminent Architect?", *Northern Architect* (Winter 1994/95, 5th Series, Issue 1).

35. E. Mackenzie, *A Descriptive and Historical Account of the Town and County of Newcastle upon Tyne* (Newcastle upon Tyne, 1827), vol. I, p.231.

36. H.M. Colvin, *A Biographical Dictionary of British Architects 1600-1840*, 3rd ed. (New Haven and London, 1995), p.739.

37. A. Rowan, *Designs for Castles and Country Villas by Robert and James Adam* (New York, 1985), p.11.

38. T.E. Faulkner and A. Greg, *John Dobson: Newcastle Architect, 1787-1865* (Newcastle upon Tyne, 1987), p.93.

39. M.J. Dobson, *Memoir of John Dobson of Newcastle Upon Tyne: Containing some Account of the Revival of Architecture in the North of England with a List of His Works* (London, 1885), p.6.

Part II

URBAN IDENTITY

We next reached Newcastle where we found nothing of interest to do but rest and sleep. The town is fairly large and has, apart from many narrow and crooked streets, a few handsome ones. It is very important to the British economy because of its trade in coal.

JOHANNA SCHOPENHAUER

A Lady Travels

(based on her Diaries, first published 1816)

IV

MORPETH: A NORTHUMBRIAN MARKET TOWN IN THE NINETEENTH CENTURY

Ian Willis

The prevailing image of the North East is still largely that of pit-heaps, shipyards and iron-works, although the present-day visitor would have to search hard to find these. Industrial heritage centres, like the Beamish North of England Open Air Museum, help to perpetuate this image. This picture of the North East is largely a legacy of the nineteenth century and especially of the period after 1850, when the rate of industrial development in the region accelerated. With the shrinkage in the region's heavy industrial base it is perhaps salutary to remind ourselves that far from acting as a unifying force, industrial and urban development in many ways strengthened intra-regional as well as inter-regional differences.[1] As industrial and urban expansion proceeded apace on Tyneside and in south-east Northumberland, the major market towns of Northumberland – Hexham, Morpeth, Alnwick and Berwick and their agricultural hinterlands – appeared even more distinctive as they remained largely outside this development.

If we wish to understand the development of the modern North East then certainly Newcastle and Middlesborough are more important than Alnwick and Morpeth, but, as Alan Everitt has reminded us,[2] the Victorian world contained both types of town and probably more than a third of English people either lived in or were dependent upon market towns. In terms of their economic and social structures, Northumberland's market towns had more in common with other country towns in the rest of England than they had with their manufacturing and mining neighbours.

One of these small towns, Morpeth, is located some fifteen miles north of Newcastle upon Tyne. In 1800 the parish of Morpeth, with the exception of the town, was entirely agricultural. In 1832 the parliamentary borough had been enlarged to a quite extraordinary degree, from under half a square mile to over twenty-three square miles, principally by adding the parish of Bedlington. Unlike Bedlington, the town of Morpeth, which in 1851 had a population of a little over 4,000, did not possess any modern industries apart from one small iron and brass foundry, and the physical appearance of the town was not much altered from the early eighteenth century (fig. 26).

By the 1840s, the expanding coal-mining areas of the region stood in marked contrast to a town like Morpeth. Its staple eighteenth century

Fig. 26 Morpeth market place, c.1830 (Newcastle City Libraries).

industries had either collapsed or were in steep decline. Cloth manufacturing had peaked by the end of the the eighteenth century and only small remnants survived. By the end of the nineteenth century the only reminders of this once flourishing industry were a small woollen factory employing a handful of people and the name Manchester Street.

The decline of tanning was much more precipitous. In 1832 it could still be described as "the most staple and important trade of this town".[3] But in 1852 the town's biggest tanner closed and by the 1870s the tanners had entirely disappeared, victims of a failure to modernise and of competition from Leeds.

Psychologically, the biggest blow which the town received was the decline of the cattle market. In 1746, Samuel Simpson, in his *The Agreeable Historian, or the Compleat English Traveller,* described it as "the greatest for live cattle excepting Smithfield". Forty years later George Culley ranked it as the third market in England for quantity of stock sold, and in 1830 it was still being described by William Cobbett in his *Rural Rides* as "a great market town, for cattle especially". A few years after Cobbett had written this the market had lost its importance with the rise of a formidable rival at Newcastle. Not only had Morpeth lost a regionally significant market, but it was even challenged as a small local market for store cattle with the emergence of local rivals at Wooler in 1845 and at Alnwick in 1850.

By the 1840s Morpeth's economy was faltering and this was reflected in a population fall of 18% between 1841-51 at a time when the region's large towns experienced significant growth. Between 1841-51 Newcastle's population grew by 20%, Gateshead's by 23%, and Sunderland's by 34%.

It was the same Newcastle to Berwick railway, which had dramatically diminished Morpeth's cattle market, which helped prevent the town from becoming a mere rural backwater. Attracted by good rail links, in addition to excellent sand for moulding and buildings recently vacated by tanners, the Swinney brothers from Tweedmouth set up the town's first engineering works in 1866. It began with eight employees making mortar mills and then brickmaking machines. It also manufactured a general range of ironmongery from lamp posts to kitchen stoves. By 1890, when the firm began to specialise, it had 130 employees.

When the Swinneys established themselves in Morpeth the numbers engaged in the classical occupations of the industrial revolution (cloth manufacture, coal, metal manufacture and fabrication and rail) were tiny (see table 1).[4]

Table 1 – Occupations in Morpeth 1841-1891

	1841 No. (%)	1851 No. (%)	1861 No. (%)	1871 No. (%)	1891 No. (%)
Food and Drink	143(11.2)	181(10.5)	164(8.7)	190(9.7)	236(11.4)
Services	37(2.9)	39(2.3)	44(2.3)	53(2.7)	82(4.0)
Building	131(10.2)	208(12.0)	232(12.3)	261(13.3)	231(11.2)
Cloth Manufacture	23(1.8)	10(0.6)	8(0.4)	8(0.4)	2(0.1)
Clothes and Shoes	238(18.6)	288(16.6)	270(14.3)	277(14.1)	226(11.0)
Ironfounders	6(0.5)	9(0.5)	6(0.3)	42(2.1)	68(3.3)
Blacksmiths, Metal Workers & Engineers	36(2.8)	35(2.0)	36(1.9)	51(2.6)	51(2.5)
Horses	57(4.4)	72(4.2)	84(4.4)	98(5.0)	96(4.7)
Coal	1(0.1)	8(0.5)	11(0.6)	30(1.50)	125(6.1)
Agriculture	112(8.7)	184(10.6)	274(14.5)	218(11.1)	221(10.7)
Central Government	8(0.6)	11(0.6)	17(0.9)	18(0.9)	24(1.2)
Local Government	13(1.0)	22(1.3)	24(1.3)	31(1.6)	38(1.8)
Labourers (unspecified)	70(5.5)	86(5.0)	33(1.7)	54(2.8)	81(3.9)
Teachers	10(0.8)	21(1.2)	32(1.7)	26(1.3)	22(1.1)
Domestic Service	214(16.7)	285(16.5)	345(18.3)	345(17.6)	251(12.2)
Rail	–	28(1.6)	88(4.7)	26(1.3)	55(2.7)
Furs & Leather	49(3.8)	54(3.1)	35(1.9)	22(1.1)	1(0.05)
Others	134(10.5)	189(10.9)	185(9.8)	209(10.7)	250(12.2)
Total	1,282	1,730	1,888	1,959	2,060

Note: Categories are generally those suggested by D.J.Rowe, "Occupations in Northumberland and Durham, 1851-1911", *Northern History*, vol.8 (1973), pp.121-23.

In the second half of the century modern manufacture (see fig. 27), coal and rail were of increasing importance. The development of collieries in the vicinity of Morpeth led to large numbers of miners living in the town; in the 1870s miners' picnics were being held by the River Wansbeck and by 1891 miners had become the largest male occupational group. By the 1880s there was also a settled corpus of railway workers after the building of railwaymen's cottages on the outskirts of the town. The growing importance of these industries to the local economy is reflected in the increasing proportion of jobs they provided, rising from 5% (66 jobs) of all occupations in 1841, to 14.5% (299 jobs) in 1891.

Fig. 27 Foundry, Morpeth, c.1898 (Beamish. The North of England Open Air Museum, Stanley, Co. Durham).

Although the economic benefits the town derived from these industries were undoubtedly significant and drew the town into a closer relationship with the industrially developed part of the county, Morpeth's prosperity primarily depended upon its role as a retail and service centre for its agricultural hinterland. The retail sector (food and drink, clothes and shoes) was the most significant element in Morpeth's employment structure (see table 2).

Table 2 – Some occupational groups in Morpeth 1841 and 1891
(Numbers and as a percentage of all occupations)

	1851		1891	
	No.	%	No.	%
Coal Miners	8	0.5	117	5.7
Gardeners & Seedsmen	56	3.2	104	5.0
Grocers	47	2.7	86	4.2
Dressmakers & Seamstresses	95	5.5	84	4.1
Joiners & Cabinet Makers	44	2.5	76	3.7
Masons	93	5.4	74	3.6
Ironfounders	9	0.5	68	3.3
Tailors	47	2.7	59	2.9
Railway Employees	28	1.6	55	2.7
Agricultural Labourers	107	6.2	51	2.5
Clerks	15	0.9	50	2.4
Butchers	31	1.8	30	1.5
Shoemakers	90	5.2	21	1.0

Although as a proportion of all occupations the retail sector declined from 30% in 1841 to 22% in 1891, the numbers involved increased by 39%, which was slightly better than the overall rate of job formation in this period. However, these figures undoubtedly underestimate the numbers engaged in the food trades. Many itinerant hawkers and market traders who sold meat would not call themselves butchers, and in addition to the high class grocer and tea-dealer there also existed the general 'shopkeeper' who sold provisions. Outside the demanding trade of the grocer and tea-dealer, food-selling could be taken up with relative ease. Little skill and comparatively little capital were required. In the 1851 census twelve people gave 'grocer' as their subsidiary occupation.

It is quite clear that the town's inhabitants alone were insufficient to support these businesses. The neighbouring parish of Bedlington, with its much larger population, had only four butchers and sixteen grocers listed in *Slater's Directory* in 1864 compared to sixteen and twenty-two respectively in Morpeth. Consequently Morpeth's traders were crucially dependent upon the agricultural hinterland. In evidence to the *Commission on the Employment of Children, Young Persons and Women in Agriculture* (1867), Dr Brummel, a Morpeth doctor, observed that in the neighbourhood of the town butchers' and grocers' carts were constantly met upon the road. In addition to these, the *Directories* indicate a substantial number of general carrying services operating out of Morpeth, at least twenty-four in 1858 and twenty-five in 1897. There were also numerous village carriers, many of them part-time, bringing farm produce to Morpeth and acting as village shopping agents in the town.

Within the retail sector there were significant changes in the second half of the century. The grocery trades continued to grow in importance but butchering, and especially shoemaking, became less significant in the town's economy. To some extent this was inevitable since Morpeth's population grew relatively slowly, from 4,333 in 1851 to 5,219 in 1891, and neighbouring villages developed their own shops and other facilities, while the rise of factory production hastened the decline of local shoemaking.

Two developments were able to compensate for this. One was the growth in mining and manufacture; the other was the town's increasing importance as a county administrative centre. The county gaol was built there in 1822, although it was moved to Newcastle in 1881; the county quarter sessions met there once a year; the county asylum was located in Morpeth in 1859, as was the county constabulary in 1886.

By the 1870s the most obvious country features of the town, the manor mill, the stockyards, the pinfold and the manor cross had gone, yet the agricultural nature of the town was still strongly marked (see figs 28 and 29). Store cattle were still sold in the public streets, a practice which continued

Fig. 28 Morpeth market place, c.1890 (Newcastle City Libraries).

Fig. 29 Sheep at Dogger Bank, Morpeth (Beamish. The North of England Open Air Museum, Stanley, Co. Durham).

until 1903. The number of agricultural labourers halved between 1851 and 1891 but agriculture remained a significant employer of labour in Morpeth. Market gardening was a thriving local industry, providing, after mining, the largest number of jobs in the town, as well as a famous gooseberry – 'Whinham's Industry'. Marriage patterns in mid-century continued to reflect the town's agricultural nature. The two busiest months for marriages were May and November, the traditional times for hiring farm servants, other than hinds, in Northumberland. It was also after the winter quarter that employment opportunities, particularly outdoor work, quickened. Casual outdoor work for women could be quite constant from March until harvest. Building and brickmaking, which virtually ceased in the winter months, picked up again in the spring, important for a town with brick and tile works and where masons and labourers made up almost 18% of the labour force.

On a more sombre note, in contrast to its industrial and mining neighbours, but in common with rural Northumberland, Morpeth had a very high proportion of illegitimate births, "the great blot" upon this part of England, as it was described by a Parliamentary Commissioner in 1867. In 1844 one in six births in the town was illegitimate. In the sub-district 11.9% of all births in the 1850s were illegitimate, but the figure in the Bedlington sub-district was only 7%, a rate much closer to the national average.

It is axiomatic that there was widespread distress and unrest in the 1830s and 1840s. But an emphasis upon social conflict in these years, derived from mining and manufacturing districts, can produce a distorted picture. In England's country towns, life generally went on much as before. The fractures and divisions which seem to have accompanied rapid and significant urbanisation were generally absent. The paucity of large employers, the scattering of small workshops and the large numbers of craftsmen and retailers militated against any class-based solidarity. In Morpeth there is more evidence for co-operation between social classes than conflict. This is not to suggest that the town was always free of social tension and violence. The annual hirings were a recurring source of trouble and not only in Morpeth. In 1875 a police sergeant was beaten to death when a crowd of 2,000-3,000 gathered at the Alnwick hirings.[5] In Morpeth it was customary for the Council to appoint up to two hundred special constables to cope with the flood of labourers. Whether the disturbances which took place during the hirings were simply due to drink, or whether they were an outburst of pent-up feelings relating to work or to other causes is impossible to say.[6] In 1848, nervous at Chartist activity at nearby collieries, troops were despatched from Newcastle after a desperate plea from the watch committee following unrest among a number of labourers, but in the event they were not actually used.

Day-to-day industrial relations in the town were generally peaceable. Only one strike is recorded in the local press in the middle years of the century. This was a masons' strike for five shillings per day in 1845 at a time of extensive strikes in the building trades throughout northern England. The strike at least demonstrates that the local tradition of deference was not wholly inviolable. Yet the calm enjoyed in Morpeth during the Chartist month of protest in 1839 was more typical. Strikes at local collieries, together with some violence at the nearby Howard pit at Netherton, aroused great alarm in Morpeth. There was little fear that the Morpeth labourers would take to the streets but the vision of hordes of colliers descending on the town caused near panic. The town council requested a military force but had to make do with a consignment of cutlasses and pistols. Once the crisis had passed the Mayor expressed his gratitude for the readiness with which people of all classes and parties in the borough had come forward to help.

All this does not mean that Morpeth was a less socially unequal town than, say, Newcastle or Gateshead. By a number of criteria it was a wealthy town in the mid-nineteenth century. In terms of assessed taxes Morpeth was taxed more heavily per head of population than any other town of comparable size in the mid-1840s and was assessed more highly than any other North East town. Since assessed taxes were levied on luxury items such as carriages and also included the window tax, the presence of large houses in the parish did distort the figures. However, Morpeth's relatively high social status can be confirmed from other sources. It had a much higher proportion of persons of independent means than did a variety of other North East towns, one in 46 of its population compared to one in 103 in Tynemouth, one in 104 in Newcastle and only one in 318 in Bedlington. The proportion of professionals (lawyers, doctors, churchmen etc.) in the occupied population was almost double the proportion recorded for these other towns and two and a half times that of Bedlington. On the other hand, all these other towns had fewer labourers as a proportion of occupied males, 10.3%, 9.6%, 8%, and 4.1% respectively in Gateshead, Newcastle, Bedlington and Tynemouth, but 11.1% in Morpeth.

So the gulf in income inequality was at least as marked in Morpeth as it was in the heavily urbanised south-east corner of the county. But there were more factors promoting social cohesion than disunity. F.M.L. Thompson has noted how urban society increasingly divided into its separate social parts so that the process of urbanisation led not to less but to more social divisiveness.[7] Residential social segregation played a key role in this process. In Morpeth, however, rich and poor still lived cheek by jowl in the mid-nineteenth century. There were few socially homogeneous areas. Until this time middle-class enclaves consisted of a few houses at most. Not one exclusively middle-class street can be identified before the 1850s, when Howard Street, "a fine row of buildings", and Dacre Street, which consisted of dwellings of a "superior character", were built.[8]

By this time also there had been little suburban development which might have taken away the town's upper-middle-class residents. Only a very few of those active in the town's professional or business affairs lived outside the town. The lack of clear-cut class antagonism in Morpeth made it more likely that the residential proximity of the social classes led to a greater degree of mutual tolerance and understanding than to mutual antipathy.

Morpeth also had a settled population which provided an additional element of continuity and stability. In 1851 41% of household heads and 41% of all those aged 20 and above had been born in the town. The latter figure was significantly higher than the 13% recorded for Gateshead, or the 30% recorded for Newcastle, although Sunderland's figure of 47% was even higher than Morpeth's.

One important factor promoting cohesion was the existence of the extended family as a common form of social organisation. The extended family was a common feature of nineteenth-century towns of different sizes and economic structures, although the relationship of kin to household head did vary significantly. In Preston, for example, there was a high incidence of co-residence of parents with their married or single non-dependent children which can be explained in economic terms – shortage of housing, high rents, the demand for child-minding to permit married women to work in the mills[9] – but the co-residence of parents and married children was unusual in Morpeth. Although we have little information about the level of house rents in Morpeth in this period, the low level of co-residence of parents and married children is best explained by the limited opportunities for regular paid employment for married women, and also by tenement dwelling and the compact nature of the town. No child would have been more than a few minutes' walking distance from its parents.

'Parentless' children (grandchildren, nephews and nieces) made up the biggest grouping of kin (42%) in Morpeth households in 1851. Most of these 'parentless' grandchildren were the illegitimate children of co-residing daughters of the household head or children who had lost parents.The remainder were simply children who were providing companionship and domestic help.

It seems very unlikely that 'parentless'children as a whole made any substantial contribution to the household budget. Only 26% had a recorded occupation and 75% were aged under 15. The reverse seems to have been the case in Preston, where 80% were above the age of 10 and the normal age for beginning full-time employment was lower than it was in Morpeth. The possibility of a small parish allowance for dependent children might have been a consideration; indeed, without it, the five dependent grandchildren of Dorothy Burn, a 76-year-old widow, would almost certainly have been in the workhouse.

Whereas 'parentless' grandchildren were more likely to be found in working-class households, nieces and nephews were more likely to be found in middle-class households, and many had the same occupation as the household head. This parallels the experiences noted in the Lancashire accounts.With their greater resources, the professional and employing classes were better placed to aid these more distant relatives, particularly when they were not burdened with unproductive grandchildren. Further support for the argument that these nephews and nieces were taking advantage of employment opportunities offered by their kin is that 85% of all 'parentless' nephews and nieces were aged 10 and above and 51% were aged 15 and above. The corresponding figures for 'parentless' grandchildren were only 45% and 18% respectively.

Despite their proximity, Morpeth provided a strong contrast in many respects to Bedlington, which lay five miles to the south-east. Although

Morpeth did not remain divorced from the rapid mining and manufacturing development which took place in south Northumberland, especially after 1850, its occupational pattern still conformed to that which distinguished many of England's country towns which did not have a dominant industry. Craftsmen, retailers and professional people commonly made up about half the working population. In Morpeth in 1851 54% of male occupations were in these groups. In Bedlington the corresponding figure was only 15%. Bedlington was dominated by coal-mining and iron-working. In 1851 over 800 men and boys, 42% of all male occupations, were employed in the coal industry and 403 (21%) were employed in metal manufacture and fabrication. Although competition from Cleveland and Cumberland brought about the final closure of the ironworks in 1867, mining continued to expand.

Gender experience was also markedly different. In the new towns and colliery villages of the North East there were high proportions of men to women. But in Northumberland's market towns there was a surplus of females and an unusually large surplus at that – 113 females for every 100 males in Morpeth in 1851 compared to 103 females for every 100 males nationally. Alnwick and Hexham had even greater gender imbalances – 116 and 115 females respectively for every 100 males. This imbalance did correct itself to some degree during the second half of the century but it was still marked at 106 females to every 100 males in Morpeth in 1891.

Bedlington was closer to the norm for North East mining communities. It had 117 males for every 100 females. One consequence of this gender imbalance was that marriage, especially for women, took place much earlier than it did in Morpeth and ultimately more women married. More than twice as many women under 25 were married in Bedlington. Another consequence was that Morpeth had an unusually high proportion of single-person households, 11.4% in 1851, made up largely of single (34%) or widowed (38%) females. A further consequence was that marriage for males took place late in Morpeth. The proportion of males ever-married in Morpeth between the ages of 25 and 34 was only 59%. In Alnwick, dominated by agriculture, 80% of males in this age group were ever-married. The corresponding proportions for Newcastle, Gateshead and Sunderland ranged from 84% to 88%.

The different marital patterns that are evident in Morpeth and Bedlington were continued in the employment opportunities for women in the two towns. The employment of women in Morpeth was very much in line with the national pattern, both in the proportions employed (see table 3) and in the nature of their employments (see table 4), although there are special difficulties in using census material to establish detailed patterns of female employment. Many women who helped their tradesmen/retailer husbands on a casual basis would not have had that help recorded. On the other hand, there is also the possibility that many women who gave an occupation such as dressmaking or bonnet-making would not have been working full-time at that occupation.

Table 3 – Proportion of occupied females aged 15 and above in Morpeth, Bedlington and in England and Wales 1851

	Morpeth	Bedlington	England and Wales
No. of females aged 15 and above	1,504	1,380	
No. of occupied females aged 15 and above	546	232	
Occupied females aged 15 and above as % of female population	24.6	16.8	25.7
All females as % of the labour force 1851	31.8	11.5	30.2

Table 4 – Major sectors of female employment 1851

	Morpeth		Bedlington Parish	
	No.	%	No.	%
Domestic service & allied occupations e.g.washerwomen	293	60.1	159	63.6
Food and drink	51	6.5	8	3.2
Clothes & shoes	130	22.0	58	23.2
Teaching	11	1.8	9	3.6
Agriculture	31	5.6	7	2.8

Female employment was overwhelmingly concentrated in indoor domestic service. Richards has argued that domestic service was a form of disguised under-employment,[10] since it operated as a substitute employment for women who earlier would have found a job in some other part of the domestic economy. Dressmaking also operated in a similar fashion. Many women turned their hands to stitching and sewing when alternatives were scarce. This was true not only of Bedlington, with its male-dominated mining and engineering economy, but also of a retail centre like Morpeth. In both, three-quarters of those engaged in the clothes and shoes sector described themselves as 'dressmakers'. At least as a retail centre Morpeth did have more jobs on offer for women than did Bedlington. If we look at the numbers of young, single women who had left school but had not yet married, i.e. those between the ages of 15 and 19 who were recorded as unoccupied, then the extent of female unemployment and underemployment becomes clear.[11] In Morpeth in 1851 only 53% of this group had jobs; in Bedlington a mere 38%. It seems unlikely that such wide differences can be explained simply by young women choosing to stay at home; rather it seems that there was a great deal of gender-based structural unemployment caused by the sexual division of labour.

An obvious difference between a town like Morpeth and the industrial towns and mining villages of the North East lies in the contrast between the slow population growth of the former and the rapid increases in population experienced by the latter. Between 1831 and 1891 Gateshead's population grew from 15,000 to 86,000, Sunderland's from 39,000 to 131,000 and Newcastle's from 54,000 to 186,000. In the same period Morpeth's population increased from 4,093 to 5,219. Since the excess of births over deaths was far higher in this period than the increase in the enumerated population, Morpeth experienced a net loss in population owing to emigration. That Morpeth's population had grown at all was thanks to the town's good rail communications and the consequent development of small-scale engineering, as well as the development of neighbouring collieries. The outflow of population from Morpeth is to be understood in terms of the slow stagnation of the neighbouring agricultural population, the demise of her native industries of tanning and weaving, the loss of the cattle market and, most importantly, her position on the edge of an expanding industrial belt with all its job opportunities.

A look at Morpeth-born inhabitants of Newcastle is interesting in this respect. In 1851 there were 400 residents in Newcastle who had been born in Morpeth, and in 1861, 599. A rapidly growing town like Newcastle offered opportunities, particularly in the building, craft and retail trades which a small, relatively static town could not match. Less than quarter of the jobs of Morpeth-born males in Newcastle were in manufacturing, mining or rail in 1861. Joiners, masons, butchers, grocers, tailors and shoemakers easily outnumbered those employed in modern manufacturing and transport. Labourers from Morpeth were a rarity; in 1861 they made up less than 3% of the Morpeth-born male labour force. Those who did work in modern industry were generally young; in 1851 65% were aged under 35.

Male migrants to Newcastle from Morpeth easily outnumbered female migrants. Newcastle's male-dominated industries offered few employment opportunities for women. It was largely in domestic service and dressmaking that they found jobs. In 1861, of those women with jobs, 71% were washerwomen and charwomen and 21% were dressmakers, milliners and seamstresses.

It is difficult to avoid the conclusion that the Morpeth trades were overstocked in mid-century, which not only helps to account for the outflow from Morpeth but is also one reason why there was little permanent immigration, although its location on the Great North Road meant it always had a large, floating population in its lodging-houses. In 1851 41% of household heads had been born in the town and another 36% were natives of Northumberland, although it should be noted that birthplace information is one of the least reliable areas of the census. Most long distance migration was from Ireland and Scotland. Household heads from these two countries accounted for 6.5% and 6% respectively of all household heads, but there were marked differences between these two groups. The generally unskilled character of the Irish labour force in Britain is well known. If we ignore the 'grey-coated' seasonal harvesters who were in the habit of turning up in large numbers, 65% of occupied Irish males in Morpeth in 1851 were labourers, a figure slightly higher but not inconsistent with the 60% found for Tyneside generally in mid-century. The next highest categories were agricultural labourers (10%) and lodging-housekeepers (8%), the latter described in 1849 by the afore-mentioned Dr Matthew Brummel as "the lowest description of Irish". The Irish were noticeably absent from the skilled trades. There was not a single joiner, tailor, tanner, grocer or butcher and only three masons and five shoemakers.

Although the Irish were conspicuously absent from Tyneside collieries, mining was the second largest category in which they were found in Bedlington in 1851. The numbers involved were small (13) and most Irishmen in Bedlington were labourers (43), yet it does demonstrate that away from Tyneside they were entering the colliery labour force. By contrast, just over half of all Scots males in Morpeth either had professional occupations or were in skilled jobs, while only 5% were labourers.

In two areas Morpeth shared in the region's least welcome characteristics, overcrowding and poor health. The former was a phenomenon not confined to large urban and industrial areas; as N. McCord and D.J. Rowe have shown, it was associated with different types of community, location and house-style.[12] However, overcrowding has resisted any convincing historical explanation other than customary low expectations. As late as 1911 Northumberland had 28.7% overcrowding; Morpeth had 32.9%, one of the worst rates for overcrowding in the country. Contemporaries frequently referred to the crowded nature of the town; even a guidebook published in 1884 noted that "A number of yards and lanes enter from the main streets and are densely populated".[13]

It was in these crowded parts of the town that epidemics spread rapidly. Although cholera spared Morpeth almost entirely in 1849 and 1853, typhus was a frequent visitor. In 1847, it struck those areas where labourers working on the Newcastle-Berwick railway line were crowded. When mortality in the town rose to 34.3 per 1,000 in 1855 the town clerk drew up a map pinpointing the location of each death. Not surprisingly, these were clustered in the packed courts and alleys.

Anecdotal evidence that the rural neighbourhood was healthier, especially for women and children, can be confirmed by comparing mortality figures for the town and the rural hinterland. For 1849-55 mortality in the sub-district averaged 18.6 per 1000; in the town it averaged 27.3 per 1,000 for 1841-51 and 28.1 per 1,000 for 1852-55.

Morpeth's death-rate may have been higher than the national average in the early Victorian period, but at least from mid-century, given the knowledge and services available, local effort was not without merit and, compared to attitudes to public health to be found in neighbouring Bedlington, Morpeth was a centre of enlightenment. If contemporaries are to be believed, later in the century, despite the persistence of overcrowding, the lanes, alleys and streets of the town were kept in a very clean state.

In education, Morpeth's experience again illustrates how much local developments could be at variance with the broad regional picture. The differences in the middle of the century between rural Northumberland, market towns like Morpeth and the industrial and mining centres were striking and are to be explained largely in terms of employment opportunities for children. The early age at which children left school in the Northern District (of England)[14] caused disquiet in educational circles. One of the region's inspectors noted that the "sole variation" in the age at which children left school was "the demand for labour" and another pinpointed the high wages which could be earned in the mining areas: six shillings for a boy of thirteen in the pits in the Tow Law or Bishop Auckland areas and even higher wages in the neighbourhood of Newcastle. But rural Northumberland did not enjoy these high-paying counter-attractions to school. In Morpeth in 1861 57% of fourteen year-old boys and 52% of girls were scholars. It is worth remembering that as late as 1922 only 31% of fourteen year-olds in England and Wales were at school. Census evidence indicates that in Morpeth regular employment below the age of ten was almost unknown and that regular employment for most boys and girls began at fourteen or fifteen. Erratic attendance at school, however, points to significant involvement in unrecorded casual work.

The proportion of boys and girls on school registers was also very much higher in Morpeth than in the large towns of the North East. In 1851 the proportion of scholars to population was 1:8.5 in Gateshead, 1:8.6 in Sunderland and 1:9.7 in Newcastle but 1:5.7 in Morpeth. Indeed, out of a national total of 178 municipal boroughs only seventeen had better ratios and some of these, such as Marlborough, only because of boarding schools within the borough. The proportion of children on school registers in Morpeth was 78.3% compared with 52.6% for England and Wales. It would be a mistake to regard these healthy figures as a continuation of traditionally high levels of educational participation. According to a Parliamentary inquiry known as the *Kerry Return* (1835), the proportion of scholars to population in the town was only 1:9. The rise in pupil numbers had been recent and it had been rapid. Prior to the Municipal Reform Act, the old Corporation jealously maintained its right of free and exclusive education for the children of freemen and freebrothers in the schools it supported from Corporation funds and from money raised from the annual stinting of Morpeth Common. The abolition of the old Corporation began a swing from private to public provision which received a further boost in the 1840s with a marked increase in voluntary provision. In 1833 there were three publicly funded and ten private schools in the town. This had increased to ten and sixteen in 1851. Private schools were generally more popular with parents than the cheaper and more efficient schools offered by the voluntary bodies, partly because the latter were identified with 'charity'. However, as the above figures indicate, the swing from private to 'public' was very well advanced in Morpeth by 1851. In that year 78% of Morpeth's scholars were being educated in publicly funded schools.

Casual attitudes to school attendance were a problem for most elementary schools in the nineteenth century. Attendance in the Northern District was sufficiently poor that it led to the Northumberland and Durham School Prize Scheme in 1855 to try to encourage, among other things, good attendance by the award of cash prizes. Morpeth schools also had to compete with the availability of casual agricultural work. Nevertheless, on census day, 1851, 84% of the town's pupils were in attendance and it was not until 1893-94 that the national average attendance at such schools rose above 80%. Even allowing for special efforts to get pupils in on census day, this was a high figure.

In addition to public and private elementary schools, boys from middle-class homes were well catered for by the grammar school, at least from the 1860s when the *Schools Inquiry Commission* recognised it as offering for a boy of ability the best education in the whole of Northumberland.

The town also had a reasonable spread of post-school educational institutions. The Mechanical and Scientific Institute (1825) peaked in terms of numbers in 1853. By the 1860s there were also Reading Rooms, a Young Men's Improvement Society (1854) and more than one venue for evening classes, although these attracted few self-improvers in this period.

If the region cannot be regarded as uniform in terms of its educational structures, the same is true when its religious character and patterns of worship are examined. The unique Religious Census of 1851 does indicate that church accommodation and attendance at worship in the North East were consistent with national patterns. Higher figures for both were generally found in small market towns and in rural areas rather than in large industrial and commercial centres, although a rural district like Alnwick was short of accommodation. Morpeth Registration District had accommodation for only 57% of potential worshippers owing to the rapid expansion of population in the Bedlington area, but the town of Morpeth had accommodation for almost 81%, or 93% if standing room is added to take account of the Roman Catholic practice of using standing room at services.

The contrast between attendance at church on Census Sunday in Morpeth (78.4%) and in Newcastle (40%) and in Gateshead (32.9%) is striking. Whereas Methodism provided the strongest challenge to Anglicanism in Durham, it was Presbyterianism which was the main rival to the Established Church in Northumberland. In Morpeth they ran neck and neck, and Presbyterianism accounted for 63% of Nonconformity in the town. Methodism was weakly represented. The Wesleyan chapel (1822) was not joined by a Primitive Methodist building until 1871, when there had been a significant increase in the number of miners living in the town.

Morpeth was also a town with church-going habits, 54.9% of the town's inhabitants worshipping on Census Sunday (see table 5). Horace Mann calculated that on Census Sunday 70% of the population was able to attend at least one service. Using his formula, 78.4% of Morpeth's inhabitants went to church on that day; using Inglis's 'index of attendance'[15] exactly the same figure is arrived at. Inglis calculated that in towns with populations above 10,000 49.7% attended church on Census Sunday and in rural areas and small towns it was 71.4%. Two North East towns, Newcastle upon Tyne (40%) and Gateshead (32.9%) had some of the lowest attendances recorded. If the most numerously attended service is preferred to either the Mann or Inglis formulae, Morpeth still emerges as one of the region's most church-going towns with 38.3% of her inhabitants attending the most popular service, a figure considerably above the Nothumberland average of 28%.

Table 5 – Attendance at religious worship in Morpeth on 30 March 1851

Denomination	Mann's Formula		Inglis's 'Index of Attendance'		Present at most numerously attended service	
	Number	%	Number	%	Number	%
C. of England	726	32.4	1,101	34.4	380	24.2
Roman Catholic	325	14.5	400	12.5	250	16.0
Presbyterian	760	33.9	1,080	33.8	600	38.3
Wesleyan	132	5.9	186	5.8	105	6.7
Independent	297	13.2	431	13.5	230	14.7
Total	2,240		3,198		1,565	
% of population attending	54.9		78.4		38.3	

Notes: (i) Mann's formula: half of those attending afternoon service were not present in the morning and one-third of those attending in the evening were not present at either of the two preceding services.
(ii) Inglis's 'Index': aggregate of attendance at all services expressed as a percentage of the population in the area.

We shall never know the extent to which church-building and attendance at religious worship represented religious devotion or social conformity. As in all parts of the North East considerable church- and chapel-building took

Fig. 30 Morpeth, c.1890 (Newcastle City Libraries).

place in Morpeth in the last sixty years of the nineteenth century. The role played by individual clergymen in widening the appeal of Christianity is also problematic. If we are to believe the town clerk, William Woodman, Christianity was almost dead in the town before the arrival of vigorous new Ministers for the leading congregations – Anglican, Presbyterian and Independent – in the 1840s. All three were destined for long stays in the town.

What this chapter has underlined is the significance of locality in regional development and the fact that the history of Morpeth in the nineteenth century was a story of continuities as well as of changes. The service sectors remained the backbone of the town although engineering, mining and county administrative services made a very significant contribution to the town's prosperity in the second half of the century. This combination ensured that Morpeth did not decline into a sleepy, large village, but maintained its identity as one of the region's most important inland towns.

References and Notes

1. D.J. Rowe, "The North-East", in F.M.L. Thompson (ed.), *The Cambridge Social History of Britain 1750-1950*, vol.1 (Cambridge, 1990), passim.

2. A. Everitt (ed.), *Perspectives in English Urban History* (London, 1973), p.235.

3. J.A. Hodgson, *A History of Morpeth* (Newcastle upon Tyne, 1832, 1973 ed.), p.90.

4. The data in tables 1-4 is derived from the decennial census.

5. N. McCord, *North East England, The Region's Development 1760-1960* (London, 1979), p.184.

6. Violence at hirings seem to have been a common phenomenon. For a discussion of hiring violence in Cumbrian market towns see J.D. Marshall, "The Rise and Transformation of the Cumbrian Market Town", *Northern History*, 19 (1983), pp.191-96.

7. F.M.L. Thompson, "Town and City", in *The Cambridge Social History of Britain 1750-1750*, vol.1 (Cambridge, 1990), p.33.

8. D.F. Wilson, *A Handbook to Morpeth and the Neighbourhood* (Morpeth, 1884), p.9.

9. M. Anderson, *Family Structure in Nineteenth Century Lancashire* (Cambridge, 1971), pp.229-31.

10. E. Richards, "Women in the British Economy Since about 1700: An Interpretation", *History*, cxcvii (October 1974), p.348.

11. For a general discussion see E. Jordan, "Female Unemployment in England and Wales 1851-1911: an Examination of the Census Figures for 15-19 year olds", *Social History*, vol.13, no.2 (May 1988), pp.175-208.

12. N. McCord and D. J. Rowe "Industrialisation and Urban Growth In North-East England", *International Review of Social History*, vol. xxii (1977), Part 1, pp.30-64.

13. Wilson, op.cit., p.9.

14. The Northern District consisted of the counties of Northumberland, Durham, Cumberland and Westmorland.

15. K.S. Inglis, "Patterns of Religious Worship in 1851", *Journal of Ecclesiastical History*, xi (1960).

V

THE SUNDERLAND COTTAGE

Angela Long

This chapter represents a series of hypotheses. I was brought up in Sunderland, and the rows of neat cottage streets (see fig. 31) were as much a part of my birthplace as the sea, the river and the ships. The meaning of the town was not demonstrated in aristocratic mansions, Regency terraces, or garden suburbs, nor was it conveyed through mill chimneys, rows of 'mean' streets, and tenement slums. To the belonger, such images fitted other places, on the Tyne or on the Clyde, not the Wear. Sunderland is viewed as special by its inhabitants and that the town developed such a successful answer to the question of housing its workforce, the cottage street, is entirely to be expected.

Fig. 31 A street of cottages in the High Barnes area, built c.1898.

Housing the working class is a complex issue – frustrating to the architectural or design historian who enters the field with visions of plans, elevations, and room sizes, public-spirited architects and the development of flush toilets, and who emerges, part way through the research, from Public Health Acts, Corporation Acts, Demographic and Economic Surveys and above all from the attentions of the Sanitary Inspector! The early history of the Sunderland cottage becomes, inevitably, anonymous history – for the form evades connections with individual architects or stylistic movements. But the roots of the form are not my central concern; I am most interested in the intrinsic merits of the design.[1]

Today the Sunderland cottage is a successful housing form. Cottages are selling in a stagnant housing market – selling as both starter homes and retirement homes while many often remain stable, family homes, with long-term residents. The houses are small, unsuitable for sub-letting, characteristic of the nuclear family: achieving territoriality and privacy. Maintenance has never been expensive and the present stock of well-maintained cottages shows how adaptable the form still is. Even in those areas nearer the river and its industries, ironically now gaining status as the riverside is reclaimed from its old heavy industrial base, cottages, which were often smaller than the fully evolved form, still have today all the signs of respectability and homeliness which modern housing estates so often fail to achieve. The cottage streets achieve a domestic pattern language of facilities, privacy and pride of ownership – albeit on a very basic level. The design of the Sunderland cottage closely fitted the cultural identity of the town at the turn of the century and continues to do so today.

To those outside the region, the North East conjures up a dreary industrial area, where the weather is dreadful and the locals speak too quickly; 'Catherine Cookson country', crossed with vague memories of the Jarrow March. To the nineteenth-century outsider, too, Sunderland was a place where industries "vomit forth their black, broad and extending columns of trailing smoke".[2] To those within the region, the North East is a place to be proud of, an area of natural beauty and historic monuments. In the nineteenth and early twentieth centuries the region was not only the proud producer of sources of energy for the nation's industry but also of artefacts for the world's markets. To the people of Sunderland this identity was further tempered by a strong town and river identity set against Newcastle and the Tyne, not only on the football field but in most commercial ventures, where the two were in fierce competition. Sunderland once claimed to be the greatest shipbuilding town in the world and was rightly proud of the fact that tonnage statistics for the Wear involved only one town – Sunderland.[3]

Sunderland expanded in the nineteenth century and even though the pattern of development seems to follow trends observable in most industrial cities, it developed its own unique form of working-class housing. The Sunderland housing form is a single-storey terrace, variously described as the 'Sunderland' or 'Wearside' cottage or as a 'terraced bungalow'.[4] The cottages have also been described as a blend of the Sunderland bye-laws and colliery housing and dated at about 1860.[5] I believe that the form predates the 1860s and would suggest that the cottages were built over a period of at least seventy to eighty years up till 1910. However, I have focused my detailed research on houses constructed in the West Ward between 1897 and 1910 – cottages built to house skilled workers in what was a boom town; houses which represent the cottage in its final and most developed phase.

If they are to be understood in the context of a pattern of housing in 1900 then it is necessary to understand the status and role of Sunderland at the time, for the final stage of the development of the Sunderland cottage is set in a town where 'modern' nineteenth-century attitudes to technology went hand in hand with 'modern' self-help attitudes to housing, but where there was little or none of the paternal, philanthropic endeavour so typical of other towns.[6] The worker in Sunderland was seen as a vital part of the enterprise and his particular talent for industry, enterprise, and even his good looks were remarked upon in the nineteenth century.[7] The cottage gave him privacy and social mobility, the chance not only to rent but even to own his home and that of his neighbour. So far I have not found evidence that the shipyard owners took responsibility for housing the work force. Certainly in the last decades of the nineteenth century, in a town where a successful system of speculative endeavour had been established, they did not need to.

There are many reasons why Sunderland deserves study – why it was in fact exceptional. In the nineteenth century it also had the world's deepest mine, the world's longest single-span cast-iron bridge, and even a geologically unique rock formation on the sea front known as the 'cannon ball' rocks. It is important to remember, too, that in the last quarter of the nineteenth century Sunderland was the commercial capital of County Durham and as such saw itself as different and distinct from Tyneside.[8] In the 1840s the town was compared to a vigorous Australian or 'Yankee' frontier settlement; onlookers were amazed at the sense of 'progress' in the town.

Sunderland meant industry and industriousness. By 1900 it was on the crest of a wave; admirers came to look at the bridge and holiday makers strolled along the Roker promenade, developed between 1860 and 1890. The town centre, which by 1860 was characterised by impressive, solid, Doric style terraces,[9] was further enriched by a neo-French Museum, its foundation stone laid by Ulysses Grant in 1877; by a new Town Hall in 1890; by a series of impressive civic utilities in 1907 (Police Station, Fire Station, Water Company); and by the Empire Theatre, with its enormous stage, which was opened by Vesta Tilley in 1909. One of the country's earliest department stores, Binns, moved to new premises in Fawcett Street in 1900, its success in part a reflection of the high wages in the shipbuilding and engineering sectors.[10] By 1900 Sunderland had a range of medical facilities, branch libraries and a technical college which can claim to be the first to run 'sandwich' courses for apprentices. There were three daily papers, sixteen building societies, and numerous informal social institutions. A network of trams brought outer areas within easy reach of the centre and an inter-urban system of tramways linked the town with the rural district. The train linked Sunderland with Newcastle and the north, and with Durham and the south, and ships sailed three times a week to London and weekly to Hamburg. Freemasonry also flourished, with names of those attending lodge meetings published in the daily newspaper.[11]

Shipbuilding was the key to Sunderland's success – an important part of its economy and perhaps an even greater part of its self-image, well into the twentieth century. By 1840 permanent yards were established as the economic base of the town underwent a fundamental change and Sunderland developed from a port to an industrial town. The town became famous for the construction of wooden ships and some of the world's finest tea clippers were built in Sunderland,[12] but when iron ships appeared the town moved into the new technology and in 1852 the first iron ship was built. For a while, wooden ships, iron ships, and combination ships were built simultaneously, but even more importantly, Sunderland turned quickly to steel when Bessemer steel became available; in 1882 four steel ships were built and by 1888 the change to steel was complete. This readiness to embrace new technologies is also reflected in the fact that, in the related engineering sector, the research and development section of Doxfords produced Britain's first marine diesel engine in 1912. Sunderland was the 'Silicon Valley' of its day and an elite workforce developed, attracted by some of the highest wages in the country.[13] That the town's shipbuilding output soared can be seen, for example, from the output of one yard, Doxfords, which, incredibly, in 1906, produced one ship per fortnight.[14] In 1834 *Lloyd's Register of Shipping* showed that Sunderland was "the most important shipbuilding centre in the country, nearly equalling, as regards number and tonnage of ships built, all the other ports together".[15] By 1900 it was a matter of great importance for Sunderland's identity to be able to claim that it was the greatest shipbuilding town in the world.[16]

In addition to shipbuilding, which in 1900 accounted for 20% of the population, 15% worked in the related marine engineering sector. Also, in the early years of the nineteenth century pioneering techniques in plate glass and paper manufacture were invented in the town, demonstrating a well-established industrial base, while the lime industry and coal were also important to the local economy.[17] As a port, Sunderland had import companies dealing mainly in timber from the Baltic and slate from Wales, and export companies connected with the coal field. Such a well-developed industrial centre was by no means parochial, and civic pride must have been raised by the connections made by the largely self-made industrialists: men like Sir James Laing (1823-1901) who, as the owner of Laings at Deptford, was chairman of the River Wear Commissioners for 32 years; he was also a director of the Suez Canal Company.[18] Many other local industrialists took their civic duty seriously, one such being Sir John Priestman, who, in 1906, invited Edward Prior and Randall Wells to build St. Andrew's Church, Roker, one of the finest examples of Arts and Crafts church architecture in the world.[19]

So it is obvious that Sunderland had a very singular, and energetic, civic identity, closely related to its industries, which gives the architecture of the town a particular meaning, a meaning which is enriched by its housing forms. In 1970 the sociologist A.H. Halsey described Sunderland as a town with a distinct character:

> It is geographically set off by its position on the river and the coast. Centred visibly and closely on its productive work, it is the antithesis of suburbia; housing is an annexe to the workplace and the community is a working community. It is, in a double sense, a working class town . . .[20]

The town had first developed near the river mouth, and when in 1837 its borough status was confirmed by the Sunderland Corporation Act, the three areas of Monkwearmouth, Sunderland-near-the-sea, and Bishopwearmouth were linked; the main part of the town centred in Sunderland parish. In the 1830s, if the antiquarian society pamphlet writer is to be believed, Sunderland:

> was all gardens from Norfolk Street to Waterloo Place . . . three-storeyed houses were occupied by well-known shipowners, doctors and tradesmen. Each house had a neat flower garden and a pear tree and a footpath in front which made a popular walk.[21]

Other references in the same article refer to the vineries surrounding a fine stone mansion on the site of the present Vine Place and the excellent walnut trees that grew in the farmland nearby. The houses of the wealthy also extend this positive image of Sunderland as wealthy inhabitants built themselves larger and more spacious houses. In 1860, for example, Hiram Craven, who owned rope works in the town, built the Briary in Ashbrooke Road. He owned extensive sisal and coffee plantations in Kenya and spent an enormous amount on his gardens, with bananas under glass, rock terraces, and lawns of Solway turf.[22] His choice of site on the south side of the town proved popular with other industrialists and other 'grand' houses were built in this area.[23]

But this rosy picture is not the whole story, and Sunderland Parish was rapidly transformed in the 1840s into an overcrowded slum as the town's industrial base expanded and more docks opened.[24] In common with all nineteenth century towns, as industry encroached, those with money moved to the outskirts; as one family moved out, four or five moved in and the gardens were soon covered with hastily thrown-up tenements. This process of relocation was further generated in Sunderland by the opening of the first bridge across the Wear in 1796.[25] Gradually the town's focus shifted, and by the end of the nineteenth century the old town was known as the East End and Sunderland town centre was now in line with the new bridge. This shift accelerated the run-down of the old town, where tenements and dilapidated property failed miserably in the race to house the town's increasing population.

In 1848 the Sunderland Parish was affected by an outbreak of cholera, which was most serious in the tenements.[26] Attention at the time concentrated on the relationship between sanitation, defective drainage, inadequate water and overcrowding on the one hand, and disease and high mortality rates on the other. Overcrowding in Sunderland is generally dismissed as being an extreme example. However, I look with some degree of suspicion on figures which are sometimes applied to the Sunderland cottage but which originally applied to the tenements and dilapidated housing stock in the old town. Official census figures[27] do not clearly differentiate between different housing types; moreover, certain tables include both landlord and lessee as occupants, and it is necessary to know whether both resided in the house before determining levels of overcrowding. So, despite official figures which appear to maintain that Sunderland had one of the highest levels of overcrowding in the country, Sunderland was not a city of slums to be compared with London or Manchester; in a sense the overcrowded courts and tenements and the decaying housing stock of the old town were a relic of an earlier phase of industrialisation and urbanisation and do not concern us here. The problems of the East End continued into the twentieth century and slums which had been described as such in the 1830s were made worse by their proximity to industry, railways, and docks. Casual dock labourers and costermongers needed to live near the docks if they were to get employment on a casual basis, but casual employment almost certainly meant slum housing. That their income was small was underlined by the reports of the 1885 commissioners.[28] These men and their families were to remain trapped in the East End throughout the period.

As in all other large industrial towns at that time, many workers found accommodation in multi-occupancy, either in tenements, in dilapidated homes abandoned by the better off, or in terraces of small two-storey houses.[29] However, a mid-nineteenth-century observer said:

> In the midst of all these disadvantages, the visitor of the poor meets with numerous instances of determined struggles for cleanliness and general purity of character and even of moral heroism of a high cast, indicating that there is an effort to stem the general effects of poverty and that commendable self-respect is not worn out.[30]

The signs of this moral worth were the whitened doorstep, the white muslin window blind, a Bible and a pair of shells, with geranium, balsam and musk.

In Sunderland the 'deserving poor', or perhaps in view of high wages in the town the 'deserving not so poor', those workers with a regular wage, were able to move out of multi-occupancy and into a Sunderland cottage without having to move too far from sources of work. Even as early as the 1840s Sunderland was praised by a Government Commission enquiring into the state of large towns and populous districts for its "single-storeyed cottages, occupied by one or at most two families; comfortably and cleanly and furnished with small yards and other conveniences".[31] These cottages at Bishopwearmouth and Monkwearmouth, which represent the earliest phases of the Sunderland type, had 'privies' in the back yard in the 1840s. They were small, single-fronted, single-storey terraced houses, but these scaled-down dwellings had one magic ingredient – privacy. The tenant, or owner, had his own front door and his own yard. The cottage evolved over the next seventy years of its known development (i.e. 1840-1910) from a single-fronted, single-storey cottage (fig. 32), to a double-fronted, single-

Fig. 32 Single-fronted cottages in the High Barnes area, built between 1898 and 1902. Most cottages now have modernised windows.

Fig. 33 A single-fronted dormer cottage in the High Barnes area, built between 1898 and 1902. The dormer is in its original form although the windows are modern.

storey cottage (see fig. 31). On the way there were the occasional dormers where bedrooms in the roof, approached by a tiny cramped staircase, extended the living space (fig. 33). But these were the exception rather than the rule. The first cottages were sited near the centres of industry – in the 1840s near the collieries at Monkwearmouth and Wearmouth, and near the glass works in Millfield. Although pit owners provided tied housing for their workers, who worked on annual contracts and who could have an extra four pounds per annum in lieu of housing, the rest of the housing provision was speculative, developers recognising that areas near work were likely in the first instance to be successful. During the 1840s the shipbuilding industry was developing, but it may be that the tentative, fluctuating nature of the early days of the industry explains the original speculative choice of the simple cottage. Between 1800 and 1860 nearly 300 shipbuilders completed at least one vessel on the Wear, but almost a third of these firms did not last a year and more than half did not survive two years,[32] even though by 1840 those firms that were to become permanent had appeared on the Wear.

By 1901 the population of Sunderland had risen to 182,074.[33] This increase necessarily led to overcrowding in the older part of the town and the town was forced to grow by spreading into the undeveloped areas on its edge. The highest growth in population occurred in the 1830s and, by 1851, as fewer people moved into the town, the population became more static.[34] As the century went on this relatively settled, homogeneous and indigenous population could also be, in part, a factor in the longevity of the original house form.[35] Where two full generations define the development between the earliest cottages and its final form, it is not too fanciful to model a family with small children moving into a small cottage in the 1840s, an artisan aged 30 plus years, i.e. out of apprenticeship and through journeying. By the time his small children were out of their own apprenticeships the next phase of cottages of the 1870s, in areas like Hendon and Roker Avenue, would be suitable for them.[36] For the children of this second generation, who would be 30 in 1900, the West End cottages came on stream at a period of high wages and building control. It is possible to see three generations settled and moving within the cottage streets.[37] By 1901 household size on average was 4.8 persons, so the two- or three-bedroomed cottage could accommodate the families reasonably well. The development from single front to double front seems to have taken two or three generations.

In the second half of the nineteenth century, wages were high in Sunderland. In 1882 engineers could earn more than thirty-seven shillings a week (higher rates than Newcastle) and by the end of the century shipwrights could earn about two pounds a week, while other key workers also had very high time-rates of over the two pound mark.[38] These high wages came at a time when the cost of living index was falling.[39] Thus in the period I am most interested in, Sunderland paid well, it attracted and housed a highly skilled workforce, and it is a feature of housing in Britain at the time that virtually all wage earners lived in rented accommodation. There were cyclical slumps, as in 1907-8 when houses in Pallion were boarded up and men had their bags packed ready to move to wherever there was work, but overall there was a generally settled environment in which the form developed.

Closely related to the question of wages is the question of rents, but it is notoriously difficult to assess the importance of rents in relation to house forms. In Sunderland, rents were generally recognised as high and arguably high for less space when compared to other towns. The fact that the working class often paid out an enormously high proportion of income in rent has been noticed by many, including the writer of a leading article in *The Times* of 1880 who noted that "the poor pay out 6 pounds a year for a space of 1,000 cubic feet which in proportion is as much as a nobleman pays for his mansion in Belgravia".[40] But the rent paid for a cottage in Sunderland, although it may not seem to account for much square footage, acquired a self-contained house. It was a measure of independence, of territoriality, that was clearly desirable to the self-confident Sunderland worker. That workers in Sunderland had a particularly high self-image may well be seen not only in descriptions of the energy drive of the workforce, e.g. "The fresh coloured vigour that characterises Sunderland",[41] but also in the widespread acceptance of union membership, and the confidence demonstrated in the relationship with the owners.[42] The cottages, established originally as a short-term response to a population explosion, can be seen to develop and improve in response to the market demands of a relatively settled population. They can also be seen as a form of investment for small-time investors in the property market.

In the West Ward of the town (see fig. 34) the Chester Road and High Barnes cottage estates developed along the southern side of the road to

Chester-le-Street, which runs in a roughly westerly direction uphill from the railway line that crosses the road near the town. The boundaries of the cottage area were marked by Chester Road, with its shops, agencies, school

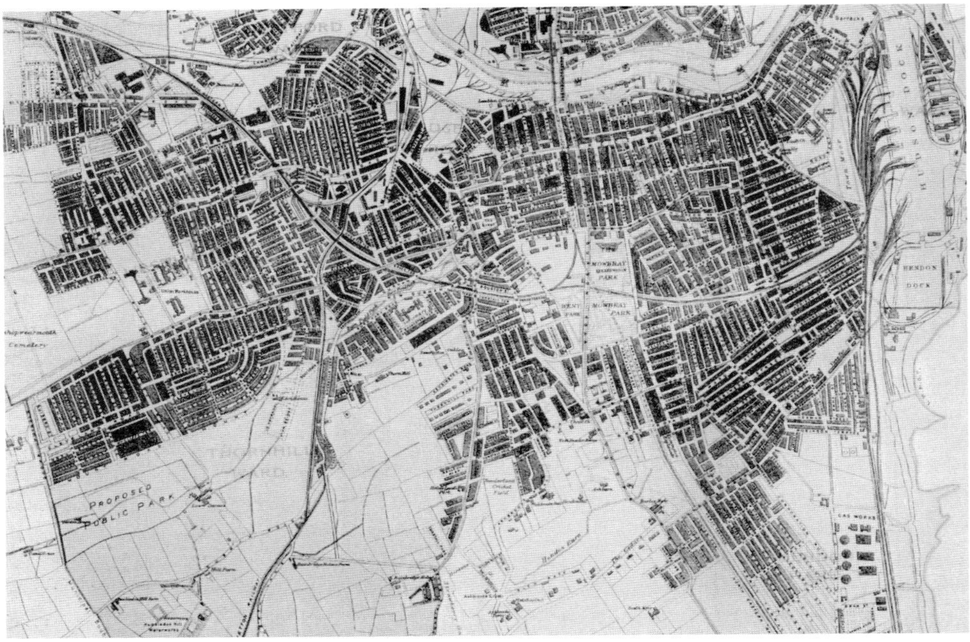

Fig. 34 Plan of Sunderland South, part of *Plan of the Borough of Sunderland* by J.W. Moncur, Borough Engineer, 1905 (City Library and Arts Centre, Sunderland).

and workhouse hospital, and higher up the hill by the Westlands and West Mount – redbrick middle-class housing, which was intersected by the 'ABC' streets of the later cottages, so-called because the street names are in alphabetical order, and where one house contained such grandiose features as a billiard room and tennis lawn.[43] The development was separated from the Thornhill and Eden Vale housing areas by the railway.[44] The area developed rapidly, cottage streets interspersed with streets of larger, more spacious, two-storey middle-class terraces, and even some detached and semi-detached houses. By 1907 Guisborough Street, the last cottage street, was complete. By 1909 there existed Ewesley Road Methodist Church and the Anglican Church of St Gabriel, impressive statements of religious faith, while Barnes School (opened in 1906) and the West branch library (opened in Kayll Road in 1909) provided visible evidence of the area's commitment to educational improvement. The Barnes park opened in 1909, providing leisure facilities with its pond, bowling greens and tennis courts. So facilities were quickly established as the houses went up. Even though the last houses in the development were only a twenty minute walk downhill into town, the clean, smart Sunderland tramways provided easy access to the town centre

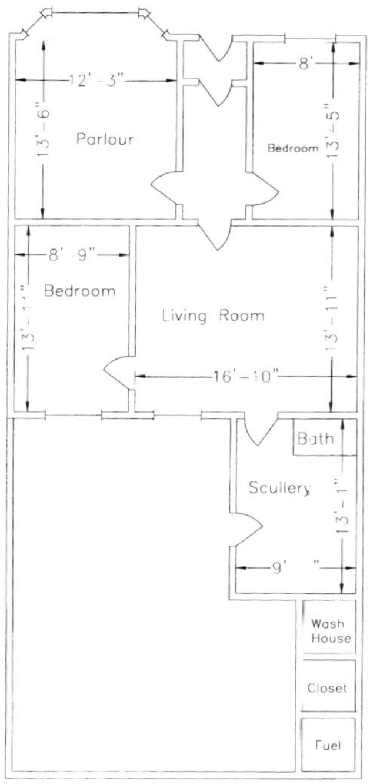

Fig. 35 Plan of a typical cottage in Abingdon Street, c.1897.

and to the promenades on the sea front.[45] In 1906 a neat tram shelter with public toilets was erected at the end of Kayll Road to further mark the area as respectable.

By 1900 the cottage had a lobby and an internal hall which measured on average 4'6" wide. Most, but not all, of the plans for the High Barnes estate bear the stamp of the Milburn Architectural Partnership, who were heavily involved in the provision of civic amenities at the time. Developments of the plan which altered the internal layout (see figs 35 and 36), eventually allowing more space in the kitchen, can be identified, but it is not really possible to point to such features as being evidence of the involvement of the architectural profession; even today it is possible for an individual purchaser to specify minor changes to an interior plan. However, at least the signature on the accession plan reveals a contact with the trained architect, and as such provides a link, however tenuous, with the 'High Design' of the day. The cottage is certainly a small house but it contained in miniature the key rooms found in larger scale housing.

The main rooms in the cottages were surprisingly big.[46] In a small double-fronted cottage in Brinkburn Street, the parlour measured 12'11" by 12'6" and the living room measured 12'9" by 14'6", while in a larger double-fronted cottage in Thelma Street built in 1897, the parlour measured 15' by 13', opening off a hall corridor which was 5'8" wide. The living room was 11'7" by 13'6", from which access was gained to a second bedroom 9'11" by 7'1"; the kitchen was accessible from the living room and formed an extension at the back. These houses all had a private yard which measured approximately 26' by 7'. If we compare these internal dimensions with rooms in Ewesley Road – a more spacious middle-class terrace built in 1902 – the front parlour measured 13'7" by 14'9" (smaller than the cottage in Thelma Street) and the main bedroom 13'6" by 11'6". Of course, the Ewesley Road house has two storeys and more rooms, but the actual

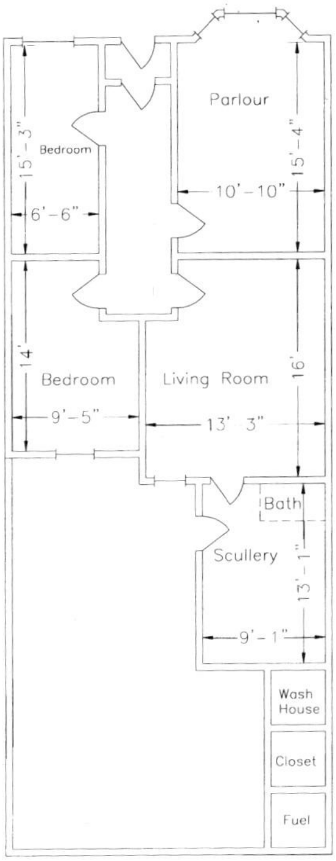

Fig. 36 Plan of a typical cottage in Guisborough Street, c.1907.

dimensions of individual rooms are not so very different, while a ceiling height of 10', fixed by regulation, adds to the sense of space within the cottage.

As I have already mentioned, it was possible to vary the basic plan to gain more space in the living room, as can be seen in figs 34 and 35, showing the varying size of the hall. This might give access to as many as four rooms. Sometimes the house was extended by putting bedrooms in the roof space (as in accession 338 no. 119), where 'Attics' were added to a house in Abingdon Street in 1900, access being via a stair out of the hall running over a corner of the existing large living room.[47] As the endorsement makes clear, the walls were constructed of brick and stone "properly bonded and solidly put together with good mortar and cement", the roof covered with slate or tiles or other appropriate incombustible material.[48] The ash closet constructed in the yard in, for example, Abingdon Street was subject to a different endorsement: "Ash closet to be built in strict conformity with a plan prepared by the Borough Engineer". Not every house had an indication of a bath in the original plans and it is also worth mentioning that the middle-class houses also had ash closets in the yard, even though there might in most cases be an internal W.C. Sunderland had access to excellent bricks made of locally excavated clay, while large deposits of limestone resulted in a ready supply of lime for mortar. Sheet glass was manufactured in the town and wood was imported from the Baltic.

None of these local materials can be said to supply a complete explanation of the town's unique housing form, but it would seem that in Sunderland the construction industry had no difficulty finding supplies for the housing estates that began to spread between and around the middle-class areas in the last quarter of the nineteenth century. These housing developments were discussed in detail by the town's politicians in the run-up to the Sunderland Corporation Act, which aimed to expand the town in order to control standards of housing which was being constructed on its boundaries.

Many writers have commented on the effects of such bye-laws on housing forms and it is obvious that the local bye-laws affected the cottage in its later stages; but those in Sunderland did not at any point limit the builder to single-storey houses, and I have not yet found evidence to support the notion that the town moved to low-rise cottages only in the bye-law phase.[49] Towns were empowered by government legislation during the last quarter of the nineteenth century but the effectiveness of such regulations was limited by the fact that the adoption of such bye-laws was not mandatory; moreover, even when the relatively energetic Sunderland Council sought to apply local Acts which extended the model bye-laws, they were opposed by local self-interest. The *Sunderland Daily Echo* on 7th January 1885 praised the moderation of the Council in pursuance of a Corporation Bill of 1885. The bill sought to extend the boundaries of the town to bring under control adjacent areas which were then being built on:

> in a word it took a single line which was at present being built on and which they thought was likely to be built on and over which they ought in the public interest, have power and over which the Corporation byelaw sought to have force.

The leader writer outlined his view of the opposition in the following terms:

> The sharp attorneys who have hope of some pickings and the building land purveyors who shrink from stating their real objection to the bill now before the Town . . . it will be for those who still object to the landowners having to pave new streets, to the building land round the town being brought under the byelaws, to the improved sanitation regulations to say why they oppose the bill.[50]

The Bill had been debated in and out of Parliament for three years and when it was eventually passed in 1885 it represented only a limited act. Not unexpectedly, speculative builders in areas which were outside the jurisdiction of the Corporation opposed the Bill, but, more significantly, opposition was also found within the Town Council. One of the biggest opponents of the clause for compelling landowners to pave and lay out streets was Robert Preston, Mayor of Sunderland in 1884. He was described as "a building landowner and not at all in favour of the proposed clause for compelling landowners to layout and pave streets before building". He was reported to have cut short the meeting, thereby preventing further discussion by his opponents.[51] He was Chairman of the Building Committee and described himself as a small landowner. If self-interest is at the heart of the problem of the effectiveness of the bye-laws, it is of considerable interest that Mr Preston is also described as "One of the largest importers of Welsh slates on Tyne and Wear". It is perhaps because of a measure of self-interest that Sunderland maintained its single-storey form, a form where an entire roof of Welsh slate houses only one family.[52]

The debates in the Commons on the Bill reveal two main issues relating to Sunderland housing at the end of the century; one is the status of land in

Sunderland and the other relates to building and planning practices. The Corporation had, in common with other big towns, great difficulty in applying bye-laws. In Sunderland's case the difficulties were not so much concerned with the structure of the houses, which was not in question, but rather with the laying out of streets, as the Sunderland Corporation Bill Committee Proceedings and newspaper reports made clear. It was obviously difficult to force speculators to lay out the street prior to building, when no single developer constructed the entire street:

> many places half built, never became streets on account of the impossibility of getting a decision from the magistrate that a piece of ground laid out for building and not already built on is a street.[53]

The Town wanted to have bye-laws enforceable as law, but this had already proved difficult; for example, in 1884 two judges decided that kerbs must be there by law under the Public Health Act, but they felt they had no right to stipulate when the kerbstones should be laid. As one of them was reputed to have remarked:

> If I had to decide them I should have held that the reasonableness or unreasonableness of a byelaw is a question altogether of the length of a judge's foot.[54]

One of the witnesses felt that "the builder had everything to gain by insisting that he would have his estate laid out before he built a brick", but another pointed out that it was unreasonable to expect builders to put in good roads with kerbstones only to have the gas and water companies tear them up when they laid supplies to the houses.[55]

Various practical measures were deemed necessary in Sunderland; for example, it was practice to put a layer of concrete over the ground to counteract the fact that the town is built on clay, while a later discussion raises the issue of pre-planning. This emerged when a questioner found it surprising that the Gas Company could tell where the house frontages would be before they were built. He asserted that, surely, "He cannot tell before a single house is put in what size the houses are to be", whereas another witness said categorically that this is not the case; in Sunderland "the landowner defines the site".[56] This acceptance of 'definition' within the street seems to point to a repetitive form and is certainly exemplified by the regularity of the cottage streets. The effects of the bye-laws in relation to street layout can be demonstrated by comparing the standard model regulated by the bye-law requiring a thirty-feet-wide front street in the High Barnes Estate (see fig. 37) with an existing row of cottages which were outside the town boundary in 1880 (see fig. 38). This row lay within the Rural District Sanitation Authority, which, according to the Commons Proceedings, had no bye-laws affecting street layout. The width of the street is considerably less than thirty feet and, in order to avoid laying out a paved

Fig. 37 A street in the High Barnes area built between 1898 and 1902 in accordance with the bye-law requiring a thirty-feet-wide street.

road, gardens have been set out in front of the cottages; while in order to avoid the problems of a public thoroughfare, gates were constructed across the end of the street.[57]

The minutes of the proceedings committee also deal with the question of land tenure. Mr Storey, M.P. for Sunderland, explained to the committee looking into the Sunderland Corporation Act that Sunderland was a town:

> Where the land is not sold, it is let on a building rent to builders. The effect is that a building speculator has a street laid out. He lets to A, B, C, D, E, F, and G. Some may have money, some may not, A and G build, their houses really are in a street, but other men do not go off, the plots are not sold, other men hesitate, the street hangs fire and the consequence is we are left with streets with houses here and there and other houses will not be built for years to come. We want to remedy that, we have tried . . . we thought a kerbline might prevent hills and holes but the byelaw is said to be bad and we can't say when it can be laid, so we came to the committee and ask them in the exceptional condition of Sunderland to give us the power to call on landowners to make the streets.[58]

This needs explanation. Sunderland is a town where the majority of properties are regulated by rent charges or by a reversionary principal sum device.[59] "The essence of the rent charge lies in the power of the owner to distrain upon lands."[60] The rent charge is not reversionary but the power of distress was a powerful incentive, for it gave the owner of the rent charge the

Fig. 38 A street of cottages built in c.1880, which at the time lay outside the town boundary. They were not subject to regulations governing street layout.

right to seize, and by the mid-nineteenth century, sell, chattels found on the land to procure rents without the necessity of legal proceedings as long as he used the services of a bailiff with a warrant.

The complexity of rents in England was addressed by the Landlord and Tenant Act of 1730, whereby all owners of rents (chief rents, rents of assize and dry rents) should have power of distress. This situation where the interest of the landlord was protected by the right of distress encouraged the small landowner and property speculator, in that when a plot of land was 'sold' it continued to generate income. In addition, in Sunderland there was a second type of rent, which was actually reversionary, the Principal Sum Device, whereby the purchase price of the land was left outstanding subject to an annual charge of about 4%. This device was related to freehold but these tenancies could revert to the original owner if payments were not maintained. These different tenurial agreements were an early means of regulating land use; moreover, the rent charge was a device whereby various covenants, inserted to run with the land in the interest of the original owner, could be kept alive. Such covenants were obviously in the interest of the owner, who did not want a factory, dyeworks, or abattoir next to his land.[61]

As an explanation for the single-storey cottage form, however, these unusual tenure arrangements are unsatisfactory, for there is nothing in law to prevent the owner from deriving more than one set of rents from the plot, as would be possible if flats were constructed. Not only cottage developments but also most of the middle-class housing in Sunderland was subject to rent charges. So, for example, within the West Ward the red brick three-storey houses on the Westlands and Ewesley Road, the comfortable semi-detatched villas on Dunelm, the link villas on Kayll Road and the cottages in the 'A.B.C.' streets were all regulated by rent charges. Cottages were advertised in *The Sunderland Daily Echo,* often giving both the rental and the ground rent, e.g. a cottage in Pallion was said to generate a rental of £13 and a ground rent of £2 2s 9d.[62] The tenurial conditions, then, cannot explain the form of the cottage, but the existence of an additional means of deriving income from land would seem to fit in well with the self-help philosophy of the speculative investors in housing in the nineteenth century, and thus it is tempting to believe that rent charges were fashionable in the town at this time.[63] Also, small owners of property did not necessarily own the ground rents and so a complex web of ownership emerged. Storey, in his comments to the select committee, carefully differentiated between land speculators and landowners:

> There is the opinion of the whole town on the one side and the opinion of two or three or perhaps a dozen men who are land speculators, one or two of them perhaps landowners, who object to this clause.[64]

The question of whether renting to the poor was a good investment concerned writers in the nineteenth century.[65] That owning and renting out on a small scale was viewed favourably in Sunderland is certain, and the tenure system within the town also supported this practice. Large scale ownership is not a dominant pattern in Sunderland (the exception being the tied housing provided by the colliery owners at Monkwearmouth Colliery). Certainly an examination of the rate books reveals page after page of streets owned by a mixture of "Self" and relatively small-scale landlords. Thus Woodbine Terrace (started in 1869) has a high proportion of either self-single occupancy in 1890, or those occupants who also owned one or two cottages. Lime Street, started in 1900, contained ten single cottage owners and three owners of multiples. The rateable value of the houses in Lime Street was between £10 10s and £11, and while this is not a real rent, it is an indication that the rental gained was a useful investment. Another factor which emerges is the listing of various building societies as owners of property, including the still operative North of England Building Society and the aptly named Working Man's Building Society.[66] There is some evidence of multiple ownerships in one street by such societies, but in general, individuals took out mortgages for their own home and not for larger scale investment projects. Overall, there was a considerable percentage of home ownership in the town, assessed as 27% in 1890, as opposed to 17% in Gateshead and 3% in Birmingham.[67] Despite restrictions on land use in force since the eighteenth century[68] and increasing during the next, the demand for rented property in Sunderland was such that both the speculative builder and the small landlord flourished.

In Sunderland it is possible to construct a model which is a synthesis of economic, social and cultural factors, one in which the desirability of maintaining economically defined social divisions within the town is seen as an essential element of the town's cultural identity. From the point of view of the wealthier landowner or speculator, benefits could be gained in solving the problem of housing the workforce, both in the economic benefits of rents and ground rents and the inevitable emergence of a reliable workforce, and in the less easily defined benefits of working-class housing that actually looked working class, and thus enhanced the relative status of middle-class housing in the town. This hypothesis was touched on by Nicholas Gibson, who in 1872 agreed with the Countess of Lothair:

> I am very much in favour of improved dwellings for the poor but then you must take care that your cottages are not villas.[69]

The Sunderland cottages' distinctive building line certainly set them apart from the houses of the middle classes, or so it would appear. To the worker, the early cottage allowed privacy and space to bring up his family, and the growing pride of the working-class artisan could be expressed by moving into an estate, either as a tenant or as owner of one or two cottages. Perhaps, too, the cottage embodies the contradictary pull between the desire to 'know your place', and the wish to avoid the pretentiousness of the middle-class suburb; after all, Sunderland had supported Cromwell in the Civil War and church and chapel flourished. However, it may also embody a striving towards middle-class pretension where the skilled worker, desiring different and better housing, used many external elements of middle-class housing to mark out his own house as significantly better than a perceived lower category of house. Thus the cottage changed, from a single-fronted to a double-fronted house with an occasional interim form described as 'one and a half front'. The high ceilings, bay windows and baths of the developed forms can all be seen as signs of betterment and status. The inclusion of such characteristics as "Venetian blinds" and "new wallpaper", "washhouse" and "good district" in advertisements for cottages in *The Sunderland Daily Echo* in the 1880s can also be seen as a sign of this.[70]

In a working-class town like Sunderland status within the working class could be defined by the built environment, albeit subtly. There was undoubtedly a hierarchy within the cottages themselves, with the better built houses occupied by skilled workers on sites further away from the river – next to fields and farms – while older, smaller, less well constructed cottages were occupied by a mix of lower group workers on sites nearer the river. The estates of Pallion and Millfield were never viewed by locals as quite as 'up-market' as Barnes and Chester Road and today this division is still marked by a price differential. The cottage was an urban form which allowed a particular sector of the working class an almost middle-class degree of control, mobility and choice in economic and social terms. It also gave the middle classes a source of investment, and added meaning to their own houses as being obviously better.[71] Thus high wages and self-interest combined to provide housing in streets of single-storey cottages where only the exceptional dormer window challenged the middle-class roofline.

A survey of the professions listed in the Sunderland trades directory for the Chester Road and High Barnes estate in 1901 include many of these middle-class categories. For example, in Abingdon Street in 1901-2 there were three clerks, an insurance agent, two 'agents' and a cashier, an art master and various merchants. Alongside these lower-middle-class occupations appear others which are more obviously working-class: two joiners, a mason, two marine engineers, four master mariners, and an engineman. Others in this forty-eight house street, such as the builder at number 28, or the painter at number 14, are more difficult to categorise. The directories for 1909 reveal a varied range of occupations which were marginally more 'blue collar': there were still three clerks and two commercial travellers, and an insurance agent; the four master mariners, the "agents" and a marine engineer, were still there too, as well as a music teacher and a gentleman; but in addition there were four fitters, two platers, two caulkers, two foremen, a horticulturist, a chemist's assistant and, significantly, one electrician. If this range of occupations is compared with streets nearer the river and the shipyards, we see a much narrower range, all well outside the range of the lower middle class. In these streets the occupations reflect the range of skilled and semi-skilled operations necessary in the shipbuilding and engineering industries. The occupations listed in the bigger middle-class homes on the Westlands in 1909-10 include the established professions (a surgeon, a Methodist minister) alongside the new technocratic elite (the marine surveyor, two Lloyds surveyors and an engineer), while the flour dealer, cycle agent, funeral furnisher, laundry proprietor and earthenware manufacturer reflect the relative prosperity of the commercial sector.

Further analysis is necessary to refine this evidence, but it would seem to point to the new cottage in the final phase (1890-1910) forming a bridge between working class and lower middle class, enabling and facilitating the upward mobility of the population; certain trades or professions seem to have found accommodation in both the cottage and the three-storey terrace.[72] What distinguishes the two housing forms is size and what that entailed; with attics and inside and outside toilets, the Westlands were designed for a family with domestic help. The visual contrast between the red brick terrace fronting the main road, and the low-rise cottage street neatly laid out behind it, is obvious (see fig. 39), but the contrast in occupancy is not so clear; however, these later cottage streets were certainly not seen as lowering the tone of the neighbourhood. The two developments went up simultaneously, and a system of direct communication between the terrace and the cottage was set up by means of the church, the chapel, the school and the library. There were music teachers, elocution teachers, and

Fig. 39 The Westlands, a terrace of middle class housing, fronts the cottage streets of High Barnes.

professors of painting in the West Ward Estates and, since private tutors are not known for their wealth, it can also be argued that these small, relatively affordable cottages enabled these representatives of the poorer educated classes to live among their clients. Seamstresses and dressmakers also lived in these areas, providing services to maintain appearances to both the middle classes and the upper or artisan group of the working class. Such interaction with the middle class is not so obvious in the areas nearer the river, while the taverns and Working Men's Clubs, so common in those areas, were apparently excluded from the later cottage estates.

It is possible to look for a prototype for the Sunderland cottage in the miners' row or the agricultural labourer's cottage. In some areas of the Durham coalfield a single-storey row model prevails (e.g. in Horden), whereas in some areas of the Northumberland coalfield the Tyneside flat and small two-storey model occur (e.g. at Boldon Colliery); however, it is also apparent that many mining villages in County Durham have two-storey developments. It is more likely that the agricultural cottage was the prototype for the miner's cottage and in Weardale (in the lead mining industry) it was customary for hill-farmers and smallholders to work as part-time miners and live at home in their cottages, only using dormitory provision if the weather was bad. However, cottages in rural Weardale are not necessarily single-storey and are certainly not built in long rows, while the only single-storey rows in most mining villages in the area are 'Aged Miners' Cottages'. Further evidence of agricultural roots can be found in the fact that shipowners like the Laing brothers came from rural areas. Laing was described as a yeoman farmer when he came to Sunderland from a village in Fifeshire, and it is just feasible that his workers erected their known model, the simple single-storey cottage, near the yard he opened in 1792.

In the development of the built environment, choices become influenced by custom and force of habit, and style becomes habitual choice.[73] In Sunderland the single-storey form could well have become the unquestioned form for working class housing, which then ultimately developed into 'would-be' middle-class housing as the circumstances changed. If we posit an agricultural source, then the cottage can be seen as transitional form between vernacular culture and 'High Style' urban design.[74]

Of course, the form of the Sunderland cottage may not be the only reason for its success. Positive attitudes to housing are not only to do with privacy and space, but also to do with amenities. The rehousing schemes of the 1950s and 60s involved relocation from some of the older cottage streets near the river, as well as from slum areas in the east end, to housing estates on the outer edge of Sunderland. These new estates were generally seen as being too far from work, from town, from the beach, from the family and from known shops and schools. In sharp contrast, the old cottage estates were all within either walking distance or, in the case of cottages on the north of the river, a short bus ride from the town centre with an acceptable bus fare to the beach in summer. The cottage streets had a network of corner shops and specialist intensive shopping streets. The schools were well established with known links from primary to secondary stages, while individual shops and pubs were apparently often named as being a positive asset to a particular area.[75] These positive attributes which applied to the less well built older areas of cottages, cleared as unhealthy by the planners because of structural problems (mostly patches of damp), also applied to the cottages of Fulwell and High Barnes which were never threatened with demolition.

In 1900 the cottage represented a good fit in the context of a working-class town. It represented the embodiment of those values desired by the artisan class. The front door was highly visible and centred, while the windows extended into a bay window on one side and a large sash window on the other, derived from forms used in more prestigious terraces.[76] The house was no longer on the street – it was stepped back behind a low wall, originally decorated with a cast iron fence, within which twin planters for, say, a laurel or privet, frame the entrance. The kitchens and other offices were tucked away at the back of the house, sheltered by a seven-foot wall. Unless there were dormer windows in the rear roof space of a neighbouring house, no one could overlook the back of the house.

Today, the cottage still represents a good fit between form and context, even when choice is not so limited, for the cottages are still popular, even though, for example, the 1995 asking price of £46,500 for a cottage in Nora Street in the High Barnes Estate would also buy a new link villa in Silksworth or a Thirties bungalow in Herrington. The price is about that for a three-bedroomed terraced house in the originally middle-class area of Ashbrooke and £7,500 more than that asked in the grandiose Toward Road, where once spacious terraces have been converted to bedsits. The cottage also costs more than twice the price of a modern link villa with the same number of rooms in Barmston, constructed as a satellite to the town in the Seventies. The cottage has maintained its fit when other, even relatively recent, forms have become misfits.

I hope that this chapter will provide an antidote to the 'doom and gloom' images of the North East encountered in many studies. I maintain an optimistic view of housing in Sunderland at the turn of the century, arising from the generally positive energy generated by the dynamism of Sunderland in the boom years, but also from seeing that the Sunderland cottage is still sought after in those 'respectable areas' where, in the 1900s, the skilled workers built or rented small, but adequate cottages.

It is difficult for a newcomer to Sunderland today to realise the sense of loss that fills those who remember the town as a vibrant hive of industry, alive in the way only shipbuilding towns can be when their products are actually part of the built environment while they are being made. In Sunderland, the bridge crosses the river only a short walk from the town centre and whenever it was necessary to cross the bridge the products of the shipyards were visible, either under construction or being taken down the river to the sea. If the public buildings and private houses of a town give it meaning, then so too did these huge artefacts, and in the 1900s, with its phenomenal output, the meaning of the town was thus reinforced. The cottages too added a further dimension to the town, one which so obviously depended on its workforce. Even though there are no longer any ships on the river, and most of the paper made in the town is used for bingo tickets, the workforce has proved ever adaptable by moving on to the newer technologies of the Japanese car plant with Nissan, or advanced glass technologies with Pyrex. Perhaps Sunderland will move easily into the age of the 'tele-cottage'.

References and Notes

1. See Kit Pearce in Bill Lancaster (ed.), *Working Class Housing on Tyneside 1850-1939* (Newcastle upon Tyne, 1994), p.76.

2. T.F. Dibdin, *A Bibliographical and Picturesque Tour of the Northern Counties* (London, 1838), p.314.

3. The statistics for the Tyne involved Newcastle, Gateshead, North and South Shields and Tyne Dock.

4. See M.J. Daunton, *House and Home in the Victorian City, Working Class Housing 1850-1914* (London, 1983); S. Muthesius, *The English Terraced House* (New York, 1982); K. Peart in Lancaster, op.cit.

5. Muthesius, op.cit., pp.41 and 130. He allows that, in common with the Tyneside flat, the Wearside cottage allowed separate access to each room, and had unusually high ceilings and unusual width.

6. See J.N. Tarn, *Working Class Housing in the Nineteenth Century* (London, 1971).

7. S. Miller, *The Book of Sunderland* (Sunderland, 1990), p.58.

8. Gateshead was in County Durham, but it was too near Newcastle to have a totally distinct identity.

9. It is interesting to note that a recent exhibition of classical architecture chose several photographs of Sunderland to illustrate the strength of the Doric style. (Royal Ontario Museum).

10. See 42, 43 and 44 below.

11. See, for example, *The Sunderland Daily Echo*, 13 November 1884.

12. For example, *The Torrens*, the last fully rigged clipper to be built in Sunderland; Joseph Conrad was second mate on this ship.

13. This extends a description in N. Dennis, *People and Planning* (London, 1970), p.136. Incidentally, Tenniel's famous carpenter in *Alice in Wonderland* was modelled on the ships' carpenters with their square hats and white aprons seen on the streets of Sunderland in the 1860s.

14. By 1904 Doxfords shipyard covered 38 acres, and in 1905-7 this Wearside yard headed the U.K. output and prided itself on maintaining a one year delivery schedule.

15. J.W. Smith and T.S. Holden, *Where Ships are Born, Sunderland 1346-1946* (Sunderland, 1946), p.1.

16. This claim was based on various key statistics which calculated that Sunderland had, in most years, a higher annual tonnage than the Clyde and the Tyne. In 1938 Sunderland produced 169,898 tons, whereas the production for the whole of the United States of America was only 201,251 tons; see Smith and Holden, op.cit., pp.1-2.

17. In 1847 Hartley patented a method of plate glass manufacture and produced a third of all plate glass manufactured; in the 1860s he granted a licence to Pilkington and Chance. The industry declined in Sunderland and in 1894 the manufacture of plate glass was discontinued. In the nineteenth century lime was used as a general fertiliser, for mortar, and as a flux for glass. See Milburn and Miller, *River, Town and People* (Sunderland, 1988), pp.20ff.

18. Smith and Holden, op.cit., p.30. It is pertinent to point out that the Suez Canal was to contribute to the expansion of trade which aided the development of Sunderland in the mid-nineteenth century.

19. The new parish of St Andrew included areas of cottage streets even though the church itself was on the edge of the parish, surrounded by middle-class housing.

20. A.H. Halsey, introduction to Dennis, op.cit., p.23.

21. L. Crangle, "Antiquities of Sunderland and its Vicinity", *Sunderland Antiquarian Society Papers* vol. xxvi (May 1974-76), extracts p.68.

22. *The Sunderland Echo*, 10 May 1961.

23. For example, Corby Hall and Langholm Tower: see T. Corfe, *Sunderland Buildings* (Sunderland, 1983).

24. According to Smith and Holden, op.cit., there were nine yards on the river in 1801 as well as ships being built in odd places, even in the street; but by 1848 when the South Dock opened, there were docks, engineering works, wood yards, and other industries along both sides of the river.

25. At the time it was the world's longest single-span cast-iron bridge, which was further remodelled by Stephenson in 1858.

26. *The Commissioners for Inquiring into the State of Large Towns and Populous Districts*: the Second Report; Appendix (HMSO, 1845), p.191, and *The Royal Commission on the Housing of the Working Classes*: First Report (HMSO, 1885), p.11.

27. *Census of England and Wales*: table 3, vol, viii (HMSO, 1911).

28. *The Royal Commission on the Housing of the Working Classes*: First Report (HMSO, 1885), p.16. See also Daunton, op.cit., p.67.

29. It is possible to see examples of multi-occupancy in the Rate Books for 1890 (Tyne & Wear Archives). Clanny Street, a street of small two-storey houses, had two occupiers in each house, while number 49 had four occupiers. Some owners lived in the street and owned corner shops.

30. J. Glyde, in D. Rubinstein, *Victorian Homes* (London, 1974), p.67.

31. *The Commission for Inquiring into the State of Large Towns and Populous Districts*: Second Report; Appendix (HMSO, 1845), p.192.

32. Milburn and Miller, op.cit., pp.102ff.

33. Potts, in Milburn and Miller, op.cit., p.57, "a six fold increase with an intercensal rate of increase running higher than the national average until the end of the century".

34. See R.C. Fox, *The Demography of Sunderland 1851*, Occasional Paper No. 1, Department of Geography and History (Sunderland Polytechnic, 1980). He refers to a 60% stasis.

35. Only about 6% of all males in the town in 1901 were not born in England, and of these 3.2% were born in Scotland, 1.6% in Ireland, and 1.5% in foreign lands. This despite the fact that the town attracted large numbers of skilled artisans to its flourishing industries. See Dennis, op.cit., p.55; source successive censuses.

36. Based on an apprenticeship lasting seven years commencing at age thirteen and a journeyman's role for a further seven years.

37. It is also likely that since 1900 a further three generations have continued in the cottage streets. I do not have detailed research on this yet.

38. A.L. Bowley and G. Wood, *The Division of the Product of Industry* (Oxford, 1919), p.29, table v.

39. From 105 in 1880, to 83 in 1896, although it then rose again to 100 in 1914; calculated by A.L. Bowley, *Wages and Incomes in the United Kingdom since 1890* (Cambridge, 1937).

40. Quoted by Rubinstein, op.cit., p.147.

41. S. Miller, op.cit.,1990, p.58.

42. Ibid., pp.40-42.

43. Middle-class housing in Sunderland generated many different responses. On the key roads out of town, terraces, semi-detached houses, and villas with fashionable Arts and Crafts detailing appeared, while on Kayll Road some remarkable link villas were completed in 1907. Here, where we would expect tunnel back layout, semi-detached houses are transformed into a terrace, the houses linked by an extension containing on the ground floor a through passage to the enclosed garden, and on the first floor a flush toilet and bathroom.

44. For layout of these estates see accession 269, p.23. (No. 7767, Tyne & Wear Archives.)

45. S.A. Staddon, *Tramways of Sunderland* (Sunderland, 1964), p.7. Trams had been introduced in the town in 1878 and after the application of electricity to the network in 1896 and the purchase of the original company in 1899, Line One, "the Circle", linked Kayll Road with the town and Sea Lane.

46. Even in a single fronted cottage in Lime Street, the living room which faced the back yard measured 14'9" by 9'11", while the front bedroom measured 13'0" by 12'6". Rooms are usually labelled: Parlour, Dining room, Bedroom (bath), Scullery and Closet. All figures based on either Building Plans submitted to Sunderland Corporation between 1890 and 1910 in Tyne & Wear Archives, or my own measurements. At this stage I must acknowledge the help given to me by the inhabitants of the cottage streets.

47. Tyne & Wear Archives. Other houses gained access to the upstairs attics by putting a stair out of the kitchen at the back of the house, this variation running over the opposite side of the living room. The dimensions of the floor space of the attics were a reasonable 12'9" by 9'8" and 11'4" by 9'8". These rooms were set within the overall area of the main body of the house, to utilise as much height as possible within the roof. Both bedrooms also incorporate cupboards in the lower parts of the roof. It is obvious, too, from the accessions, that estimates of space within the building regulations include only the three main rooms, i.e. only the space under the main roof.

48. "Space beneath all board floors is to be ventilated by means of air gratings at least 9" by 3". Every habitable room without a fireplace is to be provided with adequate means of ventilation. Drainage to be laid with full socketed pipes of approved quality to one gradient. The joints to be made with well tempered clay and where, in the opinion of the Borough Engineer, necessary the pipes to be laid in puddled clay. Conveniences are to be built in strict confirmity with a plan prepared by the Borough Engineer and approved by the Corporation. All hearth stones to be properly bedded in some approved incombustible material. The floors to all rooms on the ground floor to be at least 12" above the ground. The yard to have an incline of 1 in 30 to the back street and the back street to be 6" below level of yard"; Building Plans, dated 20 June 1898 (Tyne & Wear Archives).

49. See B.T. Robson, *Urban Analysis* (London, 1969); Daunton, op.cit.; Lancaster, op.cit.

50. *The Sunderland Daily Echo*, 7 January 1885.

51. *The Sunderland Daily Echo*, 11 November 1884.

52. *The Sunderland Daily Echo*, 10 November 1884, see also *The Sunderland Corporation Bill Committee Proceedings* (1885), p.295.

53. *The Sunderland Corporation Bill Committee Proceedings* (1885), p.259.

54. Ibid., p.260.

55. Indeed, the proceedings got thoroughly petty at one stage when the statement "Owners laying out new streets have to pay expenses", evinces the response, "But you would not lay out a street not already new". Ibid., p.286.

56. Ibid., p.291.

57. *The Sunderland Corporation Act* (1885), clause 73, and discussion of the difficulties of defining a street in *Sunderland Corporation Bill Committee Proceedings* (1885), pp.286ff.

58. Ibid., p.291.

59. I must thank Paul Maggiore and his colleague David Hodgeson for giving up so much of their time to explain the legal aspects of the land tenure system in Sunderland. See also G.C. Cheshire, *Modern Law of Real Property* (London, 1925), p.536, "A Rent charge is an annual sum of money, issuing and paying out of land, the due payment of which is secured by right of distress that is not the result of tenure but is allowed by statute".

60. Cheshire, op.cit., pp.409 and 537. He also makes the point that the owner has no tenurial interest in the land and therefore is not entitled to distress as of common right but by law.

61. It would appear that the earliest cottage developments did not maintain restrictive covenants because industrial development did encroach on housing areas.

62. *The Sunderland Daily Echo*, 13 November 1884.

63. There is anecdotal evidence linking Sunderland rent charges with those common in Lancashire. In the 1800s Mowbray, a local landowner, married the daughter of a ground rent owner in Lancashire, whose considerable means in part derived from the ground rent charges he had set up in Lancashire. Mowbray, it seems, quickly set up similar rents in Sunderland.

64. *Sunderland Corporation Bill Committee Proceedings* (1885), op.cit., p.291. *The Sunderland Daily Echo* in its reports on the Corporation Bill also refers to land jobbers; see *The Sunderland Daily Echo*, 17 December 1884.

65. See Rubinstein, op.cit., pp.113ff. *The Builder* also took up the issue of "healthful, decent and remunerative dwellings" (1 March 1884). The editorial board also wholeheartedly supported the work of the Sanitary Inspector!

66. *Wards Directory* (Sunderland, 1901) lists 16 building societies; see also the *Rate Books*, 1900 (West District), p.143 (Tyne & Wear Archives). Page 143/4 of the 1900 rate book also reveals the tantalising fact that Sunderland Corporation owned numbers 36, 37 and 38 Woodbine Terrace; as yet I do not know on what basis these houses were owned.

67. Daunton provides a table based on rent books which compares ownership in Gateshead, Sunderland and Middlesborough, at slightly different dates (1885-1901-1890) which may indicate a relationship between small house size and the needs of the small investor in housing. Daunton, op.cit., table 8, p.27.

68. Butterfield illustrates this point by reference to Samuel Johnson's letter to Boswell, "Man cannot be allowed by society to be complete master of what he calls his own, and he must submit to the restrictions placed by law on the exercise of his proprietorial rights" (Letter to Boswell, 3 February 1776); quoted in Butterfield, "Planning Law", in Cheshire, op.cit., p.853.

69. Quoted in Pearce, op.cit., p.79.

70. *The Sunderland Daily Echo*, 13 November 1884.

71. See Dennis, op.cit., p.349; Burnett, op.cit., p.98; and Marcus, in H.J. Dyos & M. Wolff (eds.), *The Victorian City*, p.260.

72. Wards, *Trade Directory*, 1900-1901 and 1909-1910. Another interesting feature that emerges from these directories is the mobility of the population, but unfortunately the Census returns for 1901 are not yet available and the absolute accuracy of the directories cannot thus be checked.

73. See A. Rapoport, *Meaning in the Built Environment* (New York, 1982), p.51.

74. See also Rapoport, *House Form and Culture* (New York, 1969).

75. Dennis, op.cit., pp.298ff.

76. The lower-middle-class villa also demonstrates this striving upwards. That such pretension or idealisation took place, can be illustrated in the small link villas in Kayll Road. When my family moved into Kayll Road Villas, as they were called (to distinguish them from the distinctly undistinguished Kayll Road at the other end of the road) in 1947, we children were delighted to discover an entire servant bell service which could have graced a stately home. The indicator box was over the dining room door, and the sitting room and the dining room had push buttons on either side of the fireplace, while each bedroom, including the tiny box room, had buttons on wires over the beds. There were no attics or cellars, so live-in help was unlikely. The house also had wooden Venetian blinds.

VI

CONSERVATION AND RENEWAL IN NEWCASTLE UPON TYNE

T.E. Faulkner

Introduction

Newcastle is proud of its record in the field of architectural conservation. The official view is that it has "kept and even enhanced so much that is good in the buildings of the past",[1] the Council's policy over the last twenty-five years having been "to safeguard and conserve the city's built heritage".[2] Even the controversial 1963 *Development Plan* had the stated intention of welding together the old and the new, while conserving "the magnificent classical stone buildings of the Victorian city".[3] In 1973, towards the end of a period of intense redevelopment which saw the destruction of such monuments as Eldon Square and the Royal Arcade, Newcastle still believed that it had kept the best of its buildings while anticipating government legislation on conservation areas by a decade: "new development and roads are fully integrated within the fabric of the city".[4] Public perception is rather different. There is a sense that much of value has been needlessly lost and, as discredited buildings from the boom years of the 1960s fall into disuse or are even demolished in their turn, attitudes to planning and further development have become uncertain and negative.

People are now increasingly conscious of 'heritage' and seek to preserve Georgian, Victorian and even selected examples of twentieth-century architecture. However, the problem remains whereby if a historic building is considered obsolete it will be allowed to decay, while if it also occupies a valuable site, it is even more likely to be redeveloped. If this occurs, the best that can usually be achieved is the retention of facades, as in the case, for example, of many buildings in Grey Street. Where complete replacement is allowed, developers today will probably play safe with vaguely traditional forms instead of modernist architecture but even these, unless handled carefully, can degenerate into pastiche.

The confidence and energy of Newcastle's early nineteenth-century developers reshaped a still essentially medieval city in classical terms. The next main phase of replanning came after about 1960. The policy-makers of this time seemed to lack confidence in the city's identity and embarked, too hastily, on a high profile programme of 'comprehensive redevelopment' which was over-ambitious and, in any case, never completely followed through. The result is now an amalgam of medieval, nineteenth-century metropolitan and international modern architecture, with isolated historic monuments, imperfectly preserved areas of Georgian and Victorian townscape and incompletely integrated modernist forms.

An air of decay, disunity and neglect persists in much of the city centre, its once pre-eminent commercial position increasingly threatened by out-of-town hypermarkets, superstores and, above all, the Metro Centre. Paradoxically, the demand for prime office space within the central business district is said to considerably exceed supply,[5] but excellent Victorian buildings remain empty for years; examples at the present time include St. Nicholas' Building, St. Nicholas' Street (now being redeveloped behind its facade), the former Post Office adjoining it, the former Barclays Bank, Collingwood Street, the former Union Club, Westgate Road, and the former Wengers' Store, Grainger Street. Even Andrews House and Magnet House in Gallowgate, built between the Wars, are currently under threat. In the words of the Newcastle *Journal*:

> The problem is that while we are quite good at looking after historic castles, cathedrals and palaces, we are not so careful with the legacy of commercial buildings which make up the urban landscape.[6]

This chapter examines changes to the 'urban landscape' of Newcastle over the last two centuries (examples of architecture discussed are or were in Newcastle unless otherwise stated); it suggests that this landscape has always been more vulnerable than we think. Indeed, fundamental to the city's collective consciousness has been, it seems, a propensity to destroy itself. An early example of this occurred in 1786 when two prominent local architects disagreed on what to do about the decaying church of All Saints, above the Quayside. A proposal by William Newton (1730-98) to restore the church was rejected, and this important Gothic structure was removed; David Stephenson (1757-1819) favoured rebuilding and won the competition for the present design, completed in 1796.[7] In this instance, the replacement of a historic building with an outstanding example of more up-to-date architecture indicates also a capacity for successful urban renewal. This capacity developed further during the early nineteenth century but since then, in spite of claims to the contrary, has not always been so evident.

Historical Perspective

In about 1760, Newcastle still centred on St. Nicholas's church, the Castle and the Quayside, from which a haphazard arrangement of streets and buildings spread up within the ancient 'town walls'. This impeded necessary expansion, but, as the city became architecturally and culturally more sophisticated, a number of 'improvements' took place, such as Charlotte Square (begun 1770) and the Assembly Rooms (1774-76), both by William Newton.

Together, Newton and Stephenson were employed by the Corporation in 1796 to remodel the north front of the Guildhall (an improvement, but seventeenth-century work by Robert Trollope was destroyed). Between 1784 and 1789 Stephenson, who was Architect to the Corporation, laid out Dean Street and Mosley Street, the latter containing his Theatre Royal of 1788, and Collingwood Street was constructed in 1810. However, communication routes were still inadequate. Newcastle's single medieval bridge, replaced after 1771 with an elegant structure by the London-based architect Robert Mylne, later widened by Stephenson, still made a tortuous entrance into the city, slightly west of the Guildhall and almost blocked by the medieval St. Thomas's Chapel; access from the river remained steep.

Meanwhile, middle-class streets were being built outside the walls. Saville Row, begun in the 1770s, was followed by Brandling Place, Claremont Place, Eldon Place, Eldon Row, Ellison Place, Higham Place (the first street by the builder and entrepreneur Richard Grainger), Lovaine Place, Summerhill, Swinburne Place and Victoria Square. By this time Grainger (1797-1861) was also laying out Blackett Street (1824) – thereby removing part of the 'town wall' – and the adjacent Eldon Square (1825-31), the latter a development of unprecedented grandeur and formality (fig. 40). Both were

Fig. 40 Eldon Square, Newcastle upon Tyne (by John Dobson, 1825-31), photographed in 1949. Largely demolished early 1970s. (Newcastle City Libraries).

by John Dobson (1787-1865), now the city's leading architect and later the first President of the Northern Architectural Association (from 1859). Grainger had also built the monumental Leazes Terrace (1829-34), by Thomas Oliver, and the Royal Arcade (1831-32), another major work by Dobson (see colour plate iii).

The demolition of the 'town wall', last repaired at the time of the Jacobite rebellion of 1745, had started with the section along the Quayside, from which masonry was used to build a fine classical church (also replacing an apparently ruinous medieval structure), St. Ann's, City Road (1764-68).[8] Another portion of the wall between the Pilgrim Street Gate and the Carliol Tower was removed in 1811 to make way for New Bridge Street, while the Gate itself had been demolished in 1802 because it had become an obstruction to traffic.[9] The New Gate (fig. 41), at the junction of Newgate Street and Blackett Street, survived until 1823, probably because of its use as a prison; however, it was the building of the new Gaol in Carliol Square (by Dobson, 1822-28) which sealed its fate, the commissioners insisting upon their right to re-use stone from the old building. This case provides one of the earliest examples in Newcastle of what might be termed a proto-conservation movement. Demolition of the Gate began with the removal of the later east and west wings and North Gate, after which, "a vigorous but unsuccessful effort was now made by the lovers of antiquity to save this venerable monument", which would have been converted into premises for Incorporated Companies with a road and footpath on either side.[10]

Fig. 41 The New Gate, Newcastle upon Tyne; demolished 1823. (From Mackenzie's *Newcastle upon Tyne*, 1827).

An interest in archaeology and antiquarianism had been growing during the late eighteenth and early nineteenth centuries. The Society of Antiquaries of Newcastle upon Tyne, one of the oldest outside London, was founded in 1813 and in the works of such local historians as Bourne, Brand and Mackenzie there is an overwhelming emphasis on architectural antiquities. Yet, despite these concerns, this period saw the destruction of one historic building after another. For example, St. James's Chapel, on the north side of Barras Bridge, was almost gone by 1800 and the 'Maison de Dieu' of 1412 (by now used as a warehouse) and Merchants' Court, at the east end of the Guildhall, were replaced in 1823 by Dobson's Fishmarket and new Merchants' Court.[11] St. Thomas's Chapel was finally pulled down in 1827 to widen the entrance to the bridge; sixty years earlier it had been partially demolished and rebuilt "in a motley manner" for the same reason.[12] The chapel's replacement, built on a site at Barras Bridge hitherto occupied by the ruins of St. Mary Magdalen's Hospital, was Dobson's church of St. Thomas the Martyr (1827-30). Even the Literary and Philosophical Society Library (1822), now one of Newcastle's best loved buildings, replaced the seventeenth-century house of Thomas Anderson.[13]

By this time the Castle Keep had become very dilapidated; its chapel was used as a beer cellar and the building was even advertised in 1782 for use as a brewery or windmill.[14] The Corporation purchased it at the time of the building of the new Moot Hall in 1810, demolishing the Bailey Gate and, sadly, the old Moot Hall, formerly the Great or King's Hall in which, in December 1292, the Scottish King John Baliol paid homage to Edward I. Described in 1649 as "an auncient [sic] building within the inner wall of the Castle Garth",[15] it had become "a curious mixture of Roman, Norman, Gothic, and modern architecture",[16] to be replaced by the local architect John Stokoe's excellent Neo-classical building (itself now partially redundant). At the same time the Corporation carried out a restoration of the Keep, re-roofing it and reconstructing the battlements. Later, after the ruthless insertion of the railway (from the new High Level Bridge) between the Keep and the Black Gate, the Keep was further restored by Dobson for the Society of Antiquaries of Newcastle upon Tyne, which took full possession of the building in 1848; Dobson's characteristic early Victorian approach, involving much recutting and replacement of medieval ornament, is much in evidence.[17]

The most important building to be demolished as a result of what Mackenzie called "the improving spirit of the age"[18] was Anderson Place or the "Newe House", a fine sixteenth-century manor built by the merchant Robert Anderson, which was later enlarged to become the town residence of the Blackett family. Together with its formal gardens and much other old property, the manor fell victim to the celebrated 'Grainger-Dobson' central redevelopment of 1834-40.

Later in the century more historic buildings were destroyed, in most cases because of redevelopment, although the old Mansion House in the Close (1691) was a casualty of indifference and neglect. Auctioned off by the Corporation with all its contents in 1837 and later used as a timber warehouse, it was burnt down in 1895. Meanwhile, major portions of the Austin Friary, including the 'King's Manor', as well as the adjacent Barber Surgeon's Hall (1730), had been replaced in 1849-51 by the Manors railway complex. Additional railway development in this area in 1894 removed further sections of the old 'town wall', other parts of which, including the Stank and West Spital Towers, had earlier made way for the new Central Station (by Dobson, begun 1847). The Station also necessitated the demolition of Forth House, which by then housed the Grammar School.[19] Subsequent railway expansion nearby caused the destruction of Westmorland Place, the former residence of the Nevilles, situated near the present Mining Institute. Meanwhile, Newcastle's fine Georgian bridge was demolished 1866-73 and replaced by Lord Armstrong's technologically advanced but utilitarian Swing Bridge.

In 1880 a "great battle was waged" between the Corporation and antiquarians as the Carliol Tower was demolished to make way for the former Public Library in New Bridge Street.[20] The fact that this was a fine classical building (by A.M. Fowler), cleverly incorporating Thomas Oliver's Mechanics' Institute of 1866 at its west end (see fig. 63, p.197) and ultimately forming a fine group with Dobson's Divine Unity Church of 1853 further to the west, and, to the east, the Laing Art Gallery by Cackett and Burns Dick (1904), did little to appease the preservationists. Measured drawings of the Tower were commissioned in May 1880 and as late as 1932 a commemorative plaque was placed on the south wall of the Library. Some stones from the Tower are now displayed, rather pathetically, under the stairs on the ground floor of the present building.

Grainger and Dobson

The 'Grainger-Dobson' scheme (so called even though it is now known that Grainger was himself almost entirely responsible for the street plan and made much use of other architects as well as Dobson) created a coherent zone of impressive new streets including Grey Street, Clayton Street, Upper Grainger Street and their intersections.[21] It is of greater importance than any other eighteenth- or nineteenth-century development because of its scale and prestige, and was also largely responsible, with Grainger's earlier schemes, for creating the city's essentially classical identity. Its rather self-contained character persists in the currently fashionable description 'Grainger Town' and, as we shall see, probably saved it, but rather at the expense of other parts of the city's classical heritage.

Perhaps rather surprisingly, the scheme was appropriated as a model for the comprehensive redevelopment policies of the post-Second World War years. This was probably because of the element of clearance and renewal. After all, Grainger was "an improver" who, according to a contemporary observer, respected "neither the claims of tradition nor prescription", if they stood directly in his path.[22] Thus he removed not only Anderson Place but also two important modern buildings, the Theatre Royal – demolished quickly before its supporters could apply for an injunction – and the Butcher Market of 1808. He also demolished the historic White, or Market Cross, using it for building material in the formation of Grey Street.[23] However, Grainger utilised a great deal of open or derelict land, inserted much more than he demolished and insisted on superlative new architecture. Also, the scheme was essentially commercial and restricted to a high prestige area; indeed, it had the effect of shifting the emphasis northward and hastening the decline of the old Quayside, an effect later exacerbated by the building of the High Level Bridge (1846) and the Town Hall (1858). Nor was it greatly concerned with public buildings, although Grainger built the Central Exchange (see fig. 66, p.208), provided impressive replacements for the Market and Theatre Royal and commissioned (unexecuted) plans for a grandiose new Town Hall, or with the problem of communication routes, especially those linking with the periphery.[24] It must also be remembered that the scheme was a private, rather than municipal, initiative.

In the case of the architect Dobson, the fact that his work acquired almost totemistic significance for those involved in the city's later redevelopment has always seemed, to the present writer at least, something of a paradox. Dobson was not, as we have seen, principally responsible for the 1834-40 scheme. Nor can he be held accountable for the replacement of earlier buildings by his own. Moreover, in this context it seems ironic that up to the present time many of the works of Dobson himself have been demolished in their turn, mostly indeed through 'comprehensive redevelopment' during the 1960s and 1970s.[25] Others have been threatened with demolition, or remain derelict or disused.[26]

Furthermore, an examination of Dobson's work and published statements confirms that he was even further than Grainger from being a forerunner of mid-twentieth-century 'comprehensive' planning ideas. For example, his attitude to historic architecture was sympathetic, as can be seen when he was required to make modifications to existing classical works. Thus the pavilions he added to James Paine's Belford Hall, Northumberland, in 1817, closely resembled the original designs. Again, his proposed alterations to Seaton Delaval Hall, Northumberland, of c.1814-17, involving the addition of a new west wing to match the one then existing, would, if built, have been completed with corner turrets carefully matching those of the main block.[27]

Dobson was also a pioneer of the Gothic Revival in the North East with a tendency to antiquarianism, making measured drawings of medieval architecture throughout his life and collecting fragments from buildings demolished or restored. When dealing with medieval work his enthusiasm, perhaps even excessive enthusiasm, for the Middle Ages is obvious. For example, in about 1820, before the decision was finally taken to build the new Gaol in Carliol Square, Dobson formulated a proposal for the conversion of the old Castle into a Debtors' Prison, to be part of a walled complex which would have included a Governor's House, Magistrates' Hall, Gaol and House of Correction, all in castellated style. However archaeologically inexact, if built it might have prevented the later incursion of the railway. After this had in fact occurred, the Society of Antiquaries of Newcastle upon Tyne not only managed to have the Castle Keep restored, but also prevented the destruction of the Black Gate, then divided into squalid tenements and now isolated both by the railway viaduct and the new street coming from the High Level Bridge. However, on this occasion elaborate proposals by Dobson to remodel the Black Gate and visually integrate it with the Keep, via a series of arcades, were not accepted.[28]

Dobson was opposed to the building of the Town Hall, suggesting that the Bigg Market should be kept open (and gothicised) as an approach to St. Nicholas's; this sensitivity to location was present also in his restoration of Westmorland Place and complementary Tudor style design for the new College of Medicine adjoining it (1852).[29] And even though his plans for the redevelopment of central Newcastle of c.1824 would have involved the replacement of Anderson Place, with a monumental "civic palace" of his own design, he would have retained the avenue of trees then leading from Pilgrim Street to the house as a ceremonial approach.[30] In 1844 Dobson was involved in a personal campaign to save the historic Hospital of St. Mary the Virgin in Westgate Street (now Road), occupied by the Grammar School since Elizabethan times and now, with its important medieval Chapel, to be demolished for the widening of Neville Street. Dobson took the unusual step of writing to the Corporation arguing that the latter was unnecessary. He himself had planned Neville Street in 1835 as an important east-west route but now expressed regret that he had not aligned it further away from the Hospital. On his own initiative, he made a survey and plan for the restoration of the building, which he persuaded a nearby landowner to be willing to implement for "the satisfaction that the restoration of such a building would occasion to the public generally",[31] although to no avail. After the Hospital's demolition, the architect salvaged two of its columns for his collection, later re-erected in the grounds of the Royal Grammar School, Eskdale Terrace.[32] A gatepost was also preserved, which, after further demolitions and rebuildings, is built into the wall of the modern structure now occupying the site, near the Station Hotel.

In the important field of church restoration, Dobson adopted an essentially orthodox, rather than antiquarian, approach, based on the Ecclesiological desire for 'authenticity'. This can be seen in his partial reconstruction of St. Andrew's, Newcastle (1844), where he replaced the late Gothic south transept with a neo-Norman version to accord, as he saw it, with the earlier parts of the church. It culminated at Hexham Abbey in his 'restoration' of the choir and complete rebuilding of the east end (1858-60) which replaced, typically, an unusual late Gothic window and the ruinous but surviving Perpendicular Lady Chapel. This, it has to be admitted, provoked considerable criticism.[33] So too did his replacement of the late Gothic east window at St. Nicholas's, Newcastle (1859).[34]

We also find Dobson coming under attack from his friend and fellow architect Anthony Salvin over his 'Early English' rebuilding of St. Gregory's, Kirknewton, Northumberland (1860). Salvin considered the restoration unnecessary and inappropriate. For two years he kept up a correspondence with a rather unsympathetic Archdeacon of Northumberland, being particularly concerned for the ancient stone vaulted chancel and south chantry. Fortunately, these were not demolished, in spite of the efforts of the clergymen involved, but Salvin was still anxious when he inspected the church in April 1862, warning the Incorporated Church Building Society that:

> The arch between the chancel and nave is so small that the chancel cannot be of much use and probably at no distant time that curious building will be removed.[35]

On the other hand, in 1852, Dobson did carry out a sensitive restoration of the late Gothic Lady Chapel at Tynemouth Priory for the Duke of Northumberland, described in the architect's paper to the Archaeological Institute of Great Britain and Ireland in that year, which was illustrated with half size drawings of the delightful sculptured roof bosses. For his restoration of the circular window above the altar, Dobson used "a common rose window of the period" as the original tracery had disappeared, "leaving no vestige to determine the character of its form".[36]

Architects and Conservationists

By this time, in any case, a more reverently conservative approach to restoration was being evolved by those sympathetic to Ruskinian ideas. Local pioneers of this were Thomas Austin (1822-67), a pupil of Dobson, who undertook a scholarly restoration of Brinkburn Priory, Northumberland (1858-61), and his partner R.J. Johnson (1832-92). The latter's *Specimens of Early French Architecture* (1864) used French examples to substantiate his conservation principles and it was Johnson, a prominent member of the

Society of Antiquaries of Newcastle upon Tyne, who was employed when the Black Gate was finally converted into a museum for the Society in 1883. His work was appropriately conservative and unspectacular. Lacking archaeological data upon which to base a restoration, he re-floored the interior and, externally, limited himself to a new roof, re-using the existing pantiles, and a few necessary additions such as a new staircase on the east side. By the provision of a new bridge, he allowed himself to suggest a little of what he saw as the original picturesque effect.[37]

Johnson was part of the growing, if loosely based conservation movement, spearheaded by the Antiquaries and the Architectural and Archaeological Society of Durham and Northumberland, which we have already encountered in connection with the Carliol Tower. He was Honorary Secretary of the latter Society 1868-81 and served on a committee which monitored "the ruthless progress of so-called restoration", opposing, for example, the replacement of the east window at St. Andrew's, Newcastle, in 1866: "a few stones inserted would answer the purpose", they argued, "and thus preserve to the town one of those memorials of its ancient importance which are being rapidly removed".[38] The approach of Austin and Johnson was continued and developed by their pupil, the distinguished ecclesiastical architect W.S. Hicks (1849-1902).

Newcastle's evolution around 1900 and up to the Second World War was mainly suburban. Such central development as had occurred up to this time tended to reinforce rather than dilute the city's character. During the late nineteenth century the business district began to centre on Mosley Street and Collingwood Street, both being rebuilt with massive banks and offices designed by prominent local architects such as R.J. Johnson, F.W. Rich and the firm of Oliver, Leeson and Wood. Given the attitude towards late Victorian architecture in the mid-twentieth century, it is remarkable that these buildings have survived, even if, as we have seen, some are now disused. Pevsner warned of "the excesses of Victorian bad taste"[39], while the historian Middlebrook, who might be taken as representative of ordinary, educated opinion, wrote of "the heavy, ornate, stone built chambers and office blocks which appeared so 'palatial' and impressive to the Victorians – and seem so dull, pretentious and pointless to us".[40]

Between the Wars a few substantial, if unconnected, buildings were added to the central area such as Carliol House, by Burnet, Tait and Lorne (1924-28) and the City Hall, by Nicholas and Dixon-Spain (1928); these were in a contemporary 'stripped classical' idiom, as were the Magistrates' Courts, Police and Fire Stations (1931-32, replacing a design of 1874 by John Lamb)[41] and the Northumberland County Council Offices, completed in 1934, both by Cackett, Burns Dick and MacKellar (principal designer:

Robert Burns Dick, 1868-1954). The Tyne Bridge (1924-28) consolidated Pilgrim Street and Northumberland Street as the main north-south route, thus foreshadowing the demise of the Royal Arcade; proposals involving alternative positions for the bridge or a by-pass from it going directly to the Great North Road, the latter advocated by Burns Dick, were shelved. Moreover, the bridge accelerated the drift northwards and confirmed the status of Northumberland Street, rather than Grainger Street, as the main shopping street. This was also reflected in the Council's controversial decision of 1934 to build a scholastic and civic centre near Barras Bridge, taken after years of debate over alternative sites for a new Town Hall; these included Eldon Square (not demolishing the buildings), Exhibition Park, the Royal Arcade, and the area between Northumberland Street and Saville Row. The recently founded Newcastle upon Tyne Society (after 1930 the Northumberland and Newcastle Society) had campaigned for the Exhibition Park site (see fig. 42), as proposed by Burns Dick, a leading member, and favoured in an independent assessment by the distinguished architect H.V. Lanchester.[42] After further delays a competition for the design of the Civic Centre was held in 1939 and won by Collins and Geens of Bournemouth, but the War intervened.

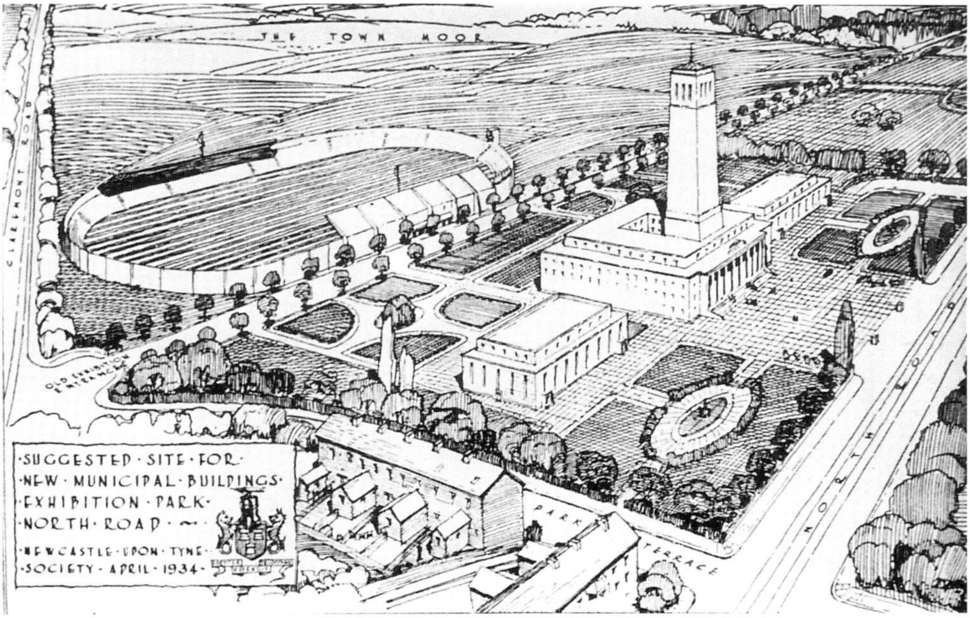

Fig. 42 Proposed site for new Civic Centre in Exhibition Park, Newcastle upon Tyne. (From *Report* of the Northumberland and Newcastle Society, 1934).

Burns Dick was the most gifted architect on Tyneside at this time. He was responsible for the architectural treatment of the Tyne Bridge and, indeed, his original scheme, involving enlarged pylons and gigantic Beaux-Arts style arch, would have provided the city with a truly magnificent approach. His 1924 *Plan for Newcastle* (fig. 43), drawn up with the assistance of the City Engineer, W.J. Steele, might, like the architect Thomas Oliver's plan nearly a century before,[43] have done much to alleviate traffic congestion and prevent some of the infamous demolitions of later years. It proposed an intersection from the Tyne Bridge, placed further south than the present Pilgrim Street roundabout, and feeding a new road to the Quayside. Also, as mentioned earlier, there would have been an axial route east of Northumberland Street (its northward section anticipating the present John Dobson Street) to Barras Bridge, and another north-south route parallel to this. An impressive feature of Burns Dick's Plan was a Parisian-style boulevard leading from Barras Bridge to his projected new Civic Centre in Exhibition Park. Burns Dick cited the names of Grainger and Dobson to justify his ideas[44] (as, for that matter, did the Councillors supporting the Barras Bridge Civic Centre scheme).[45]

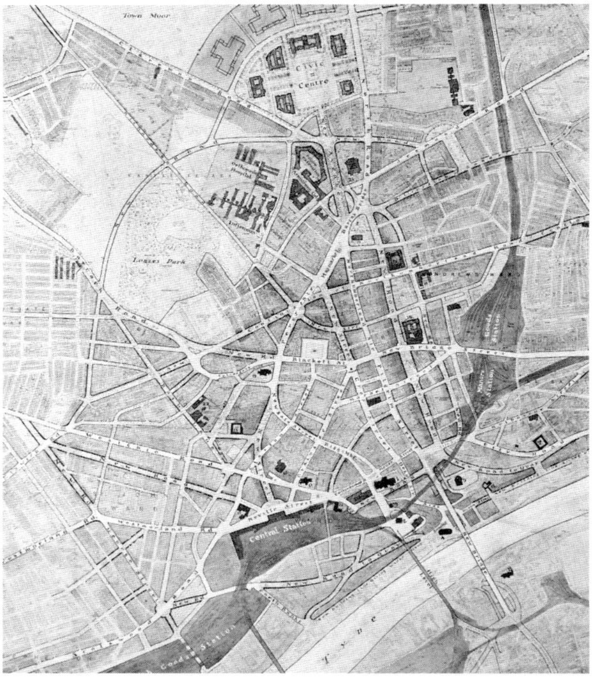

Fig. 43 Robert Burns Dick, *Newcastle upon Tyne: Suggested Plan for Future Development*, 1924 (detail). (Newcastle City Libraries).

Post-War Developments

The period after 1945 is of paramount importance in any discussion of conservation and renewal in Newcastle upon Tyne. The main activity came during the Labour Administration of 1958-67 and through to about 1973, including a period of Conservative control under Arthur Grey which, as far as planning was concerned, continued the same approach. Almost synonymous with planning and redevelopment at this time were T. Dan Smith (1915-93), who was Leader of the Council 1958-66 (see fig. 44) and Chairman of the Planning Committee, later jailed for corruption, and Wilfred Burns (1923-84), the city's first specialist Planning Officer, 1960-68, heading a new Department with the status of Chief Officer. Both adopted a similarly dynamic approach

Fig. 44 T.Dan Smith discusses a model of housing redevelopment for Scotswood Road, Newcastle upon Tyne, with Government Minister Dame Evelyn Sharp, April 1961 (*The Evening Chronicle*).

(although their personal relationship later became less harmonious).[46] Others, however, had earlier played their part. William Temple, for example, was Chairman of the Committee which produced the 1945 *Plan for Newcastle*, based on work undertaken during the War. Percy Parr, the City Engineer, was a qualified planner with the additional title of Planning Officer until his retirement in 1960. He had a major hand in the 1945 and 1951 Newcastle Plans which anticipated many features of the notorious 1963 *Development Plan*. There was also Charlton Curry (1877-1957), Leader of the Progressive (i.e. Liberal) Party, who was Temple's successor as Chairman of the Town Planning Committee until his election as Lord Mayor in 1956. Curry accepted the need for modernisation and that sometimes historic buildings had to be destroyed, but valued "these material contacts with the past"[47] and saw the function of planning as "to note what is there and the development already taking place".[48] The comparative lack of movement until the era of Smith and Burns can, however, be ascribed as much to post-war economic stringency and, perhaps, to Newcastle's geographical remoteness, as to Curry's gradualist views.

Newcastle's city centre, largely undamaged by bombing, had survived almost unchanged until the early 1960s as a coherent expression of Georgian and Victorian classicism. Unfortunately, far from being valued as an outstanding example of 'heritage', it was in the main perceived as an area "ripe for development".[49] At this time, what seems to have been a lack of confidence in the city's architectural status as a regional capital was reflected in the feeling that Newcastle was falling behind the times and needed a new image in order to compete. T. Dan Smith's notion of the "Brasilia of the North" – a phrase surely born out of the very parochialism and insularity which it purported to oppose – captured both public and political imagination. Smith demanded an international, space age city, moulded by the modernist belief that only new buildings could spearhead economic growth. As a result, once the decision was taken to rebuild along these lines, the process went ahead too quickly and too far: a classic example of the British syndrome in which a period of timid inactivity is followed by one of iconoclastic zeal.

This is not to say, however, that by the mid-twentieth century Newcastle's neglected condition and severe traffic congestion did not make a certain amount of replanning imperative. "Only by such heroic measures can the modern industrial city throw off the incubus of dirt, disorder, inconvenience and sense of inner dissatisfaction",[50] wrote Middlebrook. The 1945 Plan for Newcastle[51] caught this mood of post-war utopianism, with its modernist vision of a future city centre (fig. 45), but also addressed practical

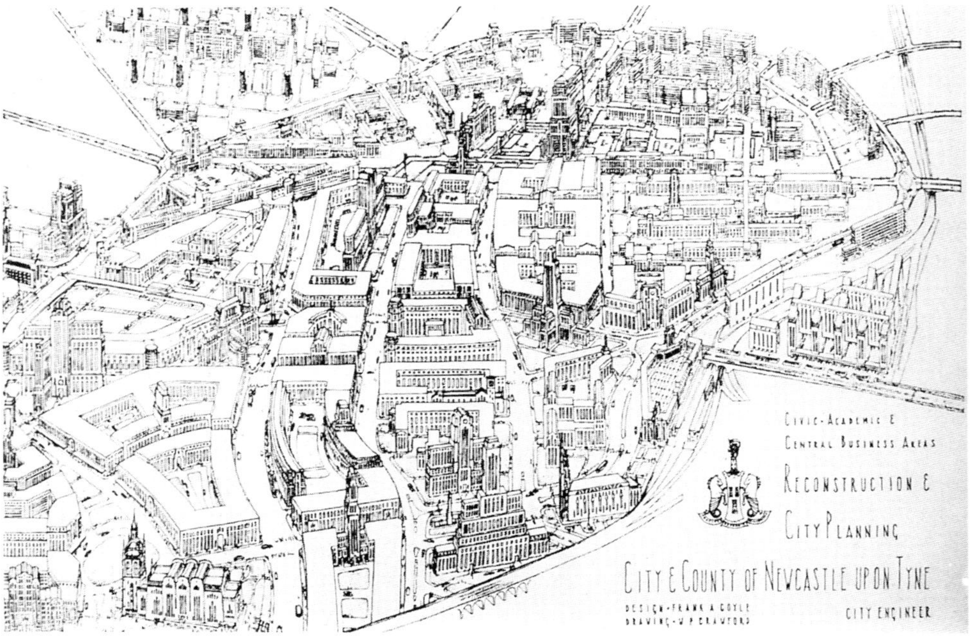

Fig. 45 Proposed reconstruciton of city centre, Newcastle upon Tyne (from the *Plan for Newcastle*, 1945).

problems such as the notorious bottle-neck north of the Tyne Bridge and the fact that, remarkably, Newcastle's principal shopping street was also part of the main route between London and Edinburgh. The Plan proposed a major new central ring road, linking the High Level Bridge and the Tyne Bridge, and joining the Great North Road at approximately the southern boundary of Brandling Park; from here the western section would have been linked to the High Level Bridge via Park Terrace, Queen Victoria Road, Richardson Road and a new road to Newgate Street and the Bigg Market. The eastern section, by-passing the city centre via a traffic intersection at the junction of Mosley Street and Pilgrim Street, would have resembled the present inner city motorway (east) although joining the Great North Road at a more southerly point. It would have destroyed the Royal Arcade and much other historic property, such as at Picton Place, but, as a result of passing closer to Jesmond Parish Church, would have avoided the demolition of Windsor Crescent and Victoria Square. Another new road, from the Pilgrim Street intersection, would have resembled that in Burns Dick's Plan as far as New Bridge Street, but then, veering left along the line of Princess Street, would have removed Dobson's Divine Unity Church; from here its rather brutal route to Barras Bridge would have gone right through Saville Row and Ridley Place. The Plan also extended the pre-War scheme for a Civic Centre and academic precinct (based on an expanded University), around Barras Bridge, adding a substantial "education centre"[52] south of St. Mary's Place. It envisaged the city's main shopping centre developing in the then comparatively run-down area bounded by Blackett Street, Percy Street and Northumberland Street.

The city's *Development Plan* of 1951[53] was generated by the requirements of the 1947 Town and Country Planning Act; it was also to some extent conditioned by the Act's new system of listing buildings of special or historic interest as Grades 1 (completely protected), 2 (protection necessary but not if, after representations to the Ministry, this would nullify replanning in the vicinity) and 3 (worthy of retention if this could be done without unduly affecting other wider interests). Twenty-two buildings in Newcastle had been listed Grade 1, all pre-eighteenth century except for the Grey Monument and St. Mary's Roman Catholic Cathedral. Twice that number were designated Grade 2, including Eldon Square, the Royal Arcade, the Holy Jesus Hospital, Leazes Terrace, the Old Jesmond Cemetery and the principal buildings in Grey Street (curiously, other sections of this street were graded as 3). There were one hundred and twenty-five buildings listed Grade 3 including the Northern Academy of Arts, the Old Infirmary and substantial sections of most Georgian and early Victorian streets (though not Brandling Place, Claremont Place or Victoria Square) and, rather surprisingly, a few later Victorian buildings such as the former Dame Allan's School in College Street (now the City Careers' Office), Lloyds Bank, Collingwood Street (both by R.J. Johnson) and A.M. Dunn's Neville Hall (Mining Institute).[54]

The Plan reiterated most of the proposals of 1945, apart from a realignment of the suggested western inner ring road to connect more directly with the Redheugh Bridge. The demolition of the Royal Arcade and Holy Jesus Hospital for the new Pilgrim Street traffic intersection was accepted as a regrettable but necessary sacrifice, although councillors again cited Grainger and Dobson as having planned what they believed was the finest city centre in the country: "we have inherited that, and it can be fitted in largely to the plan of the future".[55] There was some debate as to the exact location near Barras Bridge of the proposed Civic Centre (ultimately begun in 1958 to the designs of George Kenyon, the City Architect) but all believed that the new civic and scholastic precinct in this area would make an enormous contribution to the city's prestige. The most controversial element of the Plan concerned the projected shopping area between Blackett Street, Percy Street and Northumberland Street. Of the 1945 scheme for a road running from the Tyne Bridge east of Northumberland Street to Barras Bridge, only the New Bridge Street to St. Mary's Place section was to be retained, this to be consolidated into a shopping street rather than a major traffic route. The proposed continuation of Grey Street was abandoned. To provide better access to the shopping centre, a road from Eldon Square to Prudhoe Street (a street linking Percy Street and Northumberland Street) was suggested in its place; this was rejected because of opposition by Council members to any interference with Eldon Square.[56]

The much maligned 1963 *Development Plan* – the main proposals of which were first put before the Council in April 1961 – had to grapple with the problems of even greater traffic congestion, further economic decline and the perceived need for modernisation. It retained elements from 1945 and 1951, such as further civic development near Barras Bridge, University expansion, an education precinct south and now east of St. Mary's Place, a shopping area north of Blackett Street with a new street aligned further east of Northumberland Street (the present John Dobson Street) and a central motorway based on the earlier scheme for an inner ring road (east). The Pilgrim Street intersection, however, was completely redesigned to incorporate an underpass. Also proposed was a new central motorway (west) – only now being implemented – from the Redheugh Bridge to the Great North Road via the Haymarket; this to be linked to the eastern motorway by two major east-west routes, one parallel to the Quayside, the other passing underground from the New Bridge Street intersection to the Haymarket. Pedestrian and traffic routes were to be segregated wherever possible, and the motorways were intended to be visually interesting to pedestrians to prevent their feeling too insulated and enclosed.[57] The central motorway was seen as "a modern city wall" and the new Pilgrim Street intersection one of its major gateways.[58] Curiously, one of the more successful examples of modern architecture in the city, the Byker Wall housing development, also adopts the symbolism of a medieval city wall.

Other significant innovations were proposals for the regeneration of the Quayside and the comprehensive redevelopment of both Eldon Square, and an area adjacent to the junction of New Bridge Street and John Dobson Street, the latter involving a cultural plaza with a new Central Library and Museum overlooked by a residential tower spanning the road. Eldon Square was to be retained as an open space, surrounded by a prestigious shopping complex, with a hotel on the western side, a "tall, pencil-slim, aluminium-clad block"[59] (see fig. 46). As mentioned earlier, the 'Grainger-Dobson' central area of 1834-40 ("the first major comprehensive planning and redevelopment scheme"[60]) was regarded as a prototype for present policies. It seems also to have inspired the policy-makers to patronise eminent modern architects. Thus, Sir Robert Matthew was commissioned for the office block occupying the Pilgrim Street intersection, Sir Basil Spence for the new Central Library and Arne Jacobsen, who was personally recruited by T. Dan Smith, for the Eldon Square hotel. "Not since Grainger and Dobson left their proud mark on Newcastle, has there been a plan of such sweeping grandeur and magnificent vision", proclaimed the *Evening Chronicle*.[61]

Fig. 46 Detail of model of proposed city centre redevelopment, Newcastle upon Tyne, 1961. The scheme for Eldon Square is clearly indicated, while the new Public Library and proposed 'cultural plaza' adjacent to John Dobson Street can be seen at the top right of this photograph ("City Repro").

The city's new image was marketed through television programmes, exhibitions, newspaper reports and, not least, the effective use of models and photographs. In the overblown rhetoric of T. Dan Smith, "getting rid of the Andy Capp conception"[62] was paramount, even though this notion hardly fitted with the reality of central Newcastle's blackened but still dignified streets which, reflecting a nineteenth-century metropolitan ideal, provided "an oasis of rather sadly tarnished grace in the surrounding desert of dreariness".[63] During the 1960s a more international image was sought. Yet, curiously, there was considerable resentment at this time to what was seen as outside interference, as in the case of Ministers' decisions resulting from listed buildings legislation.

T. Dan Smith was a combative moderniser who saw reconstruction in terms of struggle and sacrifice. He had an undoubted interest in the arts, being fascinated by their capacity to express power and prestige. Hence, as we have seen, he wished to recruit 'big name' artists and architects. However, he seems to have had little understanding of the real value of historic architecture. On the other hand, Wilfred Burns's 1963 *Development Plan* showed far more sympathy for the history and character of Newcastle than is usually supposed, praising the "solidity and dignity" of its architecture.[64] Thus it proposed to conserve and improve the 'Grainger-Dobson' central-area, perceived, crucially, as a coherent entity, and other historic sites. The Plan was ahead of its time in designating conservation areas and even proposing the revitalisation of certain older areas of housing elsewhere. However, its main mistakes are equally apparent. These were the demolition of Eldon Square and the Royal Arcade, and the alignment of the central motorway (east) too close to the city centre. The situation was made worse by the over-zealous (if routine) demolition of 'outworn' Georgian and Victorian buildings – even Dobson's Jesmond Cemetery Gates only narrowly escaped destruction in 1971[65] – and by harsh juxtapositions of old and new architecture based on the modernist principle of dynamic contrast. Examples of this include the insertion of MEA House across Ellison Place (1974) and the inappropriate scale and character of buildings such as the Norwich Union office in Westgate Road (second phase, completed 1975), and the block opposite St. Nicholas's Cathedral (also 1975) which replaced the Town Hall and was originally designed to be part of an even larger scheme.[66]

The 1963 Plan's failure to achieve its aim of integrating the old with the new[67] was exacerbated by the non-completion of important developments, such as the Quayside regeneration scheme, the proposed cultural centre adjoining John Dobson Street, inherently dubious because of the removal of the fine group of buildings next to the Laing Art Gallery, and a plan to remodel the city's northern approach which involved a monumental arch across the Great North Road linking the Civic Centre and University. This would have become another of the modern gateways into Newcastle, with the motorist driving under a bridge of buildings to "emerge right into the visual excitement of the city centre proper";[68] instead, we now encounter a motorway flyover, a cutting, a concrete footbridge, and the bulk of the Civic Centre looming above. In the case of the proposed cultural centre near John Dobson Street, the new Public Library (by Basil Spence) and the high-rise block of flats were complemented only by a rather makeshift-looking and windswept concrete walkway spanning the street. Always little used, most of this is at the present moment being taken down (see fig. 47).

Fig. 47 The demolition of part of the John Dobson Street walkway, Newcastle upon Tyne, 1995.

Eldon Square and the Royal Arcade

Even the original scheme for the redevelopment of Eldon Square, with its high-rise hotel, was abandoned in 1971, because of cost. Earlier opposition to it, locally and nationally, had been unsuccessful; R.H.S. Crossman, Minister of Housing and Local Government, 1964-66, had only reluctantly accepted the demolition of the square as a "fait accompli"[69] and in 1964 demanded assurances of the Council's intention to preserve similar buildings in the central area. This led to a Council Report in November of that year which reiterated its "total preservation policy" and even considered setting up a special historic buildings fund.[70] However, in spite of this and the repeated invocation of Grainger and Dobson as planners and men of genius, no mercy was shown to the square – partly because of misapprehensions that the city possessed a superfluity of Dobson architecture, and that the square was actually being retained and enlarged as an important new focal point: "it is only the buildings surrounding the square that will be removed".[71] The square was also rather dilapidated and, like the Royal Arcade, lay outside the more highly regarded 'Grainger-Dobson' central zone. "It is only a facade at best", stated the Chairman of the Planning Committee, while a colleague observed: "In terms of planning, Eldon Square is a blank wall".[72] The present Eldon Square shopping centre, by Chapman Taylor (1972), is comparatively restrained and commercially successful but, significantly, does not have its principal entrance from the square itself. The retention of the latter as an open space and the survival by default of the eastern wing only serve as a further reminder of a particularly tragic and unnecessary loss.

The Royal Arcade was doomed by its location at the eastern entrance to Mosley Street and had been in decline for many years (fig. 48). However, the

Fig. 48 The Royal Arcade, Newcastle upon Tyne (by John Dobson, 1831-32), viewed from the south-west, 1963. The Arcade was demolished 1963-69. (Newcastle City Libraries).

redesign of the Pilgrim Street roundabout by Burns and Derek Bradshaw, the new City Engineer, included an ingenious scheme to conserve the Arcade's interior as a pedestrian thoroughfare while rebuilding the western part of the exterior in a different position; both elements were to be incorporated into the new office complex planned for the site[73] (see fig. 49). This was approved by the Minister. Accordingly, the portion of the Arcade to be rebuilt was demolished in 1963, its individual ashlar blocks being numbered and stored. However, in March 1966 the Council decided to completely demolish the Arcade, because the cost of reconstruction was

Fig. 49 Model of proposed office development, Pilgrim Street intersection, Newcastle upon Tyne, 1961, showing the incorporation of part of the Royal Arcade ("City Repro").

now considered prohibitive, especially in view of what was now seen as its distorting effect upon the new office development. Nor was it felt that the Arcade could be restored, even though, remarkably, an independent survey carried out by the architects Charlewood Curry in 1964 found that its surviving section was in "fair" or even "sound" condition.[74]

In June 1966, a deputation from the Planning Committee discussed the matter in London with the Minister, but Crossman regarded the demolition of the Arcade as extremely regrettable and a breach of faith.[75] However, after he became Leader of the House in 1966, a rather unsatisfactory compromise was reached whereby a seven-bay facsimile of the Arcade's original eight-bay interior was to be incorporated into the new office building with the restored facade. Ultimately, only the facsimile was built, the Council now claiming that restoration of the Dobson facade had become impossible owing to the irreparable deterioration of the stone already removed. The remainder of the Arcade was demolished in 1969, in spite of continuing opposition from the Georgian Group, the Royal Fine Art Commission, and locally. The resultant saving of money, and the sense of having outwitted clever London ministers, seemed to give particular satisfaction to councillors. One expressed the point of view already encountered in the case of Eldon Square:

> The Royal Arcade was an important building in the Dobson Grainger architecture, but there is still plenty of Dobson Grainger architecture left, there is still Grey Street, there is Leazes Terrace, there is Greenfield Place, there is Grainger Street.[76]

Ironically, T. Dan Smith saw the whole affair as a great conservation victory: "we fought and won the battle for the preservation of the Royal Arcade, albeit in a pseudo sense".[77] Meanwhile, the nearby Holy Jesus Hospital was reprieved only because of the redesign of the Pilgrim Street roundabout and subsequent delays in its construction; it still exists, isolated and encircled by the motorway.

Conclusion

The loss of Eldon Square and the Royal Arcade did more than anything to change attitudes towards further development, so that as early as 1973 the city's *Planning Progress and Policy* statement placed great emphasis on conservation, initiating the almost self-congratulatory tone that has characterised documents of this kind in recent years. Certainly there have been worthy achievements since this time, including the designation of further conservation areas and the restoration of important buildings such as the Castle Keep and Black Gate, Black Friars, and the Keelmen's Hospital. The Council has also carried out a major programme of stone cleaning in the central area, while the current 'Grainger Town Project' offers substantial grants for repair and re-use. The conversion of older premises for housing in the city centre has also been encouraged, although with limited success. Amenity societies are more active in Newcastle than ever before and the importance of the Conservation Areas Advisory Committee should not be underestimated. With the help of the Tyne and Wear Development Corporation, a scheme for the regeneration of the Quayside has at last been commenced, involving the restoration of the early twentieth-century CWS Warehouse (and a new 'Northern Architecture Centre' adjacent to this). Meanwhile, in this case as elsewhere, the more traditional 'modern' architecture of today is intended to harmonise with historic buildings (for example, Monument Mall at the top of Grey Street) and may well incorporate them into new developments; another example of this latter approach is Portland House, a new office complex on John Dobson Street built around Dobson's former Lying-in Hospital of 1825. This will face, incidentally, an extension and new entrance to the Laing Art Gallery, currently under construction. Whatever the merits of these developments, they show a degree of sensitivity to the past not seen for many years. Indeed, 'heritage' is now seen as a marketable commodity and there have even been efforts to promote the city as a tourist attraction in what is now seen as its 'post-industrial' phase.[78]

However, the distinction now made between 'conservation' and 'preservation' means that the latter term has become almost pejorative, with the former evolving into a flexible concept which can still permit a considerable amount of redevelopment, particularly if combined with the contemporary practice of 'facadism'. Even in today's more conservation-conscious atmosphere, in which conservation has begun to approach the status of an ideology, a feeling of disillusionment persists. Those involved in the planning and redevelopment of Newcastle have faced many difficulties, some fundamental and occasioned by the city's original haphazard growth northwards, rather than concentric development around a natural centre which could have been consolidated. However, they have not always approached their task with sensitivity, especially in the modernist period after the Second World War. Newcastle's leaders have oscillated between too short-sighted a view on the one hand and, on the other, rhetorical 'visions', as exemplified even today by the plans for 'Millennium Square', a futuristic education centre near the Central Station intended to explore new links between science and the arts.[79] This inconsistency seems to derive from a confused sense of architectural identity, which has exacerbated, as suggested earlier, the city's self-destructive tendencies. What is certain is that the process of renewal, in spite of the best intentioned efforts and a few glorious episodes, has been, and will continue to be, extremely difficult. Even so, as the patterns of change and redevelopment discussed in this chapter indicate, new developments which take positive and sympathetic account of existing elements are much more likely to stand the test of time. There are signs that, once again, this is beginning to be recognised. It seems to me that we should be aiming for the kind of architecture which has been described as "balanced, intelligent and humane, building on the best examples of the past", respecting alternative points of view yet seeking, above all, to achieve harmony.[80] A renewed reverence for the 'urban landscape' as it has evolved over the centuries, together with a more rigorous approach to architectural conservation, could be the starting point for this.

References and Notes

1. *Newcastle Now* (Newcastle upon Tyne City Libraries, 1987), p.45.

2. *Newcastle's Heritage: Planning for Conservation of the City* (Newcastle upon Tyne City Planning Department, 1987), p.8.

3. Kenneth Galley, "Newcastle upon Tyne", in John Halliday (ed.), *City Centre Redevelopment* (London, 1973), p.209; Galley succeeded Wilfred Burns (see below) as Newcastle's City Planning Officer.

4. *Planning Progress and Policy 1973, Newcastle upon Tyne* (Newcastle upon Tyne City Council, 1973), p.3.

5. Reported in *The Journal*, 8 March 1995, p.25.

6. Ibid., 26 April 1995.

7. See E. Mackenzie, *A Descriptive and Historical Account of the Town and County of Newcastle upon Tyne* (Newcastle upon Tyne, 1827), pp.293-94 and 302-4. The medieval church of All Saints is illustrated in J.R. Boyle, *Vestiges of Old Newcastle and Gateshead* (Newcastle upon Tyne, 1890), facing p.276.

8. Mackenzie, op. cit., p.361.

9. Ibid., p.113.

10. Ibid., p.112.

11. Ibid., pp.154 and 217.

12. Ibid., p.360.

13. A. Greg, "The Society's Building and its Architect", in *The Literary and Philosophical Society of Newcastle upon Tyne Bicentenary Lectures, 1993* (Newcastle upon Tyne, 1994), p.30.

14. Mackenzie, op. cit., pp.96-97.

15. Quoted by W.H.D. Longstaffe in "The New Castle upon Tyne", *Archaeologia Aeliana*, n.s. vol. iv (1860), p.110.

16. Mackenzie, op. cit., pp.96-97.

17. See *Archaeologia Aeliana*, n.s. vol. xi (1886), p.177 and T.E. Faulkner and A. Greg, *John Dobson: Newcastle Architect, 1787-1865* (Newcastle upon Tyne, 1987), pp.84-85.

18. Mackenzie, op. cit., p.112.

19. S. Middlebrook, *Newcastle upon Tyne, its Growth and Achievement* (Newcastle upon Tyne, 1950), pp.208, 215 and 217.

20. See *Proceedings of the Society of Antiquaries of Newcastle upon Tyne*, vol. 1 (1883), p.195.

21. For an account of the 'Grainger-Dobson' development see L. Wilkes and G. Dodds, *Tyneside Classical* (London, 1964), and T.E. Faulkner, "The Early Nineteenth Century Planning of Newcastle upon Tyne", *Planning Perspectives*, v. (1990), pp.149-67.

22. *The Daily Chronicle and Northern Counties Advertiser*, 5 July 1861.

23. Originally medieval, the Cross was rebuilt in 'Gothick' style by David Stephenson in 1783 and later carefully removed, stone by stone, from its site in Newgate Street to be re-erected near the new Butcher Market, above Mosley Street (1808). See R.O. Heslop, *The Market Cross of Newcastle, commonly called 'The White Cross'* (Newcastle upon Tyne, 1911).

24. Grainger had hoped that Grey Street would become the main north-south route and thought of extending it before financial problems intervened. See Faulkner, art. cit., p.161.

25. See the Catalogue of Works in Faulkner and Greg, op. cit., pp.98-109.

26. For example, at the time of writing, the former Cattle Market Office, Neville Street, the former Barber-Surgeons' Hall, Victoria Street (more recently a school), nos. 2-10 Grey Street (now being redeveloped) and St. Cuthbert's church, Bensham, Tyne & Wear.

27. Faulkner and Greg, op. cit., pp.15-16. During later repairs Dobson salvaged pilasters, mouldings, etc. from the fire-damaged building, which are still displayed on the ground floor.

28. Ibid., p.85.

29. The College was demolished c.1889, at the same time as Westmorland Place itself.

30. See Faulkner and Greg, op. cit., p.45, and Mackenzie, op cit., pp.200-1.

31. *Newcastle Council Minutes*, 1844, Introduction, p. xviii; an illustration of the building is in *Archaeologia Aeliana*, n.s. vol. xv (1892), facing p.198.

32. After his death, Dobson's architectural collection passed to the Society of Antiquaries of Newcastle upon Tyne, but, with the exception of these columns, no trace of it now remains.

33. See, for example, F.R. Wilson, "Hexham Abbey Church", a paper read before the Architectural and Archaeological Society of Durham and Northumberland, 23 July 1862 (reprinted in its *Transactions*, vol. 1, 1870 – see p.26).

34. See *Archaeologia Aeliana*, n.s. vol. iv (1860), pp.152-53.

35. Correspondence in Lambeth Palace Library (I.C.B.S. file no. 5529).

36. See J. Bell, *Collection Relative to the Meeting of the Archaeological Institute of Great Britain and Ireland at Newcastle upon Tyne* (1852, in Newcastle Central Library).

37. R.J. Johnson, "The Black Gate", *Archaeologia Aeliana*, n.s. vol. ix (1883), pp.53-56.

38. *Transactions of the Architectural and Archaeological Society of Durham and Northumberland*, vol. 1 (1870), Church Reports, p.2.

39. N. Pevsner, *The Buildings of England: Northumberland* (Harmondsworth, 1957), p.250.

40. Middlebrook, op. cit., p.316.

41. The 1874 design is illustrated in A. Greg, "Newcastle's Victorian Architecture: Patronage, Prestige and the Public Good", in T.E. Faulkner (ed.), *Northumbrian Heritage* (special issue of *Northern Architect*, 5th ser. no. 1, 1994-95), p.24.

42. The Newcastle upon Tyne Society, *Report* for 1929, pp.9-11.

43. Oliver's proposals were published in his *A New Picture of Newcastle upon Tyne* (Newcastle upon Tyne, 1831) and indicated on his *Plan of Newcastle upon Tyne* (1830); see Faulkner, art. cit., pp.152-54.

44. See C. Buckley and L. Walker, *Between the Wars: Architecture and Design on Tyneside, 1919-39*, exhibition catalogue, Newcastle Polytechnic (1982), p.8.

45. *Proceedings of the Newcastle Council*, 2 March 1938, p.482.

46. See T.D. Smith, *Dan Smith: An Autobiography* (Newcastle upon Tyne, 1970), p.58.

47. *Proceedings of the Newcastle Council*, 2 May 1951, p.1211.

48. Ibid., 16 February 1955, p.739.

49. Galley, op. cit., p.207.

50. Middlebrook, op. cit., p.315.

51. *Plan Newcastle upon Tyne 1945: Report of the Town Planning Sub-Commitee* (Newcastle upon Tyne, 1945).

52. Ibid., p.80.

53. Outlined in *Proceedings of the Newcastle Council*, 2 May 1951, pp.1187-1206.

54. See "Appendix to the Development Plan", ibid., pp.1207-10.

55. *Proceedings of the Newcastle Council*, 30 May 1951, p.68. It is significant that Charlton Curry had earlier commented: "I say to my friends who are interested in these ancient buildings that they should not forget that the greatest town planner this city ever had, Richard Grainger, destroyed more ancient buildings than any man that ever lived" (ibid., 2 May 1951, p.1212).

56. Ibid., 30 May 1951, pp. 74-85.

57. W. Burns, *Newcastle: a Study in Replanning at Newcastle upon Tyne* (London, 1967), p.34.

58. Smith, op. cit., p.51.

59. Ibid., p.57.

60. *The Development Plan Review 1963* (Newcastle upon Tyne City Council, 1963), p.4.

61. *The Evening Chronicle*, 11 April 1961.

62. *Proceedings of the Newcastle Council*, 3 February 1966, p.773.

63. T. Sharp, "The North East – Hills and Hells" in C. William-Ellis (ed.), *Britain and the Beast* (London, 1937), p.143.

64. *The Development Plan Review 1963*, p.74.

65. See *The Architects' Journal*, 1 December 1971, p.1220. The Gates were only saved by the intervention of the Minister following a Public Inquiry.

66. Illustrated in *Planning Progress and Policy 1973 Newcastle upon Tyne*, p.24.

67. For a perceptive account of Newcastle's post-war planning in relation to Conservation Areas see R.J. Buswell, "Reconciling the past with the present: conservation policy in Newcastle upon Tyne", *Cities* (August 1984), pp.500-15; Buswell argues that the city's approach has been insufficiently holistic.

68. Burns, op. cit., p.39.

69. R.H.S. Crossman, *The Diaries of a Cabinet Minister*, vol. 1 (London, 1976), pp.218-19.

70. See *Proceedings of the Newcastle Council*, 11 November 1964, pp.548-62.

71. Ibid., 18 July 1962, p.271.

72. Ibid., pp. 268-69; see also the comment in Smith, op. cit., p.55.

73. See the "Joint Report of the City Engineer and City Planning Officer", 7 June 1961, reprinted in *Proceedings of the Newcastle Council*, 28 June 1961, pp.155-58. The Pilgrim Street intersection was redesigned following a Public Inquiry held in June 1959; at this, interestingly, the Northern Architectural Association put forward an alternative proposal and in the subsequent debate stated that it had "always considered that neither the Royal Arcade and [sic] the Holy Jesus Hospital is of the first importance as a building and that their preservation could not be justified" (see *The Architects' Journal*, 6 September 1961, p.331).

74. See *Proceedings of the Newcastle Council*, 9 March 1966, pp.1100-1.

75. Ibid., 5 October 1966, pp.405-6.

76. Ibid., 6 March 1968, p.1361. Of the examples cited, Dobson designed only the lower east side of Grey Street.

77. Smith, op. cit., p.50.

78. See, for example, *Conservation Strategy: Some Possible Aims* (Report by the City Planning Officer, June 1989).

79. See *The Evening Chronicle*, 11 April 1995.

80. John Bold and Edward Chaney (eds.), *English Architecture, Public and Private: Essays for Kerry Downes* (London and Rio Grande, 1993), p.xii.

Balliol of Bywell and Barnard Castle

gules, an orle argent

Bertram of Mitford

gules crusily, an orle or

Bertram of Bothal

or, an orle azure

Eustace de Balliol

azure crusily, an orle or

Hugh de Balliol

gules, an orle argent, with an escutcheon azure, a lion rampant argent crowned or

Ingram de Umfraville

gules, an orle ermine, with a label of five points azure

Roger Fitz Richard of Warkworth

quarterly or and gules, a baston sable

Umfraville of Prudhoe and Redesdale

gules crusily, a cinquefoil or

Percy of Topcliffe and Alnwick: I

azure, a fess of five fusils or

Percy of Topcliffe and Alnwick: II

or, a lion rampant azure

Grey of Heaton and Chillingham

gules, a lion rampant and a border engrailed argent

Hilton of Hilton

argent, two bars azure

Sir Robert de Lumley I

gules, a fess between three popinjays argent and in the fess three mullets sable

Lumley of Ravensworth

gules, a fess between three popinjays argent and as many pierced mullets sable

Sir Richard Fitz Marmaduke

gules, a fess between three popinjays argent and a baston azure

Thweng of Kilton, later Lumley

argent, a fess gules between three popinjays vert

Sir John Fitz Marmaduke

gules, a fess between three popinjays argent

Lumley quartering Thornton

Thornton: sable, a chevron and a chief indented argent

Neville impaling Lumley

Neville: gules, a saltire argent

Colour Plate I. Arms of some prominent North-Eastern families. *See Chapter I, pp. 5, 10, 11.*

Colour Plate II. John Dobson, Lilburn Tower, Northumberland, 1828, from a painting by Dobson and J.W. Carmichael (the Laing Art Gallery, Newcastle upon Tyne). *See Chapter III, p.70.*

Colour Plate III. John Dobson, the Royal Arcade, Newcastle upon Tyne, 1830-31, from a painting by Dobson and J.W. Carmichael (the Laing Art Gallery, Newcastle upon Tyne). *See Chapter VI, p.126.*

Colour Plate IV. William Bell Scott, *The Building of the Roman Wall*, 1857, from "Scenes of the English Border", Wallington Hall, Northumberland (by permission of The National Trust). *See Chapter VII, p.153.*

Colour Plate V. Alan Sorrell, *Housesteads Roman Fort* (by permission of the Department of the Environment). *See Chapter VII, p.158.*

Colour Plate VI. Winslow Homer, *Perils of the Sea,* 1881, watercolour over light sketch in black chalk, 14⅝" x 21" (37 x 53.4cm). (© Sterling and Francine Clark Art Institute, Williamstown, Massachusetts, USA). *See Chapter X, p.230.*

Colour Plate VII. Winslow Homer, *Hark! Hark! The Lark!,* 1882, oil on canvas, 36⅜" x 31⅜" (92.4 x 79.9cm). (Layton Art Collection, Milwaukee Art Museum). *See Chapter X, p.232.*

Part III

HERITAGE AND REGIONAL CULTURE

Between our eastward and our westward sea
The narrowing strand
Clasps close the noblest shore . . .

A.C. SWINBURNE

(1837-1909)

Northumberland

VII

HADRIAN'S WALL AND THE NEW ROMANS

Paul Usherwood

'Adrianus murum duxit qui barbaros Romanosque divideret.'[1]

Seven to ten feet thick and between fifteen and twenty feet high, seventy-three miles long, with an accompanying system of turrets, milecastles and forts, Hadrian's Wall is an extraordinary testament to the might of the Roman Empire. Yet it would be a mistake to consider it solely in military terms. It has always been something more.

Even in Roman times the Wall had a symbolic as well as a military role. It served as a reminder to both the soldiers guarding it and the tribes whom it protected – the tribes living in that portion of Britain that had come under Roman rule and had adopted Roman ways – that they belonged to a great empire. It marked a clear boundary line between their world, the civilised world, and what lay beyond.

Nor was it only during the Roman Occupation, that is, until the fifth century A.D., that the Wall fulfilled this role. This chapter looks at the symbolic uses to which the Wall has been put at three moments in modern times: the early nineteenth century, when it became the object of scholarly research; the early part of the twentieth century, when it served as the setting of parables of empire; and today, when it functions as a piece of unproblematic past whose principal feature is the way that it supposedly enhances a certain type of northern countryside. It will be seen that although during the modern period the Wall's meanings have changed, its fundamental symbolic role has not. The Wall continues to define the space (social space rather than geographical space) of those who wish to identify themselves as superior, those who wish to see themselves as Romans rather than barbarians.

Research Wall

The early nineteenth century saw the Wall become the object of scholarly research – or as today's literature on the Wall would put it, 'scientific research'. Newcastle, the only sizeable town in the North East, was at the time enjoying a period of unprecedented prosperity as a centre of mining, trade and industry and this especially benefited the local middle-class intelligentsia (lawyers, schoolteachers, printers and coal-owners). This group was therefore keen to confirm its new-found prominence, which it did by becoming involved in various forms of appropriate scholarly activity, including Wall research. Consequently, one finds that the attitudes reflected in early nineteenth-century Wall research tended to be those particularly of the Newcastle intelligentsia, for instance, a pride in Newcastle's contemporary commercial success. It is no coincidence, for example, that the first truly 'scientific' account of the Wall, the Rev. John Hodgson's, published in 1812, is part of a guide to the contemporary town which otherwise is chiefly concerned with the burgeoning local coal trade.[2]

Even forty years later it was still common for scholars to discuss the Wall in relation to modern Newcastle's achievements. Thus in an article of 1852 on the fort at Pons Aelius, George Bouchier Richardson cites the fact that the Romans located their camp on the site of present-day Newcastle as evidence that some Roman general must have had a mysterious inkling of the town's future success.

> Did he not see these hills laved by the waters of a noble river, far broader and deeper than his own? – Did he not thus early discern that this must needs be then and after the great northern place of shipping, of trade, and import? – And that, at this place, before all others, must the river be spanned by the great northern highway.[3]

Early nineteenth-century Wall research also reflected the intelligentsia's politics, which at this time tended to be Radical. In a lecture of 1813 to the newly-founded Newcastle Society of Antiquaries, for example, John Hodgson calls upon his knowledge of contemporary industry on the Tyne to pay tribute to the Wall as a feat of construction. Nonetheless he is at pains to make clear that he is no admirer of the Romans.[4] Indeed, far from it: in his view the Romans and their allies amongst the British tribes were nothing more than "soldiers and an enervated peasantry sheltering their frontier from the northern invaders, behind the laborious, but cowardly, defence of walls and towers". His sympathies lie entirely with "the tribes of Britain contending for freedom upwards of 120 years, against the legions of the mistress of the world".

> It is not difficult to raise in one's mind an idea of some robust Pict, in attempting to scale the battlements of Pons Aelii, perishing on its glacis, by the javelin of a Roman soldier, and thus rendering the spot on which we now stand [this was the lecture-hall of the Literary and Philosophical Society, the Newcastle intelligentsia's main institutional base] sacred to liberty . . .

As the century wore on Wall research changed in line with the intelligentsia's politics. With the spread of enthusiasm for the idea of Empire in Britain in the second half of the century, support for brave Northerners gave way to admiration for their Roman conquerors. This shift is well illustrated by two paintings by the Pre-Raphaelite painter and member of the Newcastle intelligentsia, William Bell Scott. As its title suggests, the first of these, *Free Northern Britons surprising the Roman Wall between the Tyne and the Solway*, of 1843 (now unfortunately lost but known to us through an etching), took the side of the natives. Valiant Britons, bearded and blessed with Greek hero physiques, are shown overwhelming heavily armoured Roman legionaries.[5] By contrast, the second, *The Building of the Roman Wall* (colour plate iv), number one in the eight-part series that Scott painted for the central saloon at Wallington Hall, Northumberland, in the late 1850s, not only makes the Romans victorious, but it equates them with progress and order. In the foreground, a centurion is shown rebuking a group of insolent and unkempt British workers for cooking and gambling rather than getting on with job of building the Wall,[6] whilst further back, to the north, we see what happens to those who have yet to be subjected to the centurion's censorious but civilising gaze. Under a lowering sky an ill-disciplined Pictish horde led on by a crazed-looking priestess makes what appears to be a desperate and entirely futile attack on the Wall.

In mid-century accounts of the Wall, sympathy with the Roman colonisers rather than the oppressed natives became the norm: so much so that by the time the Rev. J. Collingwood Bruce wrote the preface to the second edition of his standard guide in 1884 it was axiomatic that the chief interest of the Wall lay in the fact that the "people of England are the successors of the Romans".[7]

> Through their instrumentality vast continents, of the existence of which Caesar never dreamt, have obtained the advantage of a well organized government; their rude inhabitants have been induced to engage in the pursuits of a peaceful industry; and the blessings of Christianity have been pressed upon their attention.

However, we should see the intelligentsia group as finding more in Wall research than simply a vehicle for expressing their interests and beliefs. They also found a pursuit which brought with it an image of authority and a disposition towards legitimate forms of culture which the sociologist Pierre Bourdieu calls 'cultural capital'.[8] Hence the claim which is repeatedly made in their writings that it is their form of antiquarianism which alone is worthy of respect. "The vulgar antiquary", argued John Hodgson in a lecture to the Newcastle Society of Antiquaries,

> while he walks among the ruins of a city, is struck with wonder, and fixes his observation most upon their extent, their state of preservation, the largeness of their columns, and the difficulty of lifting the massive blocks of stone into the several situations they occupy: he is an admirer of coins on account of their rarity, their age, the beauty of their rust, or from some accidental variety which marks them . . . But the judicious antiquary considers the various objects of his contemplation with a learned eye; and imposes value upon them in proportion to the quality of light they throw upon the several departments of the history of the people to which they belong. He seizes hold of objects ready to perish, and gives them "a local habitation and a name".[9]

But how to demonstrate judiciousness in relation to the Wall? One answer was to undertake excavation projects. This was what Hodgson himself favoured. During the summers of 1822, 1830 and 1831 he supervised a series of digs at the fort at Housesteads. So too, later in the century, did the Newcastle financier and politician, John Clayton. Much of the considerable fortune Clayton amassed in various railway and building ventures in and around Newcastle, he put towards purchasing and 'uncovering' stretches of the more remote, and therefore better-preserved, sections of the Wall in south-west Northumberland. This was a costly business. None the less it was an effective way of gaining prestige. Clayton found himself honoured by his fellow Newcastle antiquarians – he is the model for the stern-looking centurion in William Bell Scott's *The Building of the Roman Wall*[10] – and at the same time secure in his position as a key figure in Newcastle society.

Commissioning suitably sober-looking illustrations when it came to writing up the results of digs in books and articles was another way to win a reputation for judiciousness. Previously, Wall illustration had tended to take the form of decorative, picturesque vignettes, often as not complete with a figure of the pensive Gibbon-like philospher–antiquary musing amidst natural-looking ruins[11] (fig. 50). By the mid-century, however, such images were giving way to diagrams, maps and meticulous perspective drawings with

Fig. 50 "Nine Nicks of Thirlwall" in J. Collingwood Bruce, *The Hand-book to the Roman Wall: a Guide to Tourists Traversing the Barrier of the Lower Isthmus* (1884).

altogther different connotations. Take, for instance, the isometric study of a fort in Richard Abbatt's *History of the Wall* of 1849 (fig. 51).[12] Every trace of humanity, weather and foliage has been banished in favour of a flat, no-nonsense style seemingly borrowed from the fields of engineering or architecture.

Fig. 51 Isometric view of Mile Castle at Cawfields in R. Abbatt's *History of the Wall* (1849).

Yet merely paying for digs or showing a preference for a dry, learned, disinterested-seeming style of illustration was not itself always enough. To win recognition as a judicious antiquary, in the Hodgson sense, it was really necessary to be known to a wider, lay public. Thus one finds that in the mid-century, despite Hodgson's solemn warnings against vulgarity, members of the intelligentsia group played their part in turning the Wall into a tourist shrine. Indeed, the person who more than anybody must be regarded as responsible for popularizing the Wall was the leading Wall scholar of the period, the Rev. J. Collingwood Bruce.

Bruce's son Gainsford tells the story of how the first tour of the Wall by a non-specialist group came about. In 1848 Bruce found himself unable to undertake a planned visit to the standard Roman sites in Italy due to the revolutionary turmoil of that year so instead he made a systematic tour of the Wall, accompanied by the fourteen year-old Gainsford and two local watercolour artists, Henry and Charles Richardson. Later in the year an account of the tour was the subject of a series of five lectures at the Newcastle Literary and Philosophical Society. These were well received. However, Bruce found that "Many persons who listened to them were surprised to find that so magnificent a monument to the power of Rome existed within easy reach of their homes."[13] He therefore decided to lead a party of "ladies and gentlemen" on a "Pilgrimage by the Roman Wall" the following summer.

This duly took place and by all acounts it was a great success thanks in large part to the clever way Bruce combined scholarship with entertainment. There were brief impromptu talks at every stop and the occasional spot of light digging, but these were interspersed with jollity and fun. On Day One, for instance, the Pilgrims were treated to a banquet at the Castle Keep in Newcastle. "All went merry as a marriage-bell", Bruce records in his journal, "while we discussed and rediscussed the eighteen toasts set down for our consideration." The result was that not only did the Wall become known to a wider, non-specialist public, but that the standing of Bruce and his fellow intelligentsia group researchers in professional as well as local community terms was confirmed.

Frontier of Empire

In the first decades of the twentieth century the Wall found a new and quite different use. It became the setting for parables of the kind of selfless, disinterested service which it was believed was required by the British Empire.

The key text here, rather surprisingly, is a children's book, Rudyard Kipling's strange blend of fairytale and meditation on Englishness and English history, *Puck of Pook's Hill.* The book's most vivid chapters are set in the fifth century AD, the final years of the Roman occupation. They concern the predicament facing a centurion called Parnesius stationed on the Wall. Parnesius realises that the Wall is doomed; his masters in far-away Rome have "forsaken the Gods" and the Empire is crumbling. Meanwhile the raids of Vikings, or "Winged Hats" as he calls them, are becoming ever more daring and there is no likelihood of reinforcements from Rome. But what can he do? His sense of his identity is founded on the idea of serving the Empire which for him is symbolised in the sheer magnificence of "The Great Wall"[14] (fig. 52). He has no option therefore but to stay at his post and face his fate as stoically as he can.

In 1906, when *Puck* was first published, such ideas could not help but touch a chord with the book's readers, or rather their parents, numbering as they did the civil servants, army officers, churchmen and officials who ran the Empire. The service middle class had little difficulty in identifying with Parnesius's plight. For, often as not, they too felt beleaguered and isolated:

Fig. 52 H. R. Millar "And that is the Wall" in Rudyard Kipling's *Puck of Pook's Hill* (school edition, 1950).

oppressed, on the one hand, by memories of the recent, nearly disastrous, war in South Africa, and on the other, by the prospect of war with Germany, the new "Winged Hats". Meanwhile at home there was every sign that those in charge had lost their resolve. It is surely no coincidence that 1906, the year of *Puck's* appearance, saw the Conservatives plunge to disastrous defeat in a General Election.

Yet it was not only this particular fraction of the middle class at this particular moment in the century to whom *Puck* appealed. Over the next thirty years Kipling's story ran through some thirty editions. And even in the 1950s – indeed, especially then – when Britain's legions were being withdrawn from their far-flung posts, it continued to be influential. For example, Rosemary Sutcliffe's hugely popular children's books, *The Eagle of the Ninth* and *The Lantern Bearers,* successfully serialised on radio at the time, are both clearly very much indebted to Kipling's story.

One of the more surprising members of the middle classes to succumb to *Puck's* charm was W.H.Auden. In 1937 he and Benjamin Britten compiled a radio programme about the Wall for the BBC. The overall message of this, it has to be said, owes little to Kipling.

> That man is born savage, there needs no other proof than the Roman Wall. It characterises both nations as robbers and murderers. Our old historians always termed the Scots barbarians. To this I assent. They surprised the innocent, murdered them, laid waste the country and left the place. Julius Caesar, Agricola, Antoninus, Severus, etc. went one step further than the Scots . . . Whoever deprives an unoffending man of his right, is a barbarian.[15]

However, that was not true of the one bit of the programme which anyone remembers today, Auden's poem, *Roman Wall Blues,* which surely is very close to the spirit of *Puck.*[16]

Over the heather the wet wind blows,
I've lice in my tunic and a cold in my nose.

The rain comes pattering out of the sky,
I'm a Wall soldier, I don't know why.

The mist creeps over the hard grey stone,
My girl's in Tungria; I sleep alone.

Aulus goes hanging around her place,
I don't like his manners, I don't like his face.

Piso's a Christian, he worships a fish;
There'd be no kissing if he had his wish.
She gave me a ring but I diced it away;
I want my girl and I want my pay.

When I'm a veteran with only one eye
I shall do nothing but look at the sky.

Rustic Wall

Today, in tourist leaflets, the most widely circulated printed material on the Wall, there are traces of both the Newcastle intelligentsia's research Wall and the service middle class's frontier-of-empire Wall. As one would expect, readers are encouraged to follow up a visit to, say, Housesteads or Chesters by looking up articles in serious academic journals like *Archaeologia Aeliana* and *Britannia*, or by making a trip to the Museum of Antiquities at Newcastle University. However, they are also encouraged, by the use of Kipling-esque phrases like "The north-west frontier of the Roman empire" and Kipling-esque illustrations, often as not by Alan Sorrell, to think of the Wall in terms of the British Raj. The latter with their moody, John Piper-ish pen-and-wash manner and their emphasis on wind and rain and the general bleakness of garrison life can be seen as very much in the *Puck* mould[17] (colour plate v).

Yet while in this sense the research Wall and the frontier Wall survive intact, they also now perform another role, that of giving what might be termed a patina of scholarly authority and imperial grandeur to the Wall as an embellishment of the Northumbrian countryside. The 1990 National Garden Festival at Gateshead contained a vivid example of this other, rustic Wall: a replica of a fifteen-foot stretch of Hadrian's structure in its present ruined state standing in the middle of a fifty-foot piece of rough-looking pasture complete with a flock of grazing sheep – live sheep.

Significantly, the information panels made no mention of either the Romans or the Wall, or gave any indication of where the tableau was supposedly set. But then they did not have to. For many years there has been a tradition that it is the same relatively small area of south-west Northumberland, between the Irthing and the North Tyne, which, along with the coast line beside Bamburgh Castle and the immediate vicinity of Durham Cathedral ("Hadrian's Wall Country" and "The Land of the Prince-

Bishops" in today's brown-sign terminology) is always used to encapsulate the scenic beauty of the North East.

In their efforts to woo visitors, arbiters of North East tourist-worthiness long ago decided that the role of the Wall is to emphasise the essential quality of the region, which they believe is its roughness. As Nikolaus Pevsner put it in the Introduction to the Northumberland volume in his *Buildings of England* series: "Northumberland is a rough county; that is its great attraction".

> Rough are the winds, rough the moors, rough the miners, rough are the castles, rough the dolerite cliffs by the Roman wall and on the coast, rough is the stone of the walls which take the place of hedges, if you compare it with the walling of the Cotswolds, and rough seems even the smoother and more precisely worked stone under the black soot of Newcastle.[18]

When therefore, in 1989, *The Independent* ran a travel piece on the North East it was perhaps inevitable that their reporter should look for the real North East simply by following the line of the Wall.[19] In the event he was initially disappointed, for if one sets off from the west, as he did, the countryside for some distance is neither moor-like nor bleak. Indeed, near Carlisle it resembles, as he discovered, "the lushest bits of Dorset". It is only a little way to the east that it improves, that is, it begins to assume the qualities identified by Pevsner (fig. 53).

> This stretch was truly the high point of my ride: an arrow-straight road that rolled up and down the hills, air that smelt of clean, wet earth, and a view to the south that stretched on almost for ever. Except for a few passing cars, there was perfect silence.

Unlike *The Independent's* reporter, the painters, printmakers and sculptors who in 1988 were commissioned by the Laing Art Gallery in Newcastle to make works about the Wall were mostly resident in the region. Interestingly, however, this proved unimportant. They approached their task in the same frame of mind. That is, they too homed in on the same south-west Northumberland section of the Wall, the area of Walltown Crags, Housesteads and Chesters.[20]

Why always this stretch of the Wall? One reason certainly is that it is the best preserved. But that surely is only part of the explanation. It is also because at this point the Wall seems 'woven into the fabric of the landscape' (modern-day guides are fond of the tapestry metaphor) and at the same time utterly remote from any centre of population. Thus one finds that although there are interesting bits of the Wall in what is nowadays Newcastle and Wallsend, this is seldom acknowledged: so much so, in fact, that maps in tourist guides often suggest that the Wall stops short of urban Tyneside altogether.[21]

Not that the use of the Wall as a way of directing attention to the charms of a particular slice of countryside is new. Even in the early nineteenth century researchers took pleasure in 'Wall country' as it is now known. John Clayton,

Fig. 53 View of the wall from *The Independent*, 11 November 1989.

for instance, was keen to pay tribute to his illustrious forebear, John Hodgson, for his skill in conveying the beauty of the moors beside the Wall.[22] In an article on his own excavations at Housesteads he especially commended Hodgson's descriptions of the crags "bearded with witchwood, rowntree, ferns, bilberry, and heath . . . their heads everywhere perfumed with wild thyme, and garlanded with the little sunflower cistus."

> Those whose fortune it has been to wander through this solitude, on a calm and bright day of summer, when no sound is heard but the wild note of the curlew wheeling in the air, and the plash of the water fowl on the lake below, will acknowledge the truth of Mr Hodgson's description of the scene.

Nevertheless, whilst nineteenth-century writers duly took note of the countryside traversed by the Wall, it was really only in the 1980s that today's overriding emphasis on the rural aspect of the Wall became apparent. The reason for this surely was that at the time a thriving service sector was seen as the most likely cure for the North East's endemic economic ills. It was therefore felt that the region's nineteenth-century industrial past needed to be played down, either by pretending that it was somehow unconnected to the life of present-day Tyneside, as it was at the 1990 Gateshead Garden Festival, and as it is at the North of England Open Air Museum at Beamish, strategically placed twelve miles south of Gateshead, or by ignoring it altogether, as at the Metro Centre, purportedly Europe's largest shopping mall, on the outskirts of Gateshead. However, merely playing down the industrial past was not itself enough. Some kind of local past on which the region's identity could be based was also needed.

Accordingly, the only reference to the North East's past at the Metro Centre turns out to be one of the Centre's three themed areas, "Roman Forum"

Fig. 54 "Roman Forum", Metro Centre, Gateshead.

(fig. 54). Opened by Frankie Howerd, the TV comedian of "Up Pompeii" fame, this offers, in the words of the publicists, "classical and stylish boutiques selling unusual gifts and a touch of mystique". Why a Roman theme? Partly no doubt because 'Roman' smacked both of authority and of Mediterranean holidays, but also surely because that seemed a neat way of side-stepping the nineteenth century, a period which, it was believed, had seen the origins of so much of the urban squalor, labour troubles and unemployment that oppress the region today. Besides, 'Roman' has overtones of things rural – thanks to the Wall's now predominantly rustic image.

This may seem sad: the Wall lending prestige and credibility to a modern shopping mall. But maybe in a sense nothing has changed. The Wall today is only fulfilling the role which I have been arguing it has always fulfilled: that of separating Romans from barbarians, allowing a particular group to classify itself as superior. Perhaps all that has changed is that nowadays, unlike fifteen hundred years ago, no one has to think of themselves as barbarian. In the consumer society of today we are all allowed to feel that merely by purchasing goods and services labelled classical, stylish and unusual we can define ourselves as civilised. We are all Romans now.

References and Notes

1. Aelius Spartianus in the *Augustan History*, quoted by David Divine, *The North-West Frontier of Rome. A Military Study of Hadrian's Wall* (London, 1969), p.29. The words were used by Lady

Pauline Trevelyan as the label for William Bell Scott's painting *The Building of the Roman Wall* – see below.

2. See John Hodgson, *The Picture of Newcastle upon Tyne . . . including an account of the Roman Wall and a Detailed History of the Coal Trade,* 2nd ed. (Newcastle upon Tyne, 1812).

3. G.Bouchier Richardson, *Pons Aelii: The Site of the Roman Station at Newcastle upon Tyne, and the Course of the Wall through the Town* (Newcastle upon Tyne, 1852).

4. John Hodgson, "On the Study of Antiquities" read before the second meeting of the Society of Antiquaries of Newcastle upon Tyne, March 1813.

5. The original canvas measuring some twelve feet square has disappeared. We now must rely on a small etching in the National Gallery of Scotland to discover what it looked like.

6. It should be noted that modern archaeologists believe that, contrary to the impression given by the painting, the Wall's primary military purpose was to control movement, not to prevent it. Hence the liberal provision of gateways. See David J.Breeze and Brian Dobson, *Hadrian's Wall* (London, 1976), p.37. It should also be noted that influenced no doubt by the increasingly racist tenor of English culture at the end of the 1850s, Scott drew attention to the fact that the Roman garrison was composed of a variety of races by including a soldier of African descent in a relatively prominent position in the picture.

7. J.Collingwood Bruce, *The Hand-book to the Roman Wall: a Guide to Tourists Traversing the Barrier of the Lower Isthmus,* 2nd ed. (Newcastle upon Tyne, 1884), Preface.

8. Pierre Bourdieu, *La Distinction. Critique sociale du jugement* (Paris, 1979).

9. John Hodgson, "On the Study of Antiquities", op.cit. p.xvi.

10. In his notes on *Romans* for its exhibition at the French Gallery in Pall Mall in June 1861, Scott says that Clayton and J. Collingwood Bruce were the models for the centurion and one of the soldiers on the ramparts.

11. E.g. the illustrations in the various editions of J.Collingwood Bruce's *Hand-book to the Roman Wall.*

12. *A History of the Picts or Romano-British Wall, and of the Roman Stations and Vallum, with an Account of their Present State, taken during a Pilgrimage along that Part of the Island in the Month of June 1849* (London, 1849) (no author given but now thought to be Richard Abbatt).

13. Gainsford Bruce, *The Life and Letters of John Collingwood Bruce* (Edinburgh, 1905), pp.114-15.

14. Augmenting the awesome effect of Kipling's version of the Wall was a vast garrison town which he, fancifully, supposed ran along one side all the way from the Tyne to the Solway: "one roaring, rioting, cock-fighting, wolf-baiting, horse-racing town . . . from Tuna in the west to Segedunum on the cold eastern shore". *Puck of Pook's Hill* (school edition, London, 1950), p.174.

15. Quoted in Humphrey Carpenter, *W.H.Auden: A Biography* (London, 1981), pp.230-32.

16. Edward Mendelson (ed.), *W.H.Auden. Collected Poems* (London, 1976), p.121.

17. These were first used to illustrate articles on popular archaeology in *The Illustrated London News* in the early 1950s.

18. Nikolaus Pevsner, *The Buildings of England: Northumberland* (Harmondsworth, 1957), p.11.

19. Frank Barrett, "A Rough Ride in Roman Footsteps", *The Independent,* 11 Nov 1989, p.51.

20. "Contemporary Views of the Wall", Laing Art Gallery, Newcastle upon Tyne, 1988 (Donald Wilkinson, Ian Patience, Derek Dalton, Gilbert Ward, Paul Rogers, Tony Peart and Chris Wainwright).

21. For example, Northumberland National Park and Countryside Department, *A Visitor's Guide to Hadrian's Wall* (1989), English Heritage, *Hadrian's Wall* (1990), and The Countryside Commission and Forestry Commission, *Outdoors North* (Summer 1990).

22. John Clayton, *Notes on the Disinternment of the Mile Castle Immediately to the West of the Roman Station of Borovicius* (Newcastle upon Tyne, 1853), pp.1-2.

VIII

WHEN PARIS MEETS TEESDALE: THE BOWES MUSEUM, BARNARD CASTLE

Sarah Kane

The issue of identity is fundamental to any study of museums in the nineteenth century. Through the manipulation of architectural forms and the selection and arrangement of their collections, museums became classic sites for the production and promotion of visions of national, regional and local identity. Although such visions tended to be filtered through the ideology of the state, the municipal authorities or influential individuals, more often than not people concurred with these visions and looked to their museums as great sources of pride. The Bowes Museum, a collection of fine and decorative arts in a château-style building (fig. 55), founded by John (1811-85) and Josephine Bowes (1825-74) in 1869 and opened to the public in 1892, did not conform to this pattern. Although located in a region of Britain which was in the process of defining itself during the

Fig. 55 The façade of the Bowes Museum. Built in the neo-Renaissance style which had become the favoured idiom for public buildings in France under the Second Empire, the Museum has always appeared somewhat incongruous amid the rugged Teesdale landscape. (By courtesy of the Bowes Museum, Barnard Castle, Co. Durham, U.K.).

course of the nineteenth century, the Bowes Museum made no concession to regional or local interests, values or achievements, but instead produced a vision of metropolitan and continental taste and art production as transcending both the English and the regional.

The first part of this chapter looks at the notion of regional identity as it is manifested in nineteenth-century museums, especially French provincial museums, and questions whether museums had any role to play in the production of a regional identity in the North East of England in this period. The central section focuses on the Bowes Museum itself, on the motivations behind its creation and the ambiguous identities of its founders. The final part considers the efforts made by the people of Teesdale to appropriate the museum for themselves by donating articles proper to a 'regional' museum, and discusses the reluctance of guidebook writers to incorporate the museum into a visit to a part of the country which was still best consumed by tourists in the manner of the eighteenth-century Picturesque Tour. In this last section, there will be an attempt to explain the museum's ambivalent reception with reference to those elements which could be said to constitute the 'foreignness' of the museum, namely its French Renaissance architecture, the near total exclusion of works of the English school and indeed the incongruity of an essentially urban institution in the depths of the countryside.

National museums, regional museums, and the production of identity

Museums had an important role to play in the re-evaluation of the national (particularly medieval) heritage of European countries which followed in the wake of the French Revolution and Napoleon's rampages across the continent. Museums formed before this time in cities such as Vienna, Dresden, Florence and St Petersburg by the throwing open of royal and princely collections to the public did not fuel the popular imagination in the same way that museums of national antiquities were to do. In Germany the Germanisches Museum in Nuremberg, founded in 1852, and the Bayerisches Nationalmuseum in Munich (1854) both appealed to national sentiment by providing a record of Germanic artistic and material culture.[1] In France, Arago and Barante, arguing in favour of the state's purchase of Du Sommerard's museum of medieval and Renaissance artefacts in the Hôtel de Cluny in 1843, stated that such an institution would strengthen people's sense of national identity,[2] and they evoked memories of the Musée des monuments français, a museum in which Alexandre Lenoir had sought to tell the story of French genius as revealed in her sculptural achievements and as represented in the effigies of her heroes.[3] In 1850, the British Museum responded to concern amongst archaeologists that there was no national museum of antiquities in England by opening two small rooms for British Antiquities; it was not until 1866, however, that a Department of British and Medieval Antiquities was created.[4]

Running alongside this movement to dig up, preserve and display the relics of a glorious national culture were the parallel attempts of individuals and groups to find evidence of rich regional cultures. Such a movement clearly existed in England – the aims of the Yorkshire Philosophical Society, for example, founded in 1823, were to elucidate the geology of Yorkshire and to contribute "specimens from every part of Yorkshire to a central museum".[5] Yet it is in France – the country in which the Bowes spent most of their married life and where they built up their collections – that we find the fullest expression of this trend. Between 1830 and 1849, forty learned societies were formed (23 specialising in history and archaeology and 17 in other disciplines); besides research, publication and the preservation of ancient buildings, their aims included the accumulation of collections of local archaeology or natural history and the creation of museums. About two fifths of French provincial museums were created in this way. One such museum was the Musée de Picardie at Amiens, begun in 1855 on the initiative of the Société des Antiquaires de Picardie.

Throughout the century, successive French regimes attempted to gain some measure of control over provincial museums. From the time of Napoleon's decree of 1801 (the 'loi Chaptal'[6]) which stimulated the creation of museums in fifteen cities by distributing amongst them over eight hundred paintings acquired through conquests in Belgium, the Netherlands and Italy, the state developed a policy of dispatching to provincial museums works of art which they had either bought from the Salon or commissioned from artists, the number and quality of these 'envois' depending on the size of the museum and the importance of the city in which it was located.[7] Although provincial museums were obliged to express gratitude for the state's 'generosity', none considered themselves responsible for glorifying the nation, but saw themselves instead as heralds of local identity and indeed as places of resistance against Parisian attempts at centralisation. A sense of regional pride could be expressed in a number of different ways by a museum, but the most visually striking methods were the choice of a particular architectural form or the use of murals, such as, for example, Puvis de Chavannes' decorative schemes in four provincial museums, which are likewise powerful statements of regional identity: the artist intended *Ave Picardia Nutrix,* commissioned by the Musée de Picardie at Amiens in 1865, "to evoke ideas of the fertile earth of Picardy", whilst in painting *Massilia, porte de l'Orient,* commissioned by the town of Marseilles in 1867-69 for the Palais Longchamp, his ambition was "to express the hospitality to all boats and the warm welcome of a maritime town, of Marseilles, which is the gate of France open to the Orient".[8] An equally visual but perhaps less spectacular way of paying homage to local achievements was the depiction of local figures, in a specially appointed 'galerie des illustres', or on the façade of a museum in the form of busts or reliefs – the façade of the museum of Toulon, built by Allar in 1888, is dominated by the profiles of eminent Provençal artists, scholars and writers in ceramic medallions, and crowned by the arms of the town itself.

The other principal method by which a town could exhibit pride in its history, in the products of its soil and the works of its artists and scientists was through the composition and the organisation of its collections. The isolation of 'indigenous' works from 'foreign' works can be seen repeated in several museums throughout France and was a further way of emphasising the unique contribution which a particular town had made to the national culture. The Norman antiquary Arcisse de Caumont went as far as to state in 1864:

> Nothing is more precious than a collection of authentic local objects, and the intrusion amongst them of foreign objects, however valuable, can only have a harmful effect.[9]

Certain Southern towns such as Narbonne, Marseilles and Montpellier dissociated their museums of fine arts, which continued to be enriched by 'depots' from the state, from their archaeology museums, which came to be filled with the fruits of local excavations and around which were generated debates about the precise nature of Mediterranean identity.[10]

The situation in England was rather different. Although museums did exist in the provinces before the mid-nineteenth century, they tended to be either university museums like the Ashmolean in Oxford, founded in 1683, privately-owned museums like Sir Ashton Lever's eighteenth-century museum of natural history and ethnography near Manchester, to which only people with good references were admitted, or the private and semi-private museums of learned societies such as those of the Liverpool Royal Institution, founded in 1814, or the Cornwall Royal Institution, begun in 1818.[11] With a few notable exceptions – for example, a public museum and art gallery was founded in Manchester in 1823 on the initiative of local artists and with the financial backing of local businessmen[12] – the history of municipal museums in England does not really begin until the passing of the Museums Act in 1845, which allowed boroughs of over 10,000 people to levy half a penny on the rates in order to provide this service.[13] Over the next twenty years, several municipal galleries were set up, most of them absorbing the collections of local Literary and Philosophical Societies or other learned bodies. Given the subsequently patchy history of museums in the North East, it is ironic that it should be a town in this region which was the first to respond to the new legislation. In 1846, Sunderland Corporation took over the natural history, geology and numismatic collections of the town's Natural History and Antiquarian Society, set up in 1836, and by that time housed in the Athenaeum building in Fawcett Street.

The Corporation slowly built up the collection, keeping the emphasis on natural history but also adding items of archaeological and ethnographic interest. From 1858, the museum had to share its premises with the free library, an institution created this time in response to the Museums and Public Libraries Act of 1850 and based on the book collection of the Mechanics' Institute. Following the constant complaints on the cramped nature of both institutions, it was finally decided in 1877 that a new building would be erected on Borough Road. Designed by J. and T. Tillmann in classical style and opened in 1879, the building incorporated a museum and library on the ground floor and an art gallery, antiquities room, and rooms for science and art classes on the floor above.[14] The museum did not advertise its regional 'rootedness' in quite the same way as did many French provincial museums: it began a policy of collecting Sunderland pottery (or 'lustreware') only from 1897, and in place of a 'galerie des illustres', just two busts of eminent regional figures – the shipbuilder, William Pile, and the inventor, Robert Stephenson – were displayed in the entrance hall. Yet the mere fact of the museum's creation testified to the town's pride in itself and to its commitment to the instruction of its citizens in science and art.

By contrast, despite the encouragement of two of the city's most eminent men – William Bell Scott and William Armstrong – Newcastle was one of the last major cities in the country to establish an art gallery (as explained in another chapter of this book). The Laing finally opened its doors in 1904 with a loan exhibition, but it was far from being a major statement of regional pride or civic cultural aspirations. The same lack of commitment was again displayed in the case of the Shipley bequest. Joseph Shipley was a Newcastle lawyer who bought pictures through the 1870s, 80s and 90s at low prices (between £2 and £10), principally through the Newcastle agent S. Harris of 130, Pilgrim Street. By the time of his death in 1909 he had accumulated at his home in Saltwell Towers, Gateshead, a vast collection of 2,500 paintings; varying considerably in quality and type, the collection demonstrated, however, a marked taste for the Dutch and Netherlandish schools of the sixteenth and seventeenth century and for English nineteenth-century landscapes from Turner to Atkinson Grimshaw.[15] The city of Newcastle, which, by the terms of Shipley's will, had been offered the collection along with £30,000 for the erection of a gallery, was very reluctant to accept the bequest, feeling that a second civic gallery would represent too great an imposition on the ratepayers; one newspaper columnist summed up the general feeling: "A man may pursue throughout life a goodly hobby, but is it right that people having no interest in such a hobby should be taxed for its maintenance?"[16]

Public opinion swung decidedly against acceptance after the architect and antiquary W.H. Knowles had written to the *Newcastle Daily Chronicle* to corroborate rumours that works attributed to Rubens, Titian and Raphael were merely copies and after two independent museum curators had produced a report which classed only 361 of the paintings as worthy of exhibition and deemed none of them to be of first class merit. The Council, responding now to an anti-Shipley petition signed by a large number of local aristocrats and professional men, voted to reject the bequest. Three years having elapsed since Shipley's death, the collection was next offered to Gateshead; although public opinion was divided – Gateshead had no strong art tradition and its art school, opened in 1886, had recently been forced to close – the Council accepted the bequest on April 12th 1912, believing that with the £30,000 Shipley had left in his will they might erect a gallery that would be an "architectural adornment to the town".[17] The resistance of townspeople to the establishment of institutions which did not promise direct material benefits was a phenomenon by no means unique to the North East, but it did seem to be particularly prevalent here in the nineteenth century. The majority of Darlington ratepayers, for example, objected to the erection of a public library in their town in 1870.[18]

Thus while the Frenchman could look to his local museum for confirmation of his heritage and could gain encouragement from the artistic achievements of fellow citizens which he saw exhibited there, the 'North Easterner' had to look elsewhere for proof that he was heir to a rich and varied culture. Although important contributions had already been made to the historiography of the region – John Hodgson published most of his *History of Northumberland* between 1820 and 1840 and Robert Surtees his *History and Antiquities of the County Palatinate of Durham*, 1816-40[19] – the movement to reveal the region's identity by uncovering and appropriating its past gained further momentum towards the end of the century. This movement operated on two levels. On one level there was the scholarly historical and antiquarian research conducted by the numerous archaeological societies in the area. On another more popular level, later in the century, there was an attempt by writers and journalists to stimulate regionalist feeling through the narration of a northern past, founded less on mighty deeds and major historical events than on extraordinary stories and curious tales, on anecdote and legend, indicative of what has been described the "rebirth of Northumbria as a terrestrial unity".[20]

A glance down the contents pages of journals such as the *Monthly Chronicle of North Country Lore and Legend* reveals, besides the publication of dialect songs, examples of Northern wit and humour, and biographies of notable natives, a whole miscellany of articles of regional interest: visits to the region by famous figures, the exploits of local heroes, descriptions of places of historic interest, histories of local families, accounts of local pursuits, local trades, and local inventions, and stories of murders, mysteries and disasters. In Teesdale, the area in which the Bowes Museum is situated, a local identity was being produced in much the same way, in the latter part of the century in the pages of the *Teesdale Mercury*; the newspaper frequently printed stories about local heroes and strange occurrences in the region's past, many of them in dialect for the sake of authenticity,[21] as well as poems by the contemporary local poet Richard Watson,[22] who, writing both of the hardships of lead mining and of the beauties of the Teesdale landscape, won for himself a considerable local following. The marriage between a museum steeped in the culture of a modern forward-looking continental metropolis and a rural part of England which was searching for its roots was destined never to be a smooth one.

John and Josephine Bowes – the identities of the Museum's founders

The story of John and Josephine Bowes and of the creation of the museum which bears their name has been told over and over again since the laying of the foundation stone in 1869, but the story has at times been so over-romanticised as to obscure certain basic truths. Two examples from a century apart will suffice at present to give an idea of the overblown language often used in the narration of this familiar tale. The first is taken from an obituary of John Bowes of 1885:

> Together they rambled wherever paintings or curiosities were to be found, and spent as liberally as they admired, gradually acquiring a rare and precious collection of works of art. When the collection became unwieldy in its proportions, when every house and castle which they possessed was literally littered with articles of priceless value from every corner of the globe, and every square yard of walling was occupied by the spoils of travel, the Countess conceived the idea to bequeath the great treasure to the British nation...[23]

The second is taken from an article in *Art and Antiques Weekly* of 1975:

> Both [the lives of J. and J. Bowes] are tales of romantic purpose, a buoyant yet muddled saga of hastily seized opportunities dashed by financial reverses, a melodrama as bright at times and as dim as the Parisian stage upon which they met.[24]

A fresh look at the identities which the Bowes created for themselves as individuals and collectors should provide a clearer understanding of the motivations behind the museum project itself.

Despite having lost his claim to the title of Earl of Strathmore on account of his illegitimacy,[25] John Bowes had inherited from his father the family estates of Streatlam and Gibside, and was determined to live the life of an English country gentleman. Such a life generated wealth and privileges but it also entailed an obligation to protect the poor, advise the troubled, rebuke wrongdoers and extend hospitality to the deserving.[26] The need of the upper classes to distinguish themselves from the newly rich bourgeois led to the adoption of a code derived from Christian chivalry, so that, ideally, the English landed aristocrat was reverent to God, courteous to women, protective to his tenancy and yet at the same time tough. A typical example of this fusion between Arthurian knight and feudal baron was the first Duke of Westminster, who was seen to combine in just measure healthy aristocratic amusements with philanthropic deeds, having bred five Derby winners and also built on his estate of Eaton Hall, Cheshire, a number of cottages, schools, churches and village halls.[27]

John Bowes certainly indulged in all the pleasures of country life and earned a considerable fortune from the four Derby winners produced from the Streatlam stud and the exploitation of the rich coal seams which lay beneath the Gibside estate.[28] Yet whilst he took seriously the duties attendant on his position, and his paternalistic gestures were well viewed by the townspeople,[29] he fell some way short of the chivalric ideal. Bowes received numerous letters asking him to contribute to the building or restoration of local churches and to make donations to a variety of causes, from the town drinking fountain to a prize for Best Stallion at the local Agricultural Show. Some of his gifts were very generous – he gave £300 to Cockfield church in 1866 and promised to give £700 to St. Mary's, Barnard Castle, once he had seen a full architectural report – but his correspondence is full of laments at having to part with money and he was particularly reluctant to donate to bodies like the Wesleyans (whom he believed already sufficiently rich) or to ventures from which he could not hope to derive any direct benefit (he refused to give more that £10 to the Middleton Primitives, for example, as he had no property in the area).[30] Like many other wealthy landowners of his time, John Bowes represented his county as a Member of Parliament, successfully defending four elections from 1832 to 1841. Yet in spite of his staunch liberal views and his obvious concerns for the welfare of his constituents,[31] he tended to see politics as yet a further drain on his resources and when it came to the 1847 election, he refused to stand again, claiming that he alone had been carrying the financial burden of the Liberals in the constituency. Contrary to the high expectations of his supporters in the constituency, Bowes never made any impression as a political orator, and one obituarist was to write: "For it must be said that politics were not his *forte*, and that he did not cut a specially brilliant figure in the House".[32]

Fig. 56 Portrait of John Bowes by J.E. Feyen, 1863. Contrary to the evidence given in this painting, Bowes was not a very enthusiastic shot; he did, however, send out regular gifts of grouse and venison in an attempt to maintain good relations with his aristocratic neighbours. (The Bowes Museum, Barnard Castle, County Durham, U.K.).

Bowes tried to play the role of landed aristocrat as fully as possible (fig. 56), but his illegitimacy nonetheless proved a handicap to his being totally accepted into polite Victorian society. In 1847, therefore, he left England and settled in France, where, according to the contemporary writer John Lemoinne, Englishmen lost their 'national reserve' and were less inhibited and more informal in their dress.[33] Yet this move did not make his position any less ambivalent and he appears to have had difficulty carving out a niche for himself. His wealth and equestrian interests qualified him for membership of two of Paris's most prestigious clubs, the Jockey Club[34] and the Cercle de l'Union, but he did not apparently mix with other English expatriate aristocrats. Bowes's name does not crop up in descriptions of the fashionable literary and artistic salons of the time, and there is little to suggest that he was scintillating company: indeed, Thackeray, whom he met several times in Paris between 1832 and 1834 to discuss theatres, later expressed reluctance at having to spend an evening with him: "He has made me promise to dine with him and I must go to be killed by his melancholy gentlemanliness".[35]

If there is any justification for presenting Josephine Bowes as a smart and thoroughly respectable Parisian lady, as most writers do, it is because she herself fashioned and promoted such an image (fig. 57). Her origins were lowly – her father, Joseph Benoît Coffin-Chevallier, was a clockmaker and when she met John Bowes she was registered as an actress at the Théâtre des Variétés,[36] then part-owned by Bowes, an occupation which was at the time generally associated with that of the 'femme de galanterie'.[37] On intimate terms with Josephine after three months, Bowes installed her as his mistress first in a house on the edge of the Bois de Boulogne at Auteuil, and then at

Fig. 57 Portrait of Josephine Bowes by Antoine Dury, 1850. Rather than representing Josephine as an actress, Dury shows her as a respectable middle class woman and aspiring patron of the arts. (The Bowes Museum, Barnard Castle, County Durham, U.K.).

no 7, Cité d'Antin, in an area of Paris notorious as a haunt for bankers and kept women. In an article in *Paris-Guide* of 1867, Xavier Aubryet wrote that the Chaussée d'Antin – that 'Antinopolis' of flashy houses – had risen rapidly to prominence, but lacked both history and pedigree; in Aubryet's description of the quartier's social status, one can perhaps see a parallel with Josephine's own situation: "Nowadays the Chaussée d'Antin is radiant, prosperous, quietly revered and highly prized . . . like those successful people about whom one still loves to say 'You know that her father was only a gardener'".[38]

Josephine's marriage to John Bowes in 1852 gave her the opportunity to transcend her background and aspire to being a society lady, a challenge to which she rose with great enthusiasm. She had a taste for expensive jewellery which her husband gratified – in 1864 alone he spent 8,000 Fr on a pearl necklace, 3,650 Fr on a gold bracelet with ruby and diamond medallion and 6,840 Fr on a pair of earrings[39] – she had a six-seater box at the Opéra, a stylish 'barouche' with leather interiors, and dresses from some of the top Parisian fashion houses.[40] From 1852 to 1859 Josephine was engaged in furnishing two houses – the large townhouse of 7, Rue de Berlin and the former château of Louis XV's mistress Mme du Barry at Louveciennes (fig. 58), which Bowes bought her as a wedding present – in the fashionable historicist styles and colour schemes of the period.[41] As easily as she had once assumed the saucy and flirtatious lead roles assigned to her by the manager of the Variétés theatre, she now assumed the role of an aristocrat's wife, acting as both a society hostess and a philanthropist. She regularly gave lavish parties for over a hundred guests, but she never forgot the needy: in 1870 she sent money to the poor of Courguin for the purchase of food,[42] and in 1873 she gave instructions for the Streatlam grapes to be distributed amongst the sick people at the Teesdale Union and promised to

Fig. 58 The Château at Louveciennes in a photograph of 1862 by Pierre Rion. Built in 1685, the château was presented to Mme du Barry in 1769 as a gift from Louis XV. In May 1852, John Bowes bought the château with some land for 180,000 francs. (By courtesy of the Bowes Museum, Barnard Castle, County Durham, U.K.).

send articles for a bazaar being organised to raise money for the restoration of Barnard Castle church.[43] Yet her identity could not be fully complete without the acquisition of a title and the construction of a country seat; in 1868 her husband bought her a title from the Republic of San Marino so that she became, as one American writer has put it, 'the mail-order Countess of Montalbo';[44] in 1869 she laid the foundation stone of a museum that was to stand symbolically as her own surrogate country house.

The uncertainties of class and status which are visible in their identities as individuals are in many ways reflected in the composition of their collections. Charles Hardy has called John Bowes a 'natural collector', as if there were an uninterrupted continuum between the collecting habits of his youth and those of his married life. There was nothing 'natural', however, about his choice as a young man to build up a collection of old master paintings – collecting was simply another of those activities proper to an aristocrat, the sign of a gentleman, the cultural counterpart to breeding horses or shooting grouse.[45] Aside from a few slightly unusual purchases, like Sassetta's *A Miracle of the Eucharist* (fig. 59) and the altarpiece by the Master of the Virgo inter Virgines, both bought from the Duke of Lucca's sale at Christie's in 1840 under the advice of the dealer Edward Solly,[46] most of his

Fig. 59 *A Miracle of the Eucharist* by Sassetta, c.1423-26. Tempera on panel. The painting was bought for £6 15s as by Fra Angelico, but was re-attributed to Sano di Pietro by Bernard Berenson in 1897 and given its current attribution by R. Langton Douglas in 1904. (The Bowes Museum, Barnard Castle, County Durham, U.K.).

purchases were thoroughly in line with aristocratic taste of the time and are paralleled in other aristocratic collections of the region. John Bowes's first two paintings were the *Temptation of St Anthony*, then attributed to David Teniers the Elder, although now given to Saftleven, and Snyders's *Boar Hunt*; seventeenth-century Flemish artists were very well represented in the collections of neighbouring Raby Castle, and by 1870 the Castle possessed three fine genre scenes by Teniers alone, all bought by Bowes's friend and contemporary Harry Vane, and including his *Interior of an Artist's Studio*, purchased at Christie's in 1860.[47] Bowes's collection also included several Italian Renaissance paintings: amongst pictures bought between 1840 and 1845 were *The Entombment*, ascribed to Tintoretto, *The Martyrdom of St Agnes* by Domenichino (now demoted to 'circle of Domenichino') and a studio version of Raphael's *La Perla*.[48] By 1873 Alnwick Castle was filled with Italian Renaissance works, many of which had been bought by the Duke of Northumberland in the early 1850s; artists favoured by Bowes were amongst those represented.

Although Bowes later transferred his early purchases to the museum from Streatlam Castle, these amounted to only a fraction of the museum's contents; the bulk of the collection was formed in Paris in the 1860s and is of a somewhat different stamp. This disparity between the two collections can be attributed to two factors which are closely linked, namely the predominant role played by Josephine in the accumulation of the Paris collection and the particular nature of the collection as a 'museum' collection. There are countless cases of individuals in both England and France in the nineteenth century who brought about the creation of a museum by the donation of pre-established collections to a particular city.[49] However, it appears to have been previously quite unheard of for individuals to set out to build up a collection designed specifically for the purposes of display in a public museum. Although the Bowes Museum archives contain no absolute proof that this was their intention from the outset – indeed the archives contain no statements of intent at all concerning the museum – this is always assumed to have been the case from certain pieces of evidence, such as their purchase of a whole series of miscellaneous objects around 1860 from the dealer Jarry, and from a statement made by the Bowes' solicitor E.Y. Western in his *History of the Bowes Museum* of 1890 (see fig. 60):

> Some time previously to the year 1862 they formed the idea of not merely collecting for their own amusement but of doing so with the view of founding a public museum. From the time, therefore, of adopting this view, they systematically set themselves to acquire works of art which should be adapted to this purpose, in being representative of various classes of art and of various styles and periods.[50]

There seems no reason to doubt the basic truth of Western's statement, but it is not sufficient to explain the collection in terms of its final destination alone. Despite John Bowes's own assertions to the contrary – in 1874 he was touched to learn that a delegation of working people from Barnard Castle wanted to present him with a vote of thanks, but he declined to receive them, saying that "thanks only are due to my late wife, as the idea and project of the Museum and Park originated entirely with her"[51] – undue emphasis has often been given to the role played by him in the creation of the museum. The rather loaded title of Hardy's book *John Bowes and the Bowes Museum* spawned a number of

Fig. 60 Group of Russian objects bought from the International Exhibition of 1867: a panel carved by the monks of Troiza-Sergui, a paperweight of carved hardstones, an enamelled glass vase and a papier-mâché cigar case. At the Paris Exhibition, the Bowes bought a vast number of objects with the clear aim of gaining as wide a coverage as possible in terms of material, style, type, and country of origin. (The Bowes Museum, Barnard Castle, County Durham, U.K.).

articles referring to 'a man and his museum', 'the titanic struggle of one man' and 'a monument to one man's zeal'. Once the years of collecting were over, Bowes did indeed take it upon himself to organise the shipment of the collection to England: throughout the 1870s he sent several hundred letters from Paris to his estate manager at Streatlam giving very precise instructions as to where cases should be put, asking him to record the contents and arrival date of every case and begging him to handle them with care. He also took great interest in the museum's construction: he expected regular reports on the progress of the building and grounds from the site architect J.E. Watson[52] and the groundsman Bewick, had meetings at Streatlam with the French architect J.A.F. Pellechet,[53] and dealt with all the practicalities of sending over workmen from France to lay the parquet floor and ordering stoves for the picture galleries; even after Josephine had died in 1874 he pushed on with the completion of the museum, although it had now become for him "a most dreary and laborious occupation".[54] Yet, with the exception of the first major set of purchases (the large group of Spanish paintings bought through the dealer Gogué at the sale of the Condessa de Quinto in 1862),[55] and negotiations with foreign dealers in relation to the couple's tour of Belgium and Germany in 1868,[56] John Bowes appears to have played only a minor part in the selection and acquisition of objects for the museum. Indeed throughout the whole period of its formation (principally the years 1862-1873), there is no mention of their collecting activities in the private correspondence of John Bowes, save for a reference to their dealings with the glassmaker Emile Gallé at the London International Exhibition of 1871.

If John Bowes had been intent on pursuing the aristocratic mode of collecting begun in his youth, he might have attempted to follow the model set by fashionable Parisian collectors of the time, who included several other voluntary exiles such as Lord Hertford and Prince Demidoff. Among the innumerable private galleries recommended to the Parisian visitor in 1867 by William Bürger were those of Lord Hertford, Baron James de Rothschild, the Duc de Galliera, the Comte Duchatel, M. Lacaze and the Perreire brothers.[57] Allowing for obvious variations in individual taste, there were substantial areas of overlap in the composition of these collections. All the above collectors possessed a fine selection of pictures by seventeenth-century Dutch masters and almost all owned choice examples of French eighteenth-century Rococo painting and seventeenth-century Spanish art. Most also collected the prominent artists of the modern school (Ingres, Scheffer, Delacroix, Delaroche, Meissonnier and Decamps) and Lord Hertford and Baron de Rothschild enriched their collections with lavish examples of the decorative arts, particularly those of eighteenth-century France. This kind of collecting entailed the expenditure of vast sums of money but at the same time a high degree of discrimination. The extravagant Lord Hertford thought little of spending thousands of pounds at a single sale and was even sometimes prepared to spend thousands on a single item.[58] And yet he was also highly selective in his choices: he knew which artists belonged to the contemporary canon of 'great masters' – "I have looked it over [the catalogue of the Mayence sale] and find, as one always does, fine names – Rubens, Van Dyck and an F. Mieris . . .". He knew what he liked and always expressed strong preferences – asking his agent Mawson to go to the second Duke of Buckingham sale at Stowe in 1848, he wrote: "I think we must have the unmerciful servant by Rembrandt . . . I am also *very anxious* to have the Sybilla by Domenichino . . . ".[59]

John Bowes, however, rarely displayed the same urgency to acquire specific works by specific artists or craftsmen,[60] whilst Josephine appeared to value the activity of acquisition more highly than that of selection. In *Bricobracomania*, Remy Saisselin explains how, with the advent of mass consumption and particularly the establishment in Paris of the department stores in the 1850s, the attention of the collector moved away from 'consecrated objects' towards the luxury products of the modern city, a space in which the distinction between attractive consumer objects and objets d'art tended to become blurred. This new model of collecting was associated primarily with the bourgeoisie and was characterised by the accumulative urge, for the bourgeois now needed art "as only a glutton can require food – quantitatively".[61] Unlike previous models of collecting, it was also associated above all with women, who had been seduced by the theatricality of the department store and who saw shopping as liberation, an opportunity to leave the interior and lead a form of aristocratic life. According to Saisselin, the department stores fostered a taste for 'things' or 'bibelots' which in turn produced a unique bourgeois style of interior decoration, a style which he refers to, rather significantly, as the 'museum' style.

For Josephine Bowes, collecting did indeed resemble a shopping expedition. Throughout the 1860s she patronised a number of local dealers in art and 'curiosités', – but above all she used the services of A.C. Lamer of the Rue Drouot and Mme Lepautre of the Rue d'Amsterdam, who called almost daily at her hôtel in the Rue de Berlin. Archival evidence suggests these dealers used to leave a basketful of objects for Josephine's perusal, accompanied by descriptions and a list of prices; Josephine would put a mark beside the items which she wanted to buy and the dealer would then return later to settle the bill. A typical basket contained a few pieces of porcelain such as a Sèvres cup or a Meissen sugarbowl, statues in bronze, wood or marble, pieces of tapestry or panels of stained-glass, carved frames, a couple of paintings, and miscellaneous items such as doorknockers or keys. The result of these shopping sprees could have tended to the clutter and bric-a-brac of the average bourgeois interior, but Josephine averted the charge of being a "mere buyer of bibelots"[62] by having a vision for the collection; she bought, not for the purpose of decorating, as other women did, but for a higher purpose, one that became clear in 1863 when she built a temporary picture gallery with a workshop and curator's flat on a plot of land in the Rue Blomet.[63]

Josephine could never really expect to be seen as a Woman of Taste, for her background and her lack of any 'cultural education' precluded it; but she could avoid her collection being passed off as that of an ordinary bourgeoise, or – worse still – as that of a 'cocotte'. For a love of 'bibelots' was at the time as much associated with the kept woman as with the bourgeoise; Zola's Nana, for example, had a Renaissance-style hôtel in the Avenue de Villiers which was crammed with cabinets, caskets, bronzes, faiences, silks and tapestries. By taking the unusual step of gearing her collection towards a historical view of the development of the fine and decorative arts, she gave her collecting a purpose beyond mere 'accumulation' and her collection a prestige which it would otherwise have lacked.

It is difficult to determine whether the Bowes had a particular museum model in mind; they are certainly not known to have sought the advice of museum curators in France and England or to have studied other museums' collections.[64] And yet the encyclopedic ideal which lay behind the creation of so many nineteenth-century museums was very much in evidence in their collection. Apart from obvious gaps (the poor representation of works of the early Italian or German schools, the absence of Velázquez, Murillo and Zurbarán despite the large number of Spanish seventeenth-century works, the severe under-representation of the English school, the absence of works by the French avant-garde beyond a landscape by Courbet and one by Monticelli), there was certainly an attempt on Josephine's part to acquire examples from a range of genres (still-life, portraiture, landscape, religious and historical painting) as well as from all the major European schools. In the decorative arts, the breadth of the collection was particularly evident: a full spectrum of ceramics (1500 to 1870) was collected, from the products of Sèvres and Meissen to those of little-regarded factories such as Chantilly, Mennecy, and St Cloud, the greatest coverage being in the area of tin-glazed earthenware.

A wide range of tapestries was also acquired and the collection became able to illustrate the development of designs in the various crafts. The archive of chair coverings, for example, demonstrates the changing taste in upholstery fashions from the bold floral designs of the late seventeenth century through the popularity of animal scenes in the mid-eighteenth to the small repetitive flower motifs in vogue after 1770.[65] By the time the Bowes began collecting, the Louvre was essentially a composite of seventeen different museums (of painting, drawing, engraving, antique sculpture, modern French sculpture, enamels and jewels, Egyptian antiquities, etc.), the Victoria and Albert Museum had a policy of buying a very broad spectrum of objects from a wide range of different crafts, countries and periods, and the curators of the National Gallery had arrived at the realisation that it was more useful to the cultural education of the nation to acquire paintings from both the 'darker' and the 'brighter' periods of art history than to limit themselves only to canonical works by the 'great' masters of the past.[66] The issue as to whether Josephine Bowes was consciously trying to emulate these policies or whether the 'encyclopedic' nature of the collection was pre-determined by the miscellany of articles offered to her by her dealers has yet to be resolved.

If it were to be resolved, we might move closer to understanding why Josephine Bowes should have wanted to establish a museum in Teesdale at all. Most writers have seen it as a pure gesture of public-spiritedness, as a desire on the couple's part to share their vision of Europe with a wider world. Yet had they been truly "committed to the public domain",[67] they might rather have built their museum on Tyneside, a region from which John Bowes had derived most of his wealth and where the educational possibilites that could be offered by a museum were in strong demand.[68] A museum of decorative arts was of little practical use in an area in which the only industry that might have benefited from it, namely carpet-weaving, had already long since died out.[69] Whilst not wanting to deny the philanthropic side altogether, I would suggest that a less altruistic motive lay behind the project. A clue to this is to be found in some of the early accounts of the museum: under the title 'The New Mansion and Grounds at the end of Newgate Street', the author of an article in the *Teesdale Mercury* of 1870 wrote that Mrs Bowes had sold her château at Louveciennes "with the intention of some day replacing her late French abode with one of a somewhat similar nature in England" and that the handsome new building would be "in the nature of a museum"; an article in *The Builder* of 1871 made a similar point: "It is designed as much for a museum and picture galleries as for a mansion".[70] This slippage between museum and mansion is significant, for, although Josephine never intended it to serve as a house,[71] she would certainly have seen the possession of a 'country seat' as part of that process of self-legitimation in which she had been engaged since the time of her marriage. In this way she could be at once cultural hero and lady of the manor. It was somewhat ironic, then, that she had chosen the one style of architecture – the "revived French Renaissance style"[72] – which, although associated in France with important civic buildings, was associated in England both with hotels and with the country houses of some of the country's nouveaux riches.

The uncertain identity of the Bowes Museum

In 1848-49, the town of Barnard Castle was blighted by an epidemic of cholera; a report presented in 1850 to the Board of Health and based on the findings of a team of medical men revealed the sanitary conditions of the town to be appalling: insufficient water supply, defective drainage, poor street ventilation, overcrowding and squalor in working-class dwellings (which tended to be only feet away from pigsties, cesspools and slaughter houses), a single public burial ground, unpaved yards and courts and no public walks. Contributing to the report, the Reverend Dugard evoked a vision of a 'shameless, godless, and reprobate' working class, wholly indifferent to religion, morally and physically debased, and given to gambling, drinking, and vice. Whilst the medical officers suggested remedies to the physical ill health of the people in the way of an improved water supply and a new drainage and sewage system, it was two carpet-weavers who proposed a solution to the moral degeneration of their fellow workers:

> . . . owing to their being no place of public amusement, the time is too often spent in public houses . . . A public play-ground and baths are much wanted, the one would keep parties from the ale house, the other tend to personal cleanliness.[73]

In many other towns, the provision of libraries and museums was often seen as a way of keeping men from the ale house – indeed this motive was cited in debates surrounding the creation of both the Sunderland Museum and Darlington Free Library. The town of Barnard Castle, however, was already provided with these cultural facilities and there does not appear to have been any call to extend the services which they offered. The Mechanics Institute, founded in 1832 by H.T.M. Witham, had been transferred in 1846 into an elegant two-storey stone building in the Market Place, erected by public subscription in memory of the Institute's late founder and president; the Witham Memorial Hall contained a well-stocked library, and a spacious lecture hall, and was later to incorporate a music room for concerts. There was no municipal museum, but a museum with free public access had been set up by Witham in 1831 in a building adjacent to his home of Lartington Hall; as well as geological and mineralogical specimens, it contained "a valuable collection of paintings by the esteemed masters of the Italian and Flemish schools with others of more modern date" and was deemed to be "one of the most attractive and interesting institutions of the kind to be found in England".[74]

It is perhaps not surprising in the light of this that the Bowes Museum was never viewed by the townspeople in terms of its potential utility to either their technical education or their moral edification. This is not to imply that the museum was not well received. When the building was in course of erection, the local press enthused about its "majestic aspect" and its "grandiose proportions" and had nothing but praise for the grace, strength and solidity of its structure and its "lofty and imposing front"; the public opening of the museum on June 10th 1892 was accompanied by flowers and bunting, processions and public speeches, and the press notices which followed were full of references to "the palatial edifice" and its "varied and valuable contents". And yet apart from Edward Pease's passing reference to the museum as a "priceless boon"[75] and a public request that the museum be open on Saturdays to allow local workmen and daytrippers from Newcastle and York the opportunity to visit it – a request that was immediately granted by the curator Owen Scott – there was no attempt on the part of the town's elite (many of whom were trustees of the museum) to suggest ways in which the townspeople might usefully profit from the museum. Instead it tended to be seen rather in terms of a gift,[76] the generous and selfless gift of a couple whose example would be an inspiration to others, for "wealth so used is free from the vulgar taint, is honoured in its use, and beneficial in its effects . . ."[77] Indeed, the foundation of the museum had already been seen as a catalyst for a new and very costly building programme in the town in the early 1870s,[78] and it might well have been the inspiration behind Ellen Morritt's benefaction of 1877 which resulted in the erection of Startforth School.

Due to endless financial setbacks, resulting principally from the fluctuations of the coal trade, the museum was under construction for over twenty years. During this period a great deal of curiosity was generated as to what lay behind the hoardings, and on several occasions it was felt necessary to turn curious townsfolk away: in 1872 John Bowes, in a far from democratic move, instructed Dent to admit only the "principal Gentlemen in the Town" and their families into the Museum Park;[79] in 1880 the curator appointed by Bowes, Robert Harley, stated that he had not yet hung the pictures or written the catalogue and that the opening of the museum would be indefinitely deferred if his time was taken up with visitors both casual and serious.[80] Members of the public were finally admitted from 1887, but then only on Tuesdays and Fridays from 10-4 and on application to the new curator Owen Scott.[81] Harley's distinction between (genuine) interest and mere curiosity was a common one in nineteenth-century debates about museum visitors, but it appears here that once the curiosity of the locals was satisfied, there was little to sustain their interest: the attendance rate dropped from 69,696 in the year 1892 to an average of 10-15,000 in the decade that followed.

Giving the presidential address in the section 'Art History and Museums' at the first annual conference in 1888 of the National Association of the Advancement of Art and its Application to Industry, Lionel Cust of the British Museum spoke of the importance of depositing objects of national interest in the national collections, whilst paying special attention to "the preservation in local museums of local relics, whether works of local artists or casual objects found within the neighbourhood and intimately connected with the place".[82] The list of donations and bequests made to the Bowes Museum between 1880 and 1919 reflects current conceptions of what a 'local' museum should be and demonstrates the attempt made by local people fundamentally to alter the identity of the museum. Donations included objects of local natural history and geology, including collections of crystals and shells, exotica brought back from distant lands, including a Nile crocodile and the hairs of a Rhodesian elephant, and items of 'curiosity' such as a Brazilian bank note, a South African pipe and arms from the Crimea. They also included articles of local archaeology, objects of local interest (such as the old iron chains from the first suspension bridge over the Tees at Winch Bridge), and pieces celebratory of local figures (such as a bust of T. Emmerson Headlam, M.P. for Newcastle, 1847-74, by the Newcastle sculptor Rowe). Apart from several individual pieces of English porcelain, almost nothing was presented in this early period which in any way complemented the original collection.[83]

The same insecurity about the museum's identity and the possibility of its integration into the rural environment of Teesdale was indirectly expressed by the writers of tourist guides to the region. Since the eighteenth century Teesdale had attracted painters and poets in search of the Picturesque: Langley Dale was celebrated in a ballad by Surtees, Abbey Mill, Dairy Bridge and Raby Castle captured in the watercolours of Turner, and Rokeby immortalised in the epic poem by Sir Walter Scott. Alongside the Lake District and North Wales, Teesdale was a prime location for the production of such an aesthetic. Here was a landscape distinguished by its roughness, irregularity and abrupt variations – qualities by which Uvedale Price had separated the Picturesque from the Beautiful in the 1790s – a landscape which fitted well with William Gilpin's original definition of the Picturesque as "that kind of beauty which would look well in picture". Here was a region imbued with historical associations and rich in that other aspect of the Picturesque which revealed itself in the irregular forms and varied colours of castles, abbeys and ruins.[84]

Throughout the nineteenth century, guidebooks to Teesdale encouraged readers to visit the region as Picturesque Tourists.[85] Attention was continually drawn to the wild, rugged, or dramatic aspects of its landscape – 'the dark frowning cliffs' of the Cronckley Scars or the 'gigantic staircase of basalt' of Cauldron Snout – and to the unexpected variations to be encountered there: the Tees began as a peaceful mountain stream, became devious, then lakelike, then started leaping and bounding over rocks, and beyond High Force, where "the whole river plunges into a seething cauldron of Stygian depth",[86] it turned into a babbling brook. If the river produced unpredictable visions, so did the land:

> After the long tramp over bleak and barren moors, unrelieved by even a tree or any signs of cultivation the glimpse through High Cup Gill into the fertile and highly cultivated valley of the Eden is a striking contrast.[87]

And not only did writers persist in pointing out ideal spots from which to paint – the most popular of these evidently being the meander of the Tees near Wynch Bridge – but, in the best Picturesque tradition, the landscape itself was seen as a series of works of art: the view from the Flatts, which encompassed the ruins of Barnard Castle, the scattered village of Startforth, the woody valley of Deepdale, a bridge, corn mill, miller's dwelling in a grove, a bold crag and the rooftops of Lartington Hall was described in one guidebook of 1852 as "a scene worthy of the pencil of a Claude, to whose style the whole landscape is closely approximate".[88] No Picturesque Tour would be complete, however, without the possibility of viewing and even visiting the historic sites which over the centuries had become fully integrated into the landscape. Chief among these were Rokeby, and Raby Castle, but Streatlam Castle and Lartington Hall were also the subject of sometimes lengthy descriptions. Specialists might view the diverse elements of the landscape in isolation – the geologist could develop his theories by studying the curious rock formations, the botanist had the opportunity to discover an unsurpassed range of rare plants and flowers, whilst the historian and antiquary could explore the 'remains of feudal greatness' – but the general visitor was called upon to see the natural and the historical as complementary, as one complete experience.

The country houses and castles of Teesdale, most of which were open to the public by appointment, were deemed to be of interest because they were rooted in the countryside and in history. All writers were at pains to stress the antiquity of the buildings and often did so by quoting from the accounts of earlier authors, such as the early sixteenth-century antiquary John Leland. A sense of permanence was suggested by describing at length the noble lineage of the families who lived there, such as that of the Vanes and Nevilles of Raby, and a sense of 'greatness' by evoking memories of heroic deeds performed by members of these families, such as those of George Bowes, faithful supporter of Elizabeth I, who defended the town of Barnard Castle against Catholic insurgents in 1569. For one writer the past was clearly legible in the Barons' Hall of Raby Castle:

> Its extent produces that grand and imposing effect on the imagination, which at once recalls the manners of past times, and almost comprehends in the picture before you, that of the illustrious dead, in all their martial accoutrements, and attendant trains, performing with impressive solemnity.[89]

Tourists were invited to seek out this past, but were discouraged from paying any attention to the modern:

> The rest of the interior is modernised and of little interest, and visitors will feel, with Howitt, that 'when we step in and find ourselves at once in modern drawing-rooms, with silken couches and gilt cornices, the Nevilles and their times vanish. We forget that we are at Raby, the castle of the victors of Neville's Cross, and we feel that we are only in the saloons of the modern Duke of Cleveland'.[90]

In guidebooks written after the Bowes Museum came into existence, the museum was always mentioned – indeed it was referred to in a handbook to Barnard Castle of 1874, some eighteen years before the opening – but it generated none of the same enthusiasm produced by the wonders of nature or the region's ancient monuments. Most early accounts of the museum are restricted to a single paragraph – as opposed to the pages devoted to some other sights – and all contain the same basic core of information: the museum was begun in 1869 by the Countess of Montalbo, is built in French Renaissance style, was 300 feet long and 100 feet high and houses a valuable collection of pictures, porcelain and curiosities. The accounts are always matter-of-fact and include no information on the origins of the museum; nor do they cite examples of particular paintings worth seeing. Backhouse dispenses with the museum in one line: "The museum contains a large and beautiful collection of pictures, pottery, and other works of art, and is well worth a visit".[91] It is not that these writers lacked the necessary artistic knowledge to be able to name or describe paintings – Murray's guide, for example, gives a fairly comprehensive list of the old master paintings to be found at Raby and Streatlam Castles[92] and yet it is silent on the collections of the Museum. Perhaps it was felt that paintings by lesser and for the large part unknown artists such as Jacob Esselens, H.J. Hoet, Jacques Linard, P.B. Dandrillon, L. Tristan or A.J. Rizi could not compete with masterpieces by the consecrated artists of the past which lined the walls of neighbouring castles.

The reluctance of these writers fully to incorporate a visit to the Bowes Museum into a tour of the region must surely be attributable to the 'foreignness' of the museum, a foreignness manifested in the almost exclusively continental nature of its collections, in the neo-Renaissance style of architecture and in the peculiarity of the museum's location. The mid-nineteenth century had been a time of great sensitivity with regard to English art production. In reviews of exhibitions, the French had often sneered at English attempts in the realm of fine arts: Charles Blanc, for example, reporting in *L'Artiste* on the Manchester Art Treasures Exhibition of 1857, was outraged by the arrogance of the English who had given themselves a gallery equal in size and magnificence to the grand gallery dedicated to the old masters of Italy and Flanders; English painters might triumph in the lower regions of art and demonstrate extraordinary attention to detail, but they were wholly incapable of producing history painting or of achieving what the French called 'style'.[93]

English critics could be equally scathing about their own national art production, particularly in the field of the decorative arts: in an essay entitled "Our public art museums", J.C. Robinson claimed that around the mid-century English manufactures were as a rule "hideous and unattractive, ugly and vulgar as they were cheap and strong", in contrast to French art manufactures, which had benefited from the availability of extensive art collections at the Louvre and the Musée de Cluny in addition to well-organised schools of design.[94] Similar criticism was levelled at the decoration of the English courts at the International Exhibition of 1867.[95] An article in *Macmillan's Magazine* of the same year summed up the general mood:

> It is all very well for us to acknowledge the superiority of France in all matters of art and taste, but we don't exactly relish the acknowledgement.[96]

Newcastle was among several provincial cities which, in the second half of the nineteenth century, attempted to re-inject confidence into national art through the organisation of exhibitions. The emphasis of the Mechanics Institute exhibition of 1866 was on surveying the British school from Hogarth to the Pre-Raphaelites, just as the inaugural exhibition of the Laing Art Gallery in 1904 was intended to represent "The British school, Hogarth onwards". The limited appeal of the first two exhibitions of the Art Association in 1878 and 1879 was adjudged to be a result of the preponderance of continental exhibits. The Bowes showed little interest in English art of the past and no interest at all in the productions of the Pre-Raphaelite or Aesthetic movements which, by the the early 1870s, filled the drawing rooms of a number of industrialists on Tyneside.[97] Their only foray into the realm of English decorative arts was their purchase of some Worcester porcelain at the International Exhibition of 1862 and their acquisition of Minton, Wedgwood, Doulton and Copeland at the International Exhibition of 1871. (It must have been a conscious policy on Josephine's part not to buy works from English factories, because they were certainly available across the channel – Lady Charlotte Schreiber who formed a huge collection of English ceramics from the mid-1860s to 1885 acquired the bulk of her collection on the continent).[98] By the time the museum opened in 1892, the English collections had been enlarged by Susan Davidson's ceramics bequest of 1878 and Bowes's transfer of some of the family porcelain from Streatlam Castle, yet the predominance of the continental over the British was still very much in evidence and might even have served to reinforce for some visitors that sense of national inferiority in the realm of art.

Yet the composition of the collections probably contributed less to the 'foreignness' of the museum than did its architectural style, in combination with the remoteness of its location. The Bowes had taken a French urban style of architecture – indeed, the building quotes extensively from the Tuileries in Paris and Brunet Debaines' Hôtel de Ville at Le Havre of 1855-59[99] (fig. 61) and is perhaps also loosely modelled on Diet and Parent's Musée de Picardie at Amiens.[100] During the 1870s there had been intense

Fig. 61 The Hôtel de Ville at Le Havre, built by Brunet Debaines in 1855-59 but since destroyed. Its proportions and certain elements of its style were incorporated by Pellechet into the design of the Bowes Museum.

debate in the pages of *The Builder* on the issues of the appropriate location of museums and the appropriate style of architecture for the museum's location. In July 1873, for example, suggestions were being made for a museum in south London which should "tell morally, socially and politically on the mass of the population in the midst of which it was proposed to erect it"; the Elephant and Castle was deemed to be a perfect site because it was at the converging point of omnibuses, trams and trains, and was a densely-populated region.[101] In the same year, the following comment was made of the red-brick Bethnal Green Museum:

> The contrast between the plain, unpretending exterior of the building at Bethnal Green, and the opposite character of some of the articles at present grouped in it for exhibition [i.e. the Wallace Collection], suggests the reflection whether the outside aspect is not the more suitable of the two, more in keeping at least with the manners and associations of the district.[102]

In the context of these debates and at a time when more and more provincial museums were being built in indigenous architectural styles rather than the earlier-favoured classical idiom – in 1879 a Queen Anne design was chosen for the Ipswich Museum and a Jacobean style for the Derby Free Library and Museum – it is curious that no contemporary commentators brought out the inappropriateness of the museum's architecture to its English or more particularly its regional location. It has been left to more recent writers to highlight this anomaly in expressions such as "big, bold, and incongruous",[103] or "a Taj Mahal on the Tees".[104] And although fears were expressed at the time in the local newspaper that such an institution might be "completely lost to the world by being located in a town of comparatively insignificant importance like Barnard Castle",[105] no visitors to the region appear to have voiced any surprise at finding a characteristically urban institution in the middle of the countyside. It must, however, have seemed odd for visitors accustomed to the more 'natural' layout of paintings and objets d'art in country houses to encounter the rigid categorisations into school and type normally associated with the cultural institutions of the city.[106]

At the end of the nineteenth century, therefore, the Bowes Museum was an oddity, for it lacked the necessary attributes to be a 'regional' museum, but at the same time was too 'modern' and too 'urban' really to succeed as a tourist attraction (fig. 62). Over the years since the museum first opened, however, curators have in various ways attempted to 'redress the balance' in favour of the English and the regional in order to give the museum a wider appeal: gifts and bequests of British furniture, pictures, silver and ceramics have always been welcomed and from 1952 to 1972, examples of Baroque, Palladian and Rococo pannelling were acquired for the purpose of setting up nine English Period Rooms. When Michael Kirkby joined the museum in 1971, he was anxious that the museum collect material that would build up a clear picture of the industrial and social life of the district and he insisted that the museum "develop its regional responsibility and display the natural and human history of Teesdale";[107] in 1972 he began to redevelop five of the museum's vaults to this end and invited the Teesdale Records Society to use the museum as their base. Yet these changes little altered the essential character of the museum. Whilst most locals remain proud, but largely uninterested in the 'treasure house' on their doorstep, tourists from all over the world now make a pilgrimage to this anomalous museum, attracted by the very same qualities that were apt to bemuse and alienate people a hundred years ago.

Fig. 62 The Entrance Hall of the Bowes Museum, c.1910. At that time, the hall was hung with examples from the museum's large collection of sixteenth-, seventeenth- and eighteenth-century European tapestry. (By courtesy of the Bowes Museum, Barnard Castle, County Durham, U.K.).

References and Notes

N.B. Much of the information on French provincial museums was gleaned from a conference held at the Musée d'Orsay in April 1994 – 'Le Musée en France depuis 1815: territoires et fonctions.' Translations of French quotations are in most cases my own.

Abbreviations:

BMA = Bowes Museum Archives

TM = *The Teesdale Mercury*

JB = John Bowes

1. See C.R. Richards, *Industrial Art and the Museum* (New York, 1927).

2. For analyses of Arago and Barante's parliamentary speeches, see S. Kane, "The First Three Decades of the Musée de Cluny: From Antiquarianism to Art History" (MA dissertation, Courtauld Institute, 1993).

3. The museum, which opened to the public in 1795, had a powerful effect on the national consciousness, but was forced to close in 1816. Its history is told in L. Courajod, *Alexandre Lenoir: Son Journal et le Musée des monuments français*, vol. 1 (1878); vols. 2 and 3 (1886).

4. See J.M.A. Thompson (ed.), *The Manual of Curatorship* (Oxford, 1992), p.27.

5. S. Pearce, *Museums, Objects and Collections* (Leicester, 1992), p.101.

6. A few embryonic provincial museums had already been formed on local initiative long before this point (Besancon, 1694; Arles, 1785; Dijon, 1781), but the loi Chaptal marked the beginning of a consistent state policy with regard to museums in the provinces. For the

decree of 1/9/1801 and its implications, see D.J. Sherman, *Worthy Monuments: Art Museums and the Politics of Culture in Nineteenth Century France* (Cambridge, Mass., 1989), pp.24-26.

7. It is worth noting here the 'regional' content of these 'envois'. During the period of the Restoration and the July Monarchy (1815-48), provincial museums often received large-scale history paintings commissioned by the government and bearing some connection to local history. During the Second Empire (1852-1870) there appeared to be a trend towards sending works relating to one region of France to museums a great distance away, but, as Sherman has noted, there are too many exceptions for this to be seen as a deliberate policy to inculcate patriotic feelings (see Sherman, op.cit., p.35).

8. From an interview by Paul Gigou with Puvis de Chavannes in *Le Figaro*, 23 July 1892 (quoted in G.M. Tapley, *The Mural Paintings of Puvis de Chavannes*, 1979, p. 119). The celebration of local genius in art and industry was also the inspiration behind *Le Rhône et la Saône* of 1886 for the Palais St. Pierre at Lyon and *La Poterie* and *La Céramique* of 1891 for the Musée des Beaux-Arts at Rouen.

9. Quoted in Musée d'Orsay, op cit., p.17.

10. Towards the end of the century, in an attempt to preserve records of local customs and traditions which were fast disappearing, museums also began to build up regional ethnographical collections: by 1896, 28 French museums had ethnography departments.

11. For other private and semi-private museums, see the chapter "Entry as privilege" in K. Hudson, *A Social History of Museums* (London, 1976). For the museums of learned societies, see J.M.A. Thompson, op.cit. p.26.

12. See *Palaces of Art: Art Galleries in Britain 1790-1990*, exh. cat., Dulwich College Picture Gallery (1991-92), p.84.

13. See Acts of Parliament, 21 July 1845 (Cap. XLIII): An Act for encouraging the Establishment of Museums in large Towns. In 1850 the act was updated to include libraries as well; see Acts of Parliament, 14 August 1850 (Cap LXV): An Act for enabling Town Councils to establish Public Libraries and Museums.

14. See *The Builder*, 29 November 1879, pp.1316-18, for a plan of the layout of Sunderland Museum and Free Library and an engraving of its elevation.

15. See the small archive of auction and sale catalogues (1872-1907), letters to dealers (S. Harris, H. Gilpin and others) and receipts for pictures purchased (1869-1908) at Gateshead Public Library, Local Studies Section, under the reference 70/6.

16. See Oxberry, "The Shipley Bequest", p.20, album of newspaper cuttings, Gateshead Public Library, Local Studies Section. Cutting from which this quotation taken is dated 1 April 1909.

17. The two men chosen to examine the collection were Sir Walter Armstrong, director of the National Gallery of Ireland, and Edward Rimbault Dibdin, curator of the Walker Art Gallery in Liverpool. The 361 paintings they selected, along with 142 further paintings, chosen from his collection by two local artists, formed the nucleus of the Shipley Art Gallery. Built in classical style by A. Stockwell on Prince Consort Road in Gateshead, the gallery opened to the public on 14 September 1917 and attracted 83,000 visitors in its first year. For a fuller account of the debates over the Shipley Bequest, see A. Lang, "Joseph Shipley and his Art Gallery", unpublished dissertation, Shipley Art Gallery.

18. In 1880, Edward Pease died, leaving £10,000 for a library or for education purposes; in 1883, his trustees offered to provide a site and build and equip the library if the town adopted the Library Act. This time a majority of townspeople voted in favour, and the library opened on 23 October 1885 amid much jubilation. See V. Redhead, "Darlington Public Library: A Centenary History 1885-1985", dissertation printed by Durham County Council (1985).

19. Research had been undertaken into the history of Durham since the sixteenth century (Christopher Watson's unpublished four-volume "Books of Durham History" of 1573-74,

Dodsworth and Mickleton's collections for a history of the county in the seventeenth century and the Spearmans' attack on the powers of the Prince Bishops, written up as *An Enquiry into the Ancient and Present State of the County Palatinate of Durham* in 1729), but it was not until 1785 that a genuine county history appeared in the form of William Hutchinson's *History and Antiquities of the County Palatinate of Durham* (1785-94). The inadequacies and inaccuracies of Hutchinson's work left the field open for the more comprehensive histories of Surtees and later Fordyce (1857). Histories of Northumberland were written by W. Hutchinson (1785-94) and John Hodgson (1820-1845). See opening chapter of J. Simmons (ed.), *English County Historians* (London, 1978).

20. See R. Colls and B. Lancaster, *Geordies: Roots of Regionalism* (Edinburgh, 1992), pp.3-5.

21. Many of these have been bound in one volume under the title *Tales and Traditions from the Teesdale Mercury*, edited by R.W. Atkinson, c.1880.

22. Richard Watson (1833-91) was a leadminer who gave 'poetical addresses' in halls and inns throughout Teesdale on subjects ranging from the poor lot of the miners and the dilemmas of emigrating to the advantages of the railway. A selection of twenty of his poems was published in 1862. For more on Watson, see J. McTaggart, *Around the Hollow Hills* (Barnard Castle, 1978).

23. TM, 14 October 1885. Not only is this statement exaggerated, but it is also inaccurate, as Josephine appears to have conceived of the museum project at the very start of her collecting activities.

24. I. Barras Hill in *Art and Antiques Weekly*, 8 November 1975, p.46.

25. By a death bed marriage in 1820, the 10th Earl of Strathmore had hoped to legitimise his son under Scottish law; not being resident in Scotland, however, his attempt failed. See C. Hardy, *John Bowes and the Bowes Museum* (Newcastle upon Tyne, 1970), pp.24-25.

26. These ideas were expounded in the architect Gilbert Scott's *Remarks on Secular and Domestic Architecture* of 1858 – see M. Girouard, *The Victorian Country House* (Oxford, 1971), p.1.

27. Ibid.

28. JB had Derby winners in 1835, 1843, 1852 and 1853. (See Hardy, op.cit., pp.114-20) In 1839, JB, William Hutt and Nicholas Ward formed the Marley Hill Coal Company, engaging C.M. Palmer as a partner in 1846. In 1847, the company changed its name to John Bowes Esq. and Partners (See Hardy, op.cit., pp.75-77).

29. TM, 3 March 1875.

30. All these examples are drawn from letters of the 1860s and 1870s in the BMA.

31. See JB's address to the electors of South Durham from Streatlam Castle 11 August 1832 (quoted in The Electors' Scrapbook, 1832, p.26.). JB gave speeches at several locations throughout the division in 1832, but his most successful was at Darlington on 20 August. (Ibid., p.47).

32. *Newcastle Daily Chronicle*, 12 October 1885.

33. J. Lemoinne, 'La Colonie anglaise', *Paris-Guide, par les principaux écrivains et artistes de la France* (1867), part 2, p.1052.

34. As early as 1835, JB was made a member of the Cercle de la Société d'Encouragement pour l'Amélioration des races des chevaux en France, which was later to be renamed the Jockey Club. In 1846 he became a member of the Cercle de l'Union. For more on both clubs (history, activities, composition of membership) see C. Yriarte, *Les cercles de Paris 1828-1864* (Paris, 1864).

35. Thackeray to Mrs Brookfield, 4-5 February 1849 (quoted in Hardy, op.cit. p.87).

36. Although Josephine was already on the payroll of the theatre (she had taken the stage name of Mlle Delorme), she did not make her debut until 1847. C. Hardy, op.cit., pp.84-85.

37. On the association between the actress and the prostitute, see the final chapter of A. Delvau's *Les Plaisirs de Paris* (Paris, 1867).

38. X. Aubryet, 'La Chaussée d'Antin', *Paris-Guide . . .* (1867), part 2, p.1842.

39. The bills are dated 1 January, 25 February and 30 December 1864.

40. Josephine shopped for most of her dresses on the fashionable Rue St Honoré and the ,Rue Royale, but on March 19th 1869 she spent almost 6,000 Fr at Worth's, the imperial dressmakers.

41. The house in the Rue de Berlin was the Bowes' Parisian residence from 1855; the château at Louveciennes was their country house from 1852 until 1862. To furnish these homes (as well as the earlier house in the Cité d'Antin), the Bowes used the firm of Monbro fils aîné, who were based from 1853 in the Rue du Helder. Less cabinet-makers than purveyors, they also acted as interior decorators and as agents, hiring out equipment for the Bowes' parties and closing up their homes when they went away. See S. Medlam, "Mrs Bowes's Furniture from 19th Century Paris", *Antique Collector*, 3 (1983), pp.77-81.

42. Letter of gratitude from Mme Dessin to Mrs Bowes, 26 September 1870 (BMA). Josephine also occasionally sent game to her friends as a gesture of goodwill (See, for example, letter of thanks from Mme Lemoine in Calais of 31 December 1870, BMA).

43. Ralph Dent was the estate manager at Streatlam. As Josephine died before she had had time to gather together any items for this bazaar, JB sent a group of small articles of porcelain etc. which he was confident she had not intended for the museum. (JB to Dent, 19 July 1874, BMA).

44. D. Bowes in the *Cincinnati Post,* 14 October 1976. JB however claimed that she had obtained the title as a young girl. (JB to Vane, 31 August 1868, BMA). Her crest – a snowy mountain top – is carved alongside her husband's on the façade of the museum.

45. This was certainly true in England from the time of the Orleans sale (1798) onwards. See F. Haskell, *Rediscoveries in Art* (Oxford, 1980), p.47.

46. The two acquisitions seem less surprising if we recall that it was JB's dealer Solly who was one of the very first to buy such works; as a timber merchant resident in Berlin in the 1810s, he formed a large and important collection of early Italian, Netherlandish and German panel paintings which he sold to the Prussian state in 1821.

47. JB bought the *Temptation of St. Anthony* for £20 when he was still at Cambridge and the *Boar Hunt* in 1837 for £60. Harry Vane bought *Interior of an Artist's Studio* for £464. Also in the collection at Raby (as catalogued by Lady Vane in her *Handbook for Raby Castle* of 1870) were pictures by Van Dyck, Jan Steen, Ostade, Rembrandt, F. van Mieris and Van der Neer.

48. *The Entombment,* now demoted to 'circle of Jacopo Palma', was bought from Dawes for 18 guineas in 1840; '*La Perla*' for 100 guineas through Solly and the *Martyrdom of St Agnes* for £15, also through Solly. For a description of the paintings in the collection at Alnwick Castle, see "The Private collections of England" in *The Athenaeum,* 30 August and 6 September 1873; the collection also included 'characteristic' works by Titian, Perugino, Andrea del Sarto, Giorgione, Sebastiano del Piombo and Agostino Carracci.

49. Museums created in this way include the Ruskin Gallery and the Mappin Art Gallery, both in Sheffield, and the Musée Vivenel at Compiègne.

50. E.Y. Western, *A History of the Bowes Museum and Park at Barnard Castle* (1890), p.2.

51. JB to Ralph Dent, 5 October 1874 (BMA).

52. John Edward Watson (d. 1885) of 59, Grey Street, Newcastle. Pupil and then assistant in the practice of J. and B. Green of Newcastle. Although Watson appears only to have slightly revised the original plans of Jules Pellechet and then to have acted as site architect, he is credited in the TM of August 10th 1870 and in *The Builder* of January 1st 1871 with being the sole architect of the museum. Watson was made a Fellow of the RIBA in 1877 – in his letter

of self-recommendation to Charles Eastlake (28 March 1877, RIBA archives), he lists among his works the Bowes Museum, the New Assembly Rooms in North Shields, Dr. Gibb's Mansion, the Trustees Savings Bank and the Douglas Hotel in Newcastle, Blaydon Church and a number of buildings on the estates of John Bowes (Streatlam), Sir William Hutt (Gibside), and the Earl of Tankerville (Chillingham). For a list of prizes won by Watson in Newcastle and at International Exhibitions, see *The Architect's, Engineer's and Building Trades Directory* (1868).

53. Jules-Antoine-François Pellechet (1829-1903), Rue Laffitte 10. Pupil of Blouet and Gibert at the Ecole des Beaux-Arts from 1850 to 1853; having excelled in a number of disciplines in the first two years, he received two second class medals in 1853 for designing a military hospital and the town house of a rich collector. (See archives of EBA in the Archives Nationales, box AJ 52377). Pellechet appears to have designed several private 'hôtels' in Paris, but little is known of his activities as an architect beyond the construction of the Bowes Museum.

54. JB to Holmes, 7 April 1874 (BMA): "No-one but I can judge the labour and trouble to come especially now the superintendence of my wife is lost . . ." Josephine had also been responsible for the finer details of the museum's architecture, requesting for example in 1871 that Pellechet raise the roofs of the pavilions to give a more monumental effect.

55. Unlike most of the bills from dealers, all the correspondence concerning the Quinto sale is addressed to JB. For the circumstances surrounding this sale, see E. Conran's introduction to E. Young, *Catalogue of Spanish Paintings in the Bowes Museum* (Barnard Castle, 1988).

56. Amongst others, JB had dealings with Thaler in Munich, Heinrich in Ulm, Höppner in Dresden and Begaert-Defoort in Bruges as well as with the royal porcelain factories at Dresden and Berlin.

57. W. Bürger, "Les collections particulieres", *Paris-Guide* (1867), part 1, pp.536-49.

58. J. Ingamells (ed.), *The Hertford Mawson Letters* (London, 1981), pp.24, 32 and 38-41.

59. Ibid., p.21.

60. After the Bowes' autumn tour of 1868, JB continued to correspond with the Bruges dealer Rogiers. Certain remarks made by Rogiers in his letters ("As you requested, I went to Bruges to see the tapestry", 11 November 1868, BMA) suggest that JB did sometimes make specific requests.

61. R. Saisselin, *Bricabracomania. The Bourgeois and the Bibelot* (Newark, N.J., 1985), p.30.

62. Ibid., p.68.

63. The building was designed by Auguste-Joseph Pellechet and construction was completed under the supervision of his son Jules-Antoine-François Pellechet. The dealer Gogué was appointed curator of the Temporary Gallery in April 1864.

64. JB visited museums in Brussels and Antwerp in 1830, but this was over 30 years before the Bowes Museum project began to take shape.

65. See H. Coutts, "Josephine Bowes and the craze for collecting ceramics in the nineteenth century", *The International Ceramics Fair and Seminar* (London, 1992), pp.16-23 and J. Hashagen, "An Archive of French Chair Coverings", *Reprints of a symposium held at Colonial Williamsburg* (February 1990), pp.92-102.

66. For a description of the Louvre in 1863, see A. Joanne's *Le Guide Parisien*, pp.277-99. For a notion of the V&A's acquisitions policy, see *Classed Catalogue of the Objects in the Art Division of the Museum at South Kensington 1852-1870.* For the ways in which the 'historicist discourse' advocated by Ruskin, Prince Albert and others began to predominate at the National Gallery from the late 1840s onwards, see Colin Trodd, "Formations of Cultural Identity: Art Criticism, The National Gallery and the Royal Academy 1824-1863" (PhD thesis, Sussex University, 1992).

67. Phrase used by John House of Samuel Courtauld, who saw that the national collections were deficient in the area of modern French painting and sought to remedy this by donating £50,000 to the Tate Board in 1923. See *Impressionism for England: Samuel Courtauld as Patron and Collector*, exh. cat., Courtauld Institute Galleries, London(1994), pp.10-33.

68. This was a point made by the author of an article in *The Telegraph* of 7 October 1876: "We are of the opinion . . . that Barnard Castle, being a small and unprogressive town, is not likely to be so worthy of Mr. Bowes's munificence as a larger and more densely-populated city . . . we can well understand that the inhabitants of the great city on the Tyne may feel some natural jealousy as to the good fortune of the little city on the Tees."

69. The technical instruction of artisans had been the motive force behind the foundation of the South Kensington Museum. The carpet weaving trade in Barnard Castle, which had expanded rapidly in the early nineteenth century (seven firms were listed in 1834), had sunk into decline by the late 1850s, despite the registration of seventeen new designs following the Patent Act of 1842.

70. TM, 27 July 1870 and *The Builder*, 14 January 1871. The landscaped grounds at Louveciennes, which included an orangery, pools and watercourses, might well have been the inspiration behind the museum park; Mme du Barry's 'temple of love' was here replaced though by a Catholic chapel.

71. In terms of domestic space, Josephine had only in fact made provision for an apartment, from where she hoped to be able to supervise the arrangement of the collections.

72. Termed by Girouard the "nouveau-riche style". For an account of the origins and development of this style, see Girouard, op.cit., pp.131-40.

73. W. Ranger, *Report to the General Board of Health on Barnard Castle* (1850), p.20.

74. *Journal of North Country Lore and Legend*, February 1889, pp.75-76. According to Railton's *Handbook to Teesdale* of 1855, p.17, the museum would "excite the admiration of the visitor".

75. For a transcript his speech, see TM, 15 June 1892.

76. Ibid.

77. *Newcastle Daily Chronicle*, 11 June 1892.

78. "Thousands and thousands of pounds have been spent in improving Barnard Castle during the last few years...and the architecture of the town has been very greatly enhanced. The new buildings have all followed upon the foundation of the Bowes Museum, the erection of which may be said to have set the proverbial ball rolling" (TM, 8 July 1875).

79. JB to Ralph Dent, 14 July 1872 (BMA).

80. TM, 1 September 1880. Harley was appointed curator in mid 1879, having formerly been a drawing master at Oxford and then at Sandhurst (BMA, 5 April 1877).

81. Owen Scott took over from Harley in 1884.

82. Transactions of the NAAAAI, Liverpool, 1888, p.284.

83. See the first Acquisitions and Donations book in the BMA.

84. For more on this subject, see *The Picturesque Tour in Northumberland and Durham, c.1720-1830*, exh. cat., Laing Art Gallery, Newcastle upon Tyne(1982).

85. The following guidebooks to the region were consulted: Anon [Richard Garland] *A Tour in Teesdale* (1852) (4th edition); H. Railton, *Handbook to Teesdale* (1855); Anon, *Handbook to Barnard Castle* (1874); Anon, *Rambles in Teesdale* (1877); J. Murray (ed.) *Handbook for Travellers in Durham and Northumberland* (1890) and J. Backhouse, *Upper Teesdale Past and Present* (1896).

86. Backhouse, op.cit. p.5.

87. Ibid., p.29.

88. Garland, op.cit., p.34.

89. Ibid., p.30.

90. Murray op.cit., p.56 (Passage also to be found in editions of 1864 and 1873).

91. Backhouse, op.cit., p.14.

92. In fact by the time of the third edition of Murray's guide, many of the Streatlam paintings had actually been transferred to the museum.

93. C. Blanc, "L'Exposition de Manchester", *L'Artiste* (May 1857).

94. J.C. Robinson, "Our public art museums : a retrospect", *The Nineteenth Century* (1897), p.940.

95. *Art Journal* (1867), p.130.

96. "Gossip about the Paris Exhibition", *Macmillan's Magazine*, No. 91 (May 1867).

97. In a series of articles in *The Athenaeum* of 1873, F.G. Stephens described the private picture collections of, among others, the engineer William Armstrong, the lead manufacturer James Leathart, the shipping magnate Eustace Smith, the alkali manufacturer Jacob Burnett, the shipowner James Hall, and the scientist J. Lowthian Bell. For an analysis of avant-garde patonage on Tyneside, see essay by Dianne Sachko Macleod in *Pre-Raphaelites: Painters and Patrons in the North East*, exh. cat., Laing Art Gallery, Newcastle upon Tyne (1989-90).

98. Lady Schreiber bequeathed her collection to the South Kensington Museum in 1884.

99. This building, since destroyed, was the first of a series of new-style monumental town halls containing administrative spaces but also reception rooms, 'salons d'honneur', and an imperial apartment; it was built in Renaissance style with mansard roofs, pavilions, and a grand staircase, as a homage to the founder of Le Havre, Francis I. The Bowes Museum's pavilions do not extend as far forward as those of Brunet-Debaines, but the dimensions of the main blocks of both buildings are similar (B.M. 90x24m; Le Havre 80x31). See Isabelle Duhau's article on Le Havre in *Bulletin de la société de l'histoire de l'art en France* (1987), pp.191-206.

100. The museum at Amiens was the second purpose-built museum in France (after Brunet Debaine's Neo-classical musée-bibliothèque at Le Havre of 1841); previously museums had been located in buildings such as convents, abbeys and castles, divested of their former purpose by the Revolution, or in academies and libraries and even in corn exchanges, barracks, banks and theatres. Begun by Parent in 1855 and continued by Diet from 1869, the Musée de Picardie realised its ambition to be 'le petit Louvre de la province'; it shared with the Louvre a number of architectural features (the façade was a synthesis of the 'pavillon Mercier' and Visconti and Lefuel's new wing) and, with its galleries for official receptions, functioned as both museum and palace. The Bowes might well have seen this museum under construction on their frequent journeys between Paris and Streatlam.

101. *The Builder*, 19 July 1873, p.559. In France too, museums were always very much part of the fabric of the city: the museum of Grenoble for example (Questel, 1863-72), was sited on the city's main square in close proximity to the prefecture, military academy, theatre and university.

102. *The Builder*, 1 February 1873, p.77. Interestingly, JB's father-in-law, William Hutt, sent him the catalogue of the Wallace collection as shown at Bethnal Green, believing Josephine's to be "something analagous to it" (Hutt to JB, 11 July 1872).

103. N. Pevsner, *The Buildings of England: County Durham*, 2nd ed.(Harmondsworth, 1983), p. 87.

104. Title of article by Ian Barras Hill in *Art and Antiques Weekly*, 8 November 1975.

105. TM, 18 August 1875. Similarly an article in *Pearson's Weekly* of 25 May 1901: "It is a veritable 'South Kensington' set down in the loneliness of a northern wild".

106. In 1885, Owen Scott put foward a proposal for the display of the collections, which entailed a chronological arrangement of paintings within national schools and a division of the decorative arts by country and by type. (For more detail on the spatial arrangement see Scott to JB, February 1885, BMA).

107. Quoted in an article in *North Magazine* of June 1973. Kirkby saw no conflict between the museum retaining its international reputation as a museum of fine and decorative arts and at the same time becoming a regional museum for Teesdale.

IX

THE GENESIS OF THE LAING ART GALLERY, NEWCASTLE UPON TYNE

E. M. Atkins

Introduction

The reasons for Newcastle's comparative lateness in establishing a civic gallery (see Appendix, table 1) require investigation in various cultural directions. On 12 October 1899, a meeting of councillors, local peers, businessmen, artists and the general public was held in Newcastle Town Hall to launch an official city art gallery. "Such an institution had for a long time been a felt want",[1] George Harkus, the Mayor of Newcastle, declared, yet this *fin de siècle* consensus conceals the protracted and uneven gestation of what in 1904 became the Laing Art Gallery and which, even in its final, concrete stages, was beset by problems. Caution and frugality were evident alongside enthusiasm, witnessed in Harkus's reference to the costly development unsuccessfully mooted earlier in the decade, when "a central hall for musical entertainment and other purposes in addition to an art gallery and a better official residence for the Mayor"[2] had been planned. And yet the buoyant and unified mood of the 1899 meeting still acquiesced in the advice, "look to private subscriptions",[3] and convened a high-powered committee including Lord Armstrong (1810-1900), Earl Grey, Sir James Joicey, Sir B.C. Browne and Joseph Cowen to support the appeal. The eight hundred guineas raised that day had risen to only £1,200 four months later and in the intervening period the Mayor received an offer of £20,000 from Alexander Laing (1828-1905), a Scot who had worked in Newcastle as a wine and spirit merchant since 1849. This generous sum was not directed specifically at a gallery, but "on the suggestion of . . . George Harkus, the Council decided to use the money for the purpose of building an Art Gallery",[4] Thus the self-cancellation of vociferous support for a civic gallery on the one hand and financial recalcitrance on the other, demonstrated at the October 1899 meeting, was circumvented by the arbitrary generosity of a Scotsman.

Newcastle's stop-go art activity during the nineteenth century has to be assessed alongside the presence, in the second half of the century, of an indigenous local culture which transcended matters of class during a period of 'radical liberalism'.[5] Hegemonic decision-making with regard to the institution of a civic art gallery,[6] normally the site of predominantly elitist values, was also confused. In this chapter, this is contextualised within the broader framework of evolving social criteria in Britain during the nineteenth century, including issues of taste, leisure and the proliferation of cultural organisations. The aim here is also to gauge the degree to which regional cultural identity played a part in Newcastle's belated acquisition of a municipal gallery, and to what extent this was affected by an equivocal attitude towards 'high art' that arguably persists to the present day.

An examination of the growth of cultural organisations in nineteenth-century Newcastle highlights the complexity of the role played by the leaders of local society and their patronage of the arts. This is considered in the light of the contrasting public philanthropy and private aesthetic preferences of three prominent Newcastle industrialists in the second half of the century. This leads in two directions. Firstly, as Dianne Sachko Macleod has suggested, "producers and consumers of works of art were called upon to justify their activities in terms of their contribution to the community",[7] and when art exhibitions included a selection of innovative Pre-Raphaelite pictures from local collections, their perceived avant-garde qualities frequently provoked public criticism. Avant-garde art acted as a cultural irritant, an unwelcome display of superiority and elitism which ran contrary to the prevailing climate of 'radical liberalism', where values such as sobriety, inventiveness and thrift were esteemed, and the co-operative store stood as a striking example of social egalitarianism.[8] Secondly, employing the French philosopher Pierre Bourdieu's model of taste in relation to class and observing the invocation of connoisseurship as an effective means of identifying and discriminating against outsiders,[9] we may speculate on a dilemma faced by the middle class Newcastle Corporation[10] during the nineteenth century, aware to some degree of a high art paradigm represented by a civic gallery, reflecting civic and spiritual excellence, and of the relatively classless example of a vigorous local culture already in place. It is conjectured that this cultural dichotomy impeded hierarchical consensus and postponed the creation of an elitist art gallery.

In addition, there existed in the centre of Newcastle from 1870-95 a commercial gallery, the Central Exchange Gallery, occupying impressive premises in the three-domed Grainger development bounded by Grainger, Grey and Market Streets. It functioned as a club but tacitly acquired the mantle of civic gallery, something which it took no steps to disown. Importantly, the cultural programme the Gallery offered struck a balance between entertainment and education (and thus complemented the 'community politics' movement), whilst also employing the successful elements of nationally popular commercial exhibitions. Didactic or 'highbrow' art exhibitions were leavened by competitions, light entertainment and public speaking which addressed a broad range of tastes.

By the time the Laing Art Gallery opened its doors in 1904, however, the changing political climate had contributed to a wider gulf between the classes[11] which possibly gave greater impetus to the Corporation's desire to institute a civic gallery. As already mentioned, however, the Laing was founded on the unspecified gift of Alexander Laing, whose philanthropy became channelled towards the building of a gallery. A lack of wholehearted Corporation support, perceptible in the protracted story of a civic gallery in Newcastle, is discernible in the architectural detail, design and siting of the completed building (see fig. 63).

Fig. 63 The Laing Art Gallery and former Public Library, Newcastle upon Tyne (Newcastle City Libraries).

Additional evidence of an uncertain commitment to high art can also be traced to the longstanding antipathy between artist and middle-class citizen, common throughout the nineteenth century, but in Newcastle once again the basis of a more complicated regional scenario. The local press, speaking for the people, upheld Newcastle artists in preference to those more commonly exhibited from London or the Continent, as an expression of local character and identity. Exhibition organisers on the other hand, whilst at times sensitive to the public's wishes, were nevertheless drawn to London-based art values or an avant-garde model. Despite the mobilisation of various art organisations by the artists themselves throughout the century, their influence on the initiation of a civic gallery remained peripheral.

The growth of cultural organisations

In Britain, until the early nineteenth century, the aristocracy predominated in aesthetic matters, after which the intelligentsia and mercantile class began to found literary and philosophical societies, athenaeums and libraries, in order to exchange ideas and raise levels of education and commerce for themselves and, by example, for others. Proletarian containment and control was also an objective at a time of considerable political unrest and social upheaval at home and abroad. Thereafter, mechanics' institutes provided a more democratic cultural programme (see Appendix, table 2), stimulated by economic growth and extended franchise in the 1830s and often launched by the subscription of paternalistic local industrialists. In Newcastle, however, the juggernaut of industrialisation made a comparatively late entry and gathered pace only after 1850;[12] this resulted on the one hand in shipping magnates such as Charles Mitchell (1820-1895) only then being financially secure enough to provide for employees (for example, Bath Street Mechanics' Institute and Hall at Walker in 1861) and, on the other, a large population of working men actively seeking education at a later period. The encouragement of moral and educational levels of attainment was seen as a spur to improved commercial production and standards, at a time when international competition was pressing. Thus Newcastle's accelerated period of industrialisation in the second half of the century matched the nationwide move from the need for overt social control to that for more subtle means of manipulation in the consolidation of industrial capitalism.

The continued viability of mechanics' institutes in the Newcastle area, however, also reflects a hierarchical awareness of the need to maintain relations with a large workforce empowered by a sense of place, local identity and growing industrial muscle, as socialism and the trades union movement became more organised. Independence not only sprang from industry (or non-conformism), but also derived from Newcastle's geographical remoteness, which bred a "fierce and proud parochialism".[13] No M.P. represented Newcastle without strong local connections. During the 1860s there was a significant shift in public mood both on and off the shop floor; a mutual recognition of the role to be played by both employer and worker displaced animosity and confrontation, and contributed to "a new spirit of moderation and restraint".[14] The incipient trade union movement adopted a pragmatic approach and supported a programme of gradual improvements via teetotalism, education and co-operation. In part, this resulted from increased material prosperity (consequent upon a healthy economy) which in turn led to a greater acceptance of *laissez-faire* capitalism. Money encouraged a sense of shared values and common class interests, creating a social homogeneity that in large measure transcended religious or political differences. Even industrial conflicts, such as the lengthy strikes of 1886 and 1894, which did involve much class bitterness, took place against the backcloth of a tacitly accepted capitalism.[15]

Until the Labour Representation Committee was formed in 1900, the Liberal party attracted most working-class votes in Newcastle. Its central policies were free trade, hence cheap food, and a willingness to support legislation specifically focused on working-class interests. But it was not just a working-class party: Robert Spence Watson was a key Liberal reformer who also acted as an industrial dispute arbiter. His ability to reconcile an inherent conflict between capital and the labouring classes underlined the delicate balance struck between the classes which was of mutual benefit to both; it also saw the local hierarchy seeking to live within this harmonious framework and reluctant to disturb it. Whereas mechanics' institutes, generally founded in satellite communities around Newcastle, were tangibly beneficial in individual advancement and improved performance for the employer, the institution of a central art gallery could be interpreted as a cultural imposition, remote from the people and at odds, as will be discussed, with a strong home-grown culture.

However, major figures in the national art educational field, such as Henry Cole (1808-82), promulgated the belief that the didactic role of museums and galleries enhanced the lives of the masses. Cole was widely influential in the establishment of rules and principles of design to guide potential designers and promote industry during the period 1852-73, at a time when there was a shift from the idea of inculcating specific skills into the working classes, towards a more general notion of public education in art. The power of culture to civilise and tame the lower classes was disseminated by Matthew Arnold in *Culture and Anarchy* (1869) and suited Victorian philanthropy: it was purposeful and altruistic, but it also served as an important counterweight to materialist attitudes that, as the century progressed, posed a paradox citizens found difficult to resolve. The presence of a civic museum and gallery, therefore, could offer a bridge between spiritual values and the requirements of commerce, which many cities increasingly recognised and sought to implement. Newcastle, immersed in industrial affairs and with social needs becoming more pressing,[16] could not view the institution of a gallery so simply: a dualism arose between what was considered measurably useful to the community, in terms of derived education or improved commercial performance, and what was purely spiritual. This is illustrated by the change in Sir William Armstrong's views on education over a period of forty years. In 1848 he built the Elswick Engine Works Mechanics' Institute, which later became the Elswick Literary and Scientific Institute, providing technical education for the workers' children from 1866. "In school education, the impressionable minds of children are acted upon by precept and example. Habits of industry are acquired", Armstrong stated in his opening speech.[17] In 1887 the *Newcastle Daily Chronicle* reported him as advocating a limited vocational education for the working classes: "Long experience has taught him what may be got out of the average mechanic and he is not disposed to indulge in any Utopian dream as to the magical influence of certain forms of knowledge . . . On the contrary he pronounced the present education system unquestionably wasteful."[18] We see here one of the most prominent members of Newcastle society unequivocally expressing disapproval of money being spent on the broad education of the working classes. It is possible to speculate that the views of (the later) Lord Armstrong would be shared not only by other members of the local hierarchy but also by members of the public, and thus militate against the promotion of an art gallery for art educational reasons.

In addition, legislation such as the 1845 Museums Act or 1850 and 1855 Museums and Public Libraries Acts[19] developed not only from the growing self-education movement but also an academic and public interest in quasi-scientific subjects connected with natural history. Scientific knowledge was of vital importance to promote and consolidate industrial interests and was also highly relevant on a religious level after the publication of such major works as Charles Darwin's *On the Origin of Species by Means of Natural Selection* (1859). The Hancock Museum of natural history, which opened in 1884, is a reflection of this movement in Newcastle and, as one of its chief sponsors, William Armstrong was thus able to acknowledge and honour the scientific field from whose technological and engineering wings his wealth had been derived. The Museum, financed by public subscription, ultimately cost £42,000, of which Armstrong and his wife donated £14,000.[20]

As key members of the Newcastle hierarchy during the second half of the nineteenth century, Charles Mitchell and William Armstrong belonged to the small, interlocking group of business families who were creating the city's economic wealth.[21] Their cultural activities, however, generally sprang from autonomous, personal decisions rather than civic-minded philanthropy.[22] To consider their sphere of cultural influence their careers can be divided into two periods of time. During the 1860s and 1870s, when both were most actively concerned with industry, the popular politics of 'radical liberalism' was at its height and Mitchell and Armstrong's hegemonic roles were largely social and economic, as paternalistic employers and sponsors of didactic educational schemes, such as mechanics' institutes.[23] In other words, their philanthropy reflected the community spirit of the times (although their own political beliefs lay with the Tories).[24] Later, when their financial affairs were assured,[25] they enthusiastically pursued cultural paths. In personal terms, these paths converged as both owned Newcastle houses within a half a mile of each other in Jesmond, both collected pictures and built themselves galleries: Armstrong at Cragside in 1883 and Mitchell at Jesmond Towers (see fig. 64)

Fig. 64 The Art Gallery, Jesmond Towers, Newcastle upon Tyne; photographed in 1910 (Newcastle City Libraries).

in 1885. Their public cultural philanthropy, however, took different routes: Armstrong gave generously to the Hancock Museum in 1884,[26] while Mitchell sponsored St George's church in Jesmond, in 1887, at a cost of £30,000,[27] and donated approximately the same amount to Aberdeen University. He also underwrote seven Arts Association exhibitions in Newcastle between 1878 and 1882, partly, it should be stressed, in order to support his son, the artist Charles Mitchell.[28] This public sponsorship was generous but did not predominantly favour fine art. Overall, during this 'second phase', as both men consolidated great wealth and acquired land, their cultural influence in Newcastle grew more emblematic and indirect.[29] Added to this, they emulated the gentry in their desire to avoid heavy death duties and pass on inheritance within families[30] and thus deprived the city of potential bequests of paintings.[31]

Middle-class promotion and advancement were key goals of Victorian cultural organisations, and local autonomy in relation to central government was a primary part of the Victorian construction of power. The ensuing decentralisation suited middle-class interests by placing within their scope a significant range of executive functions such as the levying of a local rate or, indeed, the non-application of such a rate to veto or control a public service, such as an art gallery.[32] Cultural institutions were important not just as focal points for a variety of social aspirations (class, recreation, education), but as exemplars of tradition, custom, convention and unwritten rules.

In Newcastle, an exceptionally small and tight-knit hegemonic group connected by marriage and friendship as well as business reflected these practices, but its power and influence operated within the 'radical liberal' context of the 1860s, 1870s and early 1880s. Its patronage indicates a degree of sensitivity towards this movement and also might suggest recognition of the uniquely homogenising effect created by the union between popular politics and an indigenous local culture. Towards the end of the century, however, the strength of the 'radical liberal' matrix waned, and, coming up close on the heels of the relatively small Newcastle hierarchy, was a growing population, some of whose needs had been met and whose expectations had been raised by the cultural organisations they had been encouraged to join. The implementation of an art gallery in Newcastle in 1904 could be seen as evidence of a civic desire to extend cultural opportunities, but it could also be interpreted as a seigneurial statement by a local elite, conscious of both the approach of socialism and of a working class increasingly capable of self-management and less amenable to control.

Dichotomies of taste

Taste is an important issue in Newcastle cultural affairs during the nineteenth century, particularly in relation to the establishment of a civic gallery. The city followed Victorian taste in favouring mainstream academic art; its exhibitions and the collecting patterns of most local patrons generally reflected this, and can be seen as part of the middle-class desire to consolidate social status and control by association with recognised standards of excellence and superiority.

Matters of taste, however, easily get embroiled in accusations of snobbery. Newcastle's small hegemonic group readily became Art Association executives, Corporation committee members and representatives on various cultural bodies (for instance, Sir William Armstrong was President of the Arts Association in 1878), and within these organisations what have been described as "anomalies in cognition, inconsistencies in values and uncertainties in action" frequently emerged.[33] When society asserts itself in the symbolic isolation or elevation of state or civic art collections and monuments, the need also for commercial transactions can give rise to a clash of interests, for instance the purchase of a painting or the formation of a gallery which involves public subscription, land acquisition or the negotiation of a local tax. The work of art or the municipal gallery is judged to be superior to the transaction itself and its high prestige rating can thus easily be perceived as elitist. This may be seen in the charges of snobbery levelled at the Newcastle Arts Association in the 1870s and 1880s by the local press, which arose partly because of the selection of pictures in exhibition, but also because the soirées and society events that accompanied its functions were considered to be a manifestation of elitism and an imposition of upmarket art values upon the community.

The Newcastle collector James Leathart (1820-95) is interesting, not only because of his personal taste and patronage, but also as a result of the manner in which people responded to his paintings when they saw them. Leathart, lead manufacturer and Secretary of the Newcastle School of Art, was a "shy and shrewd patron"[34] who bought not only from local and London exhibitions or dealers such as Ernest Gambart – as did Charles Mitchell and William Armstrong – but also direct from the artists themselves. William Bell Scott (1811-90), the distinguished Head Master of the Newcastle School of Art, 1842-63, introduced him to "the works of the new men Holman Hunt and Millais to begin with, then Rossetti and Arthur Hughes, Martineau and above all F.M. Brown".[35] The "new men" represented an avant-garde taste that was not widely shared in Newcastle and when some of Leathart's Pre-Raphaelite pictures were exhibited at the "Fine Art and Mechanical Inventions Exhibition" in 1866,[36] the Newcastle press were derisory.[37] At this time, moral and aesthetic improvement suited the contemporary self-help movement of 'radical liberalism', and unfamiliar, innovative art was unwelcome. But little had changed thirteen years later at the Arts Association exhibition in March 1879, when work by Rossetti, including *Penelope,* lent by Leathart, was attacked by the press.[38] Elitist undercurrents were obviously still discerned, and the sensuous and radiant Pre-Raphaelites of Leathart's collection accentuated the wide gulf between the small group of men possessing wealth and sophisticated taste who dominated the region, and a large population, antagonised by an overtly hegemonic display of 'difficult' paintings, particularly as it was at odds with a popular, and relatively classless, alternative local culture. Prints of paintings by the local artist, Ralph Hedley, issued by the *Newcastle Weekly Chronicle,* and public renditions of local dialect songs and stories which celebrated the history, memories, manners and traditions of the area were, by contrast, an accessible manifestation of popular taste that could be shared by all levels of Newcastle society.

Bourdieu has pointed out how a hierarchy within the arts corresponds to a hierarchy of art consumers and therefore that cultural tastes relate to different classes. A struggle takes place within groups which have different ideas of culture, and fine art is an area of 'high' culture where social origins and education facilitate easy entry and understanding. A work of art only has meaning for someone who can 'read' it aright and the belief that looking at a work of art ('the pure gaze') explains it or makes it uplifting or educational, frequently overlooks the fact that various levels of perception and comprehension have to be brought into play before these various responses can take place. Accordingly, this rarefied cultural world is difficult to penetrate. Those with upper-class origins, implying established status and readily acquired learning, have a considerable advantage, but a regional aristocratic family such as the Trevelyans, living at Wallington in Northumberland, and with important cultural connections in London, nevertheless played a peripheral part in Newcastle artistic life, certainly in the second half of the nineteenth century.[39] The various incipient or developing levels of education thus created a middle class, typified by the businessmen of the Newcastle Corporation, who tentatively acquired notions of connoisseurship and were at times unsure how to proceed on a 'correct' cultural path.

Arguably, this was exacerbated in Newcastle by the existence of an alternative and buoyant culture centring around music hall, humour, dialect and folklore and, importantly, cutting across class barriers to a certain degree. This movement existed in the satellite districts around Newcastle: the local pit communities and factory-centred neighbourhoods created an autonomous and homogeneous entertainment resistant to the remote appeal of city centre amenities. Thus the discrete nature of these areas can be seen as a further impediment to Corporation consensus on art policy and direction. Sir Benjamin Browne, several times Mayor of Newcastle in the late century, wrote in 1901 that:

> most large towns are self-contained communities, both as regards their wealth and their social life. . . [but] on the whole Newcastle more than almost any town depends for its influence and well-being, not on what is inside its boundaries, but on what is outside them.[40]

However, the advent of a mass transport system that was affordable for working people, in the case of Newcastle the electrification of the tramways in 1901, forged an umbilical link with the city centre and centrifugal forces were then unleashed which tended to break down the self-sufficiency of 'urban villages'.[41]

Folk history was part of the indigenous 'cultural package' that emerged in the middle of the century and which "enshrined the men, memories, manners and customs of the North-East".[42] Although its roots were largely working class, it increasingly permeated middle- and upper-class Novocastrian society, and contributed to the general sense of local identity. From 1887 to 1892, W.E. Adams published the *Monthly Chronicle of North Country Lore and Legend*, at a time of growing interest in what constituted the national or dominant sense of Englishness. Adams reasserted a provincial cultural identity, with the emphasis not just on a rich folklore and history, but on dialect, local humour, songs and men of renown. A sense of classless community had already been promoted by imaginative approaches to the growing readership of the *Newcastle Weekly Chronicle*, of which Adams was editor, 1865-98: he devised competitions which encouraged kindness to animals, charity toy schemes, the introduction in 1880 of one of the first women's columns in Britain and, notably, social gatherings inaugurated in response to Adams's popular "Notes and Queries" column:

> It bound newspaper and reader in a close two-way relationship concerning the exchange of miscellaneous information and knowledge; and for their participation up to four hundred readers at a time from widely differing backgrounds were invited to unique contributors' gatherings or 'conversaziones' at the Chronicle's expense in Newcastle in the 1890s.[43]

A collective sense of identity and culture was thus satisfied and also skirted issues of class, intellectualism and, indeed, money, that decisions on the formation of a civic gallery demanded. The predominantly middle-class Corporation hierarchy, to some extent aware and supportive of this popular entertainment and yet drawn also to 'higher' cultural expressions of taste, found itself stymied. If Bourdieu is correct in suggesting that "the most intolerable thing for those who regard themselves as the possessors of legitimate culture is the sacrilegious reuniting of tastes which taste dictates shall be separated",[44] then in Newcastle it would have been difficult for the local hegemony to extrapolate a "legitimate culture" and impose it on a community satisfied with the cultural capital it already possessed.

Architectural symbolism and the Central Exchange Gallery

The nineteenth century created a "rhetoric of monuments"[45] to reflect its central concerns of nationalism, economic growth and social class. Burgeoning municipalities such as Newcastle were alert to the power and status conveyed by impressive architecture and Duncan and Wallach have demonstrated in their study "The Universal Survey Museum"[46] the symbolic trickle-down influence of design and iconography resident in a museum such as the Louvre. When designated 'The Museum of the French Republic' in 1793, it was recognised as a symbol of the state: its Roman-derived architecture, the ritualistic route taken by visitors and organised plan of exhibits, implied state authority, confidence and the epitome of civilisation. Such potent and tangible symbols of a nation's abstract and anonymous powers were absorbed by nineteenth-century England and used to promote national identity and consolidate the status of a newly constituted public, the middle class. Moral and spiritual values were also crucial to the state and the city in order to encourage obligation and respect. Museums and galleries therefore stood as guardians of these values, reflecting the highest cultural ambitions of their country. This symbolism can be recognised by all citizens and its importance is corroborated by an imposing civic site and design, and the democracy, albeit partial, of such an institution's public accessibility. In 1904 the new Laing Art Gallery stood in Newcastle as a manifestation of these symbolic civic and national values (see fig. 65), yet if the architecture and layout of the Gallery is analysed it is possible to gain further insight into the degree of commitment to high art in Newcastle.

Fig. 65 Inaugural exhibition, Laing Art Gallery, Newcastle upon Tyne, autumn, 1904. (By courtesy of the Laing Art Gallery, Newcastle upon Tyne).

A museum building was designed to overawe as a temple of culture where the nineteenth-century desire to educate and control a mass public by a demonstration of intellectual authority took the form of a series of subtle, and less subtle, power manoeuvres, often involving classical iconography, complicated internal layout and imposing architecture. In Newcastle the effect of these factors, although utilised, was diffused and perhaps suggests that either the will to impose middle-class values or the general desire for an art gallery was less than wholehearted. For instance, the route to the 'temple' was problematic (see fig. 63). Should members of the public seek to go beyond the Public Library, attracted by the rustication of architects' Cackett & Burns Dick's Gallery tower, they entered Higham Place, which was the 'side street leading to no place' it remains today. The Gallery's subsidiary position, round the corner from the Library and with its back to the town centre, is not alleviated by the entrance, which, although elaborate, is somewhat congested and would have been more so in its early days when turnstiles were in operation. In the original ground plan, private doors were immediately opposite the main entrance and the single staircase on the left, leading to the second floor gallery, although moderately clear to the visitor, did not promise the spacious airiness of, for instance, Cartwright Hall, built in Bradford in the same year, with its twinned staircases and double-height entrance hall, or the cathedral proportions of Kelvingrove, Glasgow. Both these two galleries are by the same architects, Simpson & Allen and, although very different in scale, create a welcoming ambience that continues to the present day.

It is interesting to note that one councillor, Alderman Henry Newton, gave strong and consistent personal support for a civic art gallery in Newcastle. He wanted both a library and gallery and when a public subscription was opened in October 1899 (see Introduction), Alderman Newton seconded the motion proposed by Alderman William Stephenson and reminded those present that the Library was originally intended to serve as a library and art gallery. He then offered a piece of council land adjoining the Library. But in February 1900 he appeared to renege on his offer of land by denigrating the site – perhaps he felt that the 'dead-end' street location of Higham Place was inappropriate for a fine civic gallery.

Throughout 1900, Newcastle Council procrastinated over a decision concerning the site. In May, Newton referred in a long speech to "circumstances [which] were so difficult", but "Mr Laing's determination was so fixed . . . we give Mr Laing the plot of land for the erection of this gallery upon which his heart is so set." In October 1900 a request was received by the Council to speed up the site settlement because Alexander Laing was unwell. It was also implied that the Public Library Committee, in whose hands the operation was being conducted, was dragging its feet.[47] In June 1901 the complex purchase proceedings of Higham Place were still under way, but the foundation stone was laid by Mrs Watson Armstrong, the wife of Lord Armstrong's heir and nephew, on 13 August 1901.

Fig. 66 The Central Exchange, Newcastle upon Tyne. From a painting by T.M. Richardson (The Laing Art Gallery, Newcastle upon Tyne).

Much earlier, however, T.P. Barkas (later Alderman) and T.H. Tweedy had opened the Central Exchange Gallery in Newcastle, which had been built by Richard Grainger in 1839, originally as a corn exchange but later used as a subscription newsroom and, on occasions, as a site for exhibitions. This Gallery played a major but underrated role in Newcastle's nineteenth-century art story and its imposing premises (see fig. 66) lent a convincing degree of municipal splendour which allowed it to stand in many eyes as a civic gallery manqué.[48] As its name suggests, the Central Exchange Gallery was sited in the heart of the city centre and its accessible physical presence fulfilled an important cultural role from 1870 to 1895. The scale and spaciousness of the Grainger development in the early nineteenth century, which included such buildings as the Grainger Market, Grey Street and Central Exchange Building, contributed to Newcastle's position as the premier financial, commercial and administrative centre in the North East well into the twentieth century. When other cities were considering the construction of municipal buildings in the second half of the nineteenth century, therefore, the Grainger development already stood as an exceptional example of civic architecture and mitigated the need or desire for further building.

A negative aspect of this great architectural scheme stemmed from the clash between investment interests and council membership. As a consequence, the public became increasingly critical of bureaucracy throughout the century and numerous well-publicised cases of embezzlement and corruption between 1850 and 1900 angered ratepayers,[49] who were often inclined to query rate increases. In the last twenty years of the century, as discussion of a municipal gallery was more frequently heard, projected costs to be borne by ratepayers became a constant pejorative theme which doubtless clouded councillors' decisions on the matter.

In the early years of the Central Exchange Gallery, Alderman T.P. Barkas made very little contribution to Council affairs, but as the Gallery became more established his Council attendances increased and the Central Exchange was occasionally mentioned in Council business during the 1870s, thus subtly adding to its image as the city's representative gallery. Barkas and Tweedy's letter of thanks is minuted following the loan of "Corporation pictures at the Art Gallery" in 1878, and when sculptures by J.G. Lough were offered to the Council by his widow there was an immediate suggestion that "Mr Barkas . . . be allowed some of the models for the Art Gallery".[50] But equally obviously, this false municipal status was detected: the Mayor, William Stephenson, dismissively replied that Mr Barkas "might have a few, but he could not have them all". And Ruskin's massive snub to the town on the occasion of the British Association exhibition in 1889 also indicated that he had seen through the Central Exchange's civic pretensions. He was asked to lend some Turner drawings:

> To be placed in the only art gallery of the town the Central Exchange – in order to interest the people who came to Tyneside on the occasion of the visit of the British Association. Sir Isaac Lowthian Bell, the Mayor, received a curt reply from the philosopher to the effect that he would as soon think of trusting his drawings at the bottom of one of Newcastle's coal pits as of placing them in the hands of the chief magistrate.[51]

Education versus pleasure

Paradoxically, the reason why the Central Exchange Gallery has been neglected for study is also the source of its importance: it successfully combined art exhibitions with other more populist forms of entertainment and therefore reduced the need for a civic gallery by providing a popular cultural service. Because it has been considered neither fish nor fowl, its significance has been ignored, but it stands as a uniquely successful bridge between pleasure and education and is not dissimilar to the larger-scaled commercial exhibitions increasingly common in the second half of the century, which attracted custom by the inclusion of 'entertainments' alongside more worthy didactic and commercial exhibits.

In 1888 Thomas Greenwood quoted Ruskin as saying "A museum is . . . primarily not at all a place of entertainment, but a place of Education",[52] but by 1900 there was a fragile balance between the educational element sponsors required and the cultural status aimed for, together with the entertainment sought by the public. The growth in mass exhibitions contributed to this, beginning with the popular appeal of the 1851 Crystal Palace exhibition. Being part of a social spectacle and tasting the atavistic elements of fair or carnival drew audiences, yet allayed fear of riotous assembly because the exhibitions invoked solid images of trade and Empire. Attendance figures for the fine arts sections of these expositions reveal that they were considerably less popular than the pleasure facilities,[53] and a compromise was suggested by the Duke of Argyll's address at the opening of the Imperial International Exhibition held at the White City in 1909: "amusement without excess and knowledge without fatigue".[54]

This left the possible formation of civic galleries at the turn of the century in a state of uncertainty. "It was clear by 1900 that the higher arts were perceived by the middle classes as a kind of cultural duty – a form of work which was necessary to maintain status and that art of any kind was barely perceived at all by the working classes."[55] In some respects, therefore, this cultural ambivalence further weakened the decision-making of Newcastle Corporation; added to which was the competing influence and appeal of institutions such as department stores. Bourdieu has contrasted "the paraphernalia which always announces the sacred character, separate and separating, of high culture" with the comfortable world of the department store – "in a sense the poor man's gallery" – where people "can make their own judgements rather than feel themselves measured against 'transcendent norms'".[56] Department stores offered mass audiences across all classes objects of a modern world and, perhaps, an encounter with art.[57] Newcastle stood in the vanguard of this movement with Bainbridge's and Fenwick's: their persuasive drama and promise of personal gratification represented a very attractive alternative cultural experience.

The Central Exchange Gallery also offered an appealing cultural programme which reflected a broad range of local interests. Various art exhibitions took place, including two which ran parallel to the Arts Association exhibitions in 1878 and 1879, and the British Association was the official patron of the August 1889 exhibition of local art which was held at the Central Exchange. In 1892 the Gallery was refurbished and in the mid-1890s the lease was given up and the top floor became the Vaudeville Theatre. However, throughout the period 1870-95, it arranged a wide range of popular entertainments which included "costume shows, the polytechnic, bicycle and tricycle and photographic exhibitions",[58] and greatly salted the more sober fare of its periodic art exhibitions. This shrewd combination, together with its sixpence entrance fee to non-members, guaranteed its popularity for twenty-five years. Barkas organised painting-against-the-clock competitions and controversial speakers, and in this way encouraged links between artistic and civic communities, to whom he offered an entertainment formula which suited many tastes. Only at the end of the century, when class divisions crystallised, was there a concomitant move to more demarcated cultural interests, and at this time many vaudeville theatres were opened,[59] just as the Laing Art Gallery was being founded at the other end of the class spectrum.

The role of the artist

T.M. Richardson and H.P. Parker were two local artists[60] who from 1822 "generated most of the artistic current in the region for the next 15 years or more".[61] It was their initiative which created the Northumberland Institute for the Promotion of the Fine Arts at Brunswick Place (Richardson's own home) between 1822 and 1827. We see here the establishment of a rich artistic seam which characterises Newcastle in the first half of the nineteenth century and which places the city on an equal footing with other municipal centres during this period. However, two differing cultural forces also become evident and it is notable that their incompatibility dogged art matters throughout the century: on one side were the artists and on the other was the local hierarchy.

The opening exhibition in October 1822 was criticised on two counts: firstly, that outsiders had been favoured above Newcastle artists[62] and, secondly, that the exhibition could be improved by supervision from an aristocratic committee.[63] This latter observation was acted upon,[64] but Richardson was unhappy at the inclusion of patrons such as the Marquis of Londonderry and he threatened a splinter group;[65] this was successful and titled names withdrew.[66] Corporation members were disgruntled because it was felt that the city "should surpass what Richardson was achieving merely in his own house",[67] and also that a private enterprise was masquerading as a public institution (as later happened at the Central Exchange Gallery). New premises, therefore, were built in Blackett Street by Dobson and Grainger in 1828 and the name of the institution was changed to the Northern Academy of Art.[68] Exhibitions continued to be organised here by Richardson and

Parker and, although the *Tyne Mercury* congratulated their efforts, pessimism was expressed on the grounds that "without some society of gentlemen, some general union in its welfare, its existence this year or next, is no guarantee for its permanent establishment" (9 September 1828). This pessimism was not unfounded and only three annual exhibitions were held. Significantly, four prominent reasons for this resurfaced later in the century.

First, the competing interest of Grainger's proposed music hall next to the Academy presaged the cultural situation that developed on a wider scale in the second half of the century, when music hall was a predominant local culture, together with institutions such as the Central Exchange Gallery, already discussed. Second, Richardson's exhibitions were financially unsuccessful and anticipated the series of Arts Association exhibitions between 1878 and 1882, which also proved unprofitable.

Third, only approximately 40% of the exhibiting artists organised by Richardson for the opening exhibition in 1822 were local, and many Novocastrians objected to a preponderance of London exhibitors. This provincial sensitivity was fuelled by a growing feeling that the best of local works were contributed, yet only indifferent works by London artists were shown. Underlying reasons for this were possibly even harder to accept: (a) poor sales in Newcastle were a disincentive to London artists; (b) Londoners' dissatisfaction with the Northern Academy's hanging methods; and (c) careless loan arrangements.[69] Over fifty years later, when Charles Mitchell sponsored the seven Arts Association Exhibitions, the local press were critical not simply because of elitism discerned in the surrounding social activities but also in the choice of exhibits, and only 7,000 people attended the 1878 exhibition compared, for instance, to 470,500 at the Walker Gallery, Liverpool, in the same year.[70] The third exhibition attempted to redress criticism by inviting submissions directly from the artists. An accompanying catalogue article also tried to atone for the previous criticisms: Whistler's claim that only painters could understand paintings was challenged and it was agreed that the appreciation of certain works by "knowledgeable" members of society, who insisted upon a "right appreciation" of modern painting, made others uncomfortable, leaving them feeling ill-informed and old-fashioned.[71] This attempt at amelioration was unsuccessful, however, because from 395 artists represented, only forty were local, and there was a deluge of public criticism. Perhaps it should be remembered that at this time people had easy access to engravings, and the work of a local artist such as Ralph Hedley was often widely reproduced in this highly popular way. His work was recognised elsewhere – exhibited both at the Central Exchange Gallery and the Royal Academy in 1879, for example – and its exclusion by the Arts Association was bound to cause antagonism.

In 1883 the Bewick Club opened, largely composed of local artists, some of whose patrons were former supporters of the Arts Association. It organised an Art Union and by 1889 was attracting 10,000 visitors who entered without charge. The Club promoted the notion of a civic gallery in Newcastle, as in Robert Spence Watson's address to members in 1885:

> I do not presume to advise what our Corporation should do in this matter: I simply point out what has been done elsewhere, and add that this excellent Bewick Club is at the present time unaided in its efforts to provide an Annual Art Exhibition for our City, and to furnish the highest education in the art of painting.[72]

However, the Bewick was the focus of Newcastle's final artistic débâcle before the creation of a civic gallery. It was attacked by Harry Barnett for "inferior and unrepresentative exhibitions",[73] and later, as the *Newcastle Daily Leader's* art critic, Barnett more specifically criticised the work of local artists Emmerson and Hedley.[74] In a national publication, the *Art Journal*, of the same year (1889), an unsigned article criticised Newcastle art policy as a whole,[75] and several phrases would perhaps suggest that a key source was again Barnett. Ironically, many of his goals were shared by the Bewick Club, including the formation of a civic-funded gallery, but latent in his comments was a desire to promote a forum for "first-rate" art in Newcastle, by which he generally meant work pertaining to a London-based ideal of academic excellence. And, although this contretemps reflects a dichotomy unresolved to the present day[76] between definitions of local and national taste, Barnett's views were ultimately acted upon at the beginning of the twentieth century with the establishment of the Laing Art Gallery.

A fourth and final reason for the intermittent art activity in Newcastle throughout the century is embodied in the lack of success an artist such as T.M. Richardson encountered in the 1820s and 1830s and relates in part to public perception of the artist, relegated to the fringes of society. William Bell Scott brought to the city the sophistication of his London connections (pre-eminent artists and art education figures such as Henry Cole) and an established reputation as a painter-poet, yet he could not significantly alter entrenched cultural patterns, and his time in Newcastle coincided with a relatively barren art period which he was unable to alleviate. He was aware of the difficulties he faced and spoke of the resolute philistinism of the Newcastle community and its refusal to take art seriously, but ultimately he was an outsider and belonged neither to Newcastle nor to its ruling class; he did not carry enough weight to realise ambitions on the city's behalf in the form of a municipal gallery, despite his wish to do so.[77]

The class barriers developed by the Victorians were exemplified in the views of a (fictitious) wealthy coal-owner:

> We naturally do not feel drawn to the society of artists; we have nothing in common with them – we do not admire them; neither do we feel disposed to introduce to the society of our wives and daughters a parcel of actors, artists, musicians and so forth, who have no stake in society, who have little to lose, whose capital is all invested in themselves far beyond what we practical men have had a chance of doing, and are capable of throwing us into the shade in our own houses, whilst they show that they despise us![78]

The persistence of these opinions is demonstrated by a *Northern Counties Magazine* editorial written fifty-three years later in 1901:

> Till recently, doubtless, men's minds were almost wholly occupied with commerce. . . their avocation was probably sport of some kind. . . but for art and literature the business man had something of a contempt, viewing the artist or writer in the same light as legislators of old regarded the play-actor, as a vagrant, namely, or at least an unprofitable person.[79]

When Newcastle artists organised themselves into efficient exhibiting bodies towards the end of the century,[80] their sphere of influence was still partially undermined by the status attached to their profession and, significantly, although Ralph Hedley offered warm support "on behalf of the artists"[81] at the public meeting which finally launched the foundation of a civic gallery in the autumn of 1899, the committee elected to support the appeal for public subscription included no artists.

This situation was echoed yet again as the gallery eventually got under way, following Alexander Laing's offer of £20,000 in the final months of the century. The Laing Art Gallery Committee was formed in August 1903, comprising nine members of the Council and nine "gentlemen" but, again, no artists, despite some mild council protest. Similarly, when the Laing's first Curator was to be appointed in the early summer of 1904 there were six applicants, two of whom were local: Thomas Dickinson (artist and art administrator for many Newcastle cultural organisations) and James Watson (art master of Newcastle Royal Grammar School). The Executive Committee voted 5-2 in favour of the young Nottingham Gallery candidate, C. Bernard Stevenson, but the larger Laing Art Gallery Committee awarded Stevenson and Dickinson seven votes each.[82] Alexander Laing's casting vote chose Stevenson, who remained in office for fifty-three years until his death in 1957. His early claim, "I am in touch with the highest living authorities upon art matters, and can obtain the same [i.e. advice] free of expense to the Corporation",[83] must ultimately have been decisive with its promise of elitist standards at cut-price cost.

Fig. 67 Interior of the Laing Art Gallery, Newcastle upon Tyne, in the early twentieth century. (By courtesy of the Laing Art Gallery, Newcastle upon Tyne).

Conclusion

According to Giles Waterfield, "The development of British art galleries and museums has been fragmentary, disappointing and haphazard"[84] and the protracted genesis of Newcastle's Laing Art Gallery reflects this overview. The situation in Newcastle was a microcosm of the erratic movements which impeded the foundation of many galleries during the nineteenth and twentieth centuries, but which in this case required a more complex series of evolutionary steps.

The Laing Art Gallery has now been running for over ninety years and has consistently demonstrated an awareness of regional artists, patrons, customs, locality and community which compensates for the uncertainties of its gestation, but also strikingly echoes the priority given to similar concerns in nineteenth-century Newcastle. In the late twentieth century, the Gallery's growing attendance is testament to its successful policy to attract and entertain, and it is significant that the people of Tyneside are both its central target and its key resource.

References and Notes

1. *Newcastle Daily Leader*, 13 October 1899.

2. Ibid.

3. Ibid.

4. Laing Art Gallery, *The Creation of an Art Gallery: the History of the Laing Art Gallery and the Creation of its Permanent Collections since the Opening in 1904*, n.d.[1955], p.6.

5. Radical liberal thought promoted the belief that legislation should create "the greatest happiness of the greatest number" (Jeremy Bentham, *The Commonplace Book* (*Works*, ed. J. Bowring, vol. x (Edinburgh, 1843) p.142)). As the century progressed, the writing of followers of Bentham, such as John Stuart Mill and Edwin Chadwick, formed a social philosophy which acted as a catalyst to legal, social, political and economic reform. Laissez-faire capitalism, the right of the individual to education and religious freedom, and full adult franchise were central tenets.

6. The term 'hegemony' is used loosely throughout the chapter to denote local industrialists and members of Newcastle Corporation, and draws upon the definition given by P. Anderson and R. Blackburn (eds.) in *Towards Socialism* (London, 1965): "Dominance of one social block over another, not simply by means of force or wealth, but by a total social authority whose ultimate sanction and expression is a profound cultural supremacy".

7. Dianne Sachko Macleod, "Private and Public Patronage in Victorian Newcastle", *Journal of the Warburg and Courtauld Institutes*, 52 (1989), p.193.

8. The retail cooperative societies set up the Cooperative Wholesale Society in 1862; profits were distributed to members in proportion to the value of their purchases.

9. Pierre Bourdieu, *Distinction: a Social Critique of the Judgement of Taste* (London, 1979).

10. In the second half of the nineteenth century Newcastle Corporation largely comprised "big to medium-sized industrialists supported by larger numbers of professionals, shopkeepers and merchants – although the former group was declining in significance towards the end of the period". *Benwell Community Project Final Report*, series no. 6 (1978) p.42.

11. The advent of socialism (the Labour Representation Committee was formed in 1900 in Newcastle) and the decline of liberalism (Newcastle Liberals lost to the Tories in the General Elections of 1892 and 1895), created a more divisive class consciousness.

12. N. McCord, *North-East England: an Economic and Social History* (London, 1979), p.16.

13. E.I. Waitt, "John Morley, Joseph Cowen and Robert Spence Watson: Liberal Divisions in Newcastle Politics, 1873-1895", unpublished PhD thesis, Manchester University, 1972, p.2.

14. Owen R. Ashton, *W.E. Adams: Chartist, Radical and Journalist 1832-1906* (Newcastle upon Tyne, 1991), p.97.

15. Ibid., p.99.

16. Throughout the nineteenth century problems of overcrowded housing, inadequate diet, sickness and early death were problems generally regarded with apathy and neglect by the established authorities and "these problems were worse in Newcastle than in most large towns" (J.C. Sowden, "Public Health in the 19th Century" in M. Barke and R.J. Buswell (eds.) *Historical Atlas of Newcastle upon Tyne* (Newcastle upon Tyne, 1980), p.47).

17. *Benwell Community Project Final Report*, op. cit.

18. *Newcastle Daily Chronicle*, 28 November 1887.

19. Public libraries and museums could now be extended to towns with a lower population limit (from 10,000 to 5,000) and these services could also be provided outside municipal boroughs. Importantly, council library authorities were now empowered to provide schools of science and art (from the same rate income). There was considerable general opposition

to this legislation, yet Newcastle had in fact already opened a School of Art, aided by government money, in 1844. This underlines the erratic nature of the city's art sponsorship and also shows a greater degree of support for the arts in the early century, as opposed to later on.

20. T. Russell Goddard, *History of the Natural History Society of Northumberland, Durham and Newcastle upon Tyne, 1829-1929* (Newcastle upon Tyne, 1929), p.86. The initial subscription for the Museum in 1880 raised £23,677 (p.78) and Goddard commented that "hardly any other museum in the provinces has been financially so widely supported as has this" (p.119).

21. Armstrong, for example, was persuaded to stand as a Tory candidate in the 1886 election (he was unsuccessful). Waitt, op.cit., p.298, D. Dougan, *The Great Gun-Maker* (Newcastle upon Tyne, 1971), p.159 and *Newcastle Daily Journal*, 16 June 1886.

22. With regard to Mitchell's philanthropy, for instance, McGuire says "to some his generosity was an enigma and his motives not always understood", D.F. McGuire, *Charles Mitchell, 1820-1895, Victorian Shipbuilder* (Newcastle upon Tyne, 1988), p.30.

23. Armstrong was, however, on the organising committee of the 1848 Polytechnic Exhibition, but paintings formed only a small part of its total exhibits. Similarly, the exhibitions of 1863 (British Association for the Advancement of Science Exhibition, of which Armstrong was President) and 1866 (Mechanics' Institute Exhibition) contained a mix of artefacts.

24. D.F. McGuire, op.cit., p.30; P. McKenzie, *W.G. Armstrong* (Newcastle upon Tyne, 1983), p.113.

25. 1882 partnership between Mitchell and Armstrong launched with capital of £1,575,000 (McGuire, op.cit., p.20).

26. Goddard, op.cit., p.86.

27. *Newcastle Weekly Chronicle*, 24 August 1895.

28. Macleod, art.cit., pp.202-3 and 206.

29. Lord Armstrong, for example, was given a peerage in 1897, but spoke little in the Lords (only on the Irish question). From 1889 to 1892 he represented Rothbury on the Northumberland County Council and then retired to carry out scientific experiments at Cragside and develop plans for turning Bamburgh into a convalescent home (McKenzie, op.cit. and author's conversation with staff at Cragside).

30. F.M.L. Thompson, "Life after Death: how Successful Nineteenth-Century Businessmen Disposed of their Fortunes", *Economic History Review*, second series, vol.XLIII (February 1990).

31. Dianne Sachko Macleod, "Mid-Victorian Patronage of the Arts: F. G. Stephens' 'The Private Collections of England'", *Burlington Magazine*, 128 (August 1986), p.603.

32. Because it had been allocated no purchase fund and was a subsidiary resouce of Public Library Committee expenditure, the Laing Art Gallery began in October 1904 with loaned exhibits.

33. I. Kopytoff, "The Cultural Biography of Things: Commoditization as Process", in Arjun Appadurai (ed.), *The Social Life of Things: Commodities in Cultural Perspective* (Cambridge, 1986), p.82.

34. Jeremy Maas, *Gambart, Prince of the Victorian Art World* (London, 1975), p.140.

35. W. Minto (ed.), *Autobiographical Notes of the Life of William Bell Scott*, 2 vols (London, 1892), vol ii, p.48.

36. Held at the Town Hall to raise funds for the new Mechanics' Institute in New Bridge Street.

37. Macleod, art.cit., 1989, p.199.

38. *Newcastle Daily Chronicle*, 28 March 1879.

39. Macleod, art.cit., 1989, p.192.

40. *The Northern Counties Magazine* (1901), p.334.

41. R. Dennis, *English Industrial Cities of the Nineteenth Century* (Cambridge, 1984), p.125.

42. Ashton, op.cit., p.96.

43. Ibid., p.129. Also see *Newcastle Weekly Chronicle*, 23 May 1891.

44. Bourdieu, op.cit., pp.56-57.

45. Donald Horne, *The Great Museum* (London, 1984), p.2.

46. Carol Duncan and Alan Wallach, "The Universal Survey Museum", *Art History*, Vol.3, No.4 (December 1980), p.448-69.

47. In 1880, at the opening of the Library, Joseph Cowen's inaugural speech expressed the hope that the new Library premises would also include three large rooms on the first floor for a "Sculpture and Art Gallery" (*Newcastle Daily Journal*, 16 August 1880), but at the 1882 opening of the Library, a reference library occupied the place proposed earlier for art gallery rooms. For the later events and statements mentioned, see the *Newcastle Town Council Minute Book*, 7 February 1900, 2 May 1900 and 10 October 1900.

48. Thomas Dickinson, in his privately published pamphlet *Mr. T. Dickinson's Work in the Cause of Art in Newcastle on Tyne, 1882-1907*, n.d., speaks of his desire that the Central Exchange Gallery "would in some measure fill the position of a Municipal Gallery; it was conducted on lines similar to the chief Art Galleries of the country, holding three or four different exhibitions each year" (p.6).

49. McCord, op.cit., p.167.

50. *Newcastle Town Council Minute Book*, 1875-76, p.357.

51. Central Exchange Gallery cuttings book, 19 November 1892.

52. Thomas Greenwood, *Museums and Art Galleries* (London, 1888), p.5.

53. Paul Greenhalgh, "Education, Entertainment and Politics: Lessons from the Great International Exhibitions", in P. Vergo (ed.), *The New Museology* (London, 1989), p.88.

54. *Daily Mail*, 15 May 1909.

55. Greenhalgh, op.cit., p.86.

56. Bourdieu, op.cit., p.34.

57. Prior to World War I, many department stores sought to attract custom by offering a wide range of amenities that conveyed the image of a refined club, far removed from associations of 'trade': in-house theatres or art galleries were sometimes included to reinforce this air of cultural gentility.

58. *Newcastle Daily Chronicle*, Annual Report, 1 May 1882.

59. c.1889 Cambridge Hall, headquarters of Newcastle Volunteer Artillery; venue for farce and vaudeville (closed by 1896)

c.1890 People's Palace, Percy Street: in 1900s became Palace Theatre of Varieties, Haymarket

c.1890 The Empire Theatre of Varieties, Newgate Street 1894 Olympia Music Hall, Northumberland Road

c.1895 Grand Theatre, Byker

c.1896 Ginnett's Amphitheatre, Northumberland Road

c.1896 Queen's Theatre of Varieties, Scotswood Road; became 'New Tyne Circus' in 1900

c.1900 Vaudeville Theatre in Central Exchange Building.

60. Parker was not in fact local; he had arrived in the city in 1816. Trevor Fawcett, *The Rise of English Provincial Art, Artists, Patrons and Institutions outside London, 1800-1830* (Oxford, 1974), p.16.

61. Ibid., p.195.

62. *Tyne Mercury*, 1 October 1822.

63. Ibid., 15 October 1822.

64. Fawcett, op. cit., p.196.

65. *Tyne Mercury*, 4 January 1825.

66. Ibid., 24 May 1825 and *Newcastle Courant*, 28 May 1825.

67. L. Wilkes and F. Graham, *Tyneside Portraits* (Newcastle upon Tyne, 1971), p.81.

68. After the three exhibitions mounted by Richardson for the Northern Academy of Arts in Blackett Street, three more organisations were started at a similar time, occupying the same premises:

1831 – Northern Society of Painters in Watercolours

1832 – Newcastle on Tyne Institution for the General Promotion of the Fine Arts; held two annual exhibitions (primarily an educational institution)

1835 – Newcastle Society of Artists (only one exhibition).

The Newcastle on Tyne Institution's successor was the North of England Society for the Promotion of the Fine Arts at Market Street, which again stressed educational artistic pursuits and held annual exhibitions until 1843. It was this institution which employed William Bell Scott in 1842 and also held two successful exhibitions at the Northern Academy in 1850 and 1852.

69. Paul Usherwood, *Art for Newcastle: Thomas Miles Richardson and the Newcastle Exhibitions 1822-1843* (Newcastle upon Tyne, 1984).

70. Macleod, art.cit., 1989, p.203.

71. Quoted in Dianne Sachko Macleod, "Avant-garde patronage in the North East", in *Pre-Raphaelites: Painters and Patrons in the North East*, exh.cat., Laing Art Gallery, Newcastle upon Tyne (1989-90), p.20.

72. "An address to the Members of the Bewick Club, Delivered by Dr Robert Spence Watson, LL.D., F.R.G.S., 4th November, 1885". Quoted in John Millard, *Ralph Hedley: Tyneside Painter* (Newcastle upon Tyne, 1990), pp.10-11.

73. *Newcastle Daily Leader*, 26 March 1889.

74. Ibid., 19 September 1889.

75. "Art in the Provinces: Art on Tyneside", *Art Journal* (1889), pp. 175-76.

76. *Daily Telegraph*, 8 September 1992. Criticism of the Laing's exhibiting practices expressed by art critic Richard Dorment.

77. Somewhat bitterly, he wrote to James Leathart in 1886 of his desire to make a bequest to the city: "With so many rich people about, it seemed to me absurd to a man like myself with little to leave, and no one on the spot appearing to join in the matter"; quoted by Macleod, art. cit., 1989, p.208.

78. Geraldine Jewsbury writing in 1848, quoted in B. Jeffares, *The Artist in 19th Century Fiction* (1979), p.14.

79. *The Northern Counties Magazine*, Vol.I (Oct. 1900-Mar. 1901), p.63.

80. Bewick Club and Northumberland Art Institute 1883; 1900: old School of Art affiliated to the College of Science in Barras Bridge (part of Durham University) and instigated a new exhibiting society, the Art Circle; Northumberland Handicrafts Guild opened; Pen and Palette Club, founded by Robert Jobling and Thomas Dickinson.

81. *Newcastle Daily Leader*, 13 October 1899.

82. Dickinson was so disappointed at his lack of success that he printed the pamphlet cited in note 48.

83. Laing Art Gallery Committee Minute Book, p.24.

84. Giles Waterfield (ed.), *Palaces of Art: Art Galleries in Britain 1790-1900* (London, 1991), p.28.

Appendix

TABLE 1

Civic galleries in Northern England
Opening dates of galleries 1877-1917

Year	Gallery	1901 population
1873	South Shields Library and Museum	100,858
1877	Walker Art Gallery, Liverpool	684,958
1879	Sunderland Free Library and Museum	131,686
1882	Manchester City Art Gallery	543,872
1887	Mappin Art Gallery, Sheffield	222,441
1888	Leeds City Art Gallery	428,968
1893	Carlisle Museum and Art Gallery	45,480
1894	Harris Museum and Art Gallery, Preston	112,989
1901	Bury Art Gallery and Museum	58,000
1901	Towneley Gallery and Museum, Burnley	97,350
1904	Cartwright Hall, Bradford	279,767
1904	Laing Art Gallery, Newcastle	247,000
1917	Shipley Art Gallery, Gateshead	109,888

TABLE 2

Opening dates of Mechanics' Institutes and Literary & Philosophical Societies

	Mechanics' Institute	Literary & Philosophical Society
Bradford	1832	1774
Burnley	1834	1863
Bury	1837	1887
Carlisle	1824	1835
Gateshead	1836	–
Leeds	1865	1819
Liverpool	1832	1812
Manchester	1825	1781
Middlesbrough	1840	1863
Newcastle	1824	1792
Preston	1828	1840
Sheffield	1832	1822
South Shields	1825	–
Sunderland	1837	1834

[Information acquired from Local Studies Departments of local libraries]

Part IV

REPRESENTATIONS

Who could have foreseen that the slow process of change would accelerate to an extent not experienced since the Industrial Revolution, wiping away buildings and traditions and values in the twinkling of an eye?

BERYL BAINBRIDGE

An English Journey (on Jarrow)

(1984)

X

WINSLOW HOMER AT CULLERCOATS

Kenneth McConkey

During his long lifetime, the American artist Winslow Homer (1836-1910) made only two trips to Europe.[1] On the first of these, in 1867, two of his paintings were being shown at the Exposition Universelle in Paris and he spent ten months there. The opulence of the Second Empire must have presented a stark contrast to someone who was over thirty years of age and had been seasoned by experiences of the American Civil War. The twenty month stay at Cullercoats fourteen years later, cannot so easily be explained, even though it has been regarded by all of Homer's biographers as crucial to his development as a painter. William Howe Downes in his early critical biography, for instance, refers to his selection of Cullercoats as "a happy chance" which led to "a turning point in the artist's career, so far as popular esteem was concerned".[2] Lloyd Goodrich writing in 1944 had the same conviction. Cullercoats was a "turning point . . . in every way".

> It brought him into close contact with the sea, henceforth his dominant theme. It witnessed a phenomenal maturing in mind and vision. It resulted in a long step forward in technical mastery. It brought him his greatest acclaim and his most solid financial rewards up to that time. And it settled in his mind the kind of life he wanted to lead and the kind of art he wanted to produce.[3]

These are important claims. Many young painters of the seventies and eighties followed their Paris training with a visit to an art colony. In Homer's case the long gap between these separate experiences meant that the first was thoroughly absorbed before the second was embarked upon. Homer could go to Cullercoats in 1881 with a sense of purpose, having long since rejected the classical and historical excesses of the European high art tradition. Paris may have expanded his range at a time when he was young and impressionable, but Cullercoats consolidated and confirmed his identity as a painter. The experience was crucial in supporting a hindsight view of Homer as an artist of heroic isolation who required simply to find his own *métier*. However these assumptions are not as unproblematic as they at first appear.

When he arrived in London in April 1881 Winslow Homer was not completely unknown to British artists. As an illustrator in *Scribner's Monthly* and *Harper's Weekly*, he occupied a similar role in American terms, to Frank Holl or Hubert von Herkomer in Britain. He may have begun to take the idea of establishing a reputation in London more seriously as a result of conversations at the Tile Club, formed in the autumn of 1877 by a group of artists with strong affiliations to London and Paris. The following year, Homer sent *The Cotton Pickers* (1876) to the Royal Academy.[4] This simple scene of two Negro women picking cotton, was "remarkable" to British eyes.[5] It was, however, less exceptional than it now seems, when considered in comparison to contemporary French painting. Notwithstanding their racial origin, such figures had a clear artistic lineage in the work of Jules Breton, a leading exponent of peasant genre whose work was being avidly collected in the United States.[6] Homer's relationship to the developing tradition of peasant representation in Europe in the late 1870s, immediately prior to his trip to Cullercoats, has not been studied, but certain crucial companion images such as *Answering the Horn* and *Song of the Lark* (both 1876) have been noted for their proximity to Jean-François Millet.[7] These works, however, are among the least satisfactory in Homer's *oeuvre* in that they lack the tragic, fatalistic or classical resonance of the leading European painters of *paysanneries.* This was, nevertheless, a form of painting in Europe, outside the High Art tradition, the values of which Homer could readily identify. The dissemination of pictures of this type throughout America in the years immediately after Millet's death must have supported the desire for renewed contact with the old world. The form which this contact took, however, presents an intriguing set of puzzles.

Following his initial exposure at the Royal Academy, *The Art Journal* ran a short article on Homer in 1879, illustrating *Water Melon Eaters.*[8] He was described as "not wholly a master of technique", but his resolution and strong independence were applauded. "He paints his own thoughts and not other people's."[9] Perhaps because his name had begun to be known there, Homer was persuaded of the potential benefits of a reconnaissance trip to England. Apart from Whistler, who was a special case, there were a number of East Coast Americans who were in the process of establishing reputations in London. Artists like George Faulkner Wetherbee, George Henry Boughton, Mark Fisher and William John Hennessy were all making names for themselves and Homer may have made their acquaintance, although there is no evidence of an expatriate support network operating in his favour.[10] He apparently made no effort to contact any of these artists while in Cullercoats.

Despite the early emphasis upon his originality, Homer's insistence upon naturalistic legibility and his choice of subject matter provide for more obvious parallels with mainstream Salon and Academy painting in France and England than many American writers have admitted.[11] As an illustrator he must always have been an avid consumer of illustration and it is inconceivable that he would not have been aware of the state of the art in its broadest sense, incorporating periodicals such as *The Illustrated London News, The Graphic* and *l'Illustration.*[12] The effect of popular illustration in displacing and revitalizing pictorial conventions in the 1870s has not been studied.[13] It is not unlikely that Homer would have sought out the work of painters who, like himself, had found their way as painters by first being artist-reporters. Of the British contingent, Frank Holl in recent pictures like *The Fisherman's Home,* was continuing a tradition of lugubrious interiors, begun at Cullercoats ten years earlier in *No Tidings from the Sea,* a work which had been purchased promptly by Queen Victoria.[14]

It is equally important, to establish Cullercoats as an artistic centre in the 1880s. During the period when London and Paris were lauded as the most prestigious exhibiting venues, the most successful works were often, paradoxically, those representing customs and manners of rural life. Brittany and Fontainebleau provoked almost insatiable curiosity in the annual salons, while in England artists' colonies sprang up in the 1880s at Newlyn, Walberswick and Whitby. Before Homer arrived at Cullercoats and after he left, it was a place where artists congregated.[15] Its activities were currently the subject of illustrated articles which brought artists with growing reputations, such as William Lionel Wyllie, to the region.[16] The typical, daily rhythms of launching the fleet, unloading the catch and mending the nets provided the essential subject matter at Cullercoats, as it did at Newlyn and Whitby. The dramatic lowering skies of the North Sea, the characteristic costumes and fishing cobles are what differentiate the artistic products of Cullercoats from those of other fishing ports, and some of these features are apparent from the earliest Homer watercolours produced in Cullercoats. Arriving at some point during the summer he had time to submit a watercolour to the Newcastle Arts Association exhibition which opened on 26 August.[17] It seems most likely from contemporary descriptions that this work, entitled *Cullercoats,* is now known as *Fishergirls on the Beach, Cullercoats* (fig. 68). A local reviewer described this as a "charming sketch, containing a couple of wonderfully drawn figures".[18]

The breadth of this particular exhibition has been noted by a number of recent writers on Homer.[19] Although the work of local artists predominated, there were significant pictures by painters of international status. The anglophile French artists, Tissot, Fantin-Latour and Lhermitte were represented and of these Homer would undoubtedly have been attracted to the rustic naturalism of the latter.[20] The exhibition contained the work of one other notable American expatriate, W. J. Hennessy, who exhibited an intriguing picture, *The Impressionist at Work in a Cider Orchard, Normandy.*[21] It is likely that Homer would have identified with the *plein-air* ambitions of these works. Even in a provincial setting such as the North East of England

Fig. 68 Winslow Homer: *Fishergirls on the Beach, Cullercoats*, 1881, watercolour, 13 1/8" x 19 3/8" (33.4 x 49.3 cm). The Brooklyn Museum, Museum Collection Fund, New York. Inscribed lower left: "Winslow Homer 1881".

his awareness of French naturalism seems obvious. Another perceptive reviewer declared that Homer's work was

> evidently influenced by the work of Jules Breton. There is an attempt to catch the noble forms and attitudes so frequently to be found in the toilers of the earth and sea, who are unfettered by modern conventionalities of costume. The aim is an admirable one, for on our English coasts and fields are to be found types of simple and noble beauty equal to those which inspired the Greek masters.[22]

This highly significant appraisal reveals as much understanding of the work of Jules Breton as it does of Homer. From the mid-century in the criticisms of Breton's work there had been a consistent equation between the nobility of the ancients and contemporary peasant types.[23] Attitude and gesture were similar. Their dress was unaffected by the "modern conventionalities of costume". Even in Tyneside there was a need to differentiate between middle-class fashion and the ancient garb of the poor. Divining this tendency in Homer from *Fishergirls on the Beach, Cullercoats*, was almost prophetic in view of what was to follow.

Immediately, however, Homer faced an autumn of uncertainty at Cullercoats. As the Arts Association exhibition was drawing to a close terrible storms brought him to one of his most carefully documented works.

On Friday 21 October 1881 after over a week of storms, *The Shields Daily News* reported that in heavy seas the 1,000 ton *Iron Crown* had foundered at the mouth of the Tyne. By 2.15 a.m. five crewmen had been rescued by Breeches Buoy; however it took the launch of the Tynemouth lifeboat, the *Charles Dibden*, to secure a further fifteen, together with Mrs James, the Captain's wife, who "was conveyed to Bruce's Trevelyan Hotel, where restoratives were administered under the direction of Dr Wilkinson".[24] Finally at about 11.00 a.m. a further lone crewman, attempting to launch a boat, was observed to be still on board the *Iron Crown*. It was necessary therefore for the lifeboat to put to sea again to save him. While this was going on,

> a little cab turned up with an old Cullercoats fisherman on the dicky: out stepped a dapper medium-sized man with a watercolour sketching block and sat down on the ways. He made a powerful drawing with charcoal and some pastel.[25]

This glimpse of Homer by the young George Horton shows the American illustrator-reporter back on an assignment. A number of sketches retrieved from the scene formed the basis of a large, important watercolour which portrays the lifeboat tackling mountainous waves in its efforts to rescue a tiny crewman (figs. 69 and 70).[26] For all the confusion of such a scene,

Fig. 69 Winslow Homer: *The Wreck of the Iron Crown*, 1881, charcoal and white chalk, 8½" x 12½" (21.5 x 31.9 cm). Collection: Carleton Mitchell, Esq., on extended loan to the Baltimore Museum of Art (BMA R.8613.1).

Fig. 70 Winslow Homer: *Life Boat (Wreck of the Iron Crown)*, 1881, black chalk, black wash and white gouache, 13⁷/₈" x 19¹/₁₆" (35.4 x 48.4 cm). The Cooper-Hewitt Museum, The Smithsonian Institution's, National Museum of Design, New York, Gift of Charles Savage Homer.

Homer's watercolour, *The Wreck of the Iron Crown* (fig. 71) is a precise studio production. Each of the ten oars of the lifeboat are clearly visible, raised above the water. The rigging of the *Iron Crown* is given in detail. Observing from the promontory at Tynemouth Haven, Homer's viewpoint was a high one and this merely serves to reinforce the effect.[27] His treatment of the scene is, to some extent, confirmed by Robert Jobling's version of *The Wreck of the Iron Crown*, although this may have been completed after the event and in the knowledge of Homer's version.[28] As is often the case, photographs taken at the scene while the rescue was in progress, are less dramatic (fig. 72). Unlike his other Cullercoats pictures and most of the rest of Homer's *oeuvre*, this painting is a set-piece, dutiful in its honesty, yet containing the passion of an eye-witness account. Exhibiting the picture in a Newcastle shop window after its completion, Homer clearly hoped to have provided the definitive visual record of *The Wreck of the Iron Crown*. In February 1882 the painting was dispatched to the United States.[29]

Several of Homer's drawings of 21 October 1881 show the group of seafarers gathering at the Tynemouth Life Brigade House. The general anxiety and anticipation which such a scene evokes was, on a smaller scale, part of the daily lives of the fishermen and women of Cullercoats. Many studies and sketches begun during the autumn show little gatherings at the newly

Fig. 71 Winslow Homer: *The Wreck of the Iron Crown*, 1881, watercolour, 20¼" x 29⅜" (51.4 x 74.6 cm). Collection: Carleton Mitchell, Esq., on extended loan to The Baltimore Museum of Art (BMA R.8888613.2).

Fig. 72 *The Barque 'Iron Crown' on the Black Middens*, 21 Oct 1881 (photograph, Tynemouth Volunteer Life Brigade).

constructed Look-Out, the Cullercoats Life Brigade Station, a short walk from Homer's studio. These contributed to more finished watercolours such as *Perils of the Sea and Watching the Tempest* and an oil painting, *The Gale.*[30] In *Perils of the Sea* (colour plate vi) two women stand almost with their backs to the ocean facing into a gale blowing up the coast from the Tynemouth direction. Behind them, on the slipway, the men scan the coastline for a returning coble. In a sequence of related drawings Homer gives the full account of such petty tragedies, culminating in *A Dark Hour,* which shows a dejected mother and child leaving the scene of disaster.[31] This is merely hinted at in *Perils of the Sea* in the tension suggested by the finely observed stance of the figures.[32]

Such pictures come at a crucial stage in the development of coastal genre painting in Britain. Their accumulated imagery contributed to the development of a large oil painting entitled *The Coming Away of the Gale* (fig. 73) which shows a heroic young mother approaching the Look-Out, facing into a storm with her child clinging to her back.[33] The picture was attacked by critics when it was exhibited after Homer's return to the United States and he eventually replaced the background, the Cullercoats Look-Out, with an open seascape derived from his surroundings at Prout's Neck. It was eventually re-exhibited in this form at the Chicago World's Fair in 1893. The resulting hybrid work, one of a number of reworked Cullercoats canvases, begins to reveal what Homer took away from his experience in England.

Fig. 73 Winslow Homer: *The Coming Away of the Gale,* oil on canvas, 30 1/4" x 48 3/8" (75.6 x 122.5 cm). Worcester Art Museum, Worcester, Mass.

Other pictures produced at this time show more casual arrangements, with mothers and children sitting by beached cobles or on grassy cliff tops. The longer Homer remained at Cullercoats, however, the more simplified his figure groupings became. Watercolours such as *The Watcher, Forebodings,* and *Women on Shore with Lobster Pot* all illustrate the move towards powerful monumentality.[34] As might be expected, however, the characteristic Cullercoats costume with jackets known as 'bedgowns', skirts with layers of tucking above the hem and aprons of navy 'doctor's flannel', are recorded with documentary accuracy.[35]

Early in his Cullercoats sojourn Homer turned his attention to the more informal activities of the fishergirls in works such as *Fishergirls* and *A Fishergirl Sewing,* both of which show women seated baiting fishing lines. This ritual was often performed in the courtyard of the fisherman's cottage, where women would congregate to chat and work together. Such a grouping gave rise to one of Homer's most appealing Cullercoats oil paintings, known as *Sparrow Hall, Cullercoats.*[36] The relaxed sunlit ambience of this genre piece, full of authentic detail, gives way to starker contrasts in the watercolour *Mending the Nets* (fig. 74). In both pictures women are shown knitting, but the dramatically simplified background of the latter throws out the figures in powerful silhouettes. Comparisons with the work of Jules Breton, who habitually projected his peasant figures against a background of sky, are apposite. It is difficult not to assume that Homer was familiar with some of the other closely allied imagery of British and French artists of the period. Ulysse Butin, Eugene Feyen and his brother François Feyen-Perrin frequently represented the fisherfolk of Normandy and Brittany in paintings shown at the Salons of the 1870s. One of Feyen-Perrin's most important pictures, *Retour de la peche aux huitres . . . à Cancale,* when at the Salon of 1874 was widely reproduced and may have given inspiration to Sargent's *Oyster Gatherers of Cancale,* four years

Fig. 74 Winslow Homer: *Mending the Nets,* 1882, watercolour and gouache over graphite, 27³/₈" x 19¹/₄" (69.1 x 48.9 cm). National Gallery of Art, Washington. Bequest of Julia B. Engel (1984.58.3).

later.[37] Closer to Homer, Cancale provided the setting for Stanhope Forbes's *A Street in Brittany* which was shown at the Royal Academy of 1882.[38] Working with similar ingredients at the same time, Forbes and Homer produced very different pictures. Homer's is more conventionally structured within an acknowledged genre tradition. Forbes, by contrast, as a precocious student, is more concerned to perfect an approved technique.

It is just possible that Homer could have seen Forbes's canvas if he visited the exhibition to view his own painting *Hark! Hark! The Lark!* (colour plate vii), also on display at the Royal Academy in 1882.[39] In these circumstances he would have realised that Bastien-Lepage, the acknowledged master of young painters like Forbes, was again providing controversial pictures for London exhibitions. These were often single upright compositions in which the heroism of the peasant was given added force by the powerful, almost Pre-Raphaelite precision of the surroundings. *Pauvre Fauvette*, currently on display at the United Arts Gallery and attracting much critical attention, provided all of these ingredients.[40] Bastien-Lepage was most admired in the painting colonies where most artists worked from the model *en plein air*. He insisted that each painter find his or her own *coin de terre*, or little corner of the world which could be comprehensively portrayed. Intimacy with a painter's surroundings was an essential criterion of authenticity.

Homer's intentions in *Hark! Hark! The Lark!* were much simpler, although like Bastien-Lepage he hoped to suggest the idea of labour momentarily arrested by the shrill sound of the skylark's call.[41] The association here, derived in part from Shakespeare's *Cymbeline* ("Hark! hark! the lark at heaven's gate sings, / And Phoebus 'gins arise, / His steeds to water at those springs"),[42] is to transform the three fisher girls into a group of Eumenides – or possibly Sirens – standing upon a high promontory, facing the sea, but entranced, and looking skyward. Homer is unlikely to have entertained elaborate symbolist intentions beyond the romantic associations later described by R.J. Charleton, possibly recollecting such a picture as this. "High overhead the skylark sings, and his strain sounds congenial to our ear, so full is it of joy of mere existence."[43]

In this romantic cast of mind Homer was, if anything, closer to Breton and Millet than to Bastien-Lepage. Although Breton's *The Song of the Lark* was not produced until 1884, there were already ample precedents particularly in his large single figure Gleaner subjects of the 1870s.[44] Homer regarded *Hark! Hark! The Lark!* as his most successful Tynemouth painting. It enabled him to resolve ideas which had been tested in 1876 in two less satisfactory pictures, *Answering the Horn* and *Song of the Lark*.[45] After his return to New York in November 1882, he made a part transcription of *Hark! Hark!...* in a watercolour entitled *A Voice from the Cliffs* (fig. 75). This relocates the figures on the shore with large white cliffs, visible in the background.[46] The statuesque quality of the figures is more evident in the watercolour, where, notwithstanding any marginal fading, local colour and incidental detail are subdued. These qualities were evident in 1883 when the work was reviewed by M. G. Van Rensselaer.

> The grouping of *The Voice from the Cliffs* is . . . remarkable. These outlines might almost be transferred to a relief in marble, and yet there is none of the stiffness, the immobility, with which plastically symmetrical effects are usually attended in painted work. They are statuesque figures, but they are living, moving, breathing beings and not statues; and they are as characteristic, as simply natural and unconventional, as are the most awkward of Mr Homer's Yankee children.[47]

Homer needed to come to Europe to discover these qualities. It seems as if, conditioned by the imagery of painters like Breton, Millet, Feyen-Perrin, Holl and others, he wished to remake his Cullercoats experience in avowedly European terms. *A Voice from the Cliffs* was one of the first *resumés* of the Cullercoats experience. In a sense he had found a corner of world in the North East of England which would remain with him for the rest of his career. If the dating of his pictures is to be accepted, he quickly worked up a number of drawings to finished watercolours after his return. This was the

Fig. 75 Winslow Homer: *A Voice from the Cliffs*, 1883, watercolour, 20 7/8" x 29 3/4" (53.0 x 75.6 cm). Private Collection.

case with the most arresting Cullercoats picture, *Inside the Bar, Cullercoats* (1883, fig. 76) in which a tough and solitary fishwife braces herself against the stiff offshore gust of wind. Her basket and billowing apron describe magnificent complementary arcs which hold two departing cobles on either side in precarious balance. As if to underline her emblematic presence, a rock pool reflects her feet and the whole lower portion of her dress.[48] These resonances were evident to Van Rensselaer who particularly admired the figure pose for "its rendering of strength, of motion, of rugged vitality".[49]

Although he was clearly aware of the activity of the men in this small community, and on occasion must have gone out to sea to observe the coble under sail, Homer was most clearly impressed by the women of Cullercoats.[50] They may have been selected initially because they were more picturesque than their menfolk and because they were available to pose – they did not go out to sea. However, recalling the Victorian middle-class male fascination for working women, there is the possibility of a wider context of

Fig. 76 Winslow Homer: *Inside the Bar, Cullercoats*, 1883, watercolour, 15 3/8" x 28 1/2" (39.1 x 72.4 cm). The Metropolitan Museum of Art, New York. Gift of Louise Ryals Arkell, in memory of her husband, Bartlett Arkell, 1954.

interpretation for their dominant presence. The rustic and coastal genre painting of his time tended to concentrate upon the women's work and to read in their facial expressions the off-stage dramas of life. This achieves the force of archetype in *Inside the Bar*. Such a picture could stand as Homer's contribution to the coastal genre imagery of the late nineteenth century, were it not for the fact that, inspired by his Cullercoats sojourn, the artist planned a number of dramatic compositions of rescues at sea, in works such as *The Life Line* and *Undertow*.[51] Grappling muscular figures are shown confronting the elements in a desperate effort for survival. Once again their statuesque strength recalls the work of Breton – in this instance Virginie Demont-Breton's *Femme de pêcheur venant de baigner ses enfants*, which was exhibited at the Salon of 1881 and illustrated in *The Art Journal* during Homer's stay at Cullercoats.[52] Important pictures begun and in the instance of *The Gale* completed shortly after his return from England, survived to be reworked years later in the United States.[53] This may be the case with the extraordinary *Coursing the Hare*, a work which echoes the sentiments of John Robertson Reid's Chantrey picture of 1879, *Toil and Pleasure*.[54] It is certainly true with *Early Evening*, a painting of two fishergirls standing knitting.[55] Behind the rocks on which they stand, a fisherman in a sou'wester scans the distant horizon. Thus the tension of anticipation of the fleet's return is combined with a mood of reverie reminiscent of J. F. Millet's *Tricoteuses*. It is not an overstatement to claim that all of Homer's recapitulations of this theme including *The Fishergirl* (1894), *Sunset, Saco Bay, the Coming Storm* (1896) and *A Light on the Sea* (1897) owe something to the many Cullercoats watercolours of fisherwomen gazing out to sea.[56]

These in turn are part of a rich image community in European art. It would be possible for Homer in later years to keep in touch with the Royal Academy and the Salon by means of the ever-expanding print and reproduction market. The impetus to retain some small contact with the art world in Europe might well have been prompted by the relative success of Homer's Cullercoats studies in the American exhibitions. Given the fact that, in this era, collectors and public in general were hungry for a new sensation and that artists were often placed under contract to go abroad to produce work, Homer cannot have been impervious to the immediate recognition that he received for his Cullercoats paintings.

> A few years ago he could surely not have painted the fine subtle sky in *The Coming Storm* or *Inside the Bar* . . . A few years ago his brush was stiffer, his tones were cruder than they are today; his art altogether was harsher and more angular.[57]

So wrote Van Rensselaer in 1883. At the turn of the century, as he was drawn more and more to paint seascapes, often without figures, there is an obvious truth in the recollections of A.B. Adamson that this unique experience made him alive to "atmosphere and colour".[58] The loneliness of the figure set against the immensity of the ocean has encouraged the belief in Homer of an artist in splendid isolation, especially in his later years at Prout's Neck on the coast of Maine.[59] More recently, perhaps conditioned by the climate of post-war modernism, this picture of the lonely genius has been consolidated.[60] His celebrated advice to Joseph Foxcroft Cole, "If a man wants to be an artist he should never look at pictures" is frequently quoted.[61] Certainly in later years he led an hermetic existence, claiming that he had left New York to avoid serving on juries for exhibitions. It is not surprising that later writers should have risen to the opinion that Homer was "less influenced . . . by what others had done than any other artist."[62] This does not mean that he was not totally impervious to the work of others any more than it could be claimed that at Cullercoats he imported a ready made imagery. Homer at Cullercoats broke with his own past, and he was temporarily part of a community of artists establishing its identity as a colony. In this ambience he was brought back to the essential drama of human beings facing the elements. His clifftop figures stand up in front of the rugged force of nature. It is not surprising that this austere, hermetic and ultimately heroic image of the artist should have emerged. However his English period and the general European context of the Cullercoats-inspired works, call for a more cosmopolitan Winslow Homer.

References and Notes

1. This essay is a revised form of one which first appeared in 1988 in the catalogue of an exhibition at the Centre for Contemporary Art, Sunderland, entitled *Winslow Homer, All the Cullercoats Pictures.* My interest in Homer's work began in 1977, when researching an exhibition of nineteenth-century marine and coastal genre painting, which focused upon the colony at Cullercoats. Shortly after that exhibition was staged I was given an introduction to the subject by Helen Cooper who visited the North East researching *Winslow Homer Watercolours* (1986). Armed with a kit of photographs and a camera and trying not to get our feet wet, we picked our way over the rocks to find the vantage points from which Winslow Homer would have painted. A few years later I began to correspond regularly with William H.Gerdts, doyen of American Impressionism, whose seminal article on Homer at Cullercoats had been published in 1977. He and Abigail Booth Gerdts graciously answered queries as this essay came together in its initial form. To them and to Helen Cooper's monograph I remain continually indebted. I am grateful to Tony Knipe for his enthusiastic support at the time of the Sunderland exhibition. My greatest debt is however to the late John Boon whose extensive research on Homer at Cullercoats began in the early 1970s. Following our many conversations about the village and Homer's sojourn, John Boon graciously donated his extensive files to the University of Northumbria. To his memory, and to that of his wife Molly Boon, this essay is therefore dedicated.

2. William Howe Downes, *The Life and Works of Winslow Homer* (Boston and New York, 1911), pp. 99, 106.

3. Lloyd Goodrich, *Winslow Homer* (New York, 1944), p. 82.

4. Coll. Los Angeles County Museum of Art, exhibited RA, 1878, No. 60 as *Cotton Pickers – North Carolina.*

5. Henry Blackburn, *Academy Notes* (1878), p.11, describes the work, "Landscape low in tone and rather weird in aspect; with two dark women; a remarkable work." The picture was also mentioned in *The Art Journal* (1878), p.145.

6. For further reference see Madeleine Fidell-Beaufort, "Jules Breton in America: Collecting in the 19th Century", in Hollister Sturges (ed.), *Jules Breton and the French Rural Tradition*, catalogue of an exhibition at the Joslyn Art Museum, Omaha (1983), pp. 51-59.

7. Colls. Muskegon Museum of Art and the Chrysler Museum of Art, Norfolk, Virginia, respectively. For further reference see Patricia Hills "Images of Rural America in the Work of Winslow Homer, Eastman Johnson and their Contemporaries", in Hollister Sturges (ed.), *The Rural Vision: France and America in the late 19th Century* (Omaha, 1987), pp. 122-26.

8. Anon., "American Painters: Winslow Homer and F. A. Bridgman", *The Art Journal* (1879), pp. 154-55: this article is apparently a reprint of an article by George W. Sheldon.

9. Ibid.

10. For general reference to American painters in Europe c. 1880 see Michael Quick, *American Expatriate Painters of the late Nineteenth Century*, catalogue of an exhibition at Dayton Art Institute, Ohio (1977). Wetherbee and Hennessy are not mentioned in the above and neither has been studied in recent years. For Wetherbee see Newcastle upon Tyne Polytechnic Art Gallery, *Peasantries*, catalogue of an exhibition by Kenneth McConkey (1981), pp. 48-49. For Hennessy see Anon., *The Modern School of Art*, Vol. IV, n.d. (c. 1887), pp. 122-26.

11. I except from this the recent writers to whose research I am indebted throughout this article, particularly William H. Gerdts, whose "Winslow Homer in Cullercoats", *Yale University Art Gallery Bulletin*, vol. 36, no. 2, spring 1977, pp.18-35 (herein Gerdts), is seminal and Helen A. Cooper, whose *Winslow Homer Watercolours* was published in 1986 (herein Cooper) to coincide with a major retrospective of Homer watercolours at the National Gallery of Art, Washington, the Amon Carter Museum, Fort Worth, and Yale University Art Gallery, New Haven.

12. Gerdts proposes a number of *Graphic* illustrations to account for the wider knowledge of Cullercoats, its terrain, activities and types. John Wilmerding in "Winslow Homer's English Period", *American Art Journal*, vol. VII, no. 2 (1975), pp. 60-69, looking at Homer's earlier style of illustration, relates his work to that of George du Maurier, selecting his fishwife cartoons for comparison of the "picturesque stances, costumes and manners", of the figures.

13. A high degree of receptivity can therefore be assumed prior to his arrival and after it a degree of fine tuning inevitably must have taken place. Although no evidence has survived concerning his actual activities in London, Homer took a conventional view of the Houses of Parliament (Hirschhorn Museum and Sculpture Garden, Smithsonian Institution, Washington) modifying the fiery moon-light Gloucester, Mass., watercolours to produce an image more in tune with the world of Whistler.

14. Gerdts, pp. 22-23, discusses the latter work, but not that which Homer could have seen. He and Cooper have discussed the wide range of British and Hague School painting which might have appealed to Homer. Gerdts additionally refers to the work of Charles Napier Hemy, James Clarke Hook and Myles Birket Foster. He illustrates William Quiller Orchardson's *Toilers of the Sea* (RA 1870, no. 953, Coll. Aberdeen Art Gallery) as another important image reproduced in *The Graphic* on 6 April 1870, and executed while the artist was apparently staying at Cullercoats with Henry Hetherington Emerson. It is tempting to propose that some direct contact between Holl or Orchardson and Homer resulted in the suggestion of Cullercoats as a suitable place to study, although no evidence for this exists. Cooper (op. cit., p.83) repeats the evidence supplied by Alan Adamson, a native of Cullercoats who recalled that Homer had told him that he had learned of the village from a fellow traveller on the voyage to England. John Boon, through careful study of ships' records, has confirmed that there was indeed a passenger from North Shields on board the *Parthia* with the artist. None of the reasons advanced for Homer's choice of Cullercoats in the summer of 1881 is totally satisfactory. His selection remains as enigmatic and apparently arbitrary as Whistler's trip to Valparaiso in 1867. If the decision to journey north had, in effect, been made prior to his arrival in England, the weeks spent in London in April and May 1881 must have provided him with the opportunity to acquaint himself with the latest

trends in European art. The art season of 1881 contained a number of works which were potentially of interest, but these can be considered important only in so far as their influence is manifest in Homer's later career at Cullercoats and after. London galleries were currently featuring work by Bastien-Lepage, for instance, as well as coastal genre pictures by Hook, Moore, Bartlett, Carr and others at the Grosvenor Gallery and the Royal Academy. For a general discussion of the influences of French painting upon Homer's work prior to the Cullercoats interlude, see Henry Adams, 'Winslow Homer's 'Impressionism' and its relation to his trip to France', in Nicolai Cikovsky, Jr. (ed.), *Winslow Homer, A Symposium,* National Gallery of Art, Washington (1990), pp.61-83.

15. For further reference see John Millard, 'North East Artists on the Coast', in Northern Centre for Contemporary Art, Sunderland, *Winslow Homer, All the Cullercoats Pictures* (1988), pp. 22-27.

16. Wyllie illustrated Aaron Watson's two-part article "After the Herring" in *The Magazine of Art,* vol. 5 (1882), pp. 405-11, 454-60; Robert Jobling (1841-1932) contributed one illustration.

17. Gerdts, p. 33; Cooper, pp. 87-88; Cooper has supplied much information concerning Homer's settling-in at Cullercoats, recounting his initial stay at the Huddlestone Arms, later the Bay Hotel, his renting of a fisherman's cottage off Front Street and a Studio at 12 Bank Top. She quotes Alan B. Adamson's memoir of Homer noting his American appearance – "short-tail coat and high silk hat" which were discarded for more practical fisherman's garb.

18. Homer's *Cullercoats* was no. 32 in the Arts Association Exhibition: *Newcastle Courant* 26 August 1887, p. 6; quoted in Cooper, p. 87.

19. The Arts Association had been founded in 1878 and the wide appeal of its exhibitions were a tribute to its active secretary, the classical painter T.R. Spence.

20. One of Lhermitte's two exhibits *Jeunne Fille de Plougastil, Bretagne* (no. 297), a work which had first appeared in the Dudley Gallery, Winter Exhibition of 1879 (182) and is currently unlocated, was obviously a study of a Breton fishergirl.

21. W. J. Hennessy's work was no. 419 in the exhibition and it remains unlocated. It has not been possible to discover if H. R. Bloomer, no. 647, *Evening,* was in fact the American painter Hiram Bloomer. Other works of note shown in Newcastle were James Charles's *Our Poor* and pictures by the future members of the Glasgow School like Guthrie, Christie, East, Walton and Crawhall.

22. *Tyneside Daily Echo,* 31 August 1881, p. 3; quoted by Cooper, p. 88.

23. The classical context for Breton's work has been noted recently by a number of writers. See particularly Kenneth McConkey, "Jules Breton and the French Rural Tradition" (book review), *The Burlington Magazine,* vol. cxxv (November 1983), pp. 703-4.

24. *The Shields Daily News,* 21 October 1881. *The Iron Crown* finally broke up in the early hours of Saturday 22 October. Local papers reported at the beginning of the following week that the gale had gained such renown that it brought over 20,000 visitors to Tynemouth just to see the spectacle.

25. George Horton, "Artist with a Craze for Clocks", *Sunday Sun,* 5 March 1939.

26. The perspicacious Gerdts suggested that Homer has access to photographs in producing *The Wreck of the Iron Crown.* Homer did purchase a Marion Miniature "Academy" Camera which had just become available in 1881, but no photographs by him of Cullercoats and Tynemouth appear to have survived. He may, however, have had access to a number of other photographs of the event which show the final rescue. In these the details of the *Iron Crown* are similar. Cooper, pp. 107-8, 121 (note 28), refers to Homer's copy of Chevreul's treatise on colour harmony into which a photograph of a coble was pasted.

27. Cooper, p. 102, has given a full description of the conception and execution of *The Wreck of the Iron Crown.*

28. For further reference see, John Millard, *A Romance with the North East: Robert and Isa Jobling* (Newcastle upon Tyne, 1992), pp.20-21.

29. Most authorities quote Homer's accompanying undated letter to the dealer Eastman Chase referring to the steep horizon and telling him that he may cut off the lifeboat, "If you like . . . ".

30. *Watching the Tempest*, Coll. Fogg Museum of Art, bequest of Greville L. Winthrop, has been painted from a vantage point made familiar by various illustrations by Robert Jobling, notably his *Cullercoats Harbour*, illus. *The Magazine of Art* (1882), p. 460, and the later Academy piece *Twilight falls from the Wings of the Night* (R.A. 1886 no. 311, see p. 24).

31. Illus. Cooper, pp. 106-7; Coll. Cooper-Hewitt Museum, Gift of Charles Savage Homer.

32. So successful was this arrangement of figures that Homer produced an etching of the subject, 41.6 x 55.3 cms, coll. National Museum of American Art, Smithsonian Institution, Washington DC.

33. Coll. Worcester Museum of Art, Worcester, Mass. Hendricks, *Winslow Homer* (New York, 1979), p. 169, and CL321.

34. Colls. Institute of Art, Chicago; The Hyde Collection, Glen Falls, New York; The Brooklyn Museum, respectively.

35. For a full description of the women's dresses see Tyne & Wear Museums *The Cullercoats Fishwife*, catalogue of an exhibition by Louise Hamer (1984), pp. 66-73.

36. Private Collection, USA. This work was formerly knows as *Fisherfolk, Tynemouth*; Hendricks, op.cit., p. 152, reproduces a turn-of-the-century photograph taken from almost the same angle as Homer's vantage point in this painting. The building was sometimes known as Dove Cottage after the Dove family, lords of the manor in 1682, when it was first leased. A carved lintel contained the date of the building's construction and a dove to symbolise the owner. In later years the bird was mistaken by local people, hence the nickname "Sparrow Hall", by which it was popularly known in Homer's day. A landmark of considerable interest, the building was sadly demolished in 1979.

37. For reference to fishing subjects by both Feyens see Geneviéve Lacambre, *Le Musée du Luxembourg en 1874*, catalogue of an exhibition at the Grand Palais, Paris (1974), pp. 70-72. In a sense Feyen-Perrin transposed the classical nobility of Breton's gleaners into fisherfolk. Breton had of course tackled coastal genre with his *Breton Washerwomen* (1870, untraced). For reference to Sargent see Richard Ormond, *John Singer Sargent* (Oxford, 1971), pp. 17-18.

38. For reference to *A Street in Brittany*, see Francis Greenacre and Caroline Fox, *Artists of the Newlyn School*; catalogue of an exhibition at Newlyn, Plymouth and Bristol (1979), pp. 73-74; Caroline Fox, *Stanhope Forbes and the Newlyn School* (1993), pp.14-15.

39. Coll. Milwaukee Art Center, Gift of Frederick Layton. In recent years there has been a tendency to shorten the title of this picture to *Hark! The Lark!* It was originally shown in the Academy as *Hark! Hark! The Lark!* A similar work of the same date, though smaller in scale, by Isa Thompson, the wife of Robert Jobling, passed through the art trade in Newcastle upon Tyne c. 1983.

40. See Kenneth McConkey, "Pauvre Fauvette or 'petite folle'; a Study of Jules Bastien-Lepage's 'Pauvre Fauvette'". *Arts Magazine* (January 1981), pp. 140-43.

41. The artists had, six years earlier, given this idea, in a rustic setting, in *The Song of the Lark*.

42. *Cymbeline*, Act II, Scene iii.

43. R. J. Charleton, "Cullercoats", *The Magazine of Art*, vol. 9 (1886), p. 456; quoted by Cooper, p. 155.

44. Coll. Aberdeen Art Gallery. Without labouring the comparison between Breton and Homer, the bulk of Breton's figures, his figure poses, revealing strong muscular forearms, is apposite.

45. For further discussion see Patricia Hills, op.cit. (1987), pp. 74-76; see also Roger B. Stein, "Picture and Text: The Literary World of Winslow Homer", in Nicolai Cikovsky, Jr. (ed.), *Winslow Homer, A Symposium*, National Gallery of Art, Washington (1990), pp.33-59.

46. Private Collection, Switzerland. It also raises the question of Homer having visited other east coast resorts during his stay at Cullercoats. A drawing of his Cullercoats model, Maggie Storey, standing on white chalk cliffs, entitled *Flamborough Head,* is in the Art Institute of Chicago; see Hendricks, op. cit., p. 161. It is possible that Homer merely had access to one of the many volumes of coastal photography then becoming popular. Elsewhere in his titles Yarmouth and Scarborough appear when the actual paintings contain characteristic North East fishing cobles.

47. M. G. Van Rensselaer, "An American Artist in England", *Century Magazine,* vol. 27 (November 1883), pp. 17-18.

48. Hendricks, op. cit., p. 160, reproduces a chalk drawing *Windy Day, Tynemouth Beach* (1881, private collection) showing the central portion of the composition.

49. M. G. Van Rensselaer, op. cit., p. 17.

50. Even in such works as *Returning Fishing Boats* (1883, Fogg Museum of Art), and its related drawing, the erroneously entitled *Fishing off Scarborough* (1882, Art Institute, Chicago), Homer shows a coble with, unusually, two women on board accompanying the men. A rare exclusively male sketch produced during Homer's stay at Cullercoats is *The Return* (Art Institute of Chicago).

51. Colls. Philadelphia Museum of Art; Sterling and Francine Clark Institute of Art, Williamstown, Mass.

52. Virginie Demont-Breton, the daughter of Jules Breton, was a successful Salon exhibitor in the 1880s. Despite its contemporary popularity, her work remains unstudied.

53. Coll. Worcester Art Museum, Worcester, Mass; reproduced in Hendricks, op. cit., p. 212. A photograph of the original state, Hendricks, op. cit., p. 242, is contained in Bowdoin College Museum of Art, Brunswick, Maine.

54. Reproduced in Hendricks, op. cit., p. 174; Coll. Mr and Mrs Paul Mellon.

55. Coll. Freer Gallery of Art, Smithsonian Institution, Washington DC; Hendricks, op. cit., p. 264. Homer apparently wrote to John Beatty in November 1907 that he was repainting this Cullercoats oil which was later sold to Charles L. Freer for 5,000 dollars.

56. Colls. Amherst Museum of Art, Amherst College, Mass.; Sterling and Francine Clark Institute, Williamstown, Mass.; Corcoran Art Gallery Washington DC; reproduced in Hendricks, op. cit., pp. 222 and 225.

57. M. G. Van Rensselaer, op. cit., p. 21.

58. A. B. Adamson, "The Homer That I Knew", Centre for Contemporary Art, Sunderland, op. cit., p. 17.

59. See for instance W. H. Downes, op. cit., p. 14 et passim, refers to Homer as an "exceptional" man with "instinctive vigilance against intrusion . . . he had resources within himself".

60. See for instance Philip C. Beam, *Winslow Homer at Prout's Neck,* catalogue of an exhibition at Bowdoin College Museum of Art (1966), p. 13; after Cullercoats "he would devote his energies to few subjects, talent came genius lingered".

61. Quoted by Lloyd Goodrich, *Winslow Homer,* catalogue of an exhibition at the Whitney Museum, New York (1973), p. 21.

62. Ibid., p. 21, quoting Homer's dealer, J. Eastman Chase.

XI

MODERNITY, FEMININITY AND REGIONAL IDENTITY: WOMEN AND FASHION IN THE NORTH EAST OF ENGLAND, 1914-1940

Cheryl Buckley

Various feminist writers and historians have examined women's experiences of life and culture in Britain between the Wars.[1] Initially, most writings concentrated on the political, social, and economic activities of women, to a large extent in response to their cursory or derogatory treatment at the hands of other historians and contemporary commentators.[2] Most have located their accounts within the dual contexts of the aftermath of the First World War and the success of the women's suffrage campaign, although, in most cases, feminist historians have viewed the inter-war years as a period of anti-feminism, perceiving a loss of political momentum after the gaining of the vote. The last few years, however, have seen a new interest in women's cultural, as opposed to political, activities. Writers such as Alison Light and Sally Alexander have been concerned to outline women's resistance to oppression through their engagement with a range of popular cultural forms including literature and fashion. Within Design History, historians have shown the sheer breadth of the involvement of women in design as practitioners and as consumers.[3]

Given that women's viewpoint has been shaped as much by interior as exterior experiences, this bias has clear implications for our understanding of their lives. This is particularly so in terms of our perceptions of women's relationship to modernism and modernity.[4] Certainly within the context of Design History, women's engagement with modernism and modernity has been contradictory. On the one hand, although women designers undoubtedly contributed to modernist design practice between the Wars, by the mid-1930s British modernism was a mainly masculine affair: technological, rationalist, and progressive.[5] Women designers tended to reject the rigid formalism and dogma associated with European modernist theory and practice.[6] On the other hand, the social and cultural changes which were characteristic of modernity in the inter-war years offered both working-class and middle-class women new opportunities as workers and consumers, as well as the possibility of redefining dominant notions of 'femininity'.

Significantly, women's understanding of modernism and modernity has been shaped by gender. As Alison Light has argued, the inter-war years marked "for many women their entry into modernity, a modernity which was felt and lived in the most interior and private places."[7] Emphasising gender, Sally Alexander stresses the conflict between two images which compete in the popular memory of the 1920s and 1930s, representing the feminine and the masculine:

> the cloth cap and spare frame of the unemployed man whose face and staring eyes still wrench pity from the onlooker; and the young girl – lipsticked, silk-stockinged, and dressed . . .'like an actress'[8] (figs. 77 and 78).

Both Light and Alexander explore women's experience and engagement with modernity, and the relationship between notions of modernity and contemporary perceptions of the 'feminisation' of British social, economic and cultural life.[9] Indeed, this increased 'feminisation', which was identified by several writers in the inter-war years, has a regional dimension. It can be viewed in terms of the north/south divide, as the decline of the traditional, heavy industries of shipbuilding, coal-mining, and iron and steel removed men from the labour force in the north, whilst the concurrent growth of the 'sun-rise' industries and the shift to the service sector brought women increasingly into the labour market, particularly in the south.[10] However, as the 1930s progressed, women began to penetrate the labour force in the north as the newer industries developed along arterial roads and at new trading estates such as the Team Valley in Gateshead. Furthermore, women and their concerns were foregrounded as they were targeted as consumers of domestic products:[11]

> not only is the new working class in these new industries female, but the wants and needs which the new industries supply are feminine[12] (figs. 79 and 80).

Fig. 77 Jarrow Crusaders, marching past the City Hall and Swimming Baths, Northumberland Road, Newcastle upon Tyne, October 1936. This image is probably one of the best known and most typical of representations of the North East in the inter-war period, showing the human consequences of closures in the traditional industries of ship-building, heavy engineering and mining. Significantly, it is a specifically working-class masculine experience that is being depicted. (*The Journal*).

Fig. 78 Young women enjoying a visit to the North East Coast Exhibition in 1929. This image draws into sharp relief the contradictions of life in the North East between the Wars: the Exhibition was organised to revive and develop trade and industry in an area affected by high levels of male unemployment, yet at the same time young, working women in particular experienced the pleasures of independence and more modern lifestyles, especially in the region's towns and cities. (Newcastle City Libraries).

During the 1920s and 1930s images of modernity were closely tied to popular representations of the sexually and socially emancipated lifestyles of specific groups of women. Although several writers have questioned the extent of this emancipation, particularly for working-class married women in the north, it is evident that young single women did experience more freedom than hitherto.[13] In Hartlepool, Bishop Auckland, Newcastle and Darlington they went out dancing unchaperoned, they bought and exchanged women's magazines, attended the cinema at least once a week, and avidly followed the latest fashionable styles.[14]

Fashion was an important arena for the creation of these images of modernity and sexual freedom. Interpreting fashion allowed women the opportunity to engage with modernity in a public as well as a private way. Uniquely, it combined the interior and the exterior worlds, and it afforded women the means to signify their involvement with modern social life – with the city and town, with some measure of personal choice and independence, and with the contemporary pleasures of shops, magazines, the cinema, and dancing. It provided a powerful symbol of modernity in a

Fig. 79 "Let Electricity do your drudgery. Don't do it yourself". Reyrolle promotional brochure for the latest domestic electrical switches from 1927. Women not only worked in the new electrical components factories, they also consumed the resulting electrical products. In this photograph, the vacuum cleaner symbolises the modernity of domestic life in the inter-war period, yet the dining room design represents the conservatism of the middle-class domestic interior with 'Tudorbethan' sideboard, wall panelling and ceiling beams alongside slightly 'moderne' drapes.

Fig. 80 View of the Team Valley Trading Estate in Gateshead (built in 1937-38). The layout and the main administration building of the first estate of its type in the country were designed by Sir William Holford in collaboration with the local architect, L.J. Couves. The design represents a typically British interpretation of modernism, combining red brick with ribbon windows, flat roof and a geometric, utilitarian aesthetic. (L.J. Couves & Partners).

number of specific ways: the emphasis on day and leisure wear pointed to freer, less formal lifestyles; style, cut and fashionable iconography were a testament to the influence of Hollywood glamour and particular screen idols such as Clara Bow, Greta Garbo, Joan Crawford and Jean Harlow; and new methods of manufacture, synthetic materials, stylish advertising and lower prices were indicators of the impact of the modern production strategies of 'Taylorism', and the power of American marketing and retailing techniques.[15]

As an aspect of material culture, then, fashion was as potent an image of modernity as a new house or an electric iron. However, it also served the dual purpose of allowing women to signal their questioning of sexual identity and femininity at the same time as highlighting the ambiguities of women's social, political and economic positions. On the one hand, lesbianism, female sexuality, and a woman's control over her reproduction were on the agenda, whilst on the other they were being undermined by the negative influence of D.H. Lawrence's notions of the superiority of the 'natural' as opposed to the 'modern' woman, and Oswald Moseley's view of women as "different but equal". At the same time, women were under attack for being anti-feminist, as they were castigated for their frivolity by liberal feminists such as Winifred Holtby who claimed that:

> cropped hair and serviceable shoes [are] waging a defensive war against this powerful movement to reclothe the female form in swathing trails and frills and flounces to emphasise the difference between men and women.[16]

Whilst not denying the very real difficulties experienced by women from different classes between the Wars, such as wage cuts, unemployment, and a lack of real choice in terms of jobs, education, and their personal lives, a fundamental aim of this chapter is to show the way that engagement in fashion at a number of levels enabled women from both the working and middle classes to redefine themselves in relation to femininity and modernity. Furthermore, women's responses to fashionable iconography and to the changes within fashion production and retailing, as workers and as consumers, provide an excellent focus for an examination of the relationship of these concepts to regional identity. Did women in the North East experience fashion differently to their southern sisters, especially given the structural differences in the economy which were emerging between north and south? What was the relationship between representations of femininity, particularly in fashion and women's lived experiences? Was resistance to the so-called 'feminisation' of British social and cultural life more effective in the traditional strongholds of masculine labour in the north, or did fundamental changes in British society permanently transform women's experience of what life had to offer? Finally, was modernity experienced differently as one journeyed northwards up the A1 from London to Newcastle?

Women's Labour and Representations of the North East

The unemployed male worker, most poignantly represented as a Jarrow crusader in local and national press photography, remains the dominant image of the North East during the 1920s and 1930s. Yet, as Robert Thorne has argued in discussing J.B. Priestley's celebrated account of the North East during his 1933 *English Journey*:

> The potent descriptions in Priestley's *English Journey* again underline the contrasts to be found in the period, but they are seldom linked by an understanding of how different parts of the country or different groups in society could experience such a variety of conditions.[17]

And a variety of conditions is undoubtedly what the North East experienced in the inter-war period. The historian C.L. Mowat chronicles the demise of the older industries of mining, steel and shipbuilding in some detail.[18] Tyneside's share of the world supply of shipping was drastically cut. Whereas pre-First World War, Britain had supplied 80% of the foreign market for new tonnage, by the mid-1930s increased competition had reduced this to 20%.[19] Also badly hit were the coalfields. Stevenson describes how the Kent coalfield was developed by miners transferred from the Durham area due to the large number of closures.[20] South-west Durham, which included Bishop Auckland and Ferryhill, had thirty-three mines which employed 28,000 miners after the First World War. By 1935 only thirteen remained, employing 6,500 men. The work in these pits was intermittent and frequently part-time. In pit villages such as Shildon and Tow Law, unemployment was 100% and 80% respectively.[21] A characteristic of the unemployment experienced by these ex-miners was that it was long-term. According to Mowat, 71% of the unemployed in the County Durham town of Crook had been unemployed for over five years.[22]

Women's experience of unemployment in the inter-war years was dependent on regional variations. In some of the depressed areas such as the Durham coalfields married women tended not to work outside the home, and as a result social commentators concluded: "Here there is no problem of the employment of women, but only of the effect on women of the unemployment of men."[23]

Professional women, working-class women and middle-class women employed in the service sectors in towns and cities in the North East region, were hit by unemployment to different degrees throughout the 1920s and 1930s.

Women therefore experienced unemployment and employment differently to men in the inter-war years. However, as Beddoe argues: "the typical woman worker was not only young, but she was single".[24]

On the whole, women workers tended to be single for one of three reasons: they gave up work upon marriage (sometimes voluntarily, but often compulsorily); they remained single; or they were widowed. In 1931 40% of women in the age group 15-59 were single. Although there was substantial talk of women taking men's jobs in this period, a characteristic of working class women's work was that it was low-paid and sexually segregated. Generally, working-class women took jobs in industries in which men would not work – hence their involvement in the service sector in shops, restaurants, laundries, and as domestic servants.[25] It was also due to these sexual divisions that women worked in the newer industries, which often required skills and qualities perceived to be female, such as dexterity and the ability to withstand repetitious boring work. This work was described as semi-skilled and consequently low paid.

Typical working-class women workers were Maisie Wright and Renee Rutherford. Maisie Wright, who was born in Darlington in 1919, worked at the Lily Laundry from the age of fourteen years until she married in 1937.[26] She packed clean and dirty clothes, and was initially paid nine pence halfpenny per week, which she gave to her parents. Maisie worked because it was expected that a young working-class woman should contribute to the family income to support her two brothers and six sisters. Her father was a railway worker who lived on the north side of Darlington near the heavy industries associated with the railway. Nonetheless, Maisie was allowed to go out dancing on Friday and Saturday nights, either to the Palais de Danse or the Co-op Dance, in addition to going to the cinema during the week. To afford this she walked the two miles to and from work. Renee Rutherford was an only child, born in Ferryhill Station in County Durham in 1920.[27] Her father had worked as a gardener and chauffeur in Northumberland, but after losing an arm in the First World War he became a miner at Ferryhill Colliery until his retirement at the age of sixty-five. Renee's mother also came from a mining family who lived at East Howell, near the County Durham pit village of Mainsforth. Like Maisie Gibson, Renee worked in the service sector. She worked in a general dealers' shop and, as was expected, 'tipped up' her wages to her parents each week. Also, like many young women of her class, she had worked in domestic service as a ladies' maid in Harrogate, but although this was apparently a good situation, she did not stay long. In 1938 she married Sid Chaplin, a miner at Ferryhill colliery, and gave up work.[28]

In contrast, Elizabeth Clennell's experiences were those of a woman from a lower middle-class background. Born in 1896 and brought up in Newcastle, she was the daughter of a brickworks manager at Bill Quay, Pelaw.[29] The eldest of three children, she was brought up in relative comfort – her parents lived in their own house and employed a day servant to do the washing, ironing and general cleaning. She attended a secretarial college in Newcastle and as a result worked in various offices in Newcastle.[30] In 1924 she married Henry Morin, who worked in the railway offices at Newcastle. Upon marriage, Elizabeth gave up work and moved to Darlington with her husband when he was made transport manager of North Road Railway Station.

Elizabeth Clennell, Maisie Wright and Renee Rutherford were not unusual in working outside the home. The type of work undertaken by Elizabeth Clennell as a secretary was typical of that available for women of her class, although many women in a comparable position did not work. Equally typical were the jobs undertaken in the service sector by Maisie Wright and Renee Rutherford. Significantly, however, the choice of work for working-class women in the North East expanded as national measures to improve employment in those heavy industrial areas which had been hardest hit by unemployment, brought newer industries northwards. The development of the Team Valley Trading estate was evidence of this, as was the expansion of companies such as the Newcastle-based Reyrolle Ltd, which initially responded to the massive expansion of the electrical supply industry by making switch-gear, then started making small-scale domestic appliances such as vacuum cleaners, portable electrical heaters and curling tongs, and at the same time began employing larger numbers of women workers.[31] These jobs were just one part of an increasingly visible process of progress and modernity which became evident across the region, and which paralleled the contraction of the older industries. As Sally Alexander has said:

> In the 1920s and 1930s office cleaners, packers, shop assistants, typists became the unlikely and suddenly visible shock troops of industrial restructuring.[32]

For some women, particularly younger single ones, expectations were changing. Work, some measure of financial responsibility, and more involvement in the world outside the home were tangible indicators of women's new roles. In this respect, the feminisation of British cultural, economic and social life was not merely about the interior world of home, family and consumerism, as writers such as Orwell perceived; it was also about women's engagement with modernity, both as workers and individual consumers of clothes, make-up, magazines, the cinema and dancing. Modernity for these women was experienced as growing independence and consequent visibility. To a certain extent, this contrasts markedly with the view of the inter-war years outlined by feminist historians such as Sheila Rowbotham and Deirdre Beddoe, who generally see the period as one of anti-feminism.[33] Yet, although the lives of the women that I have interviewed were clearly shaped by conflicts within the family, lack of control of their fertility, few long term prospects outside the home, and low incomes, these women did have a greater opportunity, as I will show, to engage with the diversity of social and cultural activities than had their mothers before them.

The decline of traditional, masculine skilled labour may have been part of the dominant iconography of the North East in the inter-war years, but increasingly images of modernity proliferated.[34] These images undermined regional identity, and, although it was possible to retain regional design types such as the Tyneside flat,[35] for example, these were adapted to fit the typical inter-war semi plan and consequently looked little different to the ubiquitous spec. built semi-detached house which was to be found across Britain. New housing estates (built by local councils in the 1920s and by speculative builders in the 1930s) were proliferating across the North East.[36] Elizabeth and Henry Morin bought a semi-detached house which they named 'Wanlock' in 1928 on The Mead, a garden suburb style private housing development in the Eastbourne area of Darlington.[37] The house, which had three bedrooms, lounge, dining room and kitchen, was very progressive for its day – not in terms of architectural style, which was sub-vernacular with Art Deco details, but with regard to equipment and interior design. It had, for example, a modern kitchen with a 'Revo' electric cooker.[38]

Another increasingly visible symbol of modernity in the inter-war years was the road-house pub. Changes in the design and character of the public house, brought about in part by fear of U.S. style prohibition being introduced into Britain, led to the development of this new type of modern pub. These Neo-Georgian, Tudor and occasional 'moderne' road-house pubs sprang up on the new coast and arterial roads in the north of England as well as the south. They combined cocktail bar, games room, restaurant and children's room with drinking and dancing.[39] Typical of these were the "Wheatsheaf" at Woolsington (north of Newcastle), which was designed in 1935 for Newcastle Breweries by J. Oswald & Sons.

The experience of modernity was just as important as the image of modernity to the region, and none was more powerful than the record-breaking LNER's 'Silver Jubilee' and 'Silver Link' trains (Nigel Gresley's modified Pacific-type locomotive no. 2509), which reached 112.5 mph in the four-hour journey from London to Newcastle, thus reducing the isolation of the region.[40] Experience and image were combined in Newcastle with the opening of the new bridge over the river Tyne in 1928. Engineered by Mott, Hay & Anderson, constructed by Dorman Long of Middlesbrough and with architectural detailing by the local Newcastle practice of Cackett,

Burns Dick and Mackellar, the Tyne Bridge, with its magnificent curved steel span which swept from the Newcastle to the Gateshead quaysides, was a potent image of the new Newcastle, one willing to respond to the needs of the motor-car.[41] Similarly, the excitement and commercial viability of the cinema were demonstrated by new building which gathered pace in a city such as Newcastle which had between thirty and forty cinemas, and towns such as Darlington which by 1928 had seven.[42] A regular attender at the Darlington cinemas was Maisie Wright, who saw as many as three films a week at one penny a time.[43] Finally, and importantly for my arguments, both city and town centres were transformed by the development of new shopping facilities which brought modernist frontages, with stylistic and retailing origins that were national and international, on to the region's high streets, as well as stylish, fashionable clothes.

Shopping in the North East between the Wars

During the 1920s and 1930s fourteen chain stores opened branches in Newcastle's main shopping area, Northumberland Street, including C&A, Marks & Spencer, F.W. Woolworth & Co. Ltd. and Montagu Burton Ltd.[44] C&A thrived during the depression because it specialised in cheap, off-the-peg clothes for working-class women. The Newcastle store, which was opened in 1931, was designed by company architects, North, Robin & Wilson, in the 'house-style' which was based on a combination of Art Deco and stripped classicism.[45] In Darlington, the stripped classical Binns department store re-opened in 1925 on the corner of Blackwellgate and High Row, after a fire had devastated the former building. The new, streamlined shop had a white tiled and stone facade with massive curved glass frontages, and Marks & Spencer opened its new 'moderne' style store in 1922 with a large frontage of twenty feet.[46] This combined stripped classical and Art Deco style was used for numerous commercial and retail buildings between the Wars, including those of Burton, Woolworth, Binns, and Marks & Spencer. The angular, abstracted style which incorporated stylised columns and capitals, and sunburst and ziggurat motifs represented the most visible symbol of modernity on the high street. Significantly, this modern imagery appeared across Britain, thus undermining the distinctive identity of regional shops. This erasure of regional identity in fashion retailing was not merely confined to the exterior design of shops; it also carried through to interior design, merchandise, sales methods, advertising, and distribution and production techniques, as large companies implemented national expansion plans.

Department stores and variety chain stores or multiples (which included Marks & Spencer, Woolworth, British Home Stores Ltd., and Littlewoods

Ltd.) began to dominate the country's and the region's high streets. There was a two- to three-fold increase in the number of department stores and a four-fold increase in the number of multiples in the inter-war years.[47] Accompanying this were significant changes in consumer behaviour patterns: for example, better transport facilities, lower prices, and lively advertising in the local press attracted consumers away from local shops to the region's towns and cities. Consumer expenditure also shifted from food to other goods, and, at the same time:

> fashion, style, choice and selection and therefore of window display and window shopping, led to a parallel stress on bigger, brighter and better laid-out shops in main street sites. Shops sited in the busiest streets of the towns attracted consumers. Such shops gave the consumer an opportunity to make comparisons, to see what was new, and to make a choice with relative ease.[48]

In the North East of England, Binns, which had started out as a drapery just outside Sunderland, was trading on both sides of Fawcett Street in Sunderland town centre by 1921. A new ladies' hairdressing department was opened in the same year at the Sunderland branch, costing £2,322 11s 6d.[49] The *North Mail* reported the opening of these new extensions under the heading, "Shopping Made Easy. Rivalling London's Greatest Stores".[50] The reporter delighted in explaining the new facilities which were modern and progressive:

> The model rooms are a particular feature in the drapery departments. Here goods are on direct view, and there is no taking of bundles from shelves in the old-fashioned way; no littering of counters with piles of material or garments . . . There are also revolving cases showing dresses, skirts, and other articles. You wait . . . until the right thing comes around, when the rotary motion ceases, the garment is removed, and the transaction completed . . . There are lounges, dining and tea rooms, not forgetting a very delightful band which provides the latest and most popular musical selections.[51]

The *Northern Echo* in 1923 carried an advertisement for Binns' new Darlington store showing the highly modernistic shop front, and the *Northern Evening Despatch* of the same year described the store's expansion and the planned new café.[52] It also emphasised the up-to-the-minute fashions on display: "the Millinery, Coats and Costumes Departments are showing a dainty selection of the latest and best fashion garments direct from Paris and London."[53] The stress on new improved facilities in the department stores characterised much of the reporting in the local press, which was clearly addressed at the woman customer – lunch and tea-rooms, hairdressing, bands, and rest-rooms were all perceived to be essential in attracting this increasingly important consumer.

Like many of his contemporaries, John Simpson, company director and general manager of Binns, had studied large stores in North America and had determined to open modern department stores on American lines.[54] Throughout the 1920s new stores were opened by Binns in almost all the main towns and cities of the North East: in 1922 a new store opened in Darlington, and others in Middlesbrough in 1925, West Hartlepool in 1926, South Shields in 1927, and Newcastle in 1929. The *Sunderland Echo and Shipping Gazette* reported in 1931 that Binns employed 3,500 people at Darlington, Middlesbrough, West Hartlepool, and Sunderland, and that it served a population of four million.[55] For Christmas shopping in December 1935, the *Shields Daily News* reported that eighty-five special trains had been put on by LNER to converge on seven regional stores.[56] These came from Leeds, Doncaster, Berwick-upon-Tweed, Hawes, and Carlisle. A special free lunch was offered for all those spending over two pounds. In the same year, the company offered hire purchase at an interest rate of 5% over two years.[57] With the aid of this, a store such as Sunderland could amass 30,000 family accounts.[58]

Binns' main rivals in the region were Fenwick's, and Bainbridge and Co. Ltd. of Newcastle. Following the completion of their magnificent new store extension on Northumberland Street by the architects Marshall and Tweedy in 1913, Fenwick's was established as the most prestigious and exclusive of North East department stores. Its main competitor in Newcastle, Bainbridge and Co. Ltd., boasted sixty shops under one roof by 1938 including a marble-lined food hall, a men's hairdressing department, a newly renovated restaurant and a smoke-room[59] (fig. 81). Regular interior re-modelling, expensive advertising campaigns and promotional strategies, and the combination of exclusive sections such as Fenwick's French Salon, and more competitively priced departments at both Bainbridge's and Fenwick's, enabled Newcastle to maintain and enhance its position as the shopping capital of the North East. Fenwick's

Fig. 81 Illustrations from Bi-annual Sale brochure, January 1928, Bainbridge & Co., Market Street, Newcastle upon Tyne, showing facilities for women consumers including the new hairdressing salon (opened 1927). (John Lewis Partnership Archives).

French Salon provided members of the region's aristocracy and ruling class, such as Lady Barnard of Raby Castle, Lady Danesfort, Lady Ridley, and Linda Rhodes Moorhouse of Rokeby Park, with Paris originals and excellent London originals and copies.[60] Significantly, as I will show in the next section, cheaper copies of couture garments were sold by all the region's department stores at prices which were accessible to a middle-class if not working-class market.

In terms of bringing an international image of modernity to the region's high streets, it was the massive expansion of Marks & Spencer which (arguably) had the greatest impact. With their store development and design, manufacturing and retailing strategies, and the type, quality and design of goods, Marks & Spencer transformed shopping in the region for both working-class and middle-class buyers, particularly as the company began to concentrate on clothing. Between 1926 and 1940 Marks & Spencer opened or rebuilt 218 stores,[61] and by 1939, the company had a total of 234 stores across Britain. The new store at Darlington was opened in 1922, with new stores following at West Hartlepool in 1926, Sunderland and Bishop Auckland in 1930, Middlesbrough and South Shields in 1931, Newcastle in 1932, Durham in 1937, and Stockton in 1938.[62] Characteristics of these new or rebuilt stores were design features directly drawn from North American retailers which Simon Marks had visited in 1924:

> After my first visit, I made it my business to visit the United States as often as I could . . . It was there that I learned many new things. . . learned the value of more imposing, commodious premises, modern methods of administration and the statistical control of stocks in relation to sales. . . I learned the value of counter footage, that is, that each counter foot of space had to pay wages, rent, overhead expenses, and earn a profit.[63]

The new stores in the North East showed the impact of these modern ideas. That at Darlington, for example, where the old store had closed down in 1921, had a double glass window to replace the open front which had been closed at night by shutters: it had two long wall counters instead of the old horseshoe counter, and a plain 'Marks & Spencer' fascia instead of the original fascia legend 'Originators of the Penny Bazaars', along with much improved lighting. The Newcastle Northumberland Street store, designed in 1932 by Norman Jane and Leonard Rigby, followed the almost standardised stripped classical style with abstracted and angular motifs. The ground floor display windows and gold and green fascia were mass-produced, standardised elements which recur throughout Marks & Spencer's architecture in the 1920s and 1930s.[64] This store boasted the new island counters on which goods were laid out for shoppers to examine, and lighting in this store was hung low to enable the better display of goods (fig. 82).

Fig. 82 Interior of Marks & Spencer's, Northumberland Street, Newcastle upon Tyne, 1936, showing the new island counters and improved lighting typical of the modernity of Marks & Spencer's stores across the country in the 1930s. (Marks & Spencer's Archive).

Accompanying this progressive, modern shop design and layout was a new pricing policy of "nothing over five shillings" which had serious implications for the style, range and quality of goods sold. By 1932 seventeen categories of goods had been eliminated including hardware, cutlery, china and earthenware, and fancy goods were restricted. With increased standardisation, the use of synthetic fibres such as rayon, and a limited range of products, Marks & Spencer were able to respond to the mass demand for good and inexpensive clothing.[65] By the late 1930s, Marks & Spencer had become an entirely different type of store to its competitors. Unlike department stores, it did not have all goods available under one roof, it had middle-class and working-class clienteles, and it had a successful fixed price policy.

A consequence of this latter development was that Marks & Spencer had to discover, if not create, a range of goods that could be sold within this limit at the right quality. This entailed working alongside manufacturers to persuade them to produce the right sort of goods for their stores. They adopted two merchandising strategies to achieve this. Firstly, where goods were available at prices which customers could meet, they attempted to improve the quality in order to satisfy public tastes, and secondly, where goods existed which were more expensive than their five shillings maximum, they worked with manufacturers to bring prices down, frequently through placing large orders. They also took the unusual and radical decision to try to eliminate the wholesaler by working directly with the manufacturer. To do this they had to invest in the specific manufacturers with whom they were associated.[66] However, due to the changes in the production of clothing which took place between the Wars, improvements in quality, price, and distribution were all feasible, and, according to Rees:

> despite the variations of boom and slump, popular needs and tastes, and particularly those of the working class, were changing at a speed which we now recognise to be one of the characteristic features of the twentieth century. Any retail organisation which could interpret the public's changing needs, adapt itself rapidly to them, and satisfy them at a price which was within the income of the working class household was certain to receive a rich reward. The creation of the super stores, combined with the reintroduction of the fixed price limit, placed Marks and Spencer in an exceptionally favourable position to take advantage of this opportunity.[67]

The implications of the expansion of large retailers such as Binns and Marks & Spencer for smaller, independent, regional drapers', dressmakers', and milliners' shops were enormous. According to Jefferys, the proportion of total retail sales in clothing and footwear by large scale retailers increased from 23-25.5% in 1920 to 45-50% in 1939.[68] For the small independent draper, dressmaker and milliner the main chance of survival was by offering a different service to that provided by the likes of Marks & Spencer and Binns, hence personal service, unique designs, exclusivity and individual sizing were highlighted in contrast to the standardisation of style, size, and service. However, this type of facility had limited appeal, and it depended on a more wealthy, though less numerous customer. As a consequence, shops of this type were under threat throughout the inter-war period with substantial closures, and take-overs by larger companies. In relation to the North East, it is possible to map out the contraction of the small, independent retailer during this period in a moderately affluent town such as Darlington, which supported a number of prestigious and well-established firms including Jaques & Jaques in Northgate House ("Darlington's Big Drapery Store and Fashion Centre"), Luck & Sons on High Row which sold "the latest fashions", and J.J. Robinson & Sons, popularly known as "J.J's, the shopping centre of the town" at 84 Northgate[69] (see table below).

Table 1: Showing numbers of fashion retailers in Darlington
[information taken from *Ward's Directories*, Darlington Reference Library]

	1918	1922	1925	1928	1930	1932	1934	1936
Drapers	47	46	47	43	43	39	36	40
Dressmakers	40	35	30	20	15	16	13	11
Milliners	27	25	25	26	25	18	13	10

From these numbers we can see that, although drapers appeared to experience only a 20% reduction in numbers (probably due to the fact that these numbers include the new department stores, multiples and variety stores, and that many amalgamated, or were taken over), the decline of dressmakers' and milliners' shops (mainly owned and managed by women) was particularly acute, with a 75% and 60% reduction in numbers respectively. Clearly, the demand for the specialist services offered by such shops in a town such as Darlington was far outweighed by the mass market for cheaper, more readily available clothes which could nevertheless be in the latest styles.

These facets of modernity (the visual iconography of new shop design, the new selling techniques and standardised merchandising, and the replacement of local dressmakers and drapers by new department, multiple and variety stores) which were experienced by the region's population, served to undermine regional differences by making North East high streets much like others around Britain. As I will show in the final section, women as workers in fashion production and retailing, as shoppers in the new stores, and as consumers of fashionable styles, were in the vanguard of the inter-war engagement with modernity. In this sense, women were involved in articulating a very specific version of modernity: one which drew upon their changing experience of femininity to produce what can best be described as 'a feminine modernity'.

Women and Fashion: Work, Consumption and Style

In 1931, under the heading "Alice in Sunderland: Alice learns something of the Romance of Business", the *Sunderland Gazette and Shipping Gazette* reported on conditions of employment at Binns' department store:

> She learned from one man – still on the sunny side of the street – who has jumped from £5 a week to a salary of four figures, and half that sum again, of women on the staff who earn salaries that would make a mere man's mouth water.[70]

Although large numbers of women were employed in the retail and clothing trades, it was still the case that gender mattered in terms of pay and employment prospects. Women's employment in fashion retailing and clothing production was shaped by a continuation and extension of practices established before 1914. In particular, women's work in clothing production was influenced by the sexual division of labour; they took on jobs which were designated unskilled, whilst those jobs deemed skilled, such as pattern-making and cutting, remained in male hands. However, as in other industries, the First World War had had a critical effect on women's employment in these industries, which, combined with later changes in the clothing industry in the 1920s and 1930s, served to transform their work. Increasingly they took on better paid, often semi-skilled jobs as machinists in the new factories set up to mass produce clothes, they worked in factory and store offices as typists and secretaries, and as Susan Porter Benson has argued:

> Managers selected saleswomen both for their cheapness in the labor force and for their "female" personality characteristics which coincided with the skills of selling: empathy, habits of persuasion instead of command, and a homely familiarity with the merchandise.[71]

During the First World War women sales assistants, dressmakers, and tailoresses had taken on work previously done by men, and with trade union support, their wage levels had improved.[72] The main unions to which women belonged were the National Amalgamated Union of Shop Assistants (NAUSA) which catered particularly for sales assistants, and dressmakers and milliners employed by retailers, the Amalgamated Society of Co-operative Employees and Commercial Workers (ASCECW) whose members were mainly Co-operative employees, the United Garment Workers (UGW) and the Amalgamated Society of Tailors and Tailoresses (ASTT).[73] UGW was made up of any workers, "male or female, who are engaged in any of the occupations incidental to the manufacture of male and female clothing or attire", whereas the ASTT admitted to its membership only craftsmen or journeyman tailors.[74] Female membership of these unions in 1919 was substantial: on the production side, the UGW had 100,000 members, of which 75,000 were women, the ASTT had 20,000, of which half were women, whereas on the retailing side, the NAUSA had 80,600, of which 35,300 were women, and the AUCECW had 87,000, of which 33,700 were women.[75]

Essential as women were to the fashion production and retailing industries, the changes wrought to their employment by the First World War were reinforced and extended during the 1920s and 1930s:

> A further swing to factory production further broke down the divisions between the skilled tailor, the semi-skilled workers in tailoring shops, and the factory workers and sweated outworkers.[76]

De-skilling allowed larger numbers of women into the new factories which were making the cheaper, standardised clothes required by the new multiple and variety chains. Menswear, for example, was both mass produced and made to measure by firms such as Montague Burton Ltd. and Price's Tailors Ltd., "Fifty Shilling Tailors".[77] In 1937, a new factory was opened for Henry Price's Fifty Shilling Tailors in Saltwells Road, Middlesbrough. Dubbed "Rational Tailoring", the company boasted:

> The story of the growth of 'Rational Tailoring' is the story of a modern system of tailoring which enables many a man to be well-dressed for less money than it cost a previous generation to be ill-dressed.[78]

The Fifty Shilling Tailor was the archetypal modernist clothing manufacturer, promising a fixed price and a fixed standard of values in tailoring due to:

> courageous factory planning and buying, the cleverest organisation of skilled tailoring and inspired management.[79]

With the support of the Tees District Development Board and the County Borough of Middlesbrough, Price's Tailors introduced a modernist factory into the midst of the traditional heavy industries of "magnificent works, forges and furnaces . . . shipbuilding, structural steel . . . and engineering . . . of all kinds", making products and using techniques which represented the process of 'feminisation' so detested by those critics eager to celebrate and maintain the values and principles of masculine labour in the north.[80] The rationalism of the factory organisation, the use of new technologies for power tools and garment construction, the widespread deployment of women machinists and office workers to undertake 'light' work, all contributed to the de-skilling of formerly skilled male jobs (fig. 83). The experiences and roles of these women brought a specifically 'feminine' dimension to the modernity of these new industries which served to undermine the traditional working-class regional identities originating in the skilled male labour of the heavy industries.

Women employees also formed an equally significant sector of the fashion retailing industry. They worked in department stores, multiple and variety chain stores, and in smaller drapers, dressmakers, and milliners. In these

Fig. 83 Women machinists at Henry Price's "Fifty Shilling Tailors" Ltd., Saltwells Road, Middlesbrough, 1937. These women workers were typical of those gaining employment in the new lighter industries in the 1920s. (The Dorman Museum, Middlesbrough Borough Council).

roles they were highly visible to the public as earners. Jefferys attributes women's increased employment in fashion retailing to the decline of technical skill in the retailing trades which, he argues, was characteristic of the post-First World War years.[81] In particular he refers to the decline in the practices of living-in and apprenticeships, as retailers bought in ready-made clothing instead of training and employing tailors and dressmakers to make clothes on the premises. At Marks & Spencer:

> Problems of staff did not provide great difficulty, as in the stores the company depended almost entirely on female labour, and had early established a reputation for good conditions of employment and of human and sympathetic management.[82]

It was not uncommon to find women heading departments, although, as stores amalgamated and increased in size during the 1930s, men replaced women as departmental heads except in those sections which were thought to require particular female skills such as buying and welfare.[83] Nevertheless, ladies' clothing sections in large department stores were staffed almost entirely by women. In a company brochure headed "A Walk through the Interior of the Bainbridge Store", the range of departments catering to women's needs was illustrated. In the Millinery and Blouse sections, French

Dressmaking, English Dressmaking, Mantle showroom, Gown and Costume departments, Knitted Wear section, and Underwear and Corset showroom, women were shown serving women. Men were absent from these illustrations except from those which confirmed traditional gender stereotypes, such as the General Boot department, Men's Clothing and Hat sections, the Travelling and Sports section, Hardwear and Bedsteads, and the Carpet showroom.[84]

Given the huge expansion in the range of shops available for women to make their clothing purchases from between the Wars, it was still the case that social class remained the critical factor in determining where they actually shopped and what they bought. Although variety stores such as Marks & Spencer's brought better quality clothing within the grasp of working-class and middle-class women, for the former purchasing from such stores still represented a special investment, one not made regularly. For many working-class women, home dressmaking was the main way in which they acquired new clothes.

Maisie Wright, for example, made most of her own clothes as a young woman either by hand-sewing or knitting. For inspiration, she and her friends looked at film stars' clothes illustrated in magazines such as *Picturegoer*. She shopped in Middlesbrough or Darlington very occasionally for special clothes. When she married in 1937 she bought her wedding dress from a shop called 'Charles' on Bondgate in Darlington for 12s 11d.[85] Similarly, Renee Rutherford's mother made up clothes on a sewing machine for her daughter, but also shopped at Doggart's and the Co-op in the nearby town of Bishop Auckland. Like Maisie Wright, Renee's wedding dress was shop-bought, from Saltmers, a high-class dress shop on Linthorpe Road in Middlesbrough.[86] For her wedding, Renee wore a powder blue short-sleeved crepe dress with a navy blue hat, shoes and gloves.[87] Shop-bought clothes were what most young women wanted to wear rather than home-made ones which had the stigma of poverty attached to them. Gwenyth Batey (born in 1932), whose mother, a dressmaker, made clothes for people from her home, described "how I longed to be old enough to have a job, make some money and buy *real* clothes from a shop instead of having mum's designs".[88] As a teenager in the 1940s, she bought clothes from Doggart's and the Co-op in Bishop Auckland, while customers queued for her mother's own-made originals.[89]

Gwenyth Batey's mother had been trained by her father, a cutter and tailor for his drapery business, Hunt's in Stockton. As a young woman, Gwenyth's mother was apprenticed as a full apprentice tailoress at Coates & Sidgwick's on Stockton High Street. Once married, she ran a dressmaking business from home to supplement her husband's pay which, as a railwayman, was poor.[90] She used 'The Haslam System' of dressmaking which was based on a large kidney-shaped patent board from which patterns were cut following instructions from a number of accompanying books. According to Gwenyth, she never bought a paper pattern, but made her own using the Haslam System.[91] She would travel to Lewis's in Leeds for materials and did most of her sewing on a Jones sewing machine. For design ideas, she looked at magazines and bought catalogues from Selfridges and Ponting Brothers of London.

Like her less well-off counterparts, Elizabeth Clennell also financed her aspirations for shop-bought clothing by walking to her Newcastle office job from Pelaw, although she still had most of her clothes made at home by her mother, or by a visiting dressmaker. Apparently, she sketched designs from shop windows in Newcastle during her lunch break. As a married woman in Darlington, she had clothes made up by a dressmaker from Haughton village to designs copied from magazines such as *Woman's Weekly, Home Chat,* and *Home Notes*. But with an increased income, she shopped in Darlington at Luck & Sons and Binns, which had an exceptional hat department. For special occasions she went to Newcastle; her wedding dress and matron-of-honour's dress were bought from Fenwick's, but she had her bridesmaids' dresses copied from designs in *Harper's Bazaar* and *Vogue*.[92]

It is interesting to observe that, although fashion retailing was transformed in the inter-war years (demonstrated by the shift from small-scale dressmakers and drapers to large multiples and department stores across the region) and although women had greater choice, home dressmaking persisted for largely financial reasons for the working and lower middle classes. It was supplemented to some extent by mail order catalogue purchasing from companies such as Littlewoods and Great Universal Stores Ltd., which had solid markets in the north for their particular brand of selling through agents and mail order delivery. But for young women such as Maisie Wright, Renee Rutherford and Elizabeth Clennell a machine-made garment, complete with a manufacturer's or retailer's label, was highly prized as a symbol of fashionability and modernity. As Elizabeth Wilson has argued:

> The mass production of fashionable styles . . . links the politics of fashion to fashion as art. It is connected both to the evolution of styles that circulate in 'high' and avant-garde art; and to popular culture and taste.[93]

Importantly, then, fashion linked women to modern life and contemporary culture. It drew them into the cultural arena in a very public way, as they aspired to styles which referred to Hollywood films and lifestyles in which women acted out alternative roles to the ones for which these young women working in the North East were destined. In fact, it was the whole paraphernalia of shopping which contributed to this sense of modernity and pointed to the possibility of change: the window-shopping, the magazines and sales leaflets, and the physical experience of the shops themselves, modernised, technological, and streamlined. The glamour of Hollywood and the cosmopolitanism of fashions which had originated in Paris, London, or New York, but were available in cheaper versions in the North East, represented the internationalism of modernity as opposed to the parochialism of the region. Fashion offered the possibility, however remote, of change from the routine of their everyday lives, and it signalled changes that had already taken place which raised, no matter how slightly, their expectations and opportunities. "Fashion is dress in which the key feature is rapid and continual changing of styles. Fashion, in a sense is change . . ."[94]

The visual characteristics of women's fashion between the Wars were numerous and their meanings complex. Simplistically, in the 1920s styles were tubular and androgynous in that they de-emphasised the curvaceous

Fig. 84 Illustration from James Coxon & Co. Ltd, Market Street, Newcastle upon Tyne, "Journal of New Spring and Summer Fashions", 1924. These 1920s styles called into question accepted and stereotypical ways of shaping and covering the female body by undermining and minimising sexual difference, with cloche hats covering shortened or bobbed hair, and with tubular suits and dresses which flattened the breasts and de-emphasised the hips. (Beamish. The North of England Open Air Museum, Stanley, County Durham).

Fig. 85 Illustration from Fenwick Ltd, Northumberland Street, Newcastle upon Tyne, Sales Leaflet, Spring 1933. Fashionable 1930s women's dress drew attention to the body as a site of sexual and gender ambiguity by exaggerating sexual difference rather than underplaying it as in the 1920s. Sharp tailoring delineated the hips, waist and breasts, elaborate bias-cutting allowed soft satins and crepes to be draped across the curves of the body, and daring cutting produced spectacular backless gowns, and sleeveless halter-neck tops. (Fenwick Ltd).

female form and stressed the straight vertical line, whereas from the early- to mid-1930s bias-cutting and draping brought a softer, less angular look which hung around the body, delineating its curves and fullness (figs. 84 and 85). This difference was particularly acute in dress styles; however, it was also discernible in women's suits, which tended to take on a sharp tailored outline in the 1930s as opposed to a loose, layered look in the 1920s. To account for these styles, writers have cited the influences of sport and the cult of health, modernism and modernity, Paris haute couture (Chanel and Patou in the 1920s and Schiaparelli in the 1930s), female emancipation, Hollywood films, the rationalisation of the fashion industry, and changing attitudes to sexuality and femininity.[95]

Support for this interpretation can be gained from a glance through fashion sales catalogues, company brochures and newspaper advertising for the inter-war years. Paris in particular was regularly stressed. In "A Walk through the Interior of the Bainbridge Store", there were repeated references to "knowledge of the latest Parisian whim", and "ultra stylishness . . . found only in the productions of the leading Parisian designers".[96] A Bainbridge's "Summer Sale" brochure from July 1930 lists "British and French Models greatly reduced in price in the Model Gown Salon" before going on to describe a "Pateau [sic] Model Coat Frock in navy wool georgette, handworked collar and cuffs of shell pink – Usual price $10\frac{1}{2}$ guineas at a sale price of £8 9s 6d".[97] Another Bainbridge brochure from 1928 mentions a "French Model Jumper and Three-piece suits" and illustrates garments clearly based on Chanel and Patou lines.[98] Fenwick's Summer Sale of 1933 advertised "The Model Sale" and in particular:

> This smart afternoon coat, a copy of a Patou model, is of a soft navy woollen material, cartridge piped at the collar in natural shade. Lined throughout with crepe, it is reduced for the Model Sale from 12½ guineas to £5.[99]

The same leaflet also advertised "Model Tailored Skirts for Golf, Holidays or Cruising" and "exclusive pyjama suits for the holiday cruise"; demonstrating the influence of sports and the outdoor life on fashions for a more select market. Other leaflets promoted clothes for the races, the moors, and for hunting, again hinting at a lifestyle beyond the means of most.[100]

However, alongside these were advertisements for fabrics for home-dressmaking and for much more modestly priced garments (such as two-piece suits for 20s) which highlighted one of the main problems faced by retailers: that they had to cover the whole gamut of styles and possible consumer needs due to the enormous expansion in the market for fashion which brought different groups of women into their shops. As Susan Porter Benson has argued, although retailers were at first enthusiastic about the rapid changes in fashionable styles which characterised the inter-war period, eventually it proved their undoing as they tried to compete on what appeared to be the shifting sands of price, taste, exclusivity, and economy.

> Fashion, though profitable, injected a new note of uncertainty and unpredictability into the already volatile retail environment . . . Despite their best efforts to use service and merchandise appeals to breed loyalty to a consumer-oriented way of life and to individual stores, managers signally failed to create the docile and predictable customer of their dreams. The women who shopped in their stores continued to display what managers regarded as unwonted initiative and independence.[101]

Paris couture, the outdoor life and sport were the obvious influences on women's fashion in the inter-war years, but at a subconscious level, it was shaped by both dominant and transgressive ideas of female sexuality and feminine identity. Due to its symbiotic relationship to the body, fashion gave women the means to signal this in visual form, consciously and unconsciously. For debate about both female sexuality and femininity were firmly on the agenda between the Wars.

Female sexuality had a high profile as birth control, a woman's right to sexual fulfilment, and lesbianism were more openly discussed. All were challenging to, or transgressive of, patriarchy, and therefore unacceptable. For example, birth control became much more respectable, especially for the middle classes, through the publication of Marie Stopes's *Married Love* (1918) which sold nearly half a million copies by the mid-1920s.[102] As a consequence, contraception was discussed in popular magazines and was more available to some women with the opening of her clinics, the first in London in 1921.[103] Although no new methods of contraception appeared in

Britain between the Wars, the adoption of contraceptive devices was more widespread, affecting the working class as well as the middle class.[104]

Another outcome of Stopes's work, and of sexologists and psychologists including Havelock Ellis and Sigmund Freud, was the repudiation of women's sexual passivity (Stopes) and the foregrounding of the dangers of sexual repression (Ellis and Freud). Even middle-class women's magazines such as *Good Housekeeping* were keen to persuade women that they had:

> sex desires and that these desires were not wicked; that to repress them was as difficult and dangerous to women as to men, and that they needed no longer pretend that all they wanted was at most motherhood, when it was quite as natural for them to want loverhood.[105]

During the 1920s these ideas were especially appealing to the young, who were in revolt against the ideas of the pre-War generation whom they held responsible for the hypocrisy and carnage of the First World War. However, by the 1930s, this emphasis on sexual fulfilment had been re-packaged along more conventional lines for married women. It no longer carried the same connotations of social and sexual freedom.

Similarly the 1920s also saw the issue of lesbianism dramatically at the fore with the scandal surrounding Radclyffe Hall's book *The Well of Loneliness* (published 1928 and then promptly banned as obscene).[106] Havelock Ellis attributed lesbianism to sexual inversion which was undesirable and represented women's failure to accept their inherent feminine identity. Although these views in their original form were not widely understood by the majority of women, they were discussed in magazines and represented in film. Greta Garbo in *Queen Christina* (1933), Marlene Dietrich in *Blonde Venus* (1932), and Katherine Hepburn in *Christopher Strong* (1933) played with sexual identity either with oblique references to lesbianism or by acting out masculine-type roles. In *Christopher Strong*, Hepburn plays Cynthia Darrington, a world champion aviator, who, "transgresses male discourse through the element of sex-role reversal inherent in her characterisation."[107]

In other films, such as *Front Page Woman* (1935) with Bette Davis and *The Wild Party* (1929) with Clara Bow, women challenged dominant sexual stereotypes even if they ultimately came to conform. Although Hollywood's questioning of femininity and sexual identity was usually compromised by the needs of the market place, these films nevertheless provided powerful representations of women challenging assumptions about their lives, attributes, roles and desires in an unpredecedented way.

Clothes, personal appearance and style signified this challenge. Whether it was Dietrich's blatant sexuality, or Hepburn's masculinised dress, these images contributed to the view that femininity was not fixed, but precarious, even negotiable. It is this connection between the private self and the public persona which makes fashion so interesting in relation to representations of femininity:

> A part of this strangeness of dress is that it links the biological body to the social being, and public to private. This makes it uneasy territory, since it forces us to recognize that the human body is more than a biological entity. It is an organism in culture, a cultural artefact even, and its own boundaries are unclear . . . as a cultural phenomenon, as an aesthetic medium for the expression of ideas, desires and beliefs circulating in society.[108]

In analysing the fashionable styles worn by women between the Wars, it is significant how many of these called into question accepted and conventional ways of shaping and covering the body, particularly by either undermining gender identities and minimising sexual difference (more typical of the 1920s) or by exaggerating them (a characteristic of the 1930s). Pyjama suits, short tubular skirts, trousers, cloche hats, bias-cut and draped cocktail dresses, backless gowns, and sharply tailored suits all drew attention to the body as a site of sexual and gender ambiguity.[109] Breasts, hips, legs, the stomach, back, face and waist were all at one time or another bound, straightened, delineated, obscured, and revealed. The arbitrary nature of fashion, and the sheer artificiality and transcience of femininity were highlighted as never before in these fashions, and although on a simplistic level it is possible to read the fashions of the 1930s as a reactionary response to the loosening up of gender identities in the fashionable styles of the 1920s, it is just as feasible, in my view, to see the artificiality of 1930s glamour as a parody of femininity which enabled women, particularly young ones, to playfully engage with dominant constructions of femininity. In this respect the red-lipped, silk-stockinged, young woman attacked by Priestley and the like were not merely symbols of an unwelcome 'feminine' modernity, but also prescient of the rejection of an essentially patriachial notion of femininity – one which was unchanging and universal.

Fashion, then, with these popular meanings encoded within it, provided women with the means, consciously and subconsciously, to question the values of the pre-war generation. Arguably, both the masculinised styles of the 1920s and the glamorised looks of the 1930s represented a fundamental challenge to patriarchy. Each in their way offered women opportunities to engage with new, more modern representations of feminine identity and sexuality – in essence a femininity shaped by the conditions of contemporary life.

In conclusion, this chapter has aimed to show how women's involvement with fashion, as producers and consumers, enabled them to experience modernity at first hand. At the same time, fashion provided a vehicle for them to explore the meaning of femininity within the changing context of British social, economic and cultural life between the Wars. Modernity in its many guises undermined regional identity bringing new industrial processes and systems, new retailing and marketing techniques, and new visual icons to a region whose industrial culture was in terminal decline. Although the North East experienced the modernisation process which introduced the new light industries into British culture at a slower rate than the South East of England, it was still affected by the onslaught of modernity. Women and fashion had a pivotal role in this: as workers and producers they were employed in the new industries and the service sector. They took on work deemed 'feminine' as a consequence of essentialist notions of sexual difference and the vestiges of the sexual division of labour, and due to capitalist economics as cheap semi-skilled labour. As consumers, women played a large part in stimulating the growth of new shopping facilities and the design and manufacture of a plethora of lower priced, available, fashionable goods. In the new industries and shops, in making, buying and wearing fashionable clothes, and in creating new visual representations of femininity, women were engaged in constructing new identities within the context of the social, economic and cultural life of the North East of England between the Wars. In this, they participated in and indeed helped to precipitate a modernity based on their needs and experiences – a 'feminine modernity' which called into question both national and regional notions of women's place within society and struck at the heart of patriarchal power.

References and Notes

1. For example D. Beddoe, *Back To Home and Duty: Women Between the Wars, 1918-1939* (London, 1989), A. Light, *Forever England: Femininity, Literature and Conservatism Between the Wars* (London, 1991), S. Alexander, "Becoming a Woman in London in the 1920s and 1930s", in *Metropolis, London: Histories and Representations Since 1800,* edited D. Feldman and G. Stedman Jones (London, 1989), S. Rowbotham, *Hidden From History* (London, 1977).

2. For example C.L. Mowat, *Britain Between the Wars, 1918-1940* (London, 1955), J. Stevenson, *British Society 1914-45* (London, 1984), A.J.P. Taylor, *English History 1914-1945* (Oxford, 1965).

3. See for example J. Seddon and S. Worden, *Women Designing: Redefining Design in Britain between the Wars* (Brighton, 1994). Also, in May 1993 "The Making of Modernity" conference took place at the Design Museum, London, dealing with several of these themes.

4. The term 'modernity' is used here to describe the cultural and social experience of modern life in the period 1914-1940, whereas 'modernism' refers to the specific design theories and practices which characterise the Modern Movement in architecture and design in the inter-war period.

5. See C. Buckley, '"Design, Femininity and Modernism: Interpreting the work of Susie Cooper" in *Journal of Design History,* vol.7, no.4 (Dec 1994/Jan 1995), pp.277-93 and

C. Buckley, "Women and Modernism: A Case of Grete Marks (1899-1990)", in Seddon and Worden, op.cit., pp.104-9.

6. For a discussion of this in relation to women pottery designers see C. Buckley, *Potters and Paintresses: Women Designers in the Pottery Industry, 1870-1955* (London, 1990).

7. Light, op.cit., p.10.

8. Alexander, op.cit., p.245.

9. This is critically discussed by Alexander whose aim is to re-evaluate the experiences of working-class women in London, whose aspirations were viewed by Priestley and Orwell as indicative of the 'feminisation' of everyday life. They implied that this process of 'feminisation' contributed to the undermining of authentic working-class culture and society which, significantly, originated in the experiences of skilled male industrial workers. The aspirations of these young women who were working in the service sector and in the new light industries were represented as being somewhat immoral in the context of rising male unemployment in the traditional heavy industries. Feminists such as Mary Agnes Hamilton were also critical, viewing the fashionable symbols of femininity – the clothes, make-up, and sexual bravado – as anti-feminist.

10. Significantly, these left-wing writers celebrated the implicit masculinity of the traditional industries of ship-building, coal-mining, engineering etc. and its ensuing culture. Their claims to be chroniclers of working-class experiences needs to be seen within the context of their neglect of women from the working class who sought paid employment and independent lives, and their contempt for the different, more modern, cultural and social aspirations of these women.

11. An excellent example of this can be seen in the British pottery industry which targeted women consumers in its trade journals and in the writings and speeches of key figures such as Ida Copeland, the Conservative M.P. for Stoke-on-Trent.

12. Alexander, op.cit.,p.246.

13. For example, see Rowbotham, op.cit.

14. More details of these young women will be cited later.

15. Frederick Taylor's methods of scientific management began to be more widely understood and implemented in Britain in the 1920s and 1930s. These were complemented by an increased awareness and knowledge of American sales and marketing techniques, which radically altered the image and approach of companies such as Marks & Spencer. See G. Rees, *St Michael: A History of Marks and Spencer* (London, 1969).

16. Quoted in Rowbotham, op.cit., p.190.

17. R. Thorne, "Between the Wars on Tyneside", in *Between the Wars: Architecture and Design on Tyneside, 1919-1939*, C. Buckley and L. Walker, exhibition catalogue (Newcastle, 1982), p.4. Most of the research for this catalogue and exhibition was jointly undertaken by Lynne Walker and Cheryl Buckley at Newcastle Polytechnic in 1982 with assistance from final year students studying for the B.A.(Hons) History of Modern Art, Design and Film degree. Full acknowledgement for the use of this research in this chapter is due especially to Lynne Walker.

18. Mowat, op.cit. (1987 ed.), p.481.

19. Thorne, op.cit., p.4.

20. Stevenson, op.cit., p.145.

21. Mowat, op.cit., pp.481-82.

22. Ibid., p.483.

23. Quoted from Beddoe, op.cit., p.55.

24. Ibid., p.57.

25. There is a misplaced assumption that working-class women generally failed to return to domestic service after the First World War. This was not the case. In 1921 33% of all working women were employed in domestic service and in 1931 this had risen to 35%. See C. Hardyment, *From Mangle to Microwave: The Mechanisation of Household Work* (Cambridge, 1988).

26. Interview with Maisie Gibson (née Wright), 26 August 1993. The Lily Laundry was on Russell St. West, Darlington. See *Darlington Year Book and Business Directory*, 1921, Darlington Reference Library. In 1933 when Maisie Gibson worked there it was managed by a Miss Logan.

27. Interview with Renee Chaplin (née Rutherford), 9 November 1993.

28. Sid Chaplin went on to write a number of celebrated novels about life in the North East mining communities.

29. Interview with her daughter, Mavis Robinson, 24 August 1993.

30. For example, she worked for a company that exported eggs, and c.1916 she worked for Shell as a shorthand typist. Interview with Mavis Robinson, op.cit.

31. The Team Valley Trading Estate was designed by Sir William Holford in collaboration with the local architect L.J. Couves, 1937-38. It originally covered 700 acres and by 1939 provided 2520 jobs. See Buckley and Walker, op.cit., p.28.

32. Alexander, op.cit., p. 248.

33. Rowbotham, op.cit. and Beddoe, op.cit.

34. The Mass-Observation group tended to reinforce this image and to celebrate the heroism of the skilled male worker.

35. The Tyneside flat was a regionally distinct plan for working-class housing.

36. For example the Walker Estate of council housing, designed in 1919 for Newcastle Corporation, with rents ranging from 12 shillings to 19 shillings and The Mead Garden Suburb, Eastbourne, Darlington, built in 1927 for middle-class families. See Benwell Community Project, *Private Housing and the Working Class* (1978).

37. Interview with Mavis Robinson, op.cit.

38. Ibid.

39. See Buckley and Walker, op.cit., p.22 and E.B. Musman, "Public Houses: Design and Construction", *Architects' Journal*, no.24, vol.88 (1938), pp.833-38.

40. See Buckley and Walker, pp.23-25.

41. Ibid., p.8.

42. In Newcastle these included the Paramount Super cinema, opened 1931 and designed by Frank Verity and Samuel Beverley, the Essoldo, designed in 1937 by William Stockdale, and the Blacks Regals in Byker (1934) and Gateshead (1937), designed by Edwin M. Lawson. In Darlington by 1928 there were seven cinemas: the Alhambra on Northgate, the Arcade and the Court Kinema both in Skinnergate, the Assembly Hall, in High Northgate, Central Picture Palace in the Market Square, the Empire in Crown St., and the Scala in Eldon St. See 1928 *Darlington Business Directory and Year Book.*

43. Interview with Maisie Gibson, op.cit.

44. Buckley and Walker, op.cit. p.32.

45. Ibid., p.32.

46. M. Moss & A. Turton, *A Legend of Retailing . . . House of Fraser* (London, 1989), and Darlington Reference Library.

47. Ibid., pp. 59 and 69.

48. Ibid., p.51.

49. See Minute Books 1920-27, HF2/1/3,4,5, Binns Sunderland, House of Fraser archives, Business Records Archive, Glasgow University.

50. *North Mail,* 4 November 1921, cutting HF 2/15/1, House of Fraser archives, Business Records Archive, Glasgow University.

51. Ibid.

52. *Northern Echo* August 1923, cutting HF25/4/2, and *Northern Evening Despatch,* cutting, HF/25/4/6, House of Fraser archives, Business Records Archive, Glasgow University.

53. *Northern Evening Despatch,* cutting, HF/25/4/6, House of Fraser archives, Business Records Archive, Glasgow University.

54. Moss & Turton, op.cit., pp.290-91. See also House of Fraser archives, Business Records Archive, Glasgow University.

55. *Sunderland Echo and Shipping Gazette,* 14 May 1931, cutting HF/2/5/10, House of Fraser archives, Business Records Archive, Glasgow University.

56. *Shields Daily News,* 5 December 1935, cutting HF2/14/3, House of Fraser archives, Business Records Archive, Glasgow University.

57. HF2/12/2 House of Fraser archives, Business Records Archive, Glasgow University.

58. An example of one such customer is Mrs Gilmore from Horden, County Durham, who spent £55 15s 0d between March and May 1923. Her purchases included: a Reno Blue Dress 7s 6d, Fawn Costume £3 5s 0d, Blue Dress £2 19s 6d, Tomato Hat £1 5s 9d, a Jacobean Bedstead for £5 19s 6d, a Jacobean Bedroom suite for £25 4s 0d, and a teapot and six cups and saucers for 15s. From Sunderland Minute Books 1920-27, HF2/20/1-4, House of Fraser archives, Business Records Archive, Glasgow University.

59. See "A Fair Deal", *The Gazette* (John Lewis House Magazine), 24 September 1988, pp. 783-85, and a 1938 sales leaflet from the John Lewis Archive.

60. For further information consult accession catalogue of Costume Collection, Bowes Museum, Barnard Castle.

61. Rees, op.cit., pp. 98-101.

62. Ibid.

63. Ibid., pp.74-75.

64. Buckley and Walker, op.cit., p.32.

65. Some examples of pre-War prices: men's woven poplin shirts 5s, ladies' spun rayon dresses 5s, rayon hose 1s, children's cotton frocks 1s 11d. From Rees, op.cit., p.141.

66. The first example of this was the Leicester hosiery company Corah, with which they first traded in 1926. See Rees, op.cit., pp.127-28.

67. Rees, op cit., p.119.

68. J.B. Jefferys, *Retail Trading in Britain, 1850-1950* (Cambridge, 1954), p.74.

69. See "Darlington Official Shopping Week Handbook", 16-23 June 1923. Darlington Reference Library.

70. Sunderland Echo and Shipping Gazette, 14 May 1931, cutting HF2/5/10, House of Fraser archives, Business Records Archive, Glasgow University.

71. S.P. Benson, *Counter Cultures: Saleswomen, Managers and Customers in American Department Stores, 1890-1940* (Urbana and Chicago, 1988), p.5.

72. By 1919, the UGW had secured a rate of 8½d an hour for women over 18 years old whilst the male rate was 9½d. For women over 20 years doing men's work as cutters, trimmers, or fitters-up the rate was 9½d. The rates for sales assistants were negotiated by the NAUSA at

three-quarter men's rates or four-fifths men's rates in London. The justification for this was that the three-quarter standard, as it was known, was a great improvement on women's rates at that time, and also that the physical capacity of men and women affected the value of their labour. Managers of both sexes were meant to receive equal pay. However, it was noted that as late as 1918 large numbers of women were receiving only 9s to 13s a week. In 1919 new scales were established which paid women aged 16 to 28 20s to 53s for a forty-eight hour week, and a minimum of £4 a week for managers of either sex. See B. Drake, *Women in Trade Unions* (London, 1920, reprinted 1984), p.143 and pp.165-67.

73. Ibid.

74. Ibid., p.141. The ASTT prohibited female labour in high-class cutting and pressing.

75. Ibid., Table II – Analysis of Principal Trade Unions.

76. Wilson, op.cit., p.79.

77. Both Burton and Price's Tailors Ltd. expanded during the Depression years. By 1935 Burtons had over 400 branches and Prices had over 250 branches. See Jefferys, op.cit., p.305.

78. Souvenir booklet of the Official Opening of the new Clothing factory erected in Saltwells Road, Middlesbrough, for Messrs Prices, Tailors, Limited, Wednesday 22 September, 1937, p.12 (copy in Dorman Museum, Middlesbrough).

79. Ibid., p.13.

80. Ibid., p.11.

81. Jefferys, op.cit., p.52..

82. Rees, op.cit., p.109.

83. Ibid., p.111.

84. "A Walk through the Interior of the Bainbridge Store", blotter dated mid-1920s from the John Lewis Archive.

85. Interview with Maisie Wright, op.cit.; Maisie and her husband, a railwayman (a poorly paid job) married on 25s a week.

86. Interview with Renee Chaplin, op.cit.

87. Sid, Renee's husband, earned about £3-£3 10s a week at the time of their marriage.

88. Gwenyth Batey in letter to author 5 December 1992.

89. Ibid.

90. Ibid.

91. Ibid. The fashion collection held by Tyne and Wear Museum Service in Newcastle upon Tyne has a substantial set of Haslam pattern boards and books covering children's wear, lingerie, blouses, skirts, and other accessories. Apparently these were patented by "Miss F.A. Haslam, Ord House, Berwick-upon-Tweed & North East", as the "Haslam System of Dresscutting".

92. Interview with Mavis Robinson, op.cit.

93. Wilson, op.cit., p.8.

94. Ibid., p3.

95. For example E. Ewing, *A History of 20th Century Fashion* (London, 1992); E. Wilson and L. Taylor, *Through the Looking Glass. A History of Dress From 1860 to the Present Day* (London, 1989).

96. "A Walk through the Interior . . .", op.cit., pp.16-17.

97. "Bainbridge's Summer Sale", 10 July 1930, p.7.

98. "Bainbridge & Co.'s Bi-Annual Sale", brochure dated 5 January 1928, p.22.

99. Fenwick's "The Model Sale", leaflet dated 6 June 1933.

100. Fenwick's "Spring Tailoring Opening", 1933.

101. Benson, op.cit., p.109 and p.115.

102. M. Stopes, *Married Love* (London, 1918).

103. Beddoe, op.cit., pp.106-7. According to Cate Haste in *Rules of Desire: Sex in Britain: World War I to the Present* (London, 1992), p.63, Marie Stopes's first clinic doubled its attendance each year from 518 women in 1921 to 2368 in 1923. She opened 12 more clinics in largely working-class areas around Britain by 1930.

104. Ibid., p.106.

105. Haste, op.cit., p.61.

106. R. Hall, *The Well of Loneliness* (London, 1928).

107. A. Kuhn, *Women's Pictures: Feminism and Cinema* (London, 1982), p.89.

108. Wilson, op.cit., p.2.

109. For a detailed discussion of women wearing trousers in the 1930s see K. Bill, "Attitudes Towards Women's Trousers: Britain in the 1930s", in *Journal of Design History,* vol. 6, no.1 (1993), pp.45-54.

XII

"WHEN THE GOING GETS TOUGH . . .": REPRESENTATIONS OF THE NORTH-EAST IN FILM AND TELEVISION

Peter Hutchings

Introduction

In the 1987 thriller *Stormy Monday*, a villainous American businessman stands up before an audience of Newcastle's civic dignitaries and quotes them the maxim "When the going gets tough, the tough get going". He then proceeds to apply this to the situation as he sees it in the North East, a region in industrial decline – where the going is indeed tough – which requires the investment and redevelopment that he and his company can bring.

Bound up in this short sequence, and indeed in the film as a whole, are all sorts of assumptions about the identity of the North East at the end of the 1980s, in particular a sense of it as a site of economic hardship after the erosion of its traditional industrial base throughout the preceding decades. This way of thinking about the region has been remarkably pervasive during the past twenty years, underpinning as it does virtually every film and television programme that has claimed to deal with the North East. Where these films and television programmes differ from each other is in the responses they offer to this hardship, with these ranging from celebrations of working-class identity to more comic treatments of the situation.

This chapter will explore the various ways in which the cinematic and televisual representations of the North East that have appeared since the late 1960s have addressed changes in the identity of the region, particularly those to do with shifting patterns of employment. This will necessarily involve looking back at some of the more longstanding cultural beliefs and assumptions about the industrial North, but the focus here will be on more recent films and television programmes. This is for two reasons. First, the period of the region's industrial difficulties has also seen a proliferation of film and television projects dealing with the North East. Second, whether or not one accepts the range of representations of the region available at the moment as presenting a fair and accurate picture of it, there is clearly a need to engage with the way things are now, to think critically about all those images which seek to depict what it means to be a North Easterner.

Flat Caps, Whippets and other Stereotypes

"The stereotype image of flat caps, whippets and working-men's clubs is one that persists."[1] Within the North East of England, flat caps and whippets have often come to symbolise what is seen as the inability (or unwillingness) of the rest of the country – and especially the South – to perceive the region as it really is. Equally, it has been argued, the tendency to show Geordies as "lovable, cheeky and only just on the right side of the law . . . The Cockneys of the North, you might say" distorts or oversimplifies the life of the region.[2] Frequently identified as culprits in the perpetuation of this allegedly inaccurate view of the North East are a number of television programmes and films. These include, with a greater or lesser degree of culpability, the well-known TV situation comedies *The Likely Lads* and its sequel *Whatever Happened to the Likely Lads,* (both of which feature 'lovable, cheeky' Geordies), the Depression drama series *When the Boat Comes In* (flat caps on every corner) and *Auf Wiedersehen, Pet* (yet more lovable, cheeky Geordies), as well as films such as *Get Carter* (1971, d. Mike Hodges) and the already mentioned *Stormy Monday* (1987, d. Mike Figgis). More recently, the BBC detective series *Spender* has brought a designer-gloss to representations of the North East, although the extent to which it has done away with particular stereotypes – or, for that matter, merely replaced them with different stereotypes – remains in question. The continuing popularity of the television adaptations of some of the novels of the hugely successful local author Catherine Cookson by Tyne Tees Television suggests that some of the more traditional ways of representing the North East still retain a significant hold on the public imagination.

Virtually all the television programmes and films mentioned so far boast local talent, in terms both of writers and actors, with some of them also produced within the North East. However, these projects' local credentials have often been seen as compromised by their need to appeal to a national (and sometimes international) audience. In the face of these commercial imperatives, a critical preference is sometimes expressed for the low-budget productions of the regional independent sector, with the most notable enterprise here being Amber Films, a Tyneside-based film workshop which from the late 1960s onwards has produced a variety of shorts and features about the North East.

Before moving on to a consideration of some of the representations of the North East available in British film and television – both those which exist on a national level and those which offer themselves as being more closely linked to the region – it is worth considering here some of the unspoken assumptions that underpin many of the 'common sense' statements about the subject (a number of which have been reported above), in particular those to do with the nature of the stereotype.

Usually, when an image – flat caps and whippets, for instance – is described as being a stereotype, this means that in some way it is a bad and/or distorting representation of a particular social group. However, it has been argued that seeing the world in terms of types is not in itself automatically a bad thing, that in fact one of the important ways in which we make sense of our society is through dividing it up into groups and assigning each group particular traits and characteristics. As far as films and television are concerned, types can also function as a useful shorthand, providing, in Richard Dyer's words, "a very simple, striking, easily-grasped form of representation [which] is nonetheless capable of condensing a great deal of complex information and a host of connotations".[3] It might further be argued that typing of various kinds is actually the fundamental mode of characterisation in most areas of film and television. Of course this does not mean that stereotypes are necessarily good things either, merely that we have to look carefully at particular stereotypes and the contexts within which they operate before making our judgements. To quote Richard Dyer again, "it is not stereotypes, as an aspect of human thought and representation, that are wrong, but who controls them and defines them, what interests they serve."[4]

Bearing all this in mind, it is useful to identify what exactly it is about flat caps and whippets that make them bad stereotypes. Presumably no one would want to argue that there are no flat caps or whippets in the North East – rather that these objects are an inappropriate typification of the reality of the region. But then one has to think about what sort of representation could possibly encompass the variety of social and cultural activities going on in the North East, in its various towns and cities and in its rural areas. The answer, clearly, is that no single representation can possibly perform such a task, and that in fact what is required is a wide range of images that show the various facets of the region's life. It follows from this that each individual representation of the region is necessarily going to be limited and exclusive, with any 'truth' it contains also limited. For example, Amber's strength lies in its focus on the working class, but this focus in turn means that other sectors of the North East population – most notably, the middle class – are rarely shown. Such exclusions are an inevitable aspect of any representational activity.

The basic problem, then, with flat caps and whippets is not that they are necessarily in themselves pernicious, but rather that they are seen to have assumed a disproportionate significance in the range of available representations of the North East. This problem is compounded by the fact that what might be called the kernel of meaning within this particular stereotype is perceived as being increasingly distant from the reality of the region. Flat caps and whippets refer in a very economical and highly condensed way to a whole traditional working class culture, traditional not only in terms of patterns of work and leisure (and styles of dress), but also in terms of gender roles, with the male as breadwinner pursuing his leisure activities outside the home and, as the 'natural' complement to this, the woman as housewife and nurturer. (This might seem a case of reading too much into an apparently very straightforward image, and yet one has only to think of some of the places where this type occurs – in the Catherine Cookson adaptations, for example – to see how all the elements sketched above are 'automatically' connected with, and symbolised by, the flat cap. The power of the stereotype, and the source of its usefulness to programme-makers, lies precisely in the way in which it can carry meaning without appearing to do so.)

As has already been indicated, traditional patterns of work and leisure – and the culture associated with them – have been significantly disrupted by changes in the regional economy, and this in turn has undoubtedly had an impact on both class and gender identity: hence the growing inappropriateness of flat caps and whippets, and all the values tied up with them, as even a partial summation of North Eastern life. In particular, some of the disturbances in assumptions about gender brought on by these changes have proved especially important for and influential on those film and television productions which have been dealing with the region over the past twenty years. It is certainly the case that a wide-ranging interest in the various roles offered to men and women in the North East cuts across some of the more obvious differences that divide television and film fictions about the region. For instance, the apparently diametrically opposed Cookson drama *The Fifteen Streets* and Amber's *In Fading Light* can be shown to be equally preoccupied with the erosion of traditional models of masculinity at a time of economic hardship.

It follows from this that simply dividing up various films and television programmes about the region into two groups, those which are good/truthful/'saved' and those which are bad/distorting/'damned', is perhaps not the best tactic. Instead we should be thinking about these representations as a totality. That is to say, while retaining an awareness of the differences that separate them, we should be particularly sensitive to similarities and areas of interaction. In this way, a clearer sense can be gained of those images, types and representations which, for better or worse, contribute in significant ways to the region's sense of itself (and to the nation's sense of the region), and in relation to which any new representations will have to locate themselves.

It's Grim Up North

In the 1971 thriller *Get Carter*, Carter (played by Michael Caine) returns to his Tyneside roots in order to avenge the death of his brother. Before leaving his London base for the journey north, he is warned by his gangster masters to be wary of Newcastle's criminal underworld: "Some hard nuts operate up there, Jack", as one of the gangsters put it. But Carter is not dissuaded from his mission and there follows a series of increasingly brutal killings, all of which take place against the unforgiving backdrop of various North East locations (many of which have since vanished in the process of redevelopment).

British cinema in the 1960s had given us a new sort of working-class hero: individualistic, apolitical, hedonistic, virile, out for life's pleasures with little concern for the consequences. Exemplified by, amongst others, Albert Finney, Sean Connery, Terence Stamp and Michael Caine himself, this figure had been a potent symbol of many of the aspirations and ideals of the sixties, particularly those to do with class mobility and sexual freedom. In *Get Carter*, perhaps more so than in any other British film of this period, one sees the 1960s dream turning sour, with the Jack-the-Lad persona of Caine (most evident in his performances in *Alfie* and the Harry Palmer spy films) now transformed into something altogether more vicious and sadistic. It is worth considering here why it is that this most relentless of tales seeks the physical correlate of its narrative grimness in the North Eastern landscape. Why, in *Get Carter*, is it so grim up north?

That the North of England generally might be perceived as being grim is hardly a new idea. Of course, this way of thinking about the North is inextricably linked with, and in large part is a consequence of, its history as an industrial centre of the United Kingdom. Throughout the nineteenth and twentieth centuries, the Northern industrial landscape has repeatedly been portrayed by writers and artists as a dehumanising and alienating one. Further ingredients in the North's alleged grimness include the geographical and climatic hardiness of its rural landscape as well as what has often been seen as the taciturnity and insularity of the Northern citizen (and especially the Northern male).

In choosing Newcastle as its main location, *Get Carter* is obviously tapping into this history of thought and representation. But it inflects it in such a way that those elements which elsewhere have been presented as ameliorating an industrial and natural grimness – most notably, the close-knit working-class community – are absent. What *Get Carter* offers us instead is a series of visibly decaying streets and terraces, within which no meaningful communal activity takes place and where notions of class solidarity are totally irrelevant. (At one point we are shown a march through some of these streets, but this is clearly not meant to be seen as a genuine expression of a communal solidarity. Much the same can be said of a similar march in the later film *Stormy Monday*.) Presumably the prime motivation behind the suppression of any positive elements about the city is the need to fit it to the character of Jack Carter, local boy made bad, thereby rendering it the perfect location for his merciless activities.

Carter is, technically at least, a Geordie. He is also a hard man who, like most of the other men in the film, rarely shows his feelings and habitually resorts to physical violence as a means of dealing with confrontational situations. In fact it is the connection that *Get Carter* makes between his Geordieness and his masculine hardness that makes it so interesting, for clearly the world of the film, a world in which Jack is fully at home, is given as a male-centred one, with women figuring in it as objects upon which Jack's vengeance is founded, agents of that vengeance or present only for the recreational purposes of men (and sometimes all three at once). It should be clear from this that Carter, despite his 1960s credentials as someone not apparently bound by class origins, is actually a deeply retrograde figure. He embodies a version of masculinity – seen as authoritative, inflexible, emotionally dead, prone to violence – which was increasingly being questioned at the time of *Get Carter*'s production, particularly by the growing feminist movements, and about which the film itself is decidedly ambivalent.

At the end of *Get Carter*, Carter dies in as brutal and as unforgiving a fashion as he lived, although one gets no sense that the world which has produced him will change at all. But what is clear from the film is that the grimness of its portrayal of the region is very much bound up with the essentially masculine grimness of Carter himself. He is a reactionary figure, whom we will encounter again in the following pages – the hard man of the North, another stereotype which is just as dense and complex (and perhaps more relevant) as the flat cap and whippet stereotype already discussed.

A rather unlikely connection can be drawn here between *Get Carter* and the television situation comedy *Whatever Happened to the Likely Lads?* in terms of the ways in which they engage with some of the preconceptions about Northern masculinity, although, as is usually the case with comedy, what in *Get Carter* is deadly serious becomes in *Likely Lads* a subject for witty inversion. Terry and Bob, the principal characters in *Whatever Happened to the Likely Lads?*, represent two very different types of fictional Geordie. Terry (played by James Bolam) is more in the traditional Northern mould and in many respects can be seen as a comic version of Jack Carter: that is to say, he is morbidly suspicious of any emotional displays or involvement, happy only in a masculine environment (usually a pub or a betting shop) and unwilling or unable to see beyond the narrow confines of his own small world. When informed that someone he is about to meet has come up from the South, his spectacularly insular and wholly characteristic reply is "What – from Middlesbrough?" Bob (Rodney Bewes), on the other hand, is the new Northern man of the 1970s: cosmopolitan, concerned with his personal appearance, more at home in mixed company. Significantly, Bob has a fiancée, Thelma, who is seen to embody and promote these 'new' Northern values, all of which are tied up with social aspirations, in particular the desire to rise from working-class origins towards a lifestyle more like that of a rather genteel middle class. In fact much of the humour of *Whatever Happened to the Likely Lads?* derives from Bob's oscillation between the values represented by Thelma and those associated with Terry. Implicit here is the notion that the new essentially domesticated Northern man is actually only a veneer, a feminine (and to a certain extent Southern) imposition on the 'real' man, and that, without the constant supervision of Thelma, Bob would automatically regress to a state of authentic 'Terry-ness'.

A similar sense of an 'authentic' masculinity that is antithetical to a feminising domesticity is found in *Auf Wiedersehen, Pet* (which was written by Ian La Frenais and Dick Clement, the team also responsible for *Whatever Happened to the Likely Lads?*). This drama series dealt with the exploits of a team of building workers – many of them Geordie – on various European construction sites. Here the Terry figure, the defiantly unreconstructed male, is Oz (played by Jimmy Nail, who, a few years later and suitably reconstructed, would reappear as Spender in the BBC series of that name), boozy, aggressive and generally irresponsible, while the Bob figure is Neville (played by Kevin Whateley), married, compliant and equipped with the social skills necessary for someone to fit into the domestic realm. An important difference between *Likely Lads* and *Pet* is that whereas the former is set largely in and around various domestic households, with Terry an isolated and morose figure, *Pet* shows us lads – and Oz in particular – on a spree, far away from the claims of domesticity and the confinement these are seen to bring. Nevertheless, Terry, Oz and Jack Carter are of a type. That both Terry and Oz are humorous figures, and Carter a disturbing one, indicates there is a general uneasiness here about the sort of masculinity they between them represent. Yet also evident is an enduring fascination with the sheer awfulness of these people, suggesting that this particular stereotype still has a good deal of life left in it.

But what is it about these stereotypes, if anything, which makes them North Eastern (or even Northern)? Certainly, many of the themes discussed so far – the association of the domestic with feminine values, with this in turn seen as threatening to the male – recur in a wide range of novels, plays, films and television programmes, with the majority of these having nothing at all to do with the North East region. It is not beyond the bounds of credibility that a *Get Carter*-like thriller could have been effectively staged in Manchester or that the *Likely Lads* could have hailed from Liverpool. But the fact is that in each case Newcastle was the location of choice. This suggests that the North East has lent itself to being used by film- and programme-makers as a kind of shorthand for certain qualities, so that if an earthy, no-nonsense sort of masculinity is required, then the Geordie is one of the possible candidates for the role (with, possibly, the dour Highlander as another). Or, to give another example, we all know that Sergeant Lewis, Inspector Morse's sidekick in the *Inspector Morse* series, is a down-to-earth sort of person, and the principal reason that we think of him in this way – and this is prior to anything this character actually does in the series – is the fact that, as his accent indicates, he is a Geordie.

What we can take from this is a sense of the fluidity of the regional types outlined above. The meanings attached to particular types – the hard man of the North, for example – are not unique to that type but can also be, and often are, articulated in relation to other sectors of the population. But clearly this does not obviate the need to consider what it is about the North East that appears to suit it to particular fictional types and not others. In the case of the masculine types already discussed, it does seem that the 'flat cap and whippet' picture of the North, with all it implies about the resilience and independence of the working class male in the face of industrial exploitation and hardship, provides a significant historical foundation for the dramas of male resistance that *Get Carter, Whatever Happened to the Likely Lads?* and *Auf Wiedersehen, Pet* undoubtedly are.

It might be argued that this view of the North East, as a region caught up in thematic concerns and issues which are not specific to it but which it is used to represent in the films and television programmes in question, is merely symptomatic of the fact that neither *Get Carter* nor the television series were produced by or for the local community, but rather were produced by large national companies for an accordingly national audience. This raises the question of whether there is a local film/television body of work which is separate and distinct from national views of the North East. In order to address this question, we will now consider a series of films produced by Amber, a Tyneside film workshop.

In Fading Light: Amber Films

The Amber collective was formed in 1968. A non-hierarchical and non-profit-making workshop, Amber involved itself from its inception in a range of media-related projects, including film production, distribution and exhibition, photography and educational activities. A discussion in the early 1980s of independent British cinema characterised the workshop movement in the following terms, all of which seem relevant to Amber:

> It is evident that . . . the workshops share a new consciousness about their relationship to their constituencies, that their work is often related to their social surroundings and to their locality, and that the workshops' constituencies are as a series of interrelated and overlapping groups with different needs. The workshops can be seen as mediating the audio-visual culture and re-deploying it for and with involved audiences.[5]

One of Amber's main intentions was to record the lives of working-class people on Tyneside, with this to be achieved, initially at least, through documentary forms and techniques. This combination of a working-class subject with an approach rooted in documentary is very reminiscent of the 1930s documentary work of film producer John Grierson (and indeed Amber has acknowledged a debt to Grierson).[6] However, as one critic has noted, "There is not one, but several realisms", and the realism proposed by Grierson throughout the 1930s was, to say the least, different from that offered by Amber.[7]

The films produced by Grierson – of which the most famous are probably *Coalface* and *Night Mail* – were intended to explain various social processes to a mass audience in order, supposedly, that the members of this audience might become more informed participants in a social democracy. This was in a period which saw a heightened awareness of some of the problems posed by 'the masses' for the already-existing social order, with Grierson's solution enlightenment through education. In line with this, any elements which might have disrupted the picture he sought to project of society as a kind of benevolent, integrated machine – the most notable of these elements being, of course, class division – were suppressed or ignored, so that even though many of Grierson's films deal with work, there is rarely an acknowledgement of the many social problems deriving at this time from troubled industrial relations. Also, workers tended to be presented only in terms of their work, as cogs in the machine, with no sense of how they might be away from the workplace.

Amber shares Grierson's fascination with the recording of processes of work – for example, seacoaling in *Seacoal* and sea fishing in *In Fading Light* (see fig. 86). But at the same time, and especially in those later Amber films which incorporate fictional elements, a concern with the communities which surround and support these work processes is very apparent. One consequence of this is that Amber is far more willing – in the context of trends in the North East economy in the 1970s and 1980s, perhaps inevitably so – to engage with the ways in which workers can be exploited and alienated in the interests of capital.

Fig. 86 *In Fading Light* – Amber's recording of work.

Amber's principal themes might be summarised as follows: first, there is work and, connected with this, the difficulties involved in supporting oneself in a region of high unemployment; second, there is hardship; and third, there is community, with this community often functioning to alleviate or make bearable economic hardship through imparting a sense of belonging. One of the more frequent ways in which Amber addresses these themes, especially in its later more fictional projects, is through presenting the story of an outsider entering into and becoming part of a particular community. To give a few examples, in *Double Vision: Boxing for Hartlepool* it is Ray, a television researcher looking for a suitable subject in Hartlepool's boxing community, while in *Seacoal* a woman and her daughter are introduced by her new partner, himself originally a seacoaler, into the seacoaling community, and in *In Fading Light* the captain's daughter is drawn into what is for her the unfamiliar world of sea-fishing (see fig. 87).

Clearly one function of this outsider is to act as a delegate for the audience, so that when a member of the community concerned explains some aspect of community life and work, it is as much for our benefit as it is for the character in the film to whom the explanation is ostensibly directed. A sense

Fig. 87 *In Fading Light* – the outsider: a lone woman in a man's world.

of what this community is like therefore often comes to us via what are in effect quite traditional forms of character identification, with this in turn providing a framework for the more straightforwardly documentary footage incorporated into the film. The outcome of this particular rhetorical structure – which is by no means present in all of Amber's films – is to position the audience, initially at least, apart from the community being investigated, eventually to be drawn into a sympathetic understanding of that community. To a certain extent, this also represents what in this respect is actually quite a Griersonian attitude on the part of the filmmakers themselves, that is to say a kind of sympathetic observation and commentary which is dependent for its effectiveness on there being a certain distance between filmmakers and subject. It follows from this that Amber's 'realistic' projects do not, as some of the cruder accounts of realism might suggest, present totally transparent windows onto the North East world (as opposed to the 'fantasy' of, say, *Get Carter*), but rather that their images, just like any other images, are formed in the context of particular stylistic conventions and devices, with these in turn presupposing a set of beliefs about the region.

In order to obtain a clearer picture of how Amber relates to its chosen subjects, it is worth thinking here briefly about the attitude shown by their film towards the regional landscape, whether it be urban (*Boxing for Hartlepool, Keeping Time, Dream On, T. Dan Smith*) or situated away from the city (*Seacoal, In Fading Light*). As was the case with *Get Carter,* these landscapes often have elements of grimness about them, with this taking the form of either industrial decay or a natural hardiness. Rarely are these landscapes romanticised in any way: on the few occasions where a setting might be seen as offering a kind of austere beauty (*Seacoal* and *In Fading Light,* for example), this sense of it is constantly undercut by the films' focusing on the difficulties experienced by a group or community in extracting a living from that landscape (see fig. 88). In this respect, Amber – like *Get Carter* – portrays the Northern world as dour and alienating. In other important respects, however, the films of Amber are quite different, particularly as far as the attitudes expressed towards the communities situated in this bleak world are concerned. The communities in question are generally ones that are in decline, with their wider economic life support system under threat or in the process of being shut down. Because of this and because of the obvious sympathy of the filmmakers for these communities, their work and their lifestyles, Amber's films often take on an elegiac quality (note the title *In Fading Light* in this respect), imparting as they do a sense of something that is in itself valuable but which for a number of reasons is no longer viable in the world of the 1970s and 1980s.

Fig. 88 *Seacoal* – the austere Northern landscape.

In part at least, the elegy is for a working class solidarity and communality which is being eroded by the disruption – and in some instances destruction – of traditional working practices. But it also seems that in a number of these films a particular sort of masculinity is also being mourned. This is most spectacularly the case with *In Fading Light,* which is probably the closest the North East will ever get to producing a western, and a Sam Peckinpah western at that. In this film, the North Shields Wild Bunch heads out into the wilderness of the open seas for the last time before the money men – hardly men at all in the film's scheme of things – move in (see fig. 89). Similar preoccupations are apparent in *Boxing for Hartlepool,* in which boxing functions as a source of male pride and identity in a locale which in other ways has denied this to its men, and in *Seacoal.* In the latter film, clearly the appeal of seacoaling to Ray, the principal male character, is the freedom and self-sufficiency it promises, qualities which are very much bound up in his sense of himself as a man. His failure to achieve this ideal, and his flight from the family, is a further testament to the way in which unemployment and hardship can remove a key prop in a particular sort of working-class male identity, namely the role of breadwinner.

Fig. 89 *In Fading Light* – the last hard men.

It might be argued here that, as is the case with the western, the wide open spaces found in many of Amber's films – the seascape of *In Fading Light,* the coastline of *Seacoal* – symbolise a masculine ideal of freedom, while, as is also the case with the western, the converse of this essentially masculine realm is the domestic, the space which is seen to entrap the male and which itself is symbolised by the female. As we have already seen, the stereotypical opposition implicit here – between a male desire to roam and a female desire to settle – informs, amongst others, *Whatever Happened to the Likely Lads?* and *Auf Wiedersehen, Pet.* Its trace can also be discerned in some of Amber's films discussed thus far, with many of the female characters predominantly concerned to establish a safe haven for themselves and their family (rather than yearning after careers, etc.). Of course, this does not mean that Amber's films are the same as these other projects, merely that they are all, to a certain extent, drawing upon the same pool of types and images. As important as this to an understanding of how the North East region is represented is the need to grasp the specific uses of these elements, in this case how Amber inflects and moulds certain types in order to make particular points about the North East (see figs. 90 and 91).

Fig. 90 *In Fading Light* – male freedom in the natural world.

One way of establishing what it is about Amber's treatment of these types that is so distinctive is to turn to those of its films which do explore in some detail the realm of the domestic and what this means for both women and men. *The Filleting Machine*, a film version of Tom Hadaway's play, provides a useful starting point here for virtually the entire film takes place within a domestic setting, in this case an intensely claustrophobic house which might be contrasted with the open spaces found elsewhere in Amber. This closed-in space impacts particularly upon the man of the house who in the course of the drama discovers that he has lost the job which is obviously a key element in his self-respect. His subsequent emotional breakdown can be seen in this context as standing for a much wider collapse of a particular

Fig. 91 *Seacoal* – the domestic realm of the feminine.

masculine role and identity. The contribution of the wife to this drama is, in part, to be the nurturer – initially preparing the evening meal for the family, eventually comforting the husband. But she also expresses aspirations for the children, especially the son, which are fundamentally different from those held by her husband and which, in this respect at least, place her alongside Thelma of *Whatever Happened to the Likely Lads?* While the father wants the son to follow in his footsteps and work on the docks, the mother wants him to 'improve' himself by refusing manual labour and working in an office. In this context, the confrontation between husband and wife over the son's future reveals and dwells upon, perhaps more so than in any other Amber film until *Dream On*, the more negative aspects of a particular male type, expressed here by the husband's stubborn refusal to change and his mocking of any qualities which might be seen as socially aspirational, 'genteel' or 'feminine' (like working in an office, for example).

A comparable set of concerns is found in the much gentler *Keeping Time.* This time the focus is more on mothers and their daughters, with the father figuring primarily as an intrusion into this relationship. Again the settings are mainly domestic and claustrophobic (arguably reflecting the limited possibilities for women in the world recorded by the film), again the mother has aspirations which involve her daughter 'bettering' herself through, in this case, pursuing her interest in dancing. The mother's eventual disappointment, and the sense we gradually gain of her being trapped by her environment, is rather less dramatic than the father's collapse in *The Filleting Machine,* but is arguably all the more poignant for its understatement.

This particular 'female' emphasis in Amber receives its fullest expression in *Dream On,* a feature film which depicts the lives of three women, Kathy, her daughter Julie and their friend Rita, in and around the Meadowell estate in North Shields. A listing of the problems encountered by these characters – with these including domestic violence, solvent abuse, alcohol abuse, child abuse, eating disorders, debt – suggests that this could be possibly the grimmest of all North East productions. But in actuality, *Dream On* is a more uplifting experience than one might have expected, not because these problems are in any way trivialised but rather because they are located in the context of a way of life where such difficulties are routinely endured and managed.

Importantly, most of these difficulties, which impact mainly upon the women, are shown to arise from the actions of men, and more particularly from an increasingly discredited masculine culture. Within this situation, Shorty, Kathy's partner, represents a degraded version of an 'old-fashioned' masculinity, displaying as he does an aggression and self-reliance which has here become transformed into the violent abuse of Kathy. Larry, Rita's thoroughly domesticated husband and generally a figure of fun in the film, hardly represents an attractive alternative (although the film's conclusion does imply that he is going to change). Baz, Julie's boyfriend, does change in the course of the film, however, moving away from some of the more traditional assumptions about how a man must behave – at one point walking away in disgust from Shorty – and, in true 'New Man' fashion, coming to terms with his own emotions and those of Julie. This sense of the potential, albeit fairly limited, for change amongst the men definitely contributes to the 'hopeful' tone of *Dream On,* although to what extent this represents a radical rethinking of the relations between women and men remains in question.

But what has been the role of the women in all this? At the end of *Dream On,* the three principal female characters stand on stage and sing "I will survive". The message is clear: these women will endure, no matter what, with this endurance involving a kind of stoicism, an acceptance of a precarious existence where disasters loom at every turn, a stoicism which with a remarkable degree of constancy has characterised most of Amber's representations of women. These representations have always been sympathetic, perhaps more so than in any of the other films and television programmes discussed in this chapter. But at the same time it is important to recognise that there are elements of continuity between Amber's portrayals of men and women and the representations produced elsewhere by other people, and that when seen together all these films and television programmes offer a surprisingly consistent reading of gender relations in the region. 'Men work and women wait' is probably too crude a summation of some of the assumptions about gender that circulate in this area and which are in any case always interconnected with particular notions of class, but clearly a formulation not unlike it does lurk behind a whole range of representations of the North East. Certainly Amber has displayed a greater critical awareness than have other programme-makers of some of the issues and difficulties arising from this, but this does not mean that it has escaped from certain stereotypical assumptions entirely, nor is it likely that it ever could have. This is because all representations are necessarily bounded in some way or other, have points beyond which they are unable to see or go, with these limitations enabling the existence of the representation in the first place. In the case of the representation of the North East we seem finally to have reached one of those boundaries, and it appears to be a particularly intractable one.

Conclusion

A survey of some of the better known films and television programmes which purport to deal with the North East of England in some way or other reveals a range of different approaches and attitudes, and this chapter has, I hope, given a sense of the general richness and liveliness available in this particular field of cultural activity. However, this chapter has also sought to problematise some of the more simplistic assumptions about 'the real' that dog many of the discussions about representing the region, the idea that there are subjects which are 'authentically' North Eastern and that it is the task of representation merely to reproduce or record these. It should be clear from the analyses of specific films and television programmes offered elsewhere in this chapter that representation is not, and can never be, a neutral process, that it always involves mobilising, not necessarily consciously, a whole array of value judgements and assumptions. For example, one thing that has been established through looking at a range of films and television programmes about the North East, both those produced within the region and those which in some way 'impose' on it from outside, is that they are all drawing upon quite a narrow range of stereotypical assumptions about, amongst other things, class and gender (although their various treatments of these are, of course, very different). One consequence of this is that it becomes very difficult to identify any particular film or television programme as providing an 'authentic' picture of the region as opposed to the 'false' pictures offered elsewhere. Certainly it might be the case that we would want to value certain representations above others –

seeing them, perhaps, as more useful in an attempt to delineate a cultural base for the region – but this strategic valuation should not, I think, cause us to shy away from our critical responsibilities, and the need to think through the implications of all the representations of our world that we encounter.

References and Notes

1. Steve Pratt, *The Northern Echo*, 11 June 1992, p.10.

2. Ibid.

3. Richard Dyer, "The Role of Stereotypes", in Jim Cook and Mike Lewington (eds), *Images of Alcoholism* (London, 1979), p.16.

4. Ibid., p.15.

5. Rod Stoneman and Hilary Thompson (eds), *The New Social Function of Cinema* (London, 1981), p.140.

6. See *Amber/Side Catalogue and History of Work Since 1968* (Newcastle upon Tyne, 1987) for useful background information about Amber Films.

7. André Bazin, "William Wyler, or the Jansenist of mise-en-scène", in Christopher Williams (ed.), *Realism and the Cinema* (London, 1980), p.41.

INDEX

(References to illustrations are in bold)